# Python Deep Learning

Next generation techniques to revolutionize computer vision, AI, speech and data analysis

**Valentino Zocca**

**Gianmario Spacagna**

**Daniel Slater**

**Peter Roelants**

Packt>

BIRMINGHAM - MUMBAI

# Python Deep Learning

First published: April 2017

Production reference: 1270417

Published by Packt Publishing Ltd.
Livery Place
35 Livery Street
Birmingham B3 2PB, UK.

ISBN 978-1-78646-445-3

www.packtpub.com

# Credits

**Authors**
Valentino Zocca
Gianmario Spacagna
Daniel Slater
Peter Roelants

**Reviewer**
Max Pumperla

**Commissioning Editor**
Akram Hussain

**Acquisition Editor**
Vinay Argekar

**Content Development Editor**
Mayur Pawanikar

**Technical Editor**
Vivek Arora

**Copy Editor**
Safis Editing

**Project Coordinator**
Nidhi Joshi

**Proofreader**
Safis Editing

**Indexer**
Francy Puthiry

**Graphics**
Tania Dutta

**Production Coordinator**
Arvindkumar Gupta

# About the Authors

**Valentino Zocca** graduated with a PhD in mathematics from the University of Maryland, USA, with a dissertation in symplectic geometry, after having graduated with a *laurea* in mathematics from the University of Rome. He spent a semester at the University of Warwick. After a post-doc in Paris, Valentino started working on high-tech projects in the Washington, D.C. area and played a central role in the design, development, and realization of an advanced stereo 3D Earth visualization software with head tracking at Autometric, a company later bought by Boeing. At Boeing, he developed many mathematical algorithms and predictive models, and using Hadoop, he has also automated several satellite-imagery visualization programs. He has since become an expert on machine learning and deep learning and has worked at the U.S. Census Bureau and as an independent consultant both in the US and in Italy. He has also held seminars on the subject of machine and deep learning in Milan and New York.

Currently, Valentino lives in New York and works as an independent consultant to a large financial company, where he develops econometric models and uses machine learning and deep learning to create predictive models. But he often travels back to Rome and Milan to visit his family and friends.

**Gianmario Spacagna** is a senior data scientist at Pirelli, processing sensors and telemetry data for IoT and connected-vehicle applications.

He works closely with tyre mechanics, engineers, and business units to analyze and formulate hybrid, physics-driven, and data-driven automotive models.

His main expertise is in building machine learning systems and end-to-end solutions for data products.

He is the coauthor of the Professional Data Science Manifesto (datasciencemanifesto.org) and founder of the Data Science Milan meetup community (datasciencemilan.org).

Gianmario loves evangelizing his passion for best practices and effective methodologies in the community.

He holds a master's degree in telematics from the Polytechnic of Turin and software engineering of distributed systems from KTH, Stockholm.

Prior to Pirelli, he worked in retail and business banking (Barclays), cyber security (Cisco), predictive marketing (AgilOne), and some occasional freelancing.

**Daniel Slater** started programming at age 11, developing mods for the id Software game *Quake*. His obsession led him to become a developer working in the gaming industry on the hit computer game series *Championship Manager*. He then moved into finance, working on risk- and high-performance messaging systems. He now is a staff engineer, working on big data at Skimlinks to understand online user behavior. He spends his spare time training AI to beat computer games. He talks at tech conferences about deep learning and reinforcement learning; his blog can be found at www.danielslater.net. His work in this field has been cited by Google.

I would like to thank my wife, Judit Kollo, for her love, support, and diagrams. Also thanks to my son, David; mother, Catherine; and father, Don.

**Peter Roelants** holds a master's in computer science with a specialization in artificial intelligence from KU Leuven. He works on applying deep learning to a variety of problems, such as spectral imaging, speech recognition, text understanding, and document information extraction. He currently works at Onfido as a team lead for the data extraction research team, focusing on data extraction from official documents.

# About the Reviewer

**Max Pumperla** is a data scientist and engineer specializing in deep learning and its applications. He currently holds the position of Head of Data Science at collect Artificial Intelligence GmbH and has previous experience in banking, online marketing, and the SMB market. Being an author and maintainer of several Python packages, his open source footprint includes contributions to popular machine learning libraries such as Keras and Hyperopt. He holds a PhD in algebraic geometry from the University of Hamburg.

# www.PacktPub.com

## eBooks, discount offers, and more

Did you know that Packt offers eBook versions of every book published, with PDF and ePub files available? You can upgrade to the eBook version at www.PacktPub.com and as a print book customer, you are entitled to a discount on the eBook copy. Get in touch with us at customercare@packtpub.com for more details.

At www.PacktPub.com, you can also read a collection of free technical articles, sign up for a range of free newsletters and receive exclusive discounts and offers on Packt books and eBooks.

# Mapt

https://www.packtpub.com/mapt

Get the most in-demand software skills with Mapt. Mapt gives you full access to all Packt books and video courses, as well as industry-leading tools to help you plan your personal development and advance your career.

## Why subscribe?
- Fully searchable across every book published by Packt
- Copy and paste, print, and bookmark content
- On demand and accessible via a web browser

# Customer Feedback

Thanks for purchasing this Packt book. At Packt, quality is at the heart of our editorial process. To help us improve, please leave us an honest review on this book's Amazon page at https://www.amazon.com/dp/1786464454.

If you'd like to join our team of regular reviewers, you can e-mail us at customerreviews@packtpub.com. We award our regular reviewers with free eBooks and videos in exchange for their valuable feedback. Help us be relentless in improving our products!

# Table of Contents

# Preface

With an increasing interest in AI around the world, deep learning has attracted a great deal of public attention. Every day, deep-learning algorithms are used broadly across different industries. This book will give you all the practical information available on the subject, including best practices, using real-world use cases. You will learn to recognize and extract information to increase predictive accuracy and optimize results.

Starting with a quick recap of important machine learning concepts, the book will delve straight into deep learning principles using scikit-learn. Moving ahead, you will learn to use the latest open source libraries, such as Theano, Keras, Google's TensorFlow, and H2O. Use this guide to uncover the difficulties of pattern recognition, scaling data with greater accuracy, and discussing deep-learning algorithms and techniques. Whether you want to dive deeper into deep learning or want to investigate how to get more out of this powerful technology, you'll find everything inside.

## What this book covers

*Chapter 1, Machine Learning – An Introduction,* presents different machine learning approaches and techniques and some of their applications to real-world problems. We will introduce one of the major open source packages available in Python for machine learning, scikit-learn.

*Chapter 2, Neural Networks,* formally introduces what neural networks are. We will thoroughly describe how a neuron works and will see how we can stack many layers to create and use deep feed-forward neural networks.

*Chapter 3, Deep Learning Fundamentals,* walks you toward an understanding of what deep learning is and how it is related to deep neural networks.

*Chapter 4, Unsupervised Feature Learning,* covers two of the most powerful and often-used architectures for unsupervised feature learning: auto-encoders and restricted Boltzmann machines.

*Chapter 5, Image Recognition,* starts from drawing an analogy with how our visual cortex works and introduces convolutional layers, followed up with a descriptive intuition of why they work.

*Chapter 6, Recurrent Neural Networks and Language Models,* discusses powerful methods that have been very promising in a lot of tasks, such as language modeling and speech recognition.

*Chapter 7, Deep Learning for Board Games,* covers the different tools used for solving board games such as checkers and chess.

*Chapter 8, Deep Learning for Computer Games,* looks at the more complex problem of training AI to play computer games.

*Chapter 9, Anomaly Detection,* starts by explaining the difference and similarities of concepts between outlier detection and anomaly detection. You will be guided through an imaginary fraud case study, followed by examples showing the danger of having anomalies in real-world applications and the importance of automated and fast detection systems.

*Chapter 10, Building a Production-Ready Intrusion Detection System,* leverages H2O and general common practices to build a scalable distributed system ready for deployment in production. You will learn how to train a deep learning network using Spark and MapReduce, how to use adaptive learning techniques for faster convergence and very important how to validate a model and evaluate the end to end pipeline.

# What you need for this book

You will be able to work on any of the following OSes: Windows, Linux, and Macintosh.

To be able to smoothly follow through the chapters, you will need the following:

- TensorFlow
- Theano
- Keras

- Matplotlib
- H2O .
- scikit-learn

# Who this book is for

This book is for data science practitioners as well as aspirants who have a basic foundational understanding of machine learning concepts and some programming experience with Python. A mathematical background with a conceptual understanding of calculus and statistics is also desired.

# Conventions

In this book, you will find a number of text styles that distinguish between different kinds of information. Here are some examples of these styles and an explanation of their meaning.

Code words in text, database table names, folder names, filenames, file extensions, pathnames, dummy URLs, user input, and Twitter handles are shown as follows: The code above for drawing should be immediately clear, we just notice that the line importing cm.

A block of code is set as follows:

```
(X_train, Y_train), (X_test, Y_test) = cifar10.load_data()
X_train = X_train.reshape(50000, 3072)
X_test = X_test.reshape(10000, 3072)
input_size = 3072
```

When we wish to draw your attention to a particular part of a code block, the relevant lines or items are set in bold:

```
def monte_carlo_tree_search_uct(board_state, side, number_of_
rollouts):
    state_results = collections.defaultdict(float)
    state_samples = collections.defaultdict(float)
```

Any command-line input or output is written as follows:

```
git clone https://github.com/fchollet/keras.git
cd keras
python setup.py install
```

**New terms** and **important words** are shown in bold.

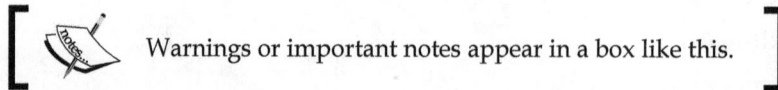

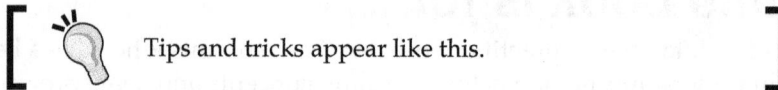

> [ 📝 Warnings or important notes appear in a box like this. ]

> [ 💡 Tips and tricks appear like this. ]

# Reader feedback

Feedback from our readers is always welcome. Let us know what you think about this book—what you liked or disliked. Reader feedback is important for us as it helps us develop titles that you will really get the most out of.

To send us general feedback, simply e-mail feedback@packtpub.com, and mention the book's title in the subject of your message.

If there is a topic that you have expertise in and you are interested in either writing or contributing to a book, see our author guide at www.packtpub.com/authors.

# Customer support

Now that you are the proud owner of a Packt book, we have a number of things to help you to get the most from your purchase.

# Downloading the example code

You can download the example code files for this book from your account at http://www.packtpub.com. If you purchased this book elsewhere, you can visit http://www.packtpub.com/support and register to have the files e-mailed directly to you.

You can download the code files by following these steps:

- Log in or register to our website using your e-mail address and password.
- Hover the mouse pointer on the **SUPPORT** tab at the top.
- Click on **Code Downloads & Errata**.
- Enter the name of the book in the Search box.

- Select the book for which you're looking to download the code files.
- Choose from the drop-down menu where you purchased this book from.
- Click on **Code Download**.

You can also download the code files by clicking on the **Code Files** button on the book's webpage at the Packt Publishing website. This page can be accessed by entering the book's name in the **Search** box. Please note that you need to be logged in to your Packt account.

Once the file is downloaded, please make sure that you unzip or extract the folder using the latest version of:

- WinRAR / 7-Zip for Windows
- Zipeg / iZip / UnRarX for Mac
- 7-Zip / PeaZip for Linux

The code bundle for the book is also hosted on GitHub at `https://github.com/PacktPublishing/Python-Deep-Learning`. We also have other code bundles from our rich catalog of books and videos available at `https://github.com/PacktPublishing/`. Check them out!

# Downloading the color images of this book

We also provide you with a PDF file that has color images of the screenshots/ diagrams used in this book. The color images will help you better understand the changes in the output. You can download this file from `https://www.packtpub.com/sites/default/files/downloads/PythonDeepLearning_ColorImages.pdf`.

# Errata

Although we have taken every care to ensure the accuracy of our content, mistakes do happen. If you find a mistake in one of our books—maybe a mistake in the text or the code—we would be grateful if you could report this to us. By doing so, you can save other readers from frustration and help us improve subsequent versions of this book. If you find any errata, please report them by visiting `http://www.packtpub.com/submit-errata`, selecting your book, clicking on the **Errata Submission Form** link, and entering the details of your errata. Once your errata are verified, your submission will be accepted and the errata will be uploaded to our website or added to any list of existing errata under the Errata section of that title.

To view the previously submitted errata, go to https://www.packtpub.com/books/content/support and enter the name of the book in the search field. The required information will appear under the **Errata** section.

# Piracy

Piracy of copyrighted material on the Internet is an ongoing problem across all media. At Packt, we take the protection of our copyright and licenses very seriously. If you come across any illegal copies of our works in any form on the Internet, please provide us with the location address or website name immediately so that we can pursue a remedy.

Please contact us at copyright@packtpub.com with a link to the suspected pirated material.

We appreciate your help in protecting our authors and our ability to bring you valuable content.

# Questions

If you have a problem with any aspect of this book, you can contact us at questions@packtpub.com and we will do our best to address the problem.

# Machine Learning – An Introduction

*"Machine Learning (CS229) is the most popular course at Stanford" –this is how a Forbes article by Laura Hamilton started, continuing- "Why? Because, increasingly, machine learning is eating the world".*

Machine learning techniques are, indeed, being applied in a variety of fields, and data scientists are being sought after in many different industries. With machine learning, we identify the processes through which we gain knowledge that is not readily apparent from data, in order to be able to make decisions. Applications of machine learning techniques may vary greatly and are applicable in disciplines as diverse as medicine, finance, and advertising.

In this chapter, we will present different Machine learning approaches and techniques, and some of their applications to real-world problems, and we will introduce one of the major open source packages available in Python for machine learning, `scikit-learn`. This will lay the background for later chapters in which we will focus on a particular type of machine learning approach using neural networks that aims at emulating brain functionality, and in particular deep learning. Deep learning makes use of more advanced neural networks than those used during the 80's, thanks not only to recent developments in the theory but also to advances in computer speed and the use of **GPUs** (**Graphical Processing Units**) versus the more traditional use of **CPUs** (**Computing Processing Units**). This chapter is meant mostly as a summary of what machine learning is and can do, and to prepare the reader to better understand how deep learning differentiates itself from popular traditional machine learning techniques.

In particular, in this chapter we will cover:

- What is machine learning?
- Different machine learning approaches
- Steps involved in machine learning systems
- Brief description of popular techniques/algorithms
- Applications in real-life
- A popular open source package

# What is machine learning?

Machine learning is often mentioned together with terms such as "big data" and "artificial intelligence", or A.I. for short, but it is quite different from both. In order to understand what machine learning is and why it is useful, it is important to understand what big data is and how machine learning applies to it. Big data is a term used to describe huge data sets that are created as the result of large increases in data gathered and stored, for example, through cameras, sensors, or Internet social sites. It is estimated that Google alone processes over 20 petabytes of information per day and this number is only going to increase. IBM estimated (http://www-01.ibm.com/software/data/bigdata/what-is-big-data.html) that every day, 2.5 quintillion bytes are created and that 90% of all the data in the world has been created in the last two years.

Clearly, humans alone are unable to grasp, let alone analyze, such a huge amount of data, and machine learning techniques are used to make sense of these very large data sets. Machine learning is the tool used for large-scale data processing and is well suited for complex datasets with huge numbers of variables and features. One of the strengths of many machine learning techniques, and deep learning in particular, is that it performs best when it can be used on large data sets improving its analytic and predictive power. In other words, machine learning techniques, and especially deep learning neural networks, "learn" best when they can access large data sets in order to discover patterns and regularities hidden in the data.

On the other hand, machine learning's predictive ability can be well adapted to artificial intelligence systems. Machine learning can be thought of as "the brain" of an artificial intelligence system. Artificial intelligence can be defined (though this definition may not be unique) as a system that can interact with its environment: artificial intelligence machines are endowed with sensors that allow them to know about the environment they are in and tools with which they can relate back. Machine learning is therefore the brain that allows the machine to analyze the data ingested through its sensors to formulate an appropriate answer. A simple example is Siri on an iPhone. Siri hears the command through its microphone and outputs an answer through its speakers or through its display, but in order to do so it needs to "understand" what it is being said to formulate the correct answer. Similarly, driverless cars will be equipped with cameras, GPS systems, sonars and lidars, but all this information needs to be processed in order to provide a correct answer, that is, whether to accelerate, brake, turn, and so on. The information processing that leads to the answer represents what machine learning is.

# Different machine learning approaches

The term machine learning, as we have seen, is used in a very general way and it refers to general techniques to extrapolate patterns from large sets or to the ability to make predictions on new data based on what is learnt by analyzing available known data. This is a very general and broad definition and it encompasses many different techniques. Machine learning techniques can be roughly divided into two large classes: Supervised and Unsupervised learning, though one more class is often added, and is referred to as Reinforcement Learning.

## Supervised learning

The first class of machine algorithms is named *supervised learning*. Supervised learning algorithms are a class of machine learning algorithms that use a set of labeled data in order to classify similar un-labeled data. Labeled data is data that has already been classified, while un-labeled data is data that has not yet been labeled. Labels, as we will see, can either be discrete or continuous. In order to better understand this concept, let's use an example.

Assume that a user receives a large amount of e-mails every day, some of which are important business e-mails and some of which are un-solicited junk e-mails, or spam. A supervised machine algorithm will be presented with a large body of e-mails that have already been labeled by the user as spam or not spam. The algorithm will run over all the labeled data and make predictions on whether the e-mail is spam or not. This means that the algorithm will examine each example and make a prediction for each example on whether the e-mail is spam or not. Typically, the first time the algorithm runs over all the un-labeled data, it will mislabel many of the e-mails and it may perform quite poorly. However, after each run, the algorithm will compare its prediction to the desired outcome (the label). In doing so, the algorithm will learn to improve its performance and accuracy. As noted above, an approach of this kind will benefit from large amounts of data on which it can better learn what characteristics (or features) cause each e-mail to be classified as spam or not.

After the algorithm has run for a while on the labeled data (often also called training data) and it stops improving its accuracy, it can then be used on new e-mails to test its accuracy on new un-labeled data.

In the example we have used, we have described a process in which an algorithm learns from labeled data (the e-mails that have been classified as spam or not spam) in order to make predictions on new unclassified e-mails. It is important to note, however, that we can generalize this process to more than simply two classes: for example, we could run the software and train it on a set of labeled e-mails where the labels are called **Personal**, **Business/Work**, **Social**, or **Spam**.

In fact, Gmail, the free e-mail service by Google, allows the user to select up to five categories, labeled as:

- **Primary**, which includes person-to-person conversations
- **Social**, which includes messages from social networks and media sharing sites
- **Promotions**, which includes marketing e-mails, offers, and discounts
- **Updates**, which includes bills, bank statements, and receipts
- **Forums**, which includes messages from online groups and mailing lists

In some cases, the outcome may not necessarily be discrete, and we may not have a finite number of classes to classify our data into. For example, we may be trying to predict the life expectancy of a group of people based on pre-determined health parameters. In this case, since the outcome is a continuous function (we can specify a life expectancy as a real number expressing the number of years that person is expected to live) we do not talk about a classification task but rather of a regression problem.

One way to think of supervised learning is by imagining we are trying to build a function $f$ defined on the dataset. Our dataset will comprise information organized by *features*. In the example of e-mail classification, those features may be specific words that may appear more frequently than others in spam e-mails. The use of explicit sex-related words will most likely identify a spam e-mail rather than a business/work e-mail. On the contrary, words, such as "meeting", "business", and "presentation" will more likely describe a work e-mail. If we have access to metadata, the sender information may also be used to better classify e-mails. Each e-mail will then have associated a set of features, and each feature will have a value (in this case, how many times the specific word is present in the e-mail body). The machine learning algorithm will then seek to map those values to a discrete range which represents the set of classes, or a real value in the case of regression. The algorithm will run over many examples until it is able to define the best function that will allow matching most labeled data correctly. It can then be run over unlabeled data to make predictions without human intervention. This defines a function:

$$f: space\ of\ features \rightarrow classes = (discrete\ values\ or\ real\ values)$$

We can also think of classification as a process seeking to separate different groups of data points. Once we have defined our features, any example, for example, an e-mail, in our dataset can be thought of as a point in the space of features, where each point represents a different example (or e-mail). The machine algorithm task will be to draw a hyper-plane (that is a plane in a high dimensional space) to separate points with different characteristics, in the same way we want to separate spam from non-spam e-mails.

While, as in the picture below, this may look trivial in a two-dimensional case, this can turn out to be very complex in examples with hundreds or thousands of dimensions.

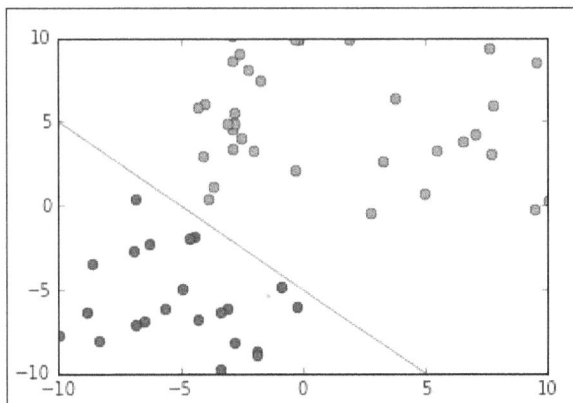

Classification can be thought of as a way of separating the input data

In later chapters, we will see several examples of either classification or regression problems. One such problem we will discuss is that of the classification of digits: given a set of images representing 0 to 9, the machine learning algorithm will try to classify each image assigning to it the digits it depicts. For such examples, we will make use of one of the most classic datasets, the MNIST dataset. In this example, each digit is represented by an image with 28 x 28 (=784) pixels, and we need to classify each of the ten digits, therefore we need to draw 9 separating hyper planes in a 784-dimensional space.

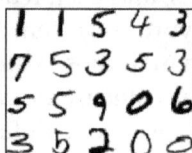

Example of handwritten digits from the MNIST dataset

# Unsupervised learning

The second class of machine learning algorithms is named *unsupervised learning*. In this case, we do not label the data beforehand, rather we let the algorithm come to its conclusion. One of the most common and perhaps simplest examples of unsupervised learning is clustering. This is a technique that attempts to separate the data into subsets.

For example, in the previous case of spam/not spam e-mails, the algorithm may be able to find elements that are common to all spam e-mails (for example, the presence of misspelled words). While this may provide a better than random classification, it isn't clear that spam/not spam e-mails can be so easily separated. The subsets into which the algorithm separates the data are different classes for the dataset. For clustering to work, each element in each cluster should in principle have high intra-class similarity and low similarity with other classes. Clustering may work with any number of classes, and the idea behind clustering methods such as k-means is to find k-subsets of the original data whose elements are closer (more similar) to each other than they are to any other element outside their class. Of course, in order to do this, we need to define what *closer* or *more similar* means, that is, we need to define some kind of metric that defines the distance between points.

In the following graph, we show how a set of points can be classified to form three subsets:

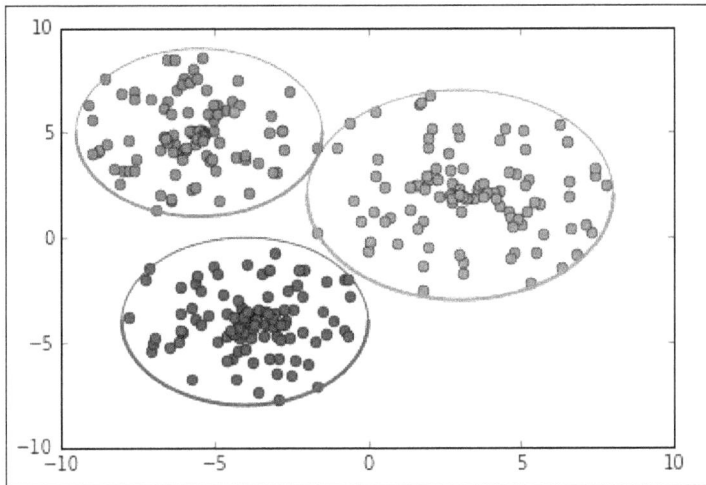

Elements of a given dataset need not necessarily cluster together to form a finite set, but clustering may also include unbounded subsets of the given dataset as in the following picture:

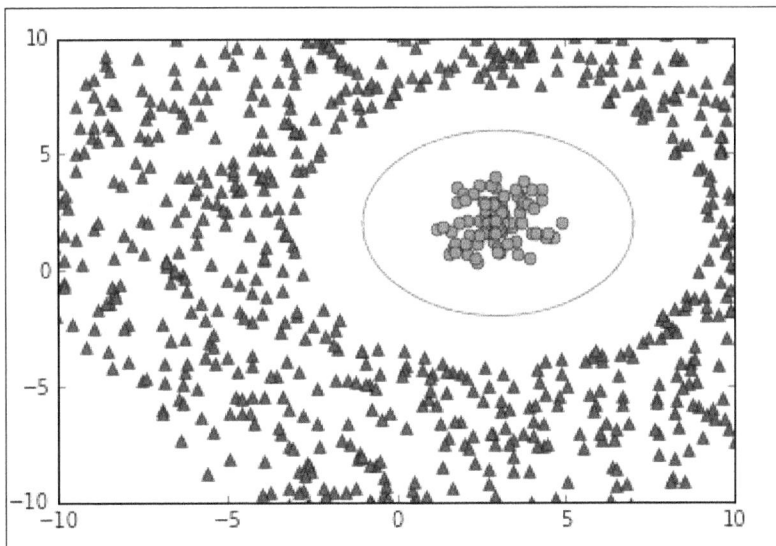

Clustering is not the only unsupervised technique and we will see that deep learning's recent successes are related to it being so effective in unsupervised learning tasks.

New data is created every day, very quickly, and labeling all the new data is quite a laborious and time-consuming activity. One advantage of unsupervised learning algorithms is that they do not need labeled data. Unsupervised deep learning techniques and methods, such as Restricted Boltzmann machines, work by abstracting features from the data. For example, using the MNIST dataset, Restricted Boltzmann machines will abstract characteristics that are unique to each digit, detecting the shape of the lines and curves for each digit. Unsupervised learning works by revealing hidden structures in the data that allow us to classify it accordingly, not by matching it to a label.

In addition, for instance with deep belief nets, we can improve performance of an unsupervised method by refining it with supervised learning.

# Reinforcement learning

The third class of machine learning techniques is called *reinforcement learning*. This works differently from supervised learning though it still uses a feedback element to improve its performance. A common application of reinforcement learning techniques is in teaching machines how to play games: in this case, we do not label each move as good or bad but the feedback comes from the game, either through the outcome of the game or through signals during the game, such as scoring or losing points. Winning a game will reflect a positive outcome, similar to recognizing the right digit or whether an e-mail is spam or not, while losing the game would require further "learning". Reinforcement learning algorithms tend to reuse actions tried in the past that led to successful results, like winning in a game. However, when in uncharted territory, the algorithm must try new actions from which, depending on the result, it will learn the structure of the game more deeply. Since usually, actions are inter-related, it is not the single action that can be valued as "good" or "bad", but rather it is the whole dynamics of actions together that is evaluated. Similar to how in playing chess sometimes sacrificing a pawn may be considered a positive action if it brings a better positioning on the chessboard, even though the loss of a piece is, in general, a negative outcome, in reinforcement learning it is the whole problem and its goal that is explored. For example, a moving cleaning robot may have to decide whether to continue cleaning a room or to start to move back to its recharging station, and such a decision could be made on the basis of whether in similar circumstances it was able to find the charging station before the battery ran out. In reinforcement learning, the basic idea is that of *reward,* where the algorithm will seek to maximize the total reward it receives.

A simple example of reinforcement learning can be used to play the classic game of tic-tac-toe. In this case, each position on the board has associated a probability (a value), which is the probability of winning the game from that state based on previous experience. At the beginning, each state is set at 50%, which is we assume that at the beginning we have an equal probability of winning or losing from any position. In general, the machine will try to move towards positions with higher values in order to win the game, and will re-evaluate them if, instead, it loses. At each position, the machine will then make a choice based on the probable outcome, rather than on a fixed determined rule. As it keeps playing, these probabilities will get refined and output a higher or lower chance of success depending on the position.

# Steps Involved in machine learning systems

So far, we have discussed different machine learning approaches, and we have roughly organized them in three different classes. Another important aspect of classical machine learning is understanding the data to better understand the problem at hand. The important aspects we need to define in order to apply machine learning can roughly be described as follows:

- **Learner**: this represents the algorithm being used and its "learning philosophy". As we will see in the next paragraph, there are many different machine learning techniques that can be applied to different learning problems. The choice of learner is important, since different problems can be better suited to certain machine learning algorithms.

- **Training data**: This is the raw dataset that we are interested in. Such data may be unlabeled for unsupervised learning, or it may include labels for supervised learning. It is important to have enough sample data for the learner to understand the structure of the problem.

- **Representation**: This is how the data is expressed in terms of the features chosen so that it can be ingested by the learner. For example, if we are trying to classify digits using images, this will represent the array of values describing the pixels of the images. A good choice of representation of the data is important to achieve better results.

- **Goal**: This represents the reason to learn from the data for the problem at hand. This is strictly related to the target, and helps define how and what learner should be used and what representation to use. For example, the goal may be to clean our mailbox of unwanted e-mails, and the goal defines what the target of our learner is, for example, detection of spam e-mails.

- **Target**: This represents what is being learned and the final output. It may be a classification of the unlabeled data, it may be a representation of the input data according to hidden patterns or characteristics, it may be a simulator for future predictions, it may be a response to an outside stimulus, or it can be a strategy in the case of reinforcement learning.

It can never be emphasized enough, though, that any machine learning algorithm can only achieve an approximation of the target, not a perfect numerical description. Machine learning algorithms are not exact mathematical solutions to problems, rather they are just approximations. In the previous paragraph, we have defined learning as a function from the space of features (the input) into a range of classes; we will later see how certain machine learning algorithms, such as neural networks, can be proved to be able to approximate any function to any degree, in theory. This theorem is called the Universal Approximation Theorem, but it does not imply that we can get a precise solution to our problem. In addition, solutions to the problem can be better achieved by better understanding of the training data.

Typically, a problem solvable with classic machine learning techniques may require a thorough understanding and cleaning of the training data before deployment. If we are to state some of the steps required in approaching a machine learning problem, we may summarize them as follows:

- **Data Collection**: This implies the gathering of as much data as possible and in the supervised learning problem also its correct labeling.

- **Data Processing**: This implies cleaning of the data (for example removing redundant or highly correlated features, or filling missing data) and understanding of the features defining the training data.

- **Creation of the test case**: Typically data can be divided into two or three sets: a training dataset, on which we train the algorithm, and a testing dataset, on which we test, after having trained the algorithm, the accuracy of the approach. Often, we also create a validation dataset, on which, after the training-testing procedure has been repeated many times and we are finally satisfied with the result, we make the final testing (or validation).

There are valid reasons to create a testing and a validation dataset. As we mentioned, machine learning techniques can only produce an approximation of the desired result. This is due to the fact that often, we can only include a finite and limited number of variables, and there may be many variables that are outside our own control. If we only used a single dataset, our model may end up "memorizing" the data and produce an extremely high accuracy value on the data it has memorized, but this result may not be reproducible on other similar datasets. One of the key desired goals of machine learning techniques is their ability to generalize. That is why we create both a testing dataset, used for tuning our model selection after training, and a final validation dataset only used at the end of the process to confirm the validity of the selected algorithm.

To understand the importance of selecting valid features in the data and the importance of avoiding "memorizing" the data (in more technical terms, this is what is referred to as "overfitting" in the literature, and this is what we will be calling it from now on), let's use a joke taken from an *xkcd* comic as an example (`http://xkcd.com/1122`): "Until 1996 no democratic US presidential candidate who was an incumbent and with no combat experience had ever beaten anyone whose first name was worth more in Scrabble". It is apparent in this example that such a "rule" is meaningless, however it underscores the importance of selecting valid features (does how much a name is worth in Scrabble bear any relevance to selecting a US president?) and that selecting random features as predictors, while it may predict the current data, cannot be used as a predictor for more general data, and that the fact that for 52 elections this had held true was simple coincidence. This is what is generally called overfitting, that is, making predictions that fit the data at hand perfectly, but do not generalize to larger datasets. Overfitting is the process of trying to make sense of what is generally called "noise" (that is, information that does not have any real meaning) and trying to fit the model to small perturbations.

Another example may be given by attempting to use machine learning to predict the trajectory of a ball thrown from the ground up in the air (not perpendicularly) until it reaches the ground again. Physics teaches us that the trajectory is shaped like a parabola, and we expect that a good machine learning algorithm observing thousands of such throws would come up with a parabola as a solution. However, if we were to zoom in on the ball and observe the smallest fluctuations in the air due to turbulence, we might notice that the ball does not hold a steady trajectory but may be subject to small perturbations. This is what we call "noise". A machine learning algorithm that tried to model these small perturbations would fail to see the big picture, and produce a result that is not satisfactory. In other words, overfitting is the process that makes the machine learning algorithm see the trees but forget about the forest.

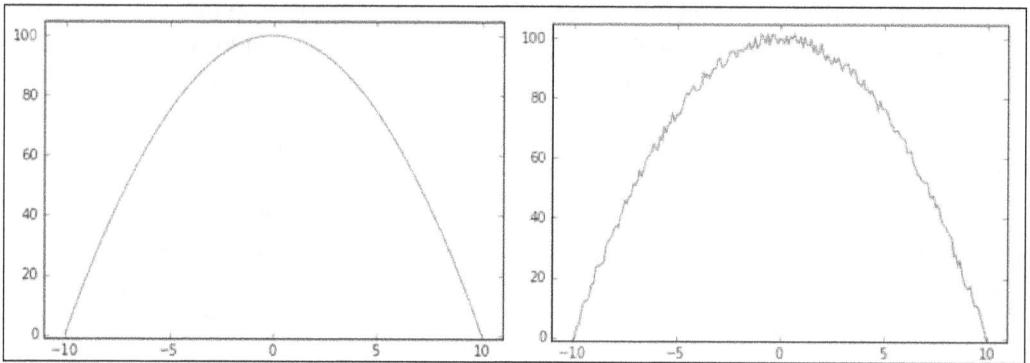

A good prediction model vs. a bad (overfitted) prediction model of the trajectory of a ball thrown from the ground

This is why we separate the training data from the test data: if the accuracy of the test data were not similar to the result achieved on the training data, that would be a good indication that we have overfitted the model. Of course, we need to make sure we don't make the opposite error either, that is, underfit the model. In practice, though, if we are aiming at making our prediction model as accurate as possible on our training data, underfitting is much less of a risk than overfitting, and most care is therefore taken in order to avoid overfitting the model.

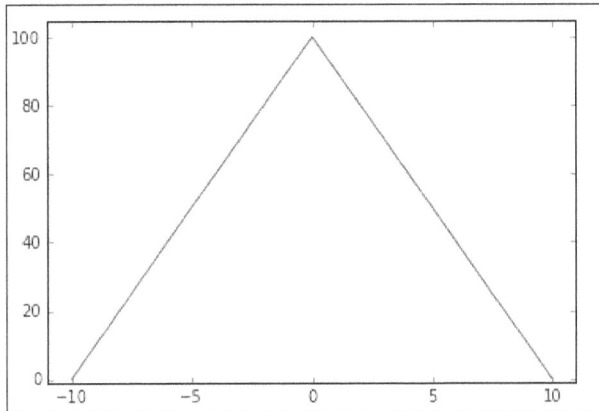

Underfitting can be a problem as well

# Brief description of popular techniques/algorithms

Besides grouping algorithms based upon their "learning style", that is, the three classes discussed at the beginning of the book, supervised learning, unsupervised learning, and reinforcement learning, we can also group them by their implementation. Clearly, each class discussed above may be implemented using different machine learning algorithms, as, for example, there are many different supervised learning techniques, where each of them may be best suited to the specific classifying or regression task at hand. In fact, the distinction between classification and regression is one of the most critical to make, and it is important to understand what we are trying to accomplish.

The following is by no means meant to be an exhaustive list or a thorough description of each machine learning method, for which we refer the reader to the book *Python Machine Learning*, Sebastian Raschka (`https://www.packtpub.com/big-data-and-business-intelligence/python-machine-learning`), rather it is meant as a simple review to provide the reader with a simple flavor of the different techniques and how deep learning differs from them. In the next chapters, we will see that deep learning is not just another machine learning algorithm, but it differs in substantial ways from classical machine learning techniques.

We will introduce a regression algorithm, linear regression, classical classifiers such as decision trees, naïve Bayes, and support vector machine, and unsupervised clustering algorithms such as k-means, and reinforcement learning techniques, the cross-entropy method, to give only a small glimpse of the variety of machine learning techniques that exist, and we will end this list by introducing neural networks, that is the main focus of this book.

# Linear regression

Regression algorithms are a kind of supervised algorithm that use features of the input data to predict a value, for example the cost of a house given certain features such as size, age, number of bathrooms, number of floors, location, and so on. Regression analysis tries to find the value of the parameters for the function that best fits an input dataset. In a linear regression algorithm, the goal is to minimize a cost function by finding appropriate parameters for the function on the input data that best approximate the target values. A cost function is a function of the error, which is how far we are from getting a correct result. A typical cost function used is the mean squared error, where we take the square of the difference between the expected value and the predicted result. The sum over all the input examples gives the error of the algorithm and it represents the cost function.

Say we have a 100-square meter house, built 25 years ago, with three bathrooms, and two floors. Furthermore, assume that we divide the city, where the houses are in 10 different areas, that we denote with integers from 1 to 10, and say this house is located in the area denoted by a 7. We can then parameterize this house with a 5-dimensional vector $x = (100, 25, 3, 2, 7)$. Say that we also know that this house has an estimated value of €10,0000. What we want to achieve is to create a function $f$ such that $f(x) = 100000$.

In linear regression, this means finding a vector $w = (w_1, w_2, w_3, w_4, w_5)$ such that $100 * w_1 + 25 * w_2 + 3 * w_3 + 2 * w_4 + 7 * w_5 = 100000$. If we had a thousand houses, we could repeat the same process for every house, and ideally we would like to find a vector $w$ that can predict the correct value (or close enough) for every house. Let's say that we initially pick some random value of $w$. In that case, we won't expect $f(x) = 100 * w_1 + 25 * w_2 + 3 * w_3 + 2 * w_4 + 7 * w_5$ to be equal to 1,00,000, so we can calculate the error $\Delta = (100000 - f(x))^2$. This is the squared error for one example $x$, and the mean of all the squared errors for all the examples represents our cost, that is, how much our function differs from the real value. Our aim is therefore to minimize this error, and to do so we calculate the derivative $\delta$ of the cost function with respect to $w$. The derivative indicates the direction where the function increases (or decreases), therefore, moving $w$ in the opposite direction to the derivative will improve our function's accuracy. This is the main point of linear regression, moving towards the minimum of the cost function, which represents the error. Of course, we need to decide how fast we want to move in the direction of the derivative, as our derivative only indicates a direction. The cost function is not linear, therefore we need to make sure we only take small steps in the direction indicated by the derivative. Taking too large a step may possibly make us overshoot our minimum, and therefore not be able to converge to it. The magnitude of this step is what is called the *learning rate*, and lets us indicate its magnitude with the symbol "*lr*".

By setting $w = w - \delta*lr$, we are therefore improving the choice of $w$ towards a better solution. Repeating this process many times will produce a value of $w$ that represents the best possible choice for the function $f$. We should emphasize, however, that this process will only work locally, and it may not find a global best value if the space is not convex. As the image suggests, if many local minima exist, the algorithm may end up being stuck in one of these local minima and not be able to escape it to reach the global minimum of the error function, similar to how a small ball, moving down from a mountain, may get stuck in a small valley and never reach the bottom of the mountain.

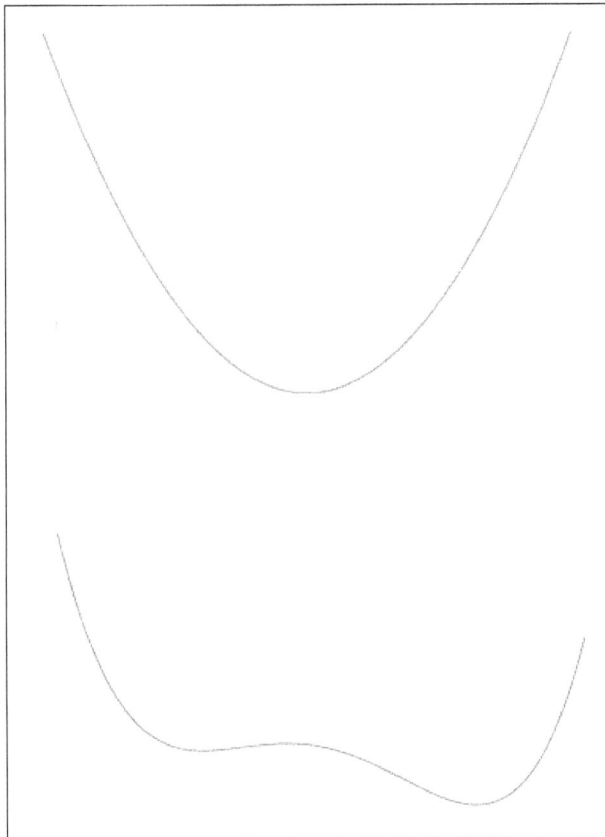

The top graph is convex, and therefore there exists just one minimum. In the bottom graph the function has two local minima, and therefore, depending on the initialization, the process may find the first local minimum that is not the global minimum.

# Decision trees

Another widely used supervised algorithm is the decision tree algorithm. A decision tree algorithm creates a classifier in the form of a "tree". A decision tree is comprised of decision nodes where tests on specific attributes are performed, and leaf nodes that indicate the value of the target attribute. Decision trees are a type of classifier that works by starting at the root node and moving down through the decision nodes until a leaf is reached.

A classic application of this algorithm is the Iris flower dataset (`http://archive.ics.uci.edu/ml/datasets/Iris`) that contains data from 50 samples of three types of Irises (Iris setosa, Iris virginica, and Iris versicolor). Ronald Fisher, who created the dataset, measured four different features of these flowers, the length and width of their sepals and the length and width of their petals. Based on the different combinations of these features, it is possible to create a decision tree to decide to which species each flower belongs. We will here describe a simple simplified decision tree that will classify correctly, almost all the flowers only using two of these features, the petal length and width.

We start with the first node and we create the first test on petal length: if the petal length is less than 2.5, then the flower belongs to the Iris setosa species. This, in fact, classifies correctly, all the setosa flowers, which all have a petal length less than 2.5 cm. Therefore, we reach a leaf node, which is labeled by the outcome Iris setosa. If the petal length is greater than 2.5, we take a different branch and we reach a new decision node, and we test whether the petal width is larger than 1.8. If the petal width is larger or equal to 1.8, we reach a leaf node and we classify our flower as an Iris virginica, otherwise we reach a new decision node, where again we test whether the petal length is longer than 4.9. If it is, we reach a leaf node labeled by the Iris virginica flower, otherwise we reach another leaf node, labeled by the Iris versicolor flower.

The decision tree discussed can be shown as follows, where the left branch reflects the positive answer to the test in the decision node, while the right branch represents the negative answer to the test in the decision node. The end nodes for each branch are the leaf nodes:

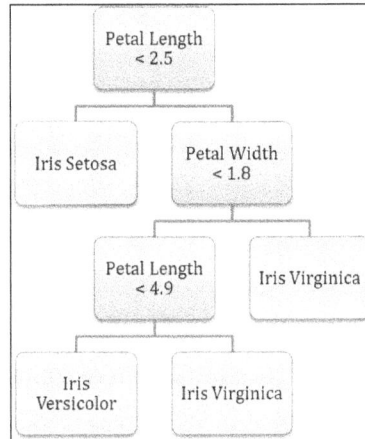

This example shows how very different the decision tree algorithm is from linear regression. In addition, when we introduce neural nets, the reader will be able to see an example of how neural nets work by using this same dataset. In that example, we will also provide Python code and we will show a few pictures of how neural nets will try to separate the flowers based on their features.

# K-means

Clustering algorithms, as we have already discussed, are a type of unsupervised machine learning method. The most common clustering technique is called k-means clustering and is a clustering technique that groups every element in a dataset by grouping them into k distinct subsets (hence the *k* in the name). K-means is a relatively simple procedure, and consists of choosing random k points that represent the distinct centers of the k subsets, which are called centroids. We then select, for each centroid, all the points closest to it. This will create k different subsets. At this point, for each subset, we will re-calculate the center. We have again, *k* new centroids, and we repeat the steps above, selecting for each centroid, the new subsets of points closest to the centroids. We continue this process until the centroids stop moving.

It is clear that for this technique to work, we need to be able to identify a metric that allows us to calculate the distance between points. This procedure can be summarized as follows:

1. Choose initial k-points, called the centroids.
2. To each point in the dataset, associate the closest centroid.
3. Calculate the new center for the sets of points associated to a particular centroid.
4. Define the new centers to be the new centroids.
5. Repeat steps 3 and 4 until the centroids stop moving.

It is important to notice that this method is sensitive to the initial choice of random centroids, and that it may be a good idea to repeat the process for different initial choices. Also, it is possible for some of the centroids not to be closest to any of the points in the dataset, reducing the number of subsets down from k. It is also worth mentioning that if we used k-means with $k=3$ in the above example discussing decision trees, we may not be getting the same classification for the iris dataset that we found using decision trees, highlighting once more how important it is to carefully choose and use the correct machine learning method for each problem.

Now, let's discuss a practical example that uses k-means clustering. Let's say a pizza delivery place wants to open four new franchises in a new city, and they need to choose the location for the four new sites. This is a problem that can be solved easily using k-means clustering. The idea is to find the locations where pizza is ordered most often; these will be our data points. Next, we choose four random points where the site locations will be located. By using k-means clustering techniques, we can later identify the four best locations that minimize the distance to each delivery place. This is an example where k-means clustering can help solve a business problem.

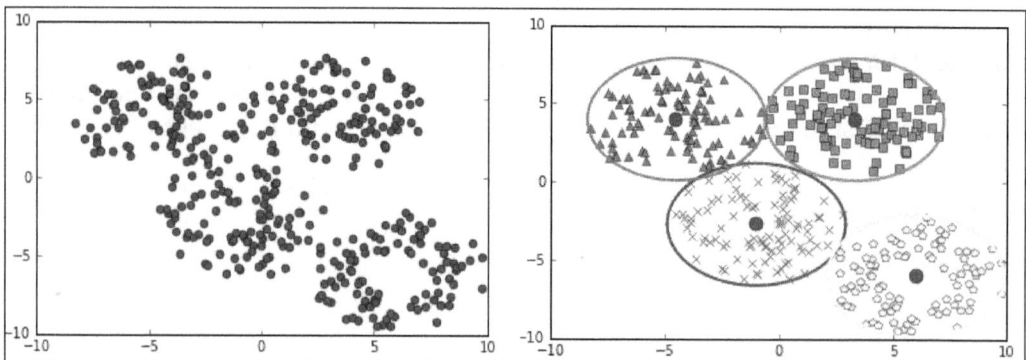

On the left the distribution of points where pizza is delivered most often. On the right, the round points indicate where the new franchises should be located and their corresponding delivery areas

# Naïve Bayes

Naïve Bayes is different from many other machine learning algorithms. Probabilistically, what most machine learning techniques try to evaluate is the probability of a certain event $Y$ given conditions $X$, which we denote by $p(Y|X)$. For example, given the picture representing a digit (that is, a picture with a certain distribution of pixels), what is the probability that that number is 5? If the pixels' distribution is such that it is close to the pixel distribution of other examples that were labeled as 5, the probability of that event will be high, otherwise the probability will be low.

Sometimes we have the opposite information, that is, given we know that we have an event Y, we know the probability that our sample is X. The Bayes theorem states: $p(X|Y) = p(Y|X)*p(X)/p(Y)$, where $p(X|Y)$ means the probability of generating instance X given Y, which is also why naïve Bayes is called a generative approach. In simple terms, we may calculate the probability that a certain pixel configuration represents the number 5, knowing what is the probability, given that we have a 5, that a random pixel configuration may match the given one.

This is best understood in the realm of medical testing. Let's say we test for a specific disease or cancer. We want to know what is the probability we may have a particular disease given that our test result was positive. Now, most tests have a reliability value, which is the percentage chance of the test being positive when administered on people with the particular disease. By reversing the expression $p(X|Y) = p(Y|X)*p(X)/p(Y)$, we have that:

$$p(cancer \mid test{=}positive) = p(test{=}positive \mid cancer) * p(cancer)/p(test{=}positive)$$

Assume that the test is 98% reliable, which means that in 98% of the cases, if the person has cancer, the test is positive, and likewise, if the person does not have cancer, the test result is negative. Also assume that this particular kind of cancer only affects older people, and only 2% of people below 50 have this kind of cancer, and the test administered on people under 50 is positive only on 3.9% of the population (we could have derived this fact from the data, but for simplicity we provide this information).

We could ask this question: if a test is 98% accurate for cancer and a 45-year-old person took the test, and it turned out to be positive, what is the probability that he/she may have cancer? Using the formula above we can calculate:

$$p(cancer \mid test{=}positive) = 0.98 * 0.02/0.039 = 0.50$$

So, despite the high accuracy of the test, naïve Bayes tells us we also need to take into account the fact that the cancer is quite rare under 50, therefore the positivity of the test alone does not give a 98% probability of cancer. The probability *p(cancer)*, or more in general the probability p for the outcome we are trying to estimate, is called the prior probability, because it represents the probability of the event without any additional information, therefore before we took the test.

At this point, we may wonder what would happen if we had more information, for example if we performed a different test with different reliability, or knew some information about the person such as recurrence of cancer in the family. In the preceding equation we used, as one of the factors in the computation, the probability *p(test=positive | cancer)*, and if we performed a second test, and it came positive, we would also have *p(test2=positive | cancer)*. The naïve Bayes technique makes the assumption that each piece of information is independent of each other (this means that the outcome of test 2 did not know about the outcome of test 1 and it was independent of it, that is, taking test 1 could not change the outcome of test 2, and therefore its result was not biased by the first test). naïve Bayes is a classification algorithm that assumes the independence of different events to calculate their probability. Hence:

*p(test1 and test2=pos | cancer) =p(test1=pos | cancer)\*p(test2=pos | cancer)*

This equation is also called the likelihood *L(test1 and test2 = pos)* that *test1* and *test2* be positive given the fact that the person does have cancer.

We can then rewrite the equation as:

*p(cancer | both tests=pos) =*

*= p(both test=pos | cancer)\*p(cancer)/p(both tests=pos)  =*

*= p(test1=pos | cancer)\*p(test2=pos | cancer) \*p(cancer)/p(both tests=pos)*

# Support vector machines

Support vector machines is a supervised machine learning algorithm mainly used for classification. The advantage of support vector machines over other machine learning algorithms is that not only does it separate the data into classes, but it does so finding a separating hyper-plane (the analog of a plane in a space with more than three dimensions) that maximizes the margin separating each point from the hyper-plane. In addition, support vector machines can also deal with the case when the data is not linearly separable. There are two ways to deal with non-linearly separable data, one is by introducing soft margins, and another is by introducing the so-called kernel trick.

Soft margins work by allowing a few miss-classified elements while retaining most predictive ability of the algorithm. As we have discussed above, in practice it is always better not to overfit any machine learning model, and we could do so by relaxing some of the support vector machine hypotheses.

The kernel trick instead involves mapping the space of features into another space where we can define a hyper-plane that, when mapped back into the space of features, is not a linear hyper-plane anymore, allowing to separate elements in the dataset that do not appear to be separable. Since this book will be mainly concerned with deep learning, we will not discuss in detail how support vector machines are implemented, that may take too much time, but rather want to emphasize the concept that support vector machines have been quite popular and effective thanks to their ability to generalize to non-linear situations. As we have seen before, the task of a supervised machine learning algorithm is to find a function from the space of features to a set of classes. Each input $x = (x_1, x_2, ..., x_n)$ represents an input example, and each $x_i$ represents the value of x for the $i^{th}$ feature. Earlier on we gave, as an example, trying to estimate the resell value of a certain house depending on some features, like number of bathrooms or location. If the $i^{th}$ feature corresponds to the number of bathrooms, $x_i$ would correspond to the number of bathrooms present in house $x$. We can create a function $k$ from the space of features to a different representation of this space, called a kernel: for example $k$ may map $x_i$ into $(x_i)^2$, and in general map the space of features non-linearly into another space $W$. So, a separating hyper-plane in $W$, can be mapped back into the space of features, where it would not be a linear hyper-plane anymore. The exact conditions under which this is true are well defined but beyond the scope of this short introduction. However, this again highlights the importance of the choice of correct features in classical machine learning algorithms, a choice that can allow finding the solution to specific problems.

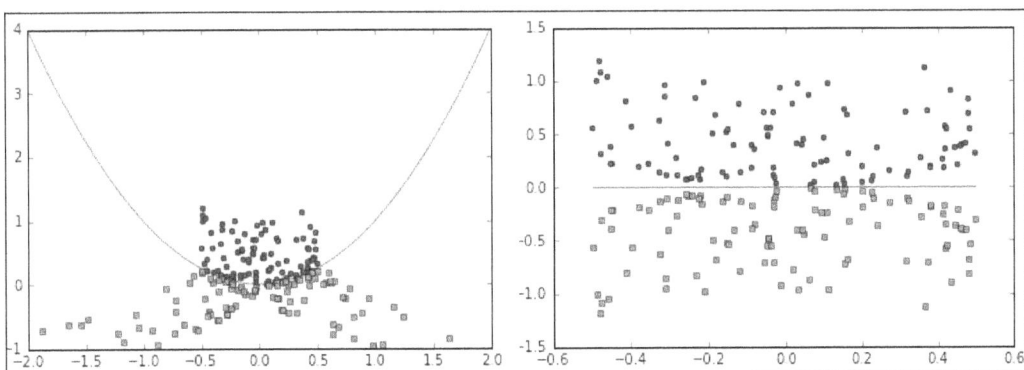

On the left a non-linearly separable set before the kernel was applied. On the right the same dataset after the kernel has been applied and the data can be linearly separated

# The cross-entropy method

So far, we have introduced supervised and unsupervised learning algorithms. The cross-entropy method belongs, instead, to the reinforcement learning class of algorithms, which will be discussed in great detail in *Chapter 7, Deep Learning for Board Games* and *Chapter 8, Deep Learning for Computer Games* of this book. The cross-entropy method is a technique to solve optimization problems, that is, to find the best parameters to minimize or maximize a specific function.

In general, the cross-entropy method consists of the following phases:

1. Generate a random sample of the variables we are trying to optimize. For deep learning these variables might be the weights of a neural network.
2. Run the task and store the performance.
3. Identify the best runs and select the top performing variables.
4. Calculate new means and variances for each variable, based on the top performing runs, and generate a new sample of the variables.
5. Repeat steps until a stop condition is reached or the system stops improving.

Suppose we are trying to solve for a function that depends on many variables, for example we are trying to build a model plane that can fly the longest when launched from a specific altitude. The distance that the plane covers will be a function of the size of its wings, their angle, the weight, and so on. Each time, we can record each variable and then launch the plane and measure the distance it flies. However, rather than trying all possible combinations, we create statistics, we select the best and worst runs, and we note at what values the variables were set during the best runs and during the worst runs. For example, if we detect that for each of the best runs the plane had wings of a specific size, we can conclude that that particular size may be optimal for the plane to fly a long distance. Conversely, if for each of the worst runs, the plane's wings were at a certain angle, we would conclude that that particular angle would be a bad choice for our plane's wings. In general, we will produce a probability distribution for each value that should produce the optimal plane, probabilities that are not random anymore, but based on the feedback we have received.

This method, therefore, uses the feedback from the run (how far the plane has flown) to determine the best solution to the problem (the value for each variable) in a typical reinforcement learning process.

# Neural networks

After having refreshed the reader with some of the popular classical machine learning algorithms, we will now introduce neural networks, and explain in deeper detail how they work and how they differ from the algorithms we have briefly summarized.

Neural networks are another machine learning algorithm and they have known periods of high popularity and periods during which they were rarely used. Understanding neural networks, to which we will dedicate the next and following chapters, is indeed key for following the content of this book.

The first example of a neural network was called the perceptron, which was invented by Frank Rosenblatt in 1957. The perceptron is a network comprised of only an input and an output layer. In case of binary classifications, the output layer has only one neuron or unit. The perceptron seemed to be very promising from the start, though it was quickly realized that it could only learn linearly separable patterns. For example, Marvin Minsky and Seymour Papert showed that it could not learn the XOR logical function. In its most basic representations, perceptrons are just simple representations of one neuron and its input, input that can be comprised of several neurons.

Given different inputs into a neuron, we define an activation value by the formula $a(x) = \sum_i w_i x_i$, where $x_i$ is the value for the input neuron, while $w_i$ is the value of the connection between the neuron $i$ and the output. We will learn this in much deeper detail in the next chapter, for now we should just notice that perceptrons share many similarities with logistic regression algorithms, and are constrained by linear classifiers as well. If the activation value, which should be thought of as the neuron internal state, is greater than a fixed threshold $b$, then the neuron will activate, that is, it will fire, otherwise it will not.

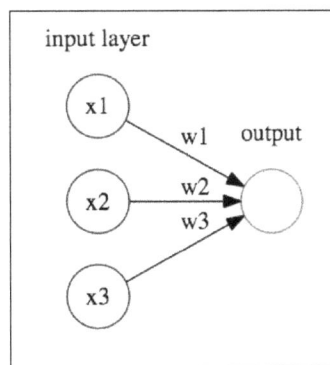

A simple perceptron with three input units (neurons) and one output unit (neuron)

The simple activation defined above can be interpreted as the dot product between the vector **w** and the vector **x**. The vector **w** is fixed, and it defines how the perceptron works, while **x** represents the input. A vector **x** is perpendicular to the weight vector **w** if <**w,x**> = 0, therefore all vectors **x** such that <**w,x**> = 0 define a hyper-plane in $\mathbf{R}^3$ (where 3 is the dimension of **x**, but it could be any integer in general). Hence, any vector **x** satisfying <**w,x**> > 0 is a vector on the side of the hyper-plane defined by **w**. This makes it clear how a perceptron just defines a hyper-plane and it works as a classifier. In general, instead of 0 we can set the threshold to be any real number *b*, this has the effect of translating the hyper-plane away from the origin. However, rather than keeping track of this value, generally we include a bias unit in our network, which is an always on (*value* = 1) special neuron with connecting weight -*b*. In this case, if the connecting weight has value –*b*, the activation value becomes $a(x) = \sum_i w_i x_i$ and setting *a(x)* > 0 is equivalent to setting $\sum_i w_i x_i > b$.

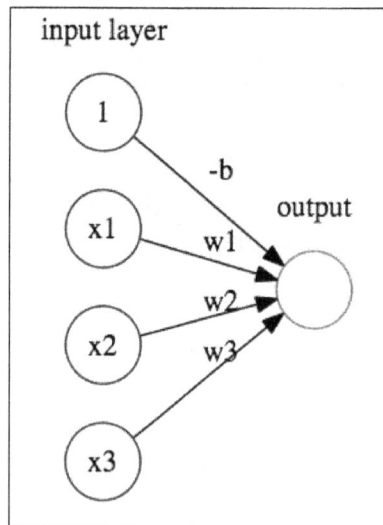

A perceptron with added a bias unit for the output vector. Bias units are always on

Perceptrons, while limited in their performance, are very important historically as they are the first examples of a neural network.

Neural networks, of course, do not need to have one single output neuron, and, in fact, in general they do not. If the network has more than one output neuron, for each output neuron we can repeat the same process. Each weight will then be labeled by two indices, *i* and *j*, to indicate that the weight is connecting the neuron *i* on the input layer to the neuron *j* on the output layer. There will also be a connection from the bias unit, with value 1, to each neuron on the output layer. It should also be noted that we can define different activity functions on the activation value. We have defined the activation value as $a(x) = \sum_i w_i x_i - b$ (from now on we will assume that the bias is included in this formula) and we have said that the neuron activates if the activation is greater than *0*. As we will see, this already defines an activity function, that is, a function defined on the activation, that is, on the neuron's internal state, and this is called the threshold activity, because the neuron activates when the activation is greater than *0*. However, we will see that neural nets can have many different activity functions that can be defined on their activation value, and we will discuss them in greater detail in the next chapter.

# Deep learning

The previous paragraph introduced a very simple example of a neural network, a feed-forward 1-layer network. They are called feed-forward because the information proceeds from the input towards the output and it never loops back, and 1-layer because there is only 1-output layer besides the input layer. This is not the general case. We have already discussed the limitations of 1-layer feed-forward networks when we mentioned that they can only work on linearly separable data, and in particular we mentioned that they cannot approximate the logical XOR function. There are, however, networks that have extra layers between the input and the output layers: these layers are called the hidden layers. A feed-forward network with hidden layers will then move the information from the input through its hidden layer to the output layer, which defines a function that takes an input and it defines an output. There exists a theorem, called the Universal Theorem, which states that any function can be approximated by a neural network with at least one hidden layer, and we will give an intuition of why this is true in the next chapter.

For a long time, given this theorem and also the difficulty in working with complex networks, people have worked with shallow networks with only one hidden layer. However, recently people have realized that more complex networks with many hidden layers can understand levels of abstraction that shallow layers cannot. In addition, recurrent networks have been introduced where neurons can also feed information back into themselves. Some neural networks' structures can also permit to define an energy function that allows for the creation of memories. All of this exciting functionality will be discussed in the next chapters as we will delve through the most recent development in deep learning.

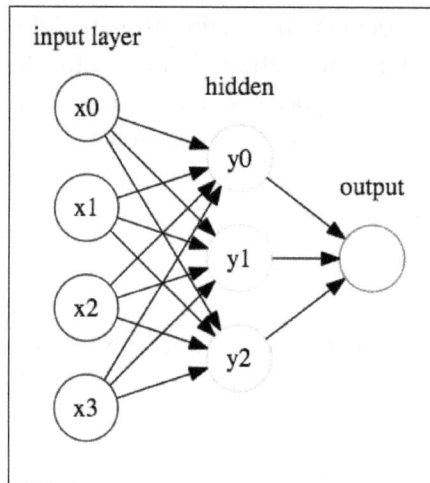

A neural network with one hidden layer

# Applications in real life

Machine learning in general, and deep learning in particular, are producing more and more astonishing results in terms of quality of predictions, feature detections, and classifications. Many of these recent results have made the news in recent years. Such is the pace of progress, that many experts are worrying that very soon machines will be more intelligent than humans. At a UN meeting, on October 14, 2015, artificial intelligence experts and researchers in many other fields warned about the need to define ethical guidelines to prevent the danger that a super-intelligent class of machines may pose to the human race. Such fears arise from some recent incredible results in which computers have been able to beat the best human champions in games where it was thought that intuition would give humans an advantage over machines.

AlphaGo is an artificial intelligence machine based on deep learning which made news in 2016 by beating world Go champion Lee Sedol. In January 2016, AlphaGo had already made the news when it beat the European champion Fan Hui, though, at the time, it seemed unlikely that it could go on to beat the world champion. Fast forward a couple of months and AlphaGo was able to achieve this remarkable feat by sweeping its opponent in a 4-1 victory series. The reason for celebration was due to the fact that Go has many more possible game variations than other games, such as chess, and it is impossible to be able to consider all possible moves in advance. In addition, in Go it is also very difficult to even judge the current position or value of a single stone on the board, unlike chess.

The strength of AlphaGo was that it had not been programmed to play, but it had *learned* to play by playing thousands of games against itself using reinforcement learning and deep learning techniques. The ability to learn is what renders machine learning, and deep learning especially, a completely different approach to solving problems. Deep learning is about creating programs that may learn by themselves with little or no help from humans.

However, the variety of fields in which deep learning has been applied with considerable success is not limited to games. Kaggle (`http://www.kaggle.com`) is a web site hosting many different machine learning competitions. These vary extensively in terms of the field they are used in and their applications. In 2013, the University of Oregon sponsored a competition in which it was asked to use machine learning techniques to detect and identify birds by using standard recording of real-world audio data. In order to gain better understanding of bird population trends, costly human effort is often required. Machine learning helps solve this problem by automatically identifying what birds are present by simply listening on an audio recording.

Amazon recently launched another competition for the problem of granting employees access to internal computers and networks, hoping that a successful solution would cut the costly delays of human supervisory intervention.

The Chicago Department of Health held a competition in 2015 where it asked "given weather location testing and spraying data ... when and where different species of mosquitoes will test positive for West Nile virus".

In August 2015, a competition asked to predict rental prices across Western Australia, and in February 2016 BNP Paribas, a French bank, launched a competition to accelerate its claim management process.

This provides some idea of the variety of problems that can be solved using machine learning, and it should be noted that all these competitions offered prizes for the best solution. In 2009, Netflix launched a one million dollar competition to improve the accuracy of its prediction system on what movies a user may enjoy based on his/her previously ranked movies, and data scientist jobs are routinely ranked among the highest paid and most sought after work occupations.

Machine learning is routinely used in applications ranging from self-driving cars, military drones, and target reconnaissance systems, to medical applications, such as applications able to read doctors' notes to spot potential health problems, and surveillance systems that can provide facial recognition.

Optical character recognition is widely used, for example by post offices, to read addresses on envelopes, and we will show how to apply neural networks to digit recognition using the MNIST dataset. Unsupervised deep learning has also found many applications and great results in **Natural Language Processing** (**NLP**), and almost each one of us has an NLP application of deep learning on his/her smartphone, as both Apple and Android use deep learning applied to NLP for their virtual assistants (for example, Siri). Machine learning also finds applications in biometrics, for example in recognizing someone's physical characteristics, such as fingerprints, DNA or retina recognition. In addition, automobile autonomous driving has improved in recent years to the point that it is now a reality.

Machine learning can also be applied to catalog pictures in a photo album, or, more importantly, satellite images, allowing the description of different images according to whether they are an urban environment or not, whether they describe forests, ice regions, water extensions, and so on.

To summarize, machine learning has recently found applications in almost every aspect of our lives, and its accuracy and performance has seen a continuous improvement thanks also to increasingly better and faster computers.

# A popular open source package

Machine learning is a popular and competitive field, and there are many open source packages that implement most of the classic machine learning algorithms. One of the most popular is `scikit-learn` (`http://scikit-learn.org`), a widely used open source library used in Python.

`scikit-learn` offers libraries that implement most classical machine-learning classifiers, regressors and clustering algorithms such as **support vector machines** (**SVM**), nearest neighbors, random forests, linear regression, k-means, decision trees and neural networks, and many more machine learning algorithms

The base class `sklearn` has several packages available, depending on the type of algorithm chosen, such as `sklearn.ensemble`, `sklearn.linear_model`, `sklearn.naive_bayes`, `sklearn.neural_network`, `sklearn.svm`, and `sklearn.tree`.

There are also helpers to do cross-validation and for helping select the best features. Rather than spending time describing all the functionality abstractly, we will instead start with one simple example using a multi-layer neural network. The `scikit-learn` library uses methods with similar signatures for each machine learning algorithm, so classifiers share the same common functionality. In addition, we want the reader to be able to quickly start getting a flavor of what neural networks can do without the need to spend time creating a neural network from scratch. The following chapters will discuss other libraries and more complex implementations for many different types of deep learning neural nets, but for now, the user can start getting a quick idea of their functionality.

For example, if one wanted to use a multi-layer neural network with scikit-learn, it would be enough to import it in our program by typing:

```
from sklearn.neural_network.multilayer_perceptron import MLPClassifier
```

Each algorithm needs to be called using pre-defined parameters, though in most instances default values may be used. In the case of the MLPClassifier, no parameter is needed and one can use the default values (all parameters are described on the scikit-learn website, and in particular for the MLPClassifier one can find them at: `http://scikit-learn.org/dev/modules/generated/sklearn.neural_network.MLPClassifier.html`).

The algorithm is then called on the training data, using the labels for tuning of the parameters, using the `fit` function:

```
MLPClassifier().fit(data, labels)
```

Once the algorithm has been fit on the training data, it can be used to make predictions on the test data, using the `predict_proba` function that will output probabilities for each class:

```
probabilities = MLPClassifier().predict_proba(data)
```

Let's write a full example of how to use a `MLPClassifier` classifier on the `iris` dataset that we discussed briefly when we introduced decision trees.

Scikit-learn makes it easy to load important classic datasets. To do this we only need:

```
from sklearn import datasets
iris = datasets.load_iris()
data = iris.data
labels = iris.target
```

This will load the dataset. Now, to load the classifier we just need:

```
from sklearn.neural_network.multilayer_perceptron import MLPClassifier
```

Now we tune the parameters using the data:

```
mlp = MLPClassifier(random_state=1)
mlp.fit(data, labels)
```

Now, since the weights are initialized randomly, the `random_state` value is simply there to force the initialization to always use the same random values in order to get consistent results across different trials. It is completely irrelevant to understanding the process. The `fit` function is the important method to call, it is the method that will find the best weights by training the algorithm using the data and labels provided, in a supervised fashion.

Now we can check our predictions and compare them to the actual result. Since the function `predict_proba` outputs the probabilities, while `predict` outputs the class with the highest probability, we will use the latter to make the comparison, and we will use one of sikit-learn helper modules to give us the accuracy:

```
pred = mlp.predict(data)
from sklearn.metrics import accuracy_score
print('Accuracy: %.2f' % accuracy_score(labels, pred))
```

And that's it. Of course, as we mentioned, it is usually better to split our data between training data and test data, and we can also improve on this simple code by using some regularization of the data. Scikit-learn provides some helper functions for this as well:

```
from sklearn.cross_validation import train_test_split
from sklearn.preprocessing import StandardScaler
data_train, data_test, labels_train, labels_test = train_test_
split(data, labels, test_size=0.5, random_state=1)
scaler = StandardScaler()
scaler.fit(data)
data_train_std = scaler.transform(data_train)
data_test_std = scaler.transform(data_test)
data_train_std = data_train
data_test_std = data_test
```

This code is self-explanatory, we split the data and we normalize it, which means we subtract the mean and scale the data to unit variance. Then we fit our algorithm on the training data and we test on the test data:

```
mlp.fit(data_train, labels_train)
pred = mlp.predict(data_test)
print('Misclassified samples: %d' % (labels_test != pred).sum())
from sklearn.metrics import accuracy_score print('Accuracy: %.2f' %
accuracy_score(labels_test, pred))
```

And we get the following output:

**Misclassified samples: 3 Accuracy: 0.96**

We can draw some pictures to show the data and how the neural net divides the space into three regions to separate the three types of flowers (since we can only draw two-dimensional pictures we will only draw two features at the time). The first graph shows how the algorithm tries to separate the flowers based on their petal width and length, without having normalized the data:

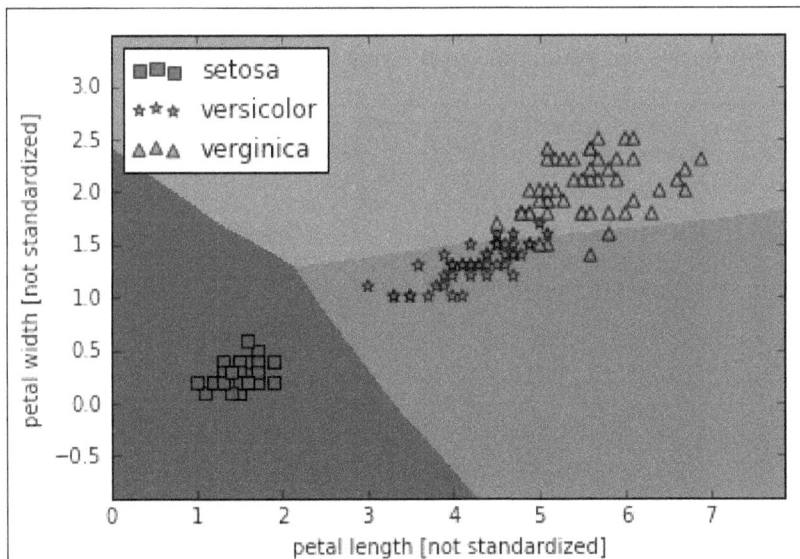

The second graph shows the same based only on the petal width and the sepal width, instead:

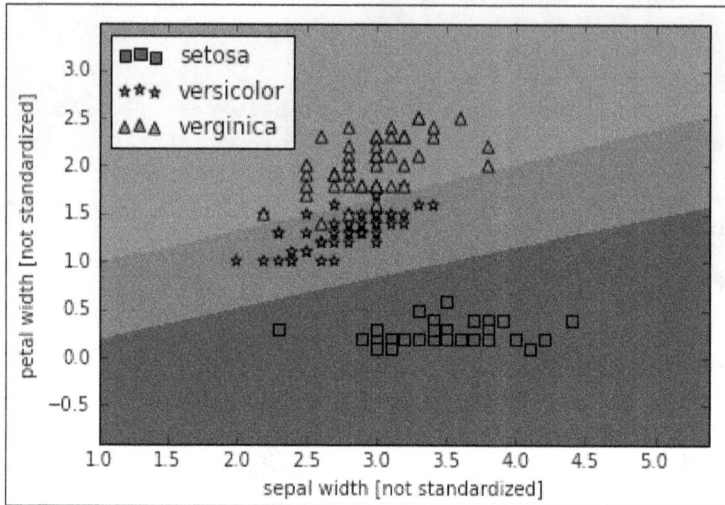

The third graph shows the same data as the first one, after normalizing the data:

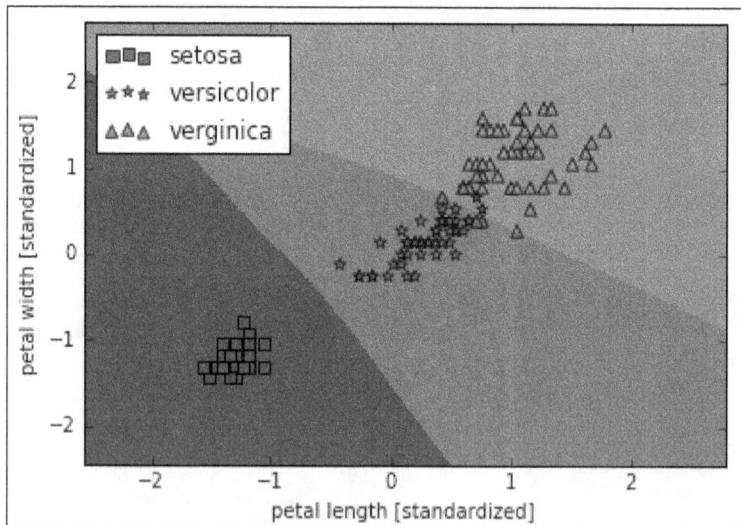

And, finally, the fourth graph is the same as the second one with the data normalized:

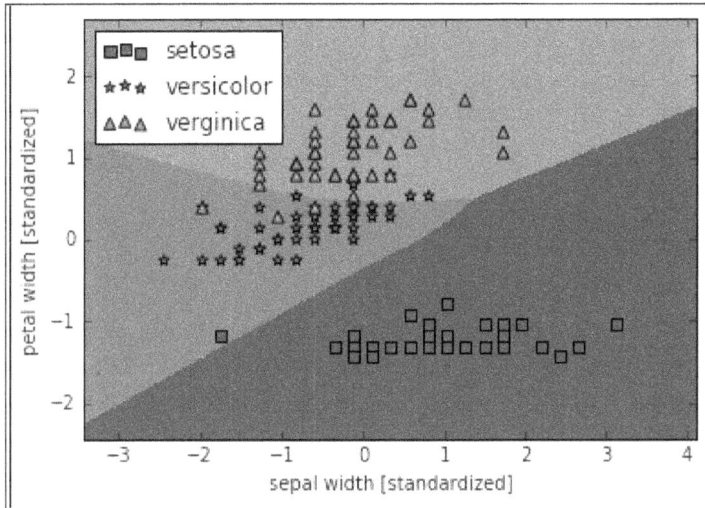

We also show the code used to create these graphs. Note that the code to draw these pictures was adapted from similar code by Sebastian Raschka in his *Python Machine Learning* book, published by Packt Publishing, and we refer the reader to it for further details.

The code to make the preceding drawings is as follows. Note that before data must be set to only contain the data relative to two variables, for example data = iris. data[:,[1,3]] for sepal and petal length, since we can only draw two-dimensional images.

```
import numpy
from matplotlib.colors import ListedColormap
import matplotlib.pyplot as plt
markers = ('s', '*', '^')
colors = ('blue', 'green', 'red')
cmap = ListedColormap(colors)
x_min, x_max = data[:, 0].min() - 1, data[:, 0].max() + 1
y_min, y_max = data[:, 1].min() - 1, data[:, 1].max() + 1
resolution = 0.01
x, y = numpy.meshgrid(numpy.arange(x_min, x_max, resolution), numpy.
arange(y_min, y_max, resolution))
Z = mlp.predict(numpy.array([x.ravel(), y.ravel()]).T)
Z = Z.reshape(x.shape)
plt.pcolormesh(x, y, Z, cmap=cmap)
plt.xlim(x.min(), x.max())
```

```
plt.ylim(y.min(), y.max())
# plot the data
classes = ["setosa", "versicolor", "verginica"]
for index, cl in enumerate(numpy.unique(labels)):
    plt.scatter(data[labels == cl, 0], data[labels == cl, 1],
    c=cmap(index), marker=markers[index], s=50, label=classes[index])
    plt.xlabel('petal length')
    plt.ylabel('sepal length')
    plt.legend(loc='upper left')
    plt.show()
```

The `MLPClassifier`, as we mentioned, does have many parameters that we can use; we will cite only the activation function and the number of hidden layers and how many neurons each may have, but the documentation for all possible parameters is available at `http://scikit-learn.org/dev/modules/generated/sklearn.neural_network.MLPClassifier.html`

The number of hidden layers and the number of neurons can be specified by adding `hidden_layer_sizes=(n_1, n_2, n_3, ..., n_m)`, where $n_i$ is the number of neurons in the $i^{th}$ layer.

For a neural net with two hidden layers with 200 and 100 neurons respectively, we would write:

```
mlp = MLPClassifier(random_state=1, hidden_layer_sizes=(200, 100,))
```

The other important parameter refers to the activation function, that we have called previously the activity function. This module supports three types defined below:

The **ReLU** is the easiest, but also one of the most popular (and the default activation function) and it is simply defined as $f(x) = \max(0, x)$

The **logistic** function is used when we are interested in calculating the probability of an event, in fact it has values between 0 and 1 and it is defined as: $f(x) = \dfrac{1}{1 + \exp(-x)}$

Finally, the **tanh** is simply defined as: $f(x) = \tanh(x) = \dfrac{\exp(x) - \exp(-x)}{\exp(x) + \exp(-x)}$

For example, to use two hidden layers with 200 and 100 neurons respectively with a logistic activation function, the code would modify to be:

```
mlp = MLPClassifier(random_state=1, hidden_layer_sizes=(200, 100,),
activation = "logistic")
```

We invite the reader to play with some of these parameters, and also to use the `max_iter` parameter that will limit the number of iterations. The number of iterations refers to the number of passes over the training data. A small value, such as `max_iter=100`, will not produce such good results, as the algorithm will not have the time to converge. Note, however, that on such a small dataset, more hidden layers will not necessarily result in better predictions, and they may instead degrade prediction accuracy.

That concludes this chapter, where we have introduced the reader to the importance of machine learning and the many applications in the real world. We have briefly mentioned some of the issues and problems, and we have touched on the topic of neural networks that will be the focus of the next chapter. We have also touched on how to use standard open source libraries such as `scikit-learn` to start implementing some simple multi-layer feed-forward networks.

We now turn to discussing neural networks in depth and the motivations behind their use.

# Summary

In this chapter, we have covered what machine learning is and why it is so important. We have provided several examples where machine learning techniques find applications and what kind of problems can be solved using machine learning. We have also introduced a particular type of machine learning algorithm, called neural networks, which is at the basis of deep learning, and have provided a coding example in which, using a popular machine learning library, we have solved a particular classification problem. In the next chapter, we will cover neural networks in better detail and will provide their theoretical justifications based on biological considerations drawn from observations of how our own brain works.

# 2
# Neural Networks

In the previous chapter, we described several machine learning algorithms and we introduced different techniques to analyze data to make predictions. For example, we suggested how machines can use data of home selling prices to make predictions on the price for new houses. We described how large companies, such as Netflix, use machine learning techniques in order to suggest to users new movies they may like based on movies they have liked in the past, using a technique that is widely utilized in e-commerce by giants such as Amazon or Walmart. Most of these techniques, however, necessitate labeled data in order to make predictions on new data, and, in order to improve their performance, need humans to describe the data in terms of features that make sense.

Humans are able to quickly extrapolate patterns and infer rules without having the data cleaned and prepared for them. It would then be desirable if machines could learn to do the same. As we have discussed, Frank Rosenblatt invented the perceptron back in 1957, over 50 years ago. The perceptron is to modern deep neural nets what unicellular organisms are to complex multi-cellular lifeforms, and yet it is quite important to understand and become familiar with how an artificial neuron works to better understand and appreciate the complexity we can generate by grouping many neurons together on many different layers to create deep neural networks. Neural nets are an attempt to mimic the functioning of a human brain and its ability to abstract new rules through simple observations. Though we are still quite far from understanding how human brains organize and process information, we already have a good understanding of how single human neurons work. Artificial neural networks attempt to mimic the same functionality, trading chemical and electrical messaging for numerical values and functions. Much progress has been made in the last decade, after neural networks had become popular and then been forgotten at least twice before: such resurgence is due in part to having computers that are getting faster, the use of **GPUs** (**Graphical Processing Units**) versus the most traditional use of **CPUs** (**Computing Processing Units**), better algorithms and neural nets design, and increasingly large datasets, as we will see in this book.

In this chapter, we will formally introduce what neural networks are, we will thoroughly describe how a neuron works, and we will see how we can stack many layers to create and use deep feed-forward neural networks.

# Why neural networks?

Neural networks have been around for many years, and they have gone through several periods during which they have fallen in and out of favor. However, in recent years, they have steadily gained ground over many other competing machine learning algorithms. The reason for this is that advanced neural net architecture has shown accuracy in many tasks that has far surpassed that of other algorithms. For example, in the field of image recognition, accuracy may be measured against a database of 16 million images named ImageNet.

Prior to the introduction of deep neural nets, accuracy had been improving at a slow rate, but after the introduction of deep neural networks, accuracy dropped from an error rate of 40% in 2010 to less than 7% in 2014, and this value is still falling. The human recognition rate is still lower, but only at about 5%. Given the success of deep neural networks, all entrants to the ImageNet competition in 2013 used some form of deep neural network. In addition, deep neural nets "learn" a representation of the data, that is, not only learn to recognize an object, but also learn what the important features that uniquely define the identified object are. By learning to automatically identify features, deep neural nets can be successfully used in unsupervised learning, by naturally classifying objects with similar features together, without the need for laborious human labeling. Similar advances have also been reached in other fields, such as signal processing. Deep learning and using deep neural networks is now ubiquitously used, for example, in Apple's Siri. When Google introduced a deep learning algorithm for its Android operating system, it achieved a 25% reduction in word recognition error. Another dataset used for image recognition is the MNIST dataset that comprises examples of digits written in different handwriting. The use of deep neural networks for digit recognition can now achieve an accuracy of 99.79%, comparable to a human's accuracy. In addition, deep neural network algorithms are the closest artificial example of how the human brain works. Despite the fact that they are still probably a much more simplified and elementary version of our brain, they contain more than any other algorithm, the seed of human intelligence, and the rest of this book will be dedicated to studying different neural networks and several examples of different applications of neural networks will be provided.

# Fundamentals

In the first chapter, we talked about three different approaches to machine learning: supervised learning, unsupervised learning, and reinforcement learning. Classical neural networks are a type of supervised machine learning, though we will see later that deep learning popularity is instead due to the fact that modern deep neural networks can be used in unsupervised learning tasks as well. In the next chapter, we will highlight the main differences between classical shallow neural networks and deep neural nets. For now, however, we will mainly concentrate on classical feed-forward networks that work in a supervised way. Our first question is, what exactly is a neural network? Probably the best way to interpret a neural network is to describe it as a mathematical model for information processing. While this may seem rather vague, it will become much clearer in the next chapters. A neural net is not a fixed program, but rather a model, a system that processes information, or inputs, in a somewhat bland analogy to how information is thought to be processed by biological entities. We can identify three main characteristics for a neural net:

- **The neural net architecture**: This describes the set of connections (feed-forward, recurrent, multi- or single-layered, and so on) between the neurons, the number of layers, and the number of neurons in each layer.

- **The learning**: This describes what is commonly defined as the training. Whether we use back-propagation or some kind of energy level training, it identifies how we determine the weights between neurons.

- **The activity function**: This describes the function we use on the activation value that is passed onto each neuron, the neuron's internal state, and it describes how the neuron works (stochastically, linearly, and so on) and under what conditions it will activate or fire, and the output it will pass on to neighboring neurons.

It should be noted, however, that some researchers would consider the activity function as part of the architecture; it may be easier, however, for a beginner to separate these two aspects for now. It needs to be remarked that artificial neural nets represent only an approximation of how a biological brain works. A biological neural net is a much more complex model; however, this should not be a concern. Artificial neural nets can still perform many useful tasks, in fact, as we will show later, an artificial neural net can indeed approximate to any degree we wish any function of the input onto the output.

The development of neural nets is based on the following assumptions:

- Information processing occurs, in its simplest form, over simple elements, called neurons

- Neurons are connected and exchange signals between them along connection links

- Connection links between neurons can be stronger or weaker, and this determines how information is processed

- Each neuron has an internal state that is determined by all the incoming connections from other neurons

- Each neuron has a different activity function that is calculated on the neuron internal state and determines its output signal

In the next section, we shall define in detail how a neuron works and how it interacts with other neurons.

# Neurons and layers

What is a neuron? A neuron is a processing unit that takes an input value and, according to predefined rules, outputs a different value.

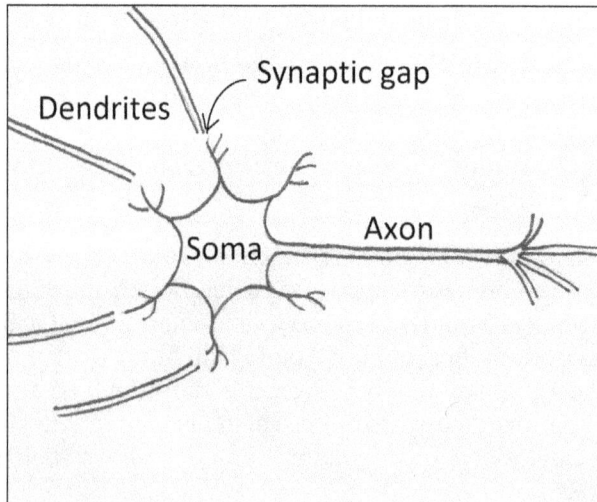

In 1943, Warren McCullock and Walter Pitts published an article (W. S. McCulloch and W. Pitts. A Logical Calculus of the Ideas Immanent in Nervous Activity, The Bulletin of Mathematical Biophysics, 5(4):115–133, 1943) in which they described the functioning of a single biological neuron. The components of a biological neuron are the dendrites, the soma (the cell body), the axons, and the synaptic gaps. Under different names, these are also parts of an artificial neuron.

The dendrites bring the input from other neurons to the soma, the neuron's body. The soma is where the inputs are processed and summed together. If the input is over a certain threshold, the neuron will "fire" and transmit a single output that is electrically sent through the axons. Between the axons of the transmitting neurons and the dendrites of the receiving neurons lies the synaptic gap that mediates chemically such impulses, altering their frequencies. In an artificial neural net, we model the frequency through a numerical weight: the higher the frequency, the higher the impulse and, therefore, the higher the weight. We can then establish an equivalence table between biological and artificial neurons (this is a very simplified description, but it works for our purposes):

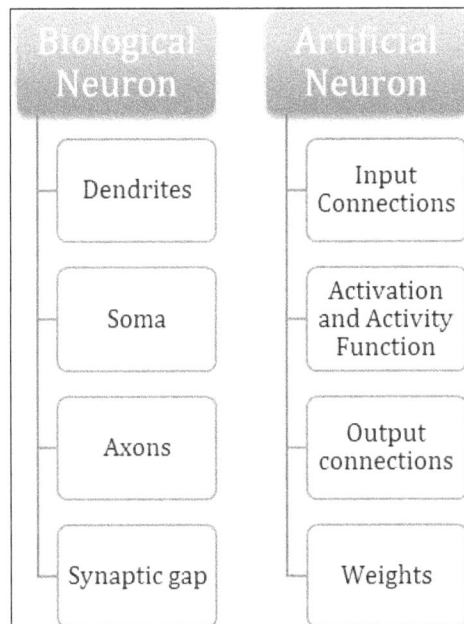

| Biological Neuron | Artificial Neuron |
| --- | --- |
| Dendrites | Input Connections |
| Soma | Activation and Activity Function |
| Axons | Output connections |
| Synaptic gap | Weights |

Schematic correspondence between a biological and an artificial neuron

We can therefore describe an artificial neuron schematically as follows:

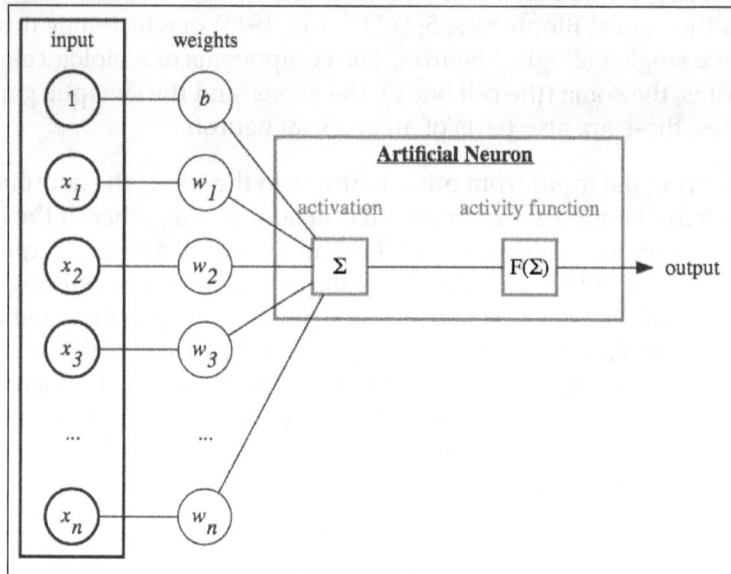

At the center of this picture we have the neuron, or the soma, which gets an input (the activation) and sets the neuron's internal state that triggers an output (the activity function). The input comes from other neurons and it is mediated in intensity by the weights (the synaptic gap).

The simple activation value for a neuron is given by $\alpha(x) = \Sigma_i \, w_i x_i$, where $x_i$ is the value of each input neuron, and $w_i$ is the value of the connection between the neuron $i$ and the output. In the first chapter, in our introduction to neural networks, we introduced the bias. If we include the bias and want to make its presence explicit, we can rewrite the preceding equation as $\alpha(x) = \Sigma_i \, w_i x_i + b$. The bias effect is to translate the hyperplane defined by the weights so it will not necessarily go through the origin (and hence its name). We should interpret the activation value as the neuron's internal state value.

As we mentioned in the previous chapter, the activation value defined previously can be interpreted as the dot product between the vector $w$ and the vector $x$. A vector $x$ will be perpendicular to the weight vector $w$ if $<w,x> = 0$, therefore all vectors $x$ such that $<w,x> = 0$ define a hyper-plane in $\mathbf{R}^n$ (where n is the dimension of $x$).

Hence, any vector $x$ satisfying $<w,x> > 0$ is a vector on the side of the hyper-plane defined by $w$. A neuron is therefore a linear classifier, which, according to this rule, activates when the input is above a certain threshold or, geometrically, when the input is on one side of the hyper-plane defined by the vector of the weights.

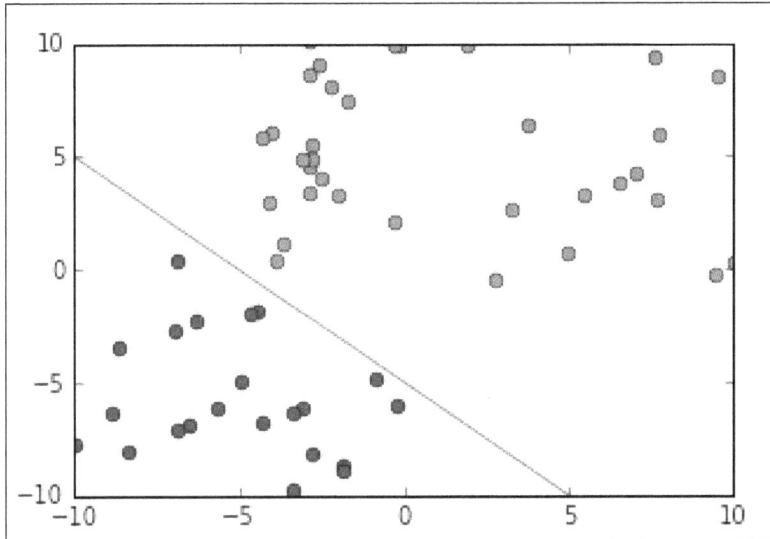

A single neuron is a linear classifier

A neural network can have an indefinite number of neurons, but regardless of their number, in classical networks all the neurons will be ordered in layers. The input layer represents the dataset, the initial conditions. For example, if the input is a grey-scale image, the input layer is represented for each pixel by an input neuron with the inner value the intensity of the pixel. It should be noted, however, that the neurons in the input layer are not neurons as the others, as their output is constant and is equal to the value of their internal state, and therefore the input layer is not generally counted. A 1-layer neural net is therefore a simple neural net with just one layer, the output, besides the input layer. From each input neuron we draw a line connecting it with each output neuron and this value is mediated by the artificial synaptic gap, that is the weight $w_{ij}$ connecting the input neuron $x_i$ to the output neuron $y_j$. Typically, each output neuron represents a class, for example, in the case of the MNIST dataset, each neuron represents a digit. The 1-layer neural net can therefore be used to make a prediction such as which digit the input image is representing. In fact, the set of output values can be regarded as a measure of the probability that the image represents the given class, and therefore the output neuron with the highest value will represent the prediction of the neural net.

It must be noted that neurons in the same layer are never connected to one another, as in the following figure; instead they are all connected to each of the neurons in the next layer, and so on:

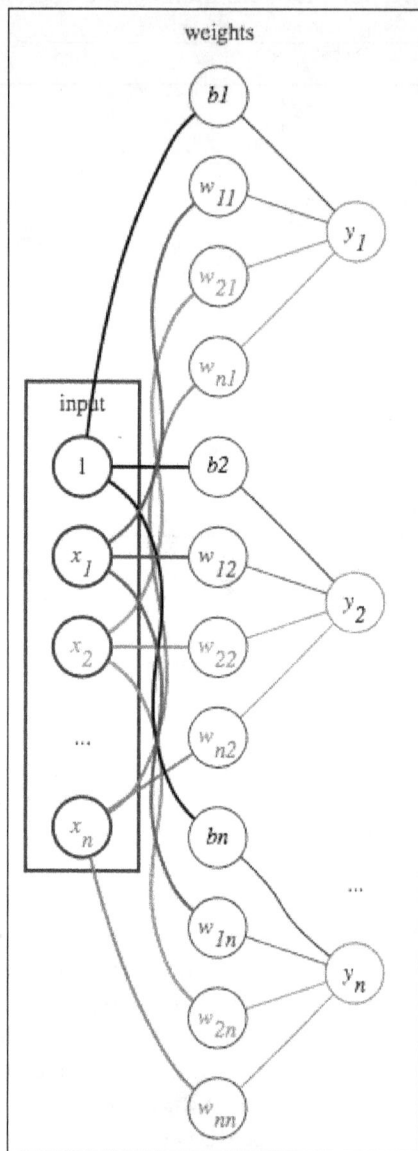

An example of a 1-layer neural network: the neurons on the left represent the input with bias b, the middle column represents the weights for each connection, while the neurons on the right represent the output given the weights *w*.

This is one of the necessary and defining conditions for classical neural networks, the absence of intra-layers connections, while neurons connect to each and every neuron in adjacent layers. In the preceding figure, we explicitly show the weights for each connection between neurons, but usually the edges connecting neurons implicitly represent the weights. The **1** represents the bias unit, the value 1 neuron with connecting weight equal to the bias that we have introduced earlier.

As mentioned many times, 1-layer neural nets can only classify linearly separable classes; however, there is nothing that can prevent us from introducing more layers between the input and the output. These extra layers are called hidden layers.

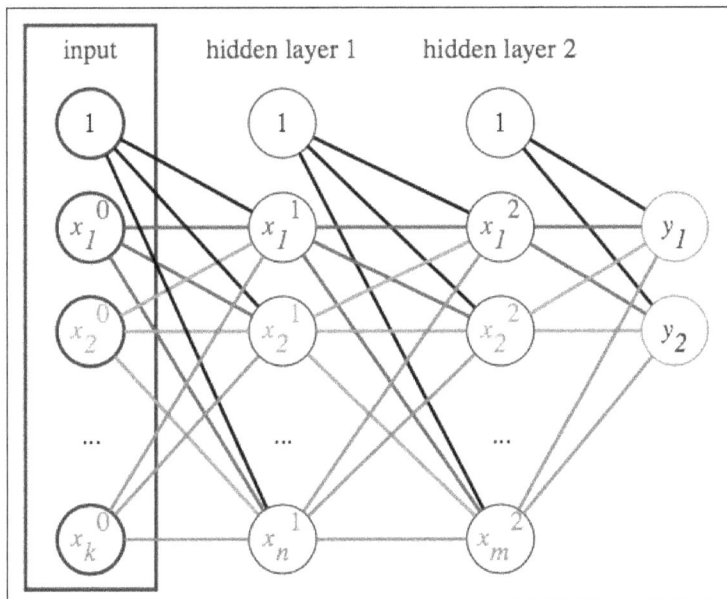

Shown is a 3-layer neural network with two hidden layers. The input layer has k input neurons, the first hidden layer has n hidden neurons, and the second hidden layer has m hidden neurons. In principle it is possible to have as many hidden layers as desired. The output, in this example, is the two classes, $y_1$ and $y_2$. On top the on always-on bias neuron. Each connection has its own weight w (not depicted for simplicity).

# Different types of activation function

Biologically, neuroscience has identified hundreds, perhaps more than a thousand different types of neurons (refer *The Future of the Brain*", by Gary Marcus and Jeremy Freeman) and therefore we should be able to model at least some different types of artificial neurons. This can be done by using different types of activity functions, that is, the function defined on the internal state of the neuron represented by the activation $a(x) = \sum_i w_i x_i$ calculated on the input from all the input neurons.

The activity function is a function defined on *a(x)* and it defines the output of the neuron. The most common activity functions used are:

- $f(a) = a$ : This function lets the activation value go through and it is called the identity function

- $f(a) = \begin{cases} 1 \, if \, a \geq 0 \\ 0 \, if \, a < 0 \end{cases}$ : This function activates the neuron if the activation is above a certain value and it is called the threshold activity function

- $f(a) = \dfrac{1}{1 + \exp(-a)}$ : This function is one of the most commonly used as its output, which is bounded between 0 and 1, and it can be interpreted stochastically as the probability for the neuron to activate, and it is commonly called the logistic function or the logistic sigmoid.

- $f(a) = \dfrac{1}{1 + \exp(-a)} - 1 = \dfrac{1 - \exp(-a)}{1 + \exp(-a)}$ : This activity function is called the bipolar sigmoid, and it is simply a logistic sigmoid rescaled and translated to have a range in (-1, 1).

- $f(a) = \dfrac{\exp(a) - \exp(-a)}{\exp(a) + \exp(-a)} = \dfrac{1 - \exp(-2a)}{1 + \exp(-2a)}$ : This activity function is called the hyperbolic tangent.

- $f(a) = \begin{cases} a \, if \, a \geq 0 \\ 0 \, if \, a < 0 \end{cases}$ : This activity function is probably the closest to its biological counterpart, it is a mix of the identity and the threshold function, and it is called the rectifier, or **ReLU**, as in **Rectfied Linear Unit**

What are the main differences between these activation functions? Often, different activation functions work better for different problems. In general, the identity activity function or threshold function, while widely used at the inception of neural networks with such implementations such as the *perceptron* or the *Adaline* (adaptive linear neuron), has recently lost traction in favor of the logistic sigmoid, the hyperbolic tangent, or the ReLU. While the identity function and the threshold function are much simpler, and therefore were the preferred functions when computers did not have quite as much calculation power, it is often preferable to use non-linear functions, such as the sigmoid functions or the ReLU. It should also be noted that if we only used the linear activity function there is no point in adding extra hidden layers, as the composition of linear functions is still just a linear function. The last three activity functions differ in the following ways:

- Their range is different
- Their gradient may vanish as we increase x

The fact that the gradient may vanish as we increase $x$ and why it is important will be clearer later; for now, let's just mention that the gradient (for example, the derivative) of the function is important for the training of the neural network. This is similar to how, in the linear regression example we introduced in the first chapter, we were trying to minimize the function following it along the direction opposite to its derivative.

The range for the logistic function is (0,1), which is one reason why this is the preferred function for stochastic networks, that is, networks with neurons that may activate based on a probability function. The hyperbolic function is very similar to the logistic function, but its range is (-1, 1). In contrast, the ReLU has a range of (0, $\infty$), so it can have a very large output.

However, more importantly, let's look at the derivative for each of the three functions. For a logistic function $f$, the derivative is $f * (1-f)$, while if $f$ is the hyperbolic tangent, its derivative is $(1+f) * (1-f)$.

If $f$ is the ReLU, the derivative is much simpler and it is simply $\begin{cases} 1 \, if \, a \geq 0 \\ 0 \, if \, a < 0 \end{cases}$.

Let's briefly see how we can calculate the derivative of the logistic sigmoid function. This can be quickly calculated by simply noticing that the derivative with respect to $a$ of the $\dfrac{1}{1+\exp(-a)}$ function is given by the following:

$$\frac{\exp(-a)}{\big(1+\exp(-a)\big)+\big(1+\exp(-a)\big)} = \frac{1}{\big(1+\exp(-a)\big)} * \frac{\big(1+\exp(-a)\big)-1}{\big(1+\exp(-a)\big)}$$

$$\frac{1}{\big(1+\exp(-a)\big)} * \left(\frac{\big(1+\exp(-a)\big)}{\big(1+\exp(-a)\big)} - \frac{1}{\big(1+\exp(-a)\big)}\right) = f * (1-f)$$

When we will talk about back-propagation, we will see that one of the problems for deep networks is that of the *vanishing gradient* (as mentioned previously), and the advantage of the ReLU activity function is that the derivative is constant and does not tend to *0* as *a* becomes large.

Typically all neurons in the same layer have the same activity function, but different layers may have different activity functions. But why are neural networks more than 1-layer deep (2-layer or more) so important? As we have seen, the importance of neural networks lies in their predictive power, that is, in their ability to approximate a function defined on the input with the required output. There exists a theorem, called the Universal Approximation Theorem, which states that any continuous functions on compact subsets of $R_n$ can be approximated by a neural network with at least one hidden layer. While the formal proof of such a theorem is too complex to be explained here, we will attempt to give an intuitive explanation only using some basic mathematics, and for this we will make use of the logistic sigmoid as our activity function.

The logistic sigmoid is defined as $\dfrac{1}{1+\exp(-a)}$ where $\alpha(x) = \sum_i w_i x_i + b$. Let's now assume that we have only one neuron $x = x_i$:

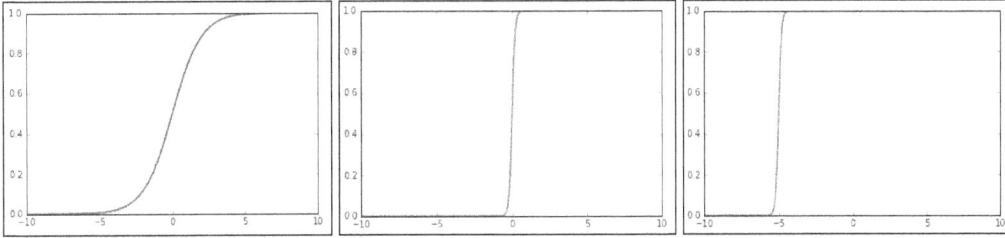

On the left is a standard sigmoid with weight 1 and bias 0. In the center is a sigmoid with weight 10, while on the right is a sigmoid with weight 10 and bias 50.

Then it can be easily shown that if $w$ is very large, the logistic function becomes close to a step function. The larger $w$ is, the more it resembles a step function at 0 with height 1. On the other hand, $b$ will simply translate the function, and the translation will be equal to the negative of the ratio $b/w$. Let's call $t = -b/w$.

With this in mind, let's now consider a simple neural net with one input neuron and one hidden layer with two neurons and only one output neuron in the output layer:

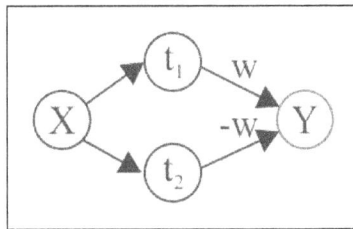

X is mapped on the two hidden neurons with weights and biases such that on the top hidden neuron the ratio $-b/w$ is $t_1$ while on the bottom hidden neuron it is $t_2$. Both hidden neurons use the logistic sigmoid activation function.

The input x is mapped to two neurons, one with weight and bias such that the ratio is $t_1$ and the other such that the ratio is $t_2$. Then the two hidden neurons can be mapped to the output neuron with weights $w$ and $-w$, respectively. If we apply the logistic sigmoid activity function to each hidden neuron, and the identity function to the output neuron (with no bias), we will get a step function, from $t_1$ to $t_2$, and height $w$, like the one depicted in the following figure. Since the series of step functions like the one in the figure can approximate any continuous function on a compact subset of **R**, this gives an intuition of why the Universal Approximation Theorem holds (this is, in simplified terms, the content of a mathematical theorem called "The simple function approximation theorem").

With a little more effort, this can be generalized to $\mathbf{R}^n$.

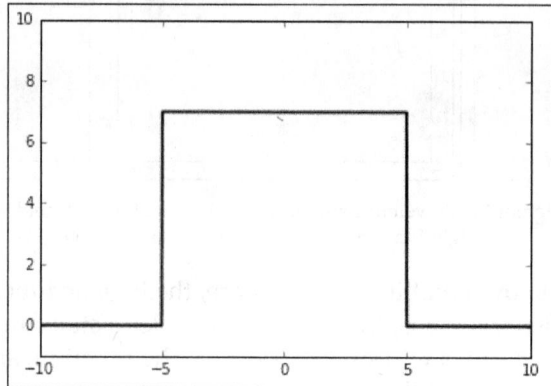

The code to produce the preceding figure is as follows:

```
#The user can modify the values of the weight w
#as well as biasValue1 and biasValue2 to observe
#how this plots to different step functions

import numpy
import matplotlib.pyplot as plt
weightValue = 1000
#to be modified to change where the step function starts
biasValue1 = 5000
#to be modified to change where the step function ends
biasValue2 = -5000

plt.axis([-10, 10, -1, 10])

print ("The step function starts at {0} and ends at {1}"
        .format(-biasValue1/weightValue,
        -biasValue2/weightValue))

y1 = 1.0/(1.0 + numpy.exp(-weightValue*x - biasValue1))
y2 = 1.0/(1.0 + numpy.exp(-weightValue*x - biasValue2))
#to be modified to change the height of the step function
w = 7
y = y1*w-y2*w
plt.plot(x, y, lw=2, color='black')
plt.show()
```

# The back-propagation algorithm

We have seen how neural networks can map inputs onto determined outputs, depending on fixed weights. Once the *architecture* of the neural network has been defined (feed-forward, number of hidden layers, number of neurons per layer), and once the activity function for each neuron has been chosen, we will need to set the weights that in turn will define the internal states for each neuron in the network. We will see how to do that for a 1-layer network and then how to extend it to a deep feed-forward network. For a deep neural network the algorithm to set the weights is called the back-propagation algorithm, and we will discuss and explain this algorithm for most of this section, as it is one of the most important topics for multi-layer feed-forward neural networks. First, however, we will quickly discuss this for 1-layer neural networks.

The general concept we need to understand is the following: every neural network is an approximation of a function, therefore each neural network will not be equal to the desired function, and instead it will differ by some value. This value is called the error and the aim is to minimize this error. Since the error is a function of the weights in the neural network, we want to minimize the error with respect to the weights. The error function is a function of many weights; it is therefore a function of many variables. Mathematically, the set of points where this function is zero represents therefore a hypersurface and to find a minimum on this surface we want to pick a point and then follow a curve in the direction of the minimum.

## Linear regression

We have already introduced linear regression in the first chapter, but since we are now dealing with many variables, to simplify things we are going to introduce matrix notation. Let $x$ be the input; we can think of $x$ as a vector. In the case of linear regression, we are going to consider a single output neuron $y$; the set of weights $w$ is therefore a vector of dimension the same as the dimension of $x$. The activation value is then defined as the inner product $<x, w>$.

Let's say that for each input value $x$, we want to output a target value $t$, while for each $x$ the neural network will output a value $y$, defined by the activity function chosen, in this case the absolute value of the difference $(y-t)$ represents the difference between the predicted value and the actual value for the specific input example $x$. If we have $m$ input values $x_i$, each of them will have a target value $t_i$. In this case, we calculate the error using the mean squared error $\Sigma_i \left( y^i - t^i \right)^2$, where each $y_i$ is a function of $w$. The error is therefore a function of $w$ and it is usually denoted with $J(w)$.

As mentioned previously, this represents a hyper-surface of dimension equal to the dimension of $w$ (we are implicitly also considering the bias), and for each $w_j$ we need to find a curve that will lead towards the minimum of the surface. The direction in which a curve increases in a certain direction is given by its derivative with respect to that direction, in this case by the following:

$$\vec{d} = \frac{\partial \Sigma_i \left( y^i - t^i \right)^2}{\partial w_j}$$

And in order to move towards the minimum we need to move in the opposite direction set by $\vec{d}$ for each $w_j$.

Let's calculate the following:

$$\vec{d} = \frac{\partial \Sigma_i \left( y^i - t^i \right)^2}{\partial_{wj}} = \Sigma_i = \frac{\partial \left( y^i - t^i \right)^2}{\partial_{wj}} = 2 * \Sigma_i = \frac{\partial y^i}{\partial w_j} \left( y^i - t^i \right)$$

If $y^i = <x^i, w>$, then $\frac{\partial y^i}{\partial w_j} = x^i_j$ and therefore

$$\vec{d} = \frac{\partial \Sigma_i \left( y^i - t^i \right)^2}{\partial w_j} = 2 * \Sigma_i x^i_j \left( y^i - t^i \right)$$

> The notation can sometimes be confusing, especially the first time one sees it. The input is given by vectors $\mathbf{x}^i$, where the superscript indicates the $i^{th}$ example. Since $\mathbf{x}$ and $\mathbf{w}$ are vectors, the subscript indicates the $j^{th}$ coordinate of the vector. $y^i$ then represents the output of the neural network given the input $x^i$, while $t^i$ represents the target, that is, the desired value corresponding to the input $\mathbf{x}_i$.

In order to move towards the minimum, we need to move each weight in the direction of its derivative by a small amount l, called the *learning rate*, typically much smaller than 1, (say 0.1 or smaller). We can therefore redefine in the derivative and incorporate the "2 in the learning rate, to get the update rule given by the following:

$$w_j \rightarrow w_j \rightarrow \lambda \Sigma_i x^i_j \left( y^i - t^i \right)$$

Or, more generally, we can write the update rule in matrix form as follows:

$$w \rightarrow w \rightarrow \lambda \nabla \left( \sum_i \left( y^i - t^i \right)^2 \right) = w - \lambda \nabla \left( J(w) \right)$$

Here, $\nabla$ (also called nabla) represents the vector of partial derivatives. This process is what is often called gradient descent.

$\nabla = \left( \dfrac{\partial}{\partial w_1}, \ldots, \dfrac{\partial}{\partial w_n} \right)$ is a vector of partial derivatives. Instead of writing the update rule for $w$ separately for each of its components $wj$, we can write the update rule in matrix form where, instead of writing the partial derivative for each $j$, we use $\nabla$ to indicate each partial derivative, for each $j$.

One last note; the update can be done after having calculated all the input vectors, however, in some cases, the weights can be updated after each example or after a defined preset number of examples.

# Logistic regression

In logistic regression, the output is not continuous; rather it is defined as a set of classes. In this case, the activation function is not going to be the identity function like before, rather we are going to use the logistic sigmoid function. The logistic sigmoid function, as we have seen before, outputs a real value in (0,1) and therefore it can be interpreted as a probability function, and that is why it can work so well in a 2-class classification problem. In this case, the target can be one of two classes, and the output represents the probability that it be one of those two classes (say *t=1*).

Again, the notation can be confusing. *t* is our target, and it can have, in this example, two values. These two values are often defined to be class 0 and class 1. These values 0 and 1 are not to be confused with the values of the logistic sigmoid function, which is a continuous real-valued function between 0 and 1. The real value of the sigmoid function represents the probability that the output be in class 0 or class 1.

If $a$ is the neuron activation value as defined previously, let's denote with the s($a$) the logistic sigmoid function, therefore, for each example x, the probability that the output be the class $y$, given the weights $w$, is:

$$P(t|x,w) = \begin{cases} \sigma(a) & \text{if } t = 1 \\ 1 - \sigma(a) & \text{if } t = 0 \end{cases}$$

We can write that equation more succinctly as follows:

$$P(t|x,w) = \sigma(a)^t \left(1 - \sigma(a)\right)^{1-t}$$

And since for each sample $x^i$ the probabilities $P(t_i | x_i, w)$ are independent, the global probability is as follows:

$$P(t|x,w) = \prod_i P\left(t^i \middle| x^i, w\right) = \prod_i \sigma(a^i)^{t^i} \left(1 - \sigma(a)\right)^{(1-t^i)}$$

If we take the natural log of the preceding equation (to turn products into sums), we get the following:

$$\log\left(P(t|x,w)\right) = \log\left(\prod_i \sigma(a)^{t^i} \left(1 - \sigma(a)\right)^{(1-t^i)}\right)$$

$$= \sum_i t^i \log\left(\sigma(a^i)\right) + \left(1 - t^i\right) \log\left(1 - \sigma(a^i)\right)$$

The object is now to maximize this log to obtain the highest probability of predicting the correct results. Usually, this is obtained, as in the previous case, by using gradient descent to minimize the cost function $J(w)$ defined by $J(w) = -log(P(y | \mathbf{x}, w))$.

As before, we calculate the derivative of the cost function with respect to the weights $w_j$ to obtain:

$$\frac{\partial \sum_i t^i \log\left(\sigma(a^i)\right) + \left(1 - t^i\right) \log\left(1 - \sigma(a^i)\right)}{\partial w_j}$$

$$= \sum_i \frac{\partial \sum_i t^i \log\left(\sigma(a^i)\right) + \left(1 - t^i\right) \log\left(1 - \sigma(a^i)\right)}{\partial w_j} =$$

$$\sum_i t^i \frac{\partial \log\left(\sigma\left(a^i\right)\right)}{\partial w_j} + \left(1-t^i\right)\frac{\partial \log\left(1-\sigma\left(a^i\right)\right)}{\partial w_j}$$

$$= \sum_i t^i \left(1-\sigma\left(a^i\right)\right)x_j^i + \left(1-t^i\right)\sigma\left(a^i\right)x_j^i$$

To understand the last equality, let's remind the reader of the following facts:

$$\frac{\partial \sigma\left(a^i\right)}{\partial a^i} = \sigma\left(a^i\right)\left(1-\sigma\left(a^i\right)\right)$$

$$\frac{\partial \sigma\left(a^i\right)}{\partial a_j} = 0$$

$$\frac{\partial a^i}{\partial w_j} = \frac{\partial \sum_k w_k x_k^i + b}{\partial w_j} = x_j^i$$

Therefore, by the chain rule:

$$\sum_i \frac{\partial \log\left(\sigma\left(a^i\right)\right)}{\partial w_j} = \sum_i \frac{\partial \log\left(\sigma\left(a^i\right)\right)}{\partial a_j}\frac{\partial a^i}{\sigma\left(a^i\right)}\sigma\left(a^i\right)\left(1-\sigma\left(a^i\right)\right)x_j^i$$

$$= \left(1-\sigma\left(a^i\right)\right)x_j^i$$

Similarly:

$$\sum_i \frac{\partial \log\left(1-\sigma\left(a^i\right)\right)}{\partial w_j} = \sigma\left(a^i\right)x_j^i$$

In general, in case of a multi-class output **t**, with **t** a vector $(t_1, \ldots, t_n)$, we can generalize this equation using $J(w) = -\log\big(P(y|x, w)\big) = E_{i,j}\, t_j^i \log\big(\ (a^i)\big)$ that brings to the update equation for the weights:

$$w_j \rightarrow w_j \rightarrow \lambda \sum_i x_j^i \left(\sigma\left(a^i\right) - t^i\right)$$

This is similar to the update rule we have seen for linear regression.

# Back-propagation

In the case of 1-layer, weight-adjustment is easy, as we can use linear or logistic regression and adjust the weights simultaneously to get a smaller error (minimizing the cost function). For multi-layer neural networks we can use a similar argument for the weights used to connect the last hidden layer to the output layer, as we know what we would like the output layer to be, but we cannot do the same for the hidden layers, as, a priori, we do not know what the values for the neurons in the hidden layers ought to be. What we do, instead, is calculate the error in the last hidden layer and estimate what it would be in the previous layer, propagating the error back from the last to the first layer, hence the name back-propagation.

Back-propagation is one of the most difficult algorithms to understand at first, but all is needed is some knowledge of basic differential calculus and the chain rule. Let's introduce some notation first. We denote with $J$ the cost (error), with $y$ the activity function that is defined on the activation value $a$ (for example, y could be the logistic sigmoid), which is a function of the weights $w$ and the input $x$. Let's also define $w_{ij}$, the weight between the $i^{\text{th}}$ input value, and the $j$th output. Here we define input and output more generically than for a 1-layer network: if $w_{ij}$ connects a pair of successive layers in a feed-forward network, we denote as "input" the neurons on the first of the two successive layers, and "output" the neurons on the second of the two successive layers. In order not to make the notation too heavy, and have to denote on which layer each neuron is, we assume that the $i$th input $y_i$ is always in the layer preceding the layer containing the $j^{\text{th}}$ output $y_j$.

> Note that the letter $y$ is used to both denote an input and the output of the activity function. $y_j$ is the input to the next layer, and $y_j$ is the output of the activity function, but it is then also the input to the next layer. Therefore we can think of the $y_j$'s as functions of the $y_j$'s.

We also use subscripts *i* and *j*, where we always have the element with subscript *i* belonging to the layer preceding the layer containing the element with subscript *j*.

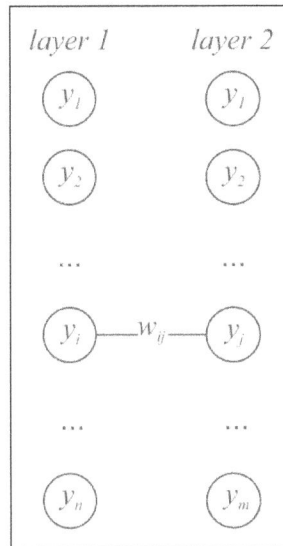

Figure 10

In this example, layer 1 represents the input, and *layer 2* the output, so $w_{t_j}$ is a number connecting the $y_j$ value in a layer, and the $y_j$ value in the following layer.

Using this notation, and the chain-rule for derivatives, for the last layer of our neural network we can write the following:

$$\frac{\partial J}{\partial w_{i,j}} = \frac{\partial J}{\partial y_j} \frac{\partial y_j}{\partial a_j} \frac{\partial a_j}{\partial w_{i,j}}$$

Since we know that $\frac{\partial a_j}{\partial w_{i,j}} = y_i$ , we have the following:

$$\frac{\partial J}{\partial w_{i,j}} = \frac{\partial J}{\partial y_j} \frac{\partial y_j}{\partial a_j} y_i$$

If *y* is the logistic sigmoid defined previously, we get the same result we have already calculated at the end of the previous section, since we know the cost function and we can calculate all derivatives.

For the previous layers the same formula holds:

$$\frac{\partial J}{\partial w_{i,j}} = \frac{\partial J}{\partial y_j} \frac{\partial y_j}{\partial a_j} \frac{\partial a_j}{\partial w_{i,j}}$$

In fact, $a_j$ is the activity function, which, as we know, is a function of the weights. The $y_j$ value, which is the activity function of the neuron in the "second" layer, is a function of its activation value, and, of course, the cost function is a function of the activity function we have chosen.

> Even though we have several layers, we always concentrate on pairs of successive layers and so, perhaps abusing the notation somewhat, we always have a "first" layer and a "second" layer, as in *Figure 10*, which is the "input" layer and the "output" layer.

Since we know that $\frac{\partial a_j}{\partial w_{i,j}} = y_i$ and we know that $\frac{\partial y_j}{\partial a_j}$ is the derivative of the activity function that we can calculate, all we need to calculate is the derivative $\frac{\partial J}{\partial y_j}$. Let's notice that this is the derivative of the error with respect to the activation function in the "second" layer, and, if we can calculate this derivative for the last layer, and have a formula that allows us to calculate the derivative for one layer assuming we can calculate the derivative for the next, we can calculate all the derivatives starting from the last layer and move backwards.

Let us notice that, as we defined by the $y_j$, they are the activation values for the neurons in the "second" layer, but they are also the activity functions, therefore functions of the activation values in the first layer. Therefore, applying the chain rule, we have the following:

$$\frac{\partial J}{\partial y_j} = \Sigma_j \frac{\partial J}{\partial y_j} \frac{\partial y_j}{\partial y_i} \Sigma_j \frac{\partial J}{\partial y_j} \frac{\partial y_j}{\partial a_j} \frac{\partial a_j}{\partial y_i}$$

And once again we can calculate both $\frac{\partial y_j}{\partial a_j}$ and $\frac{\partial a_j}{\partial y_i} = w_{i,j}$, so once we know $\frac{\partial J}{\partial y_j}$ we can calculate $\frac{\partial J}{\partial y_i}$, and since we can calculate $\frac{\partial J}{\partial y_j}$ for the last layer, we can move backward and calculate $\frac{\partial J}{\partial y_i}$ for any layer and therefore $\frac{\partial J}{\partial w_{i,j}}$ for any layer.

To summarize, if we have a sequence of layers where

$$y_i \rightarrow y_j \rightarrow y_k$$

We then have these two fundamental equations, where the summation in the second equation should read as the sum over all the outgoing connections from $y_j$ to any neuron $y_k$ in the successive layer.

$$\frac{\partial J}{\partial w_{i,j}} = \frac{\partial J}{\partial y_j} \frac{\partial y_j}{\partial a_j} \frac{\partial a_j}{\partial w_{i,j}}$$

$$\frac{\partial J}{\partial y_i} = \Sigma_k \frac{\partial J}{\partial y_k} \frac{\partial y_k}{\partial y_j}$$

By using these two equations we can calculate the derivatives for the cost with respect to each layer.

If we set $\delta_j = \frac{\partial J}{\partial y_j} \frac{\partial y_j}{\partial a_j}$, $\delta_j$ represents the variation of the cost with respect to the activation value, and we can think of $\delta_j$ as the error at the $y_j$ neuron. We can then rewrite

$$\frac{\partial J}{\partial y_i} = \Sigma_j \frac{\partial J}{\partial y_j} \frac{\partial y_j}{\partial y_i} = \Sigma_j \frac{\partial J}{\partial y_j} \frac{\partial y_j}{\partial a_j} \frac{\partial a_j}{\partial y_i} = \Sigma_j \delta_j w_{i,j}$$

This implies that $\delta_i = \left( \Sigma_j \delta_j w_{i,j} \right) \frac{\partial y_i}{\partial a_i}$. These two equations give an alternate way of seeing back-propagation, as the variation of the cost with respect to the activation value, and provide a formula to calculate this variation for any layer once we know the variation for the following layer:

$$\delta_i = \frac{\partial J}{\partial y_j} \frac{\partial y_j}{\partial a_j}$$

$$\delta_i = \left( \Sigma_j \delta_i w_{i,j} \right) \frac{\partial y_i}{\partial a_i}$$

We can also combine these equations and show that:

$$\frac{\partial J}{\partial w_{i,j}} = \delta_j \frac{\partial a_j}{\partial w_{i,j}} = \delta_j y_i$$

The back-propagation algorithm for updating the weights is then given on each layer by

$$w_{i,j} \rightarrow w_{i,j} - \lambda \delta_j y_i$$

In the last section, we will provide a code example that will help understand and apply these concepts and formulas.

# Applications in industry

We mentioned in the previous chapter some examples where machine learning finds its applications. Neural networks, in particular, have many similar applications. We will review some of the applications for which they were used when they became popular in the late 1980's and early 1990's, after back-propagation had been discovered and deeper neural networks could be trained.

## Signal processing

There are many applications of neural networks in the area of signal processing. One of the first applications of neural nets was to suppress echo on a telephone line, especially on intercontinental calls, as developed starting from 1957 by Bernard Widrow and Marcian Hoff. The *Adaline* makes use of the identity function as its activity function for training and seeks to minimize the mean squared error between the activation and the target value. The Adaline is trained to remove the echo from the signal on the telephone line by applying the input signal both to the *Adaline* (the filter) and the telephone line. The difference between the output from the telephone line and the output from the *Adaline* is the error, which is used to train the network and remove the noise (echo) from the signal.

## Medical

The instant physician was developed by Anderson in 1986 and the idea behind it was to store a large number of medical records containing information about symptoms, diagnosis, and treatment for each case. The network is trained to make predictions on best diagnosis and treatment on different symptoms.

More recently, using deep neural networks, IBM worked on a neural network that could make predictions on possible heart failures, reading doctor's notes, similarly to an experienced cardiologist.

## Autonomous car driving

Nguyen and Widrow in 1989, and Miller, Sutton, and Werbos in 1990, developed a neural network that could provide steering directions to a large trailer truck backing up to a loading dock. The neural net is made up of two modules: the first module is able to calculate new positions using a neural net with several layers, by learning how the truck responds to different signals. This neural net is called the emulator. A second module, called the controller, learns to give the correct commands using the emulator to know its position. In recent years, autonomous car driving has made huge strides and it is a reality, though much more complex deep learning neural networks are used in conjunction with inputs from cameras, GPS, lidar, and sonar units.

## Business

In 1988, Collins, Ghosh, and Scofield developed a neural net that could be used to assess whether mortgage loans should be approved and given. Using data from mortgage evaluators, neural networks were trained to determine whether applicants should be given a loan. The input was a number of features, such as the number of years the applicant had been employed, income level, number of dependents, appraised value of the property, and so on.

## Pattern recognition

We have discussed this problem many times. One of the areas where neural networks have been applied is the recognition of characters. This, for example, can be applied to the recognition of digits, and it can be used for recognizing hand-written postal codes.

## Speech production

In 1986, Sejnowski and Rosenberg produced the widely known example of NETtalk that produced spoken words by reading written text. NETtalk's requirement is a set of examples of the written words and their pronunciation. The input includes both the letter being pronounced and the letters preceding it and following it (usually three) and the training is made using the most widely spoken words and their phonetic transcription. In its implementation, the net learns first to recognize vowels from consonants, then to recognize word beginnings and endings. It typically takes many passes before the words pronounced can become intelligible, and its progress sometimes resembles children's learning on how to pronounce words.

# Code example of a neural network for the function xor

It is a well-known fact, and something we have already mentioned, that 1-layer neural networks cannot predict the function XOR. 1-layer neural nets can only classify linearly separable sets, however, as we have seen, the Universal Approximation Theorem states that a 2-layer network can approximate any function, given a complex enough architecture. We will now create a neural network with two neurons in the hidden layer and we will show how this can model the XOR function. However, we will write code that will allow the reader to simply modify it to allow for any number of layers and neurons in each layer, so that the reader can try simulating different scenarios. We are also going to use the hyperbolic tangent as the activity function for this network. To train the network, we will implement the back-propagation algorithm discussed earlier.

We will only need to import one library, numpy, though if the reader wished to visualize the results, we also recommend importing matplotlib. The first lines of code are therefore:

```
import numpy
from matplotlib.colors import ListedColormap
import matplotlib.pyplot as plt
```

Next we define our activity function and its derivative (we use tanh(x) in this example):

```
def tanh(x):
    return (1.0 - numpy.exp(-2*x))/(1.0 + numpy.exp(-2*x))

def tanh_derivative(x):
    return (1 + tanh(x))*(1 - tanh(x))
```

Next we define the NeuralNetwork class:

```
class NeuralNetwork:
```

To follow Python syntax, anything inside the NeuralNetwork class will have to be indented. We define the "constructor" of the NeuralNetwork class, that is its variables, which in this case will be the neural network architecture, that is, how many layers and how many neurons per layer, and we will also initialize at random the weights to be between negative 1 and positive 1. net_arch will be a 1-dimensional array containing the number of neurons per each layer: for example [2,4,1] means an input layer with two neurons, a hidden layer with four neurons, and an output layer with one neuron.

Since we are studying the XOR function, for the input layer we need to have two neurons, and for the output layer only one neuron:

```
#net_arch consists of a list of integers, indicating
#the number of neurons in each layer, i.e. the network
#architecture
def __init__(self, net_arch):
    self.activity = tanh
    self.activity_derivative = tanh_derivative
    self.layers = len(net_arch)
    self.steps_per_epoch = 1000
    self.arch = net_arch

    self.weights = []
    #range of weight values (-1,1)
    for layer in range(self.layers - 1):
        w = 2*numpy.random.rand(net_arch[layer] + 1,
                                net_arch[layer+1]) - 1
        self.weights.append(w)
```

In this code, we have defined the activity function to be the hyperbolic tangent and we have defined its derivative. We have also defined how many training steps there should be per epoch. Finally, we have initialized the weights, making sure we also initialize the weights for the biases that we will add later. Next, we need to define the `fit` function, the function that will train our network. In the last line, nn represents the `NeuralNetwork` class and `predict` is the function in the `NeuralNetwork` class that we will define later:

```
#data is the set of all possible pairs of booleans
#True or False indicated by the integers 1 or 0
#labels is the result of the logical operation 'xor'
#on each of those input pairs
def fit(self, data, labels, learning_rate=0.1, epochs=100):
    #Add bias units to the input layer
    ones = numpy.ones((1, data.shape[0]))
    Z = numpy.concatenate((ones.T, data), axis=1)
    training = epochs*self.steps_per_epoch
    for k in range(training):
        if k % self.steps_per_epoch == 0:
            print('epochs: {}'.format(k/self.steps_per_epoch))
            for s in data:
                print(s, nn.predict(s))
```

All we have done here is to add a "1" to the input data (the always-on bias neuron) and set up code to print the result at the end of each epoch to keep track of our progress. We will now go ahead and set up our feed-forward propagation:

```
sample = numpy.random.randint(data.shape[0])
y = [Z[sample]]
for i in range(len(self.weights)-1):
    activation = numpy.dot(y[i], self.weights[i])
    activity = self.activity(activation)
    #add the bias for the next layer
    activity = numpy.concatenate(((numpy.ones(1),
                numpy.array(activity)))
    y.append(activity)

#last layer
activation = numpy.dot(y[-1], self.weights[-1])
activity = self.activity(activation)
y.append(activity)
```

We are going to update our weights after each step, so we randomly select one of the input data points, then we set up feed-forward propagation by setting up the activation for each neuron, then applying the `tanh(x)` on the activation value. Since we have a bias, we add the bias to our matrix y that keeps track of each neuron output value.

Now we do our back-propagation of the error to adjust the weights:

```
#error for the output layer
error = labels[sample] - y[-1]
delta_vec = [error * self.activity_derivative(y[-
1])]
#we need to begin from the back,
#from the next to last layer
for i in range(self.layers-2, 0, -1):
    error = delta_vec[-
1].dot(self.weights[i][1:].T)
    error =
error*self.activity_derivative(y[i][1:])
    delta_vec.append(error)
#Now we need to set the values from back to front
delta_vec.reverse()
```

```
#Finally, we adjust the weights,
#using the backpropagation rules
for i in range(len(self.weights)):
    layer = y[i].reshape(1, nn.arch[i]+1)
    delta = delta_vec[i].reshape(1, nn.arch[i+1])
    self.weights[i]
    +=learning_rate*layer.T.dot(delta)
```

This concludes our back-propagation algorithm; all that is left to do is to write a predict function to check the results:

```
def predict(self, x):
    val = numpy.concatenate((numpy.ones(1).T, numpy.array(x)))
    for i in range(0, len(self.weights)):
        val = self.activity(numpy.dot(val, self.weights[i]))
        val = numpy.concatenate((numpy.ones(1).T,
                                 numpy.array(val)))
    return val[1]
```

At this point we just need to write the main function as follows:

```
if __name__ == '__main__':
numpy.random.seed(0)
#Initialize the NeuralNetwork with
#2 input neurons
#2 hidden neurons
#1 output neuron
nn = NeuralNetwork([2,2,1])
X = numpy.array([[0, 0],
                [0, 1],
                [1, 0],
                [1, 1]])

#Set the labels, the correct results for the xor operation
y = numpy.array([0, 1, 1, 0])

#Call the fit function and train the network
#for a chosen number of epochs
nn.fit(X, y, epochs=10)

print "Final prediction"
for s in X:
   print(s, nn.predict(s))
```

Notice the use of `numpy.random.seed(0)`. This is simply to ensure that the weight initialization is consistent across runs to be able to compare results, but it is not necessary for the implementation of a neural net.

This ends the code, and the output should be a four-dimensional array, such as: (0.003032173692499, 0.9963860761357, 0.9959034563937, 0.0006386449217567) showing that the neural network is learning that the output should be (0,1,1,0).

The reader can slightly modify the code we created in the `plot_decision_regions function` used earlier in this book and see how different neural networks separate different regions depending on the architecture chosen.

The output picture will look like the following figures. The circles represent the (**True**, **True**) and (**False**, **False**) inputs, while the triangles represent the (**True**, **False**) and (**False**, **True**) inputs for the XOR function.

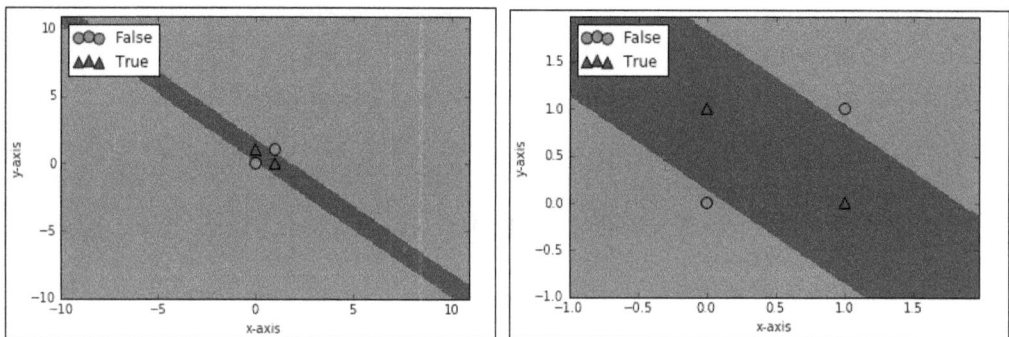

The same figure, on the left zoomed out, and on the right zoomed in on the selected inputs. The neural network learns to separate those points, creating a band containing the two **True** output values.

Different neural network architectures (for example, implementing a network with a different number of neurons in the hidden layer, or with more than just one hidden layer) may produce a different separating region. In order to do this, the reader can simply change the line in the code `nn = NeuralNetwork([2,2,1])`. While the first 2 must be kept (the input does not change), the second 2 can be modified to denote a different number of neurons in the hidden layer. Adding another integer will add a new hidden layer with as many neurons as indicated by the added integer. The last 1 cannot be modified. For example, `([2,4,3,1])` will represent a 3-layer neural network, with four neurons in the first hidden layer and three neurons in the second hidden layer.

The reader would then see that, while the solution is always the same, the curves separating the regions will be quite different depending on the architecture chosen. In fact, choosing nn = `NeuralNetwork([2,4,3,1])` will give the following figure:

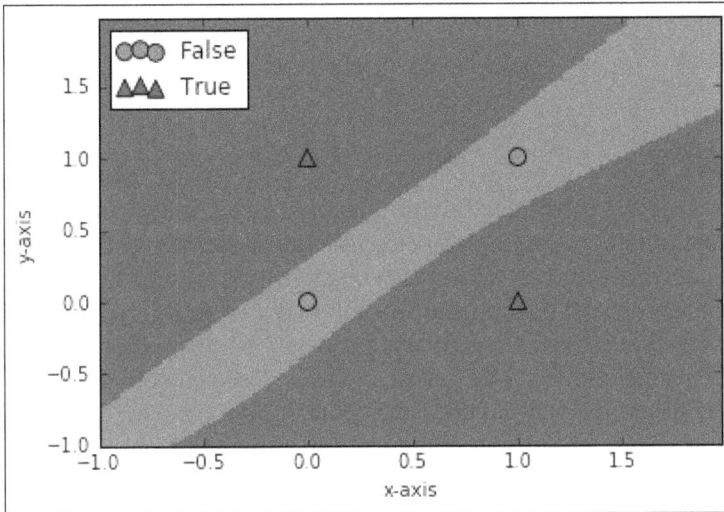

While choosing nn = `NeuralNetwork([2,4,1])`, for example, would produce the following:

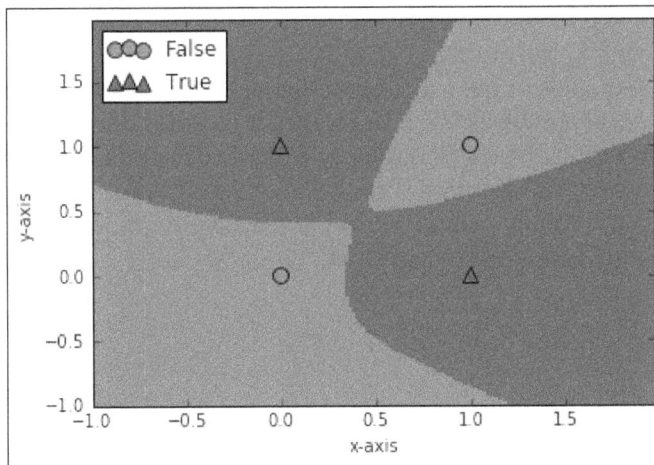

The architecture of the neural network defines therefore the way the neural net goes about to solve the problem at hand, and different architectures provide different approaches (though they may all give the same result) similarly to how human thought processes can follow different paths to reach the same conclusion. We are now ready to start looking more closely at what deep neural nets are and their applications.

# Summary

In this chapter, we have introduced neural networks in detail and we have mentioned their success over other competing algorithms. Neural networks are comprised of the "units", or neurons, that belong to them or their connections, or weights, that characterize the strength of the communication between different neurons and their activity functions, that is, how the neurons process the information. We have discussed how we can create different architectures, and how a neural network can have many layers, and why inner (hidden) layers are important. We have explained how the information flows from the input to the output by passing from each layer to the next based on the weights and the activity function defined, and finally we have shown how we can define a method called back-propagation to "tune" the weights to improve the desired level of accuracy. We have also mentioned many of the areas where neural networks are and have been employed.

In the next chapter, we will continue discussing deep neural networks, and in particular we will explain the meaning of "deep", as in deep learning, by explaining that it not only refers to the number of hidden layers in the network, but more importantly to the quality of the learning of the neural network. For this purpose, we will show how neural networks learn to recognize features and put them together as representations of the objects recognized, which will open the way to use neural networks for unsupervised learning. We will also describe a few important deep learning libraries, and finally, we will provide a concrete example where we can apply neural networks for digit recognition.

# 3
# Deep Learning Fundamentals

In *Chapter 1*, *Machine Learning – An Introduction*, we introduced machine learning and some of its applications, and we briefly talked about a few different algorithms and techniques that can be used to implement machine learning. In *Chapter 2*, *Neural Networks*, we concentrated on neural networks; we have shown that 1-layer networks are too simple and can only work on linear problems, and we have introduced the Universal Approximation Theorem, showing how 2-layer neural networks with just one hidden layer are able to approximate to any degree any continuous function on a compact subset of $R_n$.

In this chapter, we will introduce deep learning and deep neural networks, that is, neural networks with at least two or more hidden layers. The reader may wonder what is the point of using more than one hidden layer, given the Universal Approximation Theorem, and this is in no way a naïve question, since for a long period the neural networks used were very shallow, with just one hidden layer. The answer is that it is true that 2-layer neural networks can approximate any continuous function to any degree, however, it is also true that adding layers adds levels of complexity that may be much harder and may require many more neurons to simulate with shallow networks. There is also another, more important, reason behind the term *deep* of deep learning that refers not just to the depth of the network, or how many layers the neural net has, but to the level of "learning". In deep learning, the network does not simply learn to predict an output $Y$ given an input $X$, but it also understands basic features of the input. In deep learning, the neural network is able to make abstractions of the features that comprise the input examples, to understand the basic characteristics of the examples, and to make predictions based on those characteristics. In deep learning, there is a level of abstraction that is missing in other basic machine learning algorithms or in shallow neural networks.

In this chapter, we will cover the following topics:

- What is deep learning?
- Fundamental concepts of deep learning
- Applications of deep learning
- GPU versus CPU
- Popular open source libraries

# What is deep learning?

In 2012, Alex Krizhevsky, Ilya Sutskever, and Geoff Hinton published an article titled *ImageNet Classification with Deep Convolutional Neural Networks* in Proceedings of Neural Information Processing Systems (NIPS) (2012) and, at the end of their paper, they wrote:

> *"It is notable that our network's performance degrades if a single convolutional layer is removed. For example, removing any of the middle layers results in a loss of about 2% for the top-1 performance of the network. So the depth really is important for achieving our results."*

In this milestone paper, they clearly mention the importance of the number of hidden layers present in deep networks. Krizheysky, Sutskever, and Hilton talk about convolutional layers, and we will not discuss them until *Chapter 5, Image Recognition*, but the basic question remains: *What do those hidden layers do?*

A typical English saying is *a picture is worth a thousand words*. Let's use this approach to understand what Deep Learning is. In H. Lee, R. Grosse, R. Ranganath, and A. Ng, *Convolutional deep belief networks for scalable unsupervised learning of hierarchical representations* in Proceedings of International Conference on Machine Learning (ICML) (2009) (Refer to http://web.eecs.umich.edu/~honglak/icml09-ConvolutionalDeepBeliefNetworks.pdf) the authors use a few images, which we copy here.

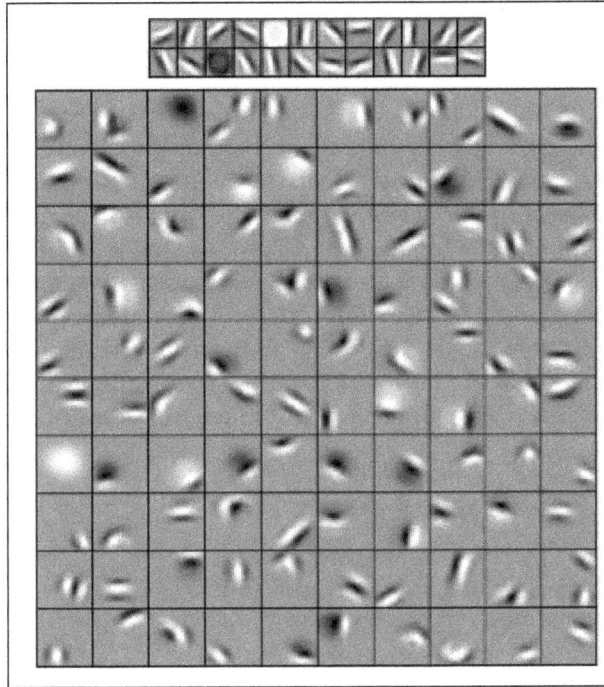

In their example, they showed neural network pictures of different categories of objects and/or animals, and the network learned some basic features for each category. For instance, the network can learn some very basic shapes, like lines or edges, which are common to every category. In the next layer, however, the network can learn how those lines and edges fit together for each category to make images that feature the eyes of a face, or the wheels of a car. This is similar to how the visual cortex in humans works, where our brain recognizes features more and more complex starting from simple lines and edges.

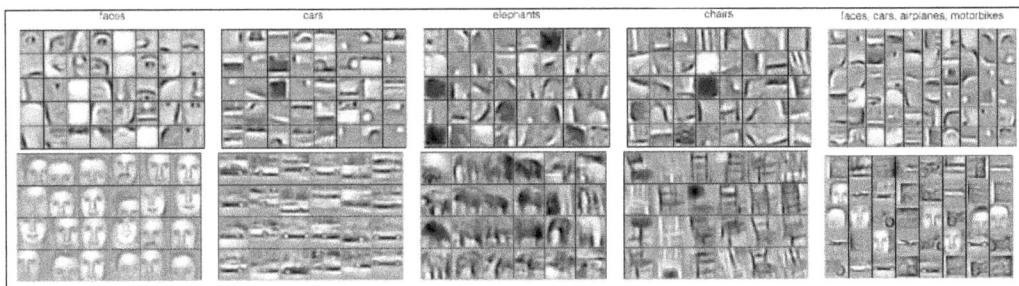

The hidden layers in a deep neural network work similarly by understanding more and more complex features in each hidden layer. If we want to define what makes a face, we need to define its parts: the eyes, the nose, the mouth, and then we need to go a level up and define their position with respect to each other: the two eyes are on the top middle part, at the same height, the nose in the middle, the mouth in the lower middle part, below the nose. Deep neural networks catch these features by themselves, first learning the components of the image, then its relative position and so on, similarly to how, in Images 1 and 2, we see the level of deeper abstraction working in each layer. Some deep learning networks can, in fact, be considered generative algorithms, as in the case of **Restricted Boltzmann Machines (RBMs)**, rather than simply a predictive algorithm, as they learn to generate a signal, and then they make the prediction based on the generation assumptions they have learned. As we will progress through this chapter, we will make this concept clearer.

# Fundamental concepts

In 1801, Joseph Marie Charles invented the Jacquard loom. Charles named the Jacquard, hence the name of its invention, was not a scientist, but simply a merchant. The Jacquard loom used a set of punched cards, and each punched card represented a pattern to be reproduced on the loom. Each punched card represented an abstraction of a design, a pattern, and each punched card was an abstract representation of that pattern. Punched cards have been used afterwards, for example in the tabulating machine invented by Herman Hollerith in 1890, or in the first computers where they were used to feed code to the machine. However, in the tabulating machine, for example, punched cards were simply abstractions of samples to be fed into the machine to calculate statistics on a population. In the Jacquard loom, the use of punched cards was subtler; in it, each card represented the abstraction of a pattern that could then be combined together with others to create more complex patterns. The punched card is an abstract representation of a feature of a reality, the final weaved design.

In a way, the Jacquard loom had the seed of what makes deep learning today: the definition of a reality through the representations of its features. In deep learning, the neural network does not simply recognize what makes a cat a cat, or a squirrel a squirrel, but it understands what features are present in a cat and what features are present in a squirrel, and it learns to *design* a cat or a squirrel using those features. If we were to design a weaving pattern in the shape of a cat using a Jacquard loom, we would need to use punched cards that have *moustaches* on the nose, like those of a cat, and an elegant and slender body. Instead, if we were to design a squirrel, we would need to use the punched card that makes a furry tail, for example. A deep network that learns basic representations of its output can make classifications using the assumptions it has made; therefore, if there is no furry tail it will probably not be a squirrel, but rather a cat. This has many implications, as we will see, not least that the amount of information that the network learns is much more complete and robust. By learning to *generate* the model (in technical parlance by learning the joint probability $p(x,y)$ rather than simply $p(y \mid x)$, the network is much less sensitive to *noise*, and it learns to recognize images even when there are other objects present in the scene or the object is partially obscured. The most exciting part is that deep neural networks learn to do this automatically.

# Feature learning

The Ising model was invented by the physicist Wilhelm Lenz in1920, and he gave it as a problem to his student Ernst Ising. The model consists of discrete variables that can be in two states (positive or negative) and that represent magnetic dipoles.

In *Chapter 4, Unsupervised Feature Learning*, we will introduce Restricted Boltzmann machines and auto-encoders, and we will start going deeper into how to build multi-layer neural networks. The type of neural networks that we have seen so far all have a feed-forward architecture, but we will see that we can define networks with a feedback loop to help tune the weights that define the neural network. Ising models, though not directly used in deep learning, are a good physical example that helps us understand the basic inner workings of tuning deep neural architectures, including Restricted Boltzmann machines, and in particular help us understand the concept of representation.

What we are going to discuss in this section is a simple adaption (and simplification) of the Ising model to deep learning. In *Chapter 2, Neural Networks*, we discussed how important it is to tune the weights of the connections between neurons. In fact, it is the weights in a neural network that make the network learn. Given an input (fixed), this input propagates to the next layer and sets the internal state of the neurons in the next layer based on the weights of their connections. Then, these neurons will fire and move the information over to the following layer through new connections defined by new weights, and so on. The weights are the only variables of the network, and they are what make the network learn. In general, if our activity function were a simple threshold function, a large positive weight would tend to make two neurons fire together. By firing together, we mean that, if one neuron fires, and the connecting weight is high, then the other neuron will also fire (since the input times the large connecting weight will likely make it over the chosen threshold). In fact, in 1949, in his *The organization of behavior*, Donald Hebb (`http://s-f-walker.org.uk/pubsebooks/pdfs/The_Organization_of_Behavior-Donald_O._Hebb.pdf`) proposed that the opposite should also be true. Donald Hebb was a Canadian psychologist, who lived during the 20th century, who proposed the rule that goes by his name, the Hebb rule, which says that when neurons fire together their connection strengthens; when they do not fire together, their connection weakens.

In the following example, we think of an Ising model as a network of neurons that acts in a binary way, that is, where they can only activate (fire) or not, and that, the stronger their relative connection, the more likely they are to fire together. We assume that the network is stochastic, and therefore if two neurons are strongly connected they are only very likely to fire together.

Stochastic means probabilistic. In a stochastic network, we define the probability of a neuron to fire: the higher the probability, the more likely the neuron is to fire. When two neurons are strongly connected, that is, they are connected by a large weight, the probability that one firing will induce the other one to fire as well is very high (and vice versa, a weak connection will give a low probability). However, the neuron will only fire according to a probability, and therefore we cannot know with certainty whether it will fire.

On the other hand, if they are inversely correlated (a large negative weight), they are very likely not to fire together. Let's show some examples:

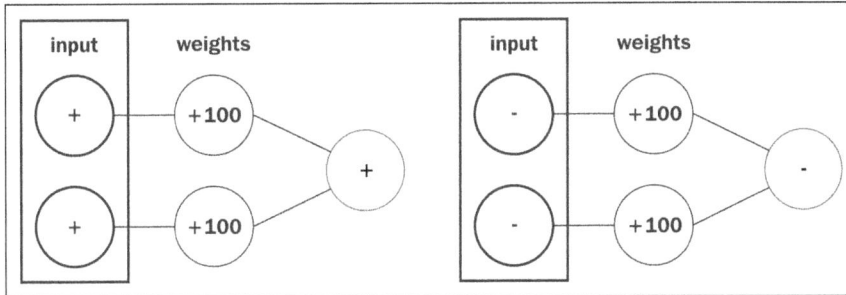

In the first figure, the first two neurons are active, and their connection with the third neuron is large and positive, so the third neuron will also be active. In the second figure, the first two neurons are off, and their connection with the third neuron is positive, so the third neuron will also be off.

In the second figure, the first two neurons are off, and their connection with the third neuron is positive, so the third neuron will also be off.

There are several combinations that may be present; we will show only a few of them. The idea is that the state of the neurons in the first layer will probabilistically determine the state of the neurons in the following layer, depending on the sign and strength of the connection. If the connections are weak, the connected neurons in the following layer may have equal or almost equal probability to be in any state. But if the connections are very strong, then the sign of the weight will make the connected neurons act in a similar or opposite way. Of course, if the neuron on the second layer has more than one neuron as its input, we will weigh all the input connections as usual. And if the input neurons are not all on or off, and their connections are equally strong, then again, the connected neuron may have equal or an almost equal chance of being on or off.

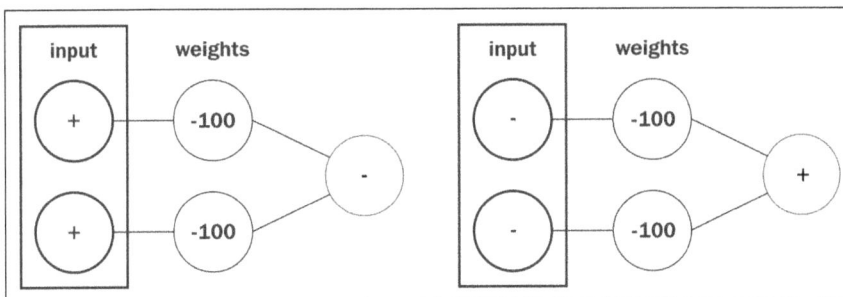

In the first figure, the first two neurons are active, and their connection with the third neuron is large and negative, so the third neuron will also be off. In the second figure, the first two neurons are off, and their connection with the third neuron is large and negative, so the third neuron will likely be on.

It is then clear that, to most likely determine the state of the neurons in the following layers, the neurons in the first layer should all be in similar states (on or off) and all be connected with strong (that is, large weights) connections. Let's see more examples:

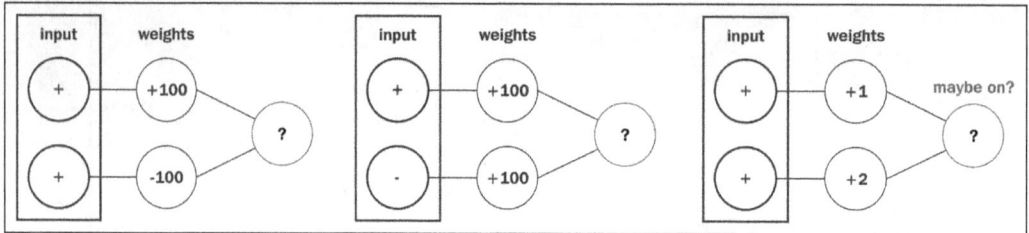

In the first figure, the first two neurons are active, and their connection with the third neuron is large but opposite, so the third neuron could be equally likely to be on or off. In the second figure, the first two neurons are, one on and one off, and their connections with the third neuron are both large and positive, so the third neuron will also be equally likely to be on or off. In the last figure, the first two neurons are active, but their connection with the third neuron is small, so the third neuron is slightly more likely to be on but it has a relatively high chance to be off as well.

The point of introducing this adaptation of the Ising model is to understand how representation learning works in deep neural networks. We have seen that setting the correct weights can make a neural network turn on or off certain neurons, or in general, affect their output. Picturing neurons in just two states, however, helps our intuition and our visual description of what goes on in a neural network. It also helps our visual intuition to represent our network layers in 2-dimensions, rather than as a 1-dimensional layer. Let's picture our neural network layer as in a 2-dimensional plane. We could then imagine that each neuron represents the pixel on a 2-dimensional image, and that an "on" neuron represents a (visible) dark dot on a white plane, while an "off" neuron blends in (invisibly) with the white background. Our input layer of on/off neurons can then be seen as a simple 2-dimensional black and white image. For example, let's suppose we want to represent a smiley face, or a sad face—we would just turn on (activate) the correct neurons to get the following figures:

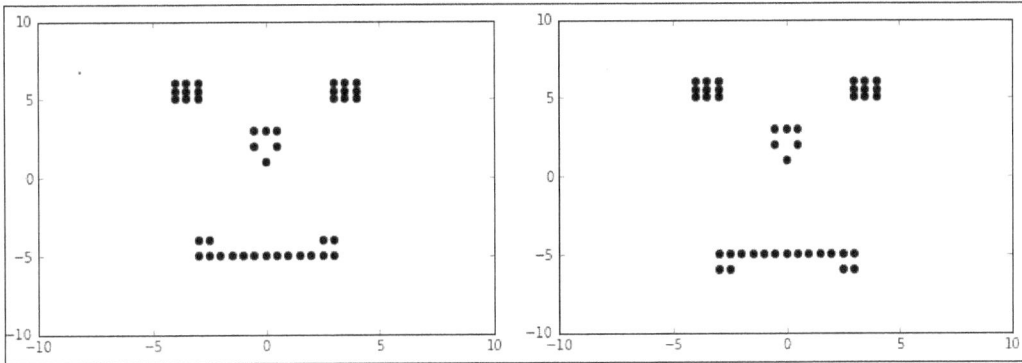

A happy and a sad face: the difference lies in a few neurons on the side of the mouth that can be on or off.

Now let's suppose that this corresponds to the input layer, so this layer would be connected to another layer, one of the hidden layers. There would then be connections between each pixel in this image (both black and white) and each neuron in the following layer. In particular, each black (on) pixel would be connected to each neuron in the following layer. Let's now assume that the connections from each neuron making the left eye has a strong (large positive weight) connection to a particular pixel in the hidden layer, but it has a large negative connection to any other neuron in the hidden layer:

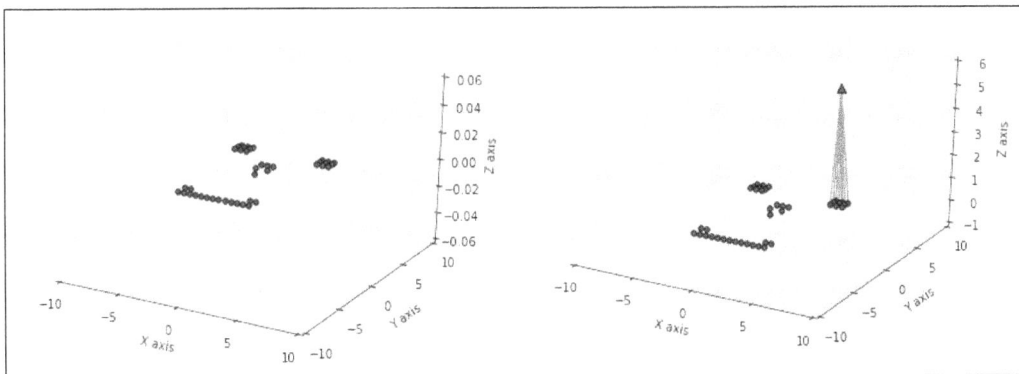

On the left a smiley face, on the right, the same smiley face and the connections between its left eye and a hidden neuron.

What this means is that if we set large positive weights between the hidden layer and the left eye, and large negative connections between the left eye and any other hidden neuron, whenever we show the network a face that contains a left eye (which means those neurons are on) this particular hidden neuron will activate, while all the other neurons will tend to stay off. This means that this particular neuron will be able to detect when a left eye is present or not. We can similarly create connections between the right eye, the nose and the main part of the mouth, so that we can start detecting all those face features.

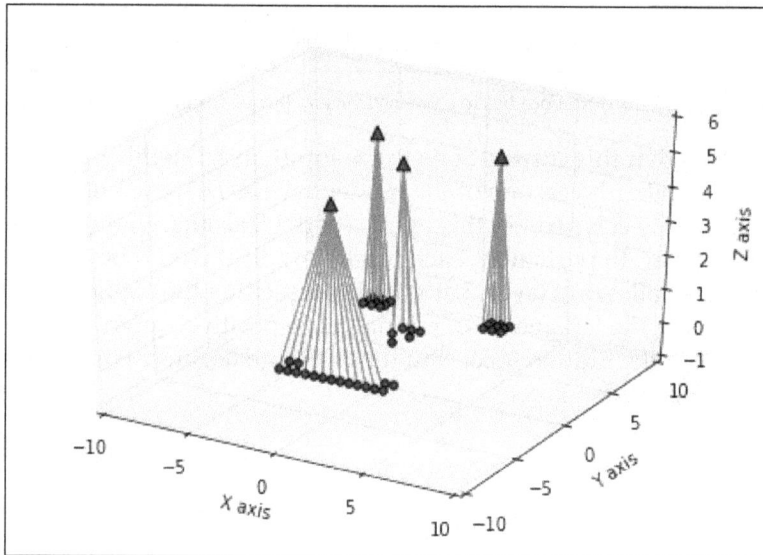

Each face feature, the eyes, the nose and the mouth, has large positive connections with certain hidden neurons and large but negative connections with the others.

This shows how we can select weights for our connections, to have the hidden neurons start recognizing features of our input.

> As an important reminder, we want to point out to the reader that, in fact, we do not select the weights for our connections to start recognizing features of the input. Instead, those weights are automatically selected by the network using back-propagation or other tuning methods.

In addition, we can have more hidden layers that can recognize features of the features (*is the mouth in our face smiling or is it sad?*) and therefore get more precise results.

There are several advantages to deep learning. The first is, as we have seen, that it can recognize features. Another, even more important, is that it will recognize features automatically. In this example, we have set the weights ourselves to recognize the features we chose. This is one of the disadvantages of many machine learning algorithms, that the user must use his/her own experience to select what he/she thinks are the best features. A lot of time goes therefore, into feature selection that must still be performed by a human being. Deep Learning algorithms, instead, automatically select the best features. This can be done, as we have seen in the previous chapter, using back-propagation, but in fact, other techniques also exist to select those weights, and those will be the important points that will be treated in the next chapter, such as auto-encoders and restricted Boltzmann machines (or *Harmoniums*, as Paul Smolensky, who invented them in 1986, called them). We should, however, also caution the reader that the advantage we get from the automatic feature selection has to pay the price of the fact that we need to choose the correct architecture for the neural network.

In some deep learning systems (for example in Restricted Boltzmann Machines, as we will see in the next chapter), the neural network can also learn to "repair" itself. As we mentioned in the previous example, we could produce a general face by activating the four neurons we have associated to the right/left eye, the nose, and the mouth respectively. Because of the large positive weights between them and the neurons in the previous layer, those neurons will turn on and we will have the neurons corresponding to those features activated, generating a general image of a face. At the same time, if the neurons corresponding to the face are turned on, the four corresponding neurons to the eyes, nose, and mouth will also activate. What this means is that, even if not all the neurons defining the face are on, if the connections are strong enough, they may still turn on the four corresponding neurons, which, in turn, will activate the missing neurons for the face.

This has one more extra advantage: robustness. Human vision can recognize objects even when the view is partly obscured. We can recognize people even when they wear a hat, or a scarf that covers their mouth; we are not sensitive to noise in the image. Similarly, when we create this correspondence, if we alter the face slightly, for example by modifying the mouth by one or two pixels, the signal would still be strong enough to turn the "mouth" neuron on, which in turn would turn on the correct pixel and off the wrong pixel making up the modified eye. This system is not sensitive to noise and can make auto-corrections.

Let's say, for example, that the mouth has a couple of pixels off (in the figure those are the pixels that have an **x**).

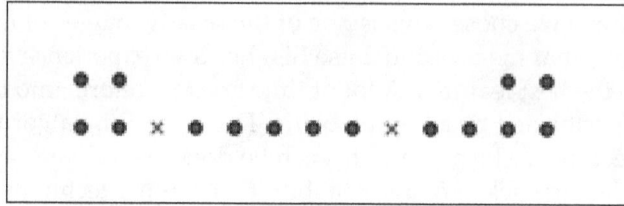

This image has a couple of pixels making the mouth that are not turned on.

However, the mouth may still have enough neurons in the right place to be able to turn on the corresponding neuron representing it:

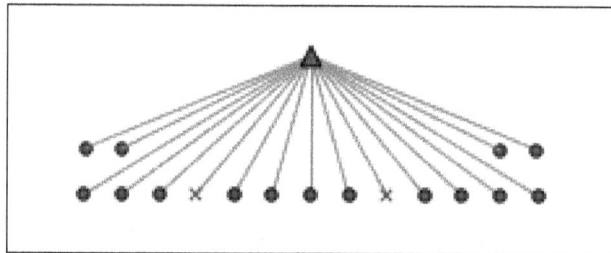

Even though a couple of neurons are off, the connections with the other neurons are strong enough that the neuron representing the mouth in the next layer will turn on anyway.

On the other hand, we could now travel the connections backwards and whenever the neuron representing the mouth is on, this would turn on all the neurons comprising the mouth, including the two neurons that were previously off:

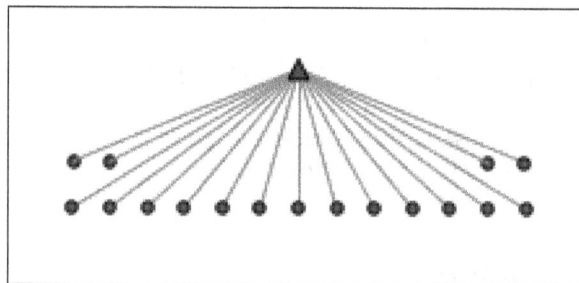

The two neurons have been activated by the neuron on top

In summary, deep learning advantages with respect to many other machine learning algorithms and shallow neural networks in particular are:

- Deep learning can learn representations
- Deep learning is less sensitive to noise
- Deep learning can be a generative algorithm (more on this in the next chapter)

To further understand why many hidden layers may be necessary, let's consider the task of recognizing a simple geometric figure, a cube. Say that each possible line in 3D is associated with a neuron (let's forget for a moment that this will require an infinite number of neurons).

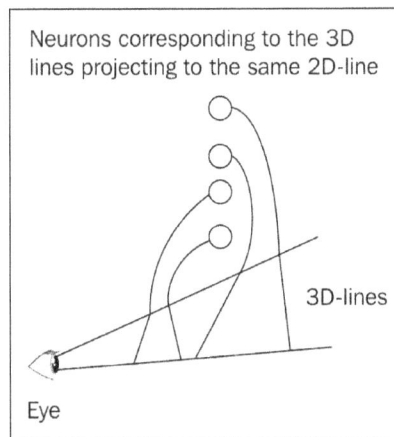

Each line on the same visual field is associated to a different neuron.

If we restrict ourselves to a single eye, lines at different angles in our vision will project to the same line on a 2-dimensional plane. Each line we see could therefore be given by any corresponding 3D-line that projects to the same line onto the retina. Assume that any possible 3D-line is associated to a neuron. Two distinct lines that make up the cube are therefore associated to a family of neurons each. However, the fact that these two lines intersect, allows us to create a connection between two neurons each belonging to a different family. We have many neurons for the line making up one of the edges of the cube, and many other neurons for the line making up another of the edges of the cube, but since those two lines intersect, there are two neurons that will be connected. Similarly, each of these lines connects to other lines that make up the cube, allowing us to further redefine our representation. At a higher level, our neural net can also start to identify that these lines are not connected at just any angle, but they are connected at exactly 90 degree angles. This way we can make increasingly more abstract representations that allow us to identify the set of lines drawn on a piece of paper as a cube.

Neurons in different layers, organized hierarchically, represent different levels of abstraction of basic elements in the image and how they are structured. This toy example shows that each layer can, in an abstract system, link together what different neurons at a lower level are seeing, making connections between them, similar to how we can make connections between abstract lines. It can, using those connections, realize that those abstract lines are connected at a point, and, in a further up layer, are in fact connected at 90 degrees and make up a cube, the same way we described how we can learn to recognize a face by recognizing the eyes, the nose, and the mouth, and their relative position.

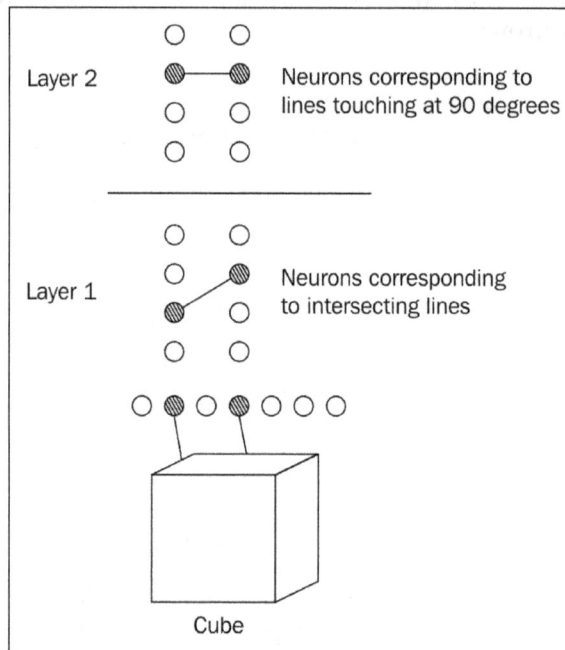

Each line is associated with a neuron, and we can create basic representations by associating neurons that represent lines that intersect, and more complex representations by associating neurons that represent lines at specific angles.

# Deep learning algorithms

In the previous paragraph, we have given an intuitive introduction to deep learning. In this section, we will give a more precise definition of key concepts that will be thoroughly introduced in the next chapters. Deep Neural Networks with many layers also have a biological reason to exist: through our study of how humans understand speech, it has in fact become clear that we are endowed with a layered hierarchical structure that transforms the information from the audible sound input into the linguistic level. Similarly, the visual system and the visual cortex have a similar layered structure, from the V1 (or striate cortex), to the V2, V3 and V4 visual area in the brain. Deep neural networks mimic the nature of our brains, though in a very primitive way. We should warn the reader, however, that while understanding our brain can help us create better artificial neural networks, in the end, we may be creating a completely different architecture, the same way we may have created airplanes by trying to mimic birds, but ended up with a very different model.

In *Chapter 2, Neural Networks*, we introduced the back-propagation algorithm as a popular training algorithm. In practice, when we have many layers, back-propagation may be a slow and difficult algorithm to use. Back-propagation, in fact, is mainly based on the gradient of the function, and often the existence of local minima may prevent convergence of the method. However, the term deep learning applies to a class of deep neural networks algorithms that may use different training algorithms and weight tuning, and they are not limited to back-propagation and classical feed-forward neural networks. We should then more generally define deep learning as a class of machine learning techniques where information is processed in hierarchical layers, to understand representations and features from the data in increasing levels of complexity. In this class of algorithms, we can generally include:

- **Multi-Layer Perceptrons (MLP)**: A neural network with many hidden layers, with feed-forward propagation. As discussed, this is one of the first examples of deep learning network but not the only possible one.

- **Boltzmann Machines (BM)**: A stochastic symmetric network with a well-defined energy function.

- **Restricted Boltzmann Machines (RBM)**: Similar to the Ising model example above, restricted Boltzmann machines are comprised of symmetric connections between two layers, one visible and one hidden layer, but unlike general Boltzmann machines, neurons have no intra-layers connections. They can be stacked together to form DBNs.

- **Deep Belief Networks (DBN)**: a stochastic generative model where the top layers have symmetric connections between them (undirected, unlike feed-forward networks), while the bottom layers receive the processed information from directed connections from the layers above them.

- **Autoencoders**: A class of unsupervised learning algorithms in which the output shape is the same as the input, that allows the network to better learn basic representations.

- **Convolutional Neural Networks (CNN)**: Convolutional layers apply filters to the input image (or sound) by sliding this filter all across the incoming signal to produce a bi-dimensional activation map. CNNs allow the enhancement of features hidden in the input.

Each of these deep learning implementations has its own advantages and disadvantages, and they can be easier or harder to train depending on the number of layers and neurons in each layer. While simple feed-forward Deep Neural Networks can generally be trained using the back-propagation algorithm discussed in the second chapter, different techniques exist for the other types of networks, as will be discussed further in the next chapter.

# Deep learning applications

In the next couple of paragraphs, we will discuss how deep neural networks have applications in the field of speech recognition and computer vision, and how their application in recent years has vastly improved accuracy in these two fields by completely outperforming many other machine learning algorithms not based on deep neural networks.

# Speech recognition

Deep learning has started to be used in speech recognition starting in this decade (2010 and later, see for example the 2012 article titled *Deep Neural Networks for Acoustic Modeling in Speech Recognition* by Hinton et al., available online at http://static.googleusercontent.com/media/research.google.com/en//pubs/archive/38131.pdf); until then, speech recognition methods were dominated by algorithms called GMM-HMM methods (Hidden Markov Models with Gaussian Mixture Emission). Understanding speech is a complex task, since speech is not, as is naively thought, made up of separate words with clear boundaries between them. In reality, in speech there are no really distinguishable parts, and there are no clear boundaries between spoken words. In studying sounds when composing words, we often look at so-called triphones, which are comprised of three regions where the first part depends on the previous sound, the middle part is generally stable, and the next one depends on the following sound. In addition, typically it is better to detect only parts of a triphone, and those detectors are called senones.

In *Deep Neural Networks for Acoustic Modeling in Speech Recognition*, several comparisons were made between the then state-of-the art models and the model used by the authors that comprised five hidden layers with 2048 units per layer. The first comparison was using the Bing voice search application, achieving a 69.6% accuracy vs. a 63.8% accuracy with a classical method, named the GMM-HMM model, on 24 hours of training data. The same model was also tested on the Switchboard speech recognition task, a public speech-to-text transcription benchmark (similar to the MNIST dataset used for digit recognition) that includes about 2500 conversations by 500 speakers from around the US. In addition, tests and comparisons were performed using Google Voice input speech, YouTube data, and English Broadcast News speech data. In the next table, we summarize the results from the article, showing the error rate for DNN versus GMM-HMM.

| Task | Total number of hours of training data | DNN (error rate) | GMM-HMM with same training (error rate) | GMM-HMM with longer training (error rate) |
|---|---|---|---|---|
| Switchboard (test1) | 309 | 18.5 | 27.4 | 18.6 (2000hrs) |
| Switchboard (test2) | 309 | 16.1 | 23.6 | 17.1 (2000hrs) |
| English Broadcast News | 50 | 17.5 | 18.8 | |
| Bing Voice Search | 24 | 30.4 | 36.2 | |
| Google Voice | 5870 | 12.3 | | 16.0 (>>5870hrs) |
| YouTube | 1400 | 47.6 | 52.3 | |

In another article, *New types of Deep Neural Network Learning for Speech Recognition and Related Applications: An overview*, by Deng, Hinton, and Kingsbury (`https://www.microsoft.com/en-us/research/publication/new-types-of-deep-neural-network-learning-for-speech-recognition-and-related-applications-an-overview/`), the authors also notice how DNNs work particularly well for noisy speech.

Another advantage of DNNs is that before DNNs, people had to create transformations of speech spectrograms. A spectrogram is a visual representation of the frequencies in a signal. By using DNNs, these neural networks can autonomously and automatically pick primitive features, in this case represented by primitive spectral features. Use of techniques such as convolution and pooling operations, can be applied on this primitive spectral feature to cope with typical speech variations between speakers. In recent years, more sophisticated neural networks that have recurrent connections (RNN) have been employed with great success (A. Graves, A. Mohamed and G. Hinton , *Speech Recognition with Deep Recurrent Neural Networks* in Proceedings of International Conference on Acoustic Speech and Signal Processing (ICASSP) (2013); refer to `http://www.cs.toronto.edu/~fritz/absps/RNN13.pdf`) for example, a particular type of deep neural network called **LSTM (long short-term memory** neural network) that will be described in a later chapter.

In *Chapter 2*, *Neural Networks*, we have discussed different activity functions, and although the logistic sigmoid and the hyperbolic tangent are often the best known, they are also often slow to train. Recently, the ReLU activity function has been used successfully in speech recognition, for example in an article by G. Dahl, T. Sainath, and G. Hinton in *Improving Deep Neural Networks for LVCSR Using Rectified Linear Units and Dropout* in Proceeding of International Conference on Acoustics Speech and Signal Processing (ICASSP) (2013) (`http://www.cs.toronto.edu/~gdahl/papers/reluDropoutBN_icassp2013.pdf`). In *Chapter 5*, *Image Recognition*, we will also mention the meaning of "Dropout", as discussed in this paper (and also mentioned in its title).

# Object recognition and classification

This is perhaps the area where deep neural networks, success is best documented and understood. As in speech recognition, DNNs can discover basic representations and features automatically. In addition, handpicked features were often able to capture only low-level edge information, while DNNs can capture higher-level representations such as edge intersections. In 2012, results from the ImageNet Large Scale Visual Recognition Competition (the results are available online at `http://image-net.org/challenges/LSVRC/2012/results.html`) showed the winning team, composed of Alex Krizhevsky, Ilya Sutskever, and Geoff Hinton, using a large network with 60 million parameters and 650,000 neurons with five convolutional layers and followed by max-pooling layers, beat the second placed team with an error rate of 16.4% versus an error rate of 26.2%. Convolutional layers and max-pooling layers will be the focus of *Chapter 5*, *Image Recognition*. It was a huge and impressive result, and that breakthrough result sparked the current renaissance in neural networks. The authors used many novel ways to help the learning process by bringing together convolutional networks, use of the GPU, and some tricks like dropout methods and the use of the ReLU activity function instead of the sigmoid.

The network was trained using GPUs (we will talk about GPU advantages in the next section) and showed how a large amount of labeled data can greatly improve the performance of deep learning neural nets, greatly outperforming more conventional approaches to image recognition and computer vision. Given the success of convolutional layers in deep learning, Zeiler and Fergus in two articles (M. Zeiler and R. Fergus, *Stochastic pooling for regularization of deep convolutional neural networks*, in Proceeding of International Conference on Learning Representations (ICLR), 2013 (`http://www.matthewzeiler.com/pubs/iclr2013/iclr2013.pdf`) and M. Zeiler and R. Fergus, *Visualizing and Understanding Convolutional Networks*, arXiv:1311.2901, pages 1-11, 2013, (`http://www.matthewzeiler.com/pubs/arxive2013/arxive2013.pdf`)) tried to understand why using convolutional networks in deep learning worked so well, and what representations were being learned by the network. Zeiler and Fergus set to visualize what the intermediate layers captured by mapping back their neural activities. They created a de-convolutional network attached to each layer, providing a loop back to the image pixels of the input.

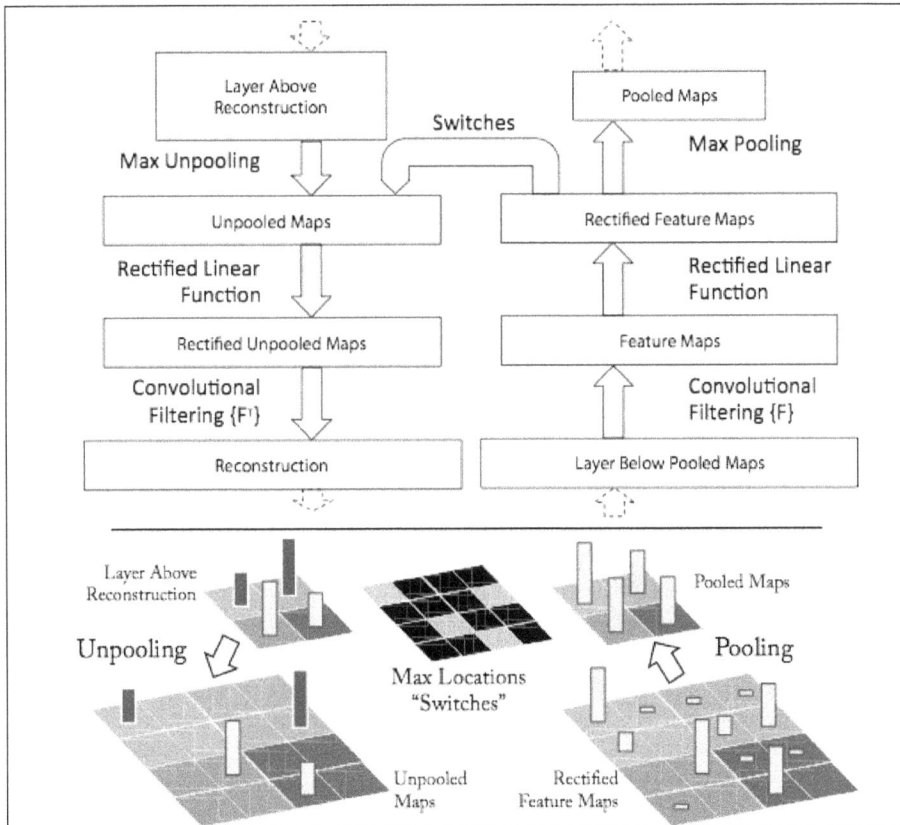

Image taken from M. Zeiler and R. Fergus, Visualizing and Understanding Convolutional Networks

The article shows what features are being revealed, where **layer 2** shows corner and edges, **layer 3**, different mesh patterns, **layer 4**, dog faces and bird legs, and **layer 5** shows entire objects.

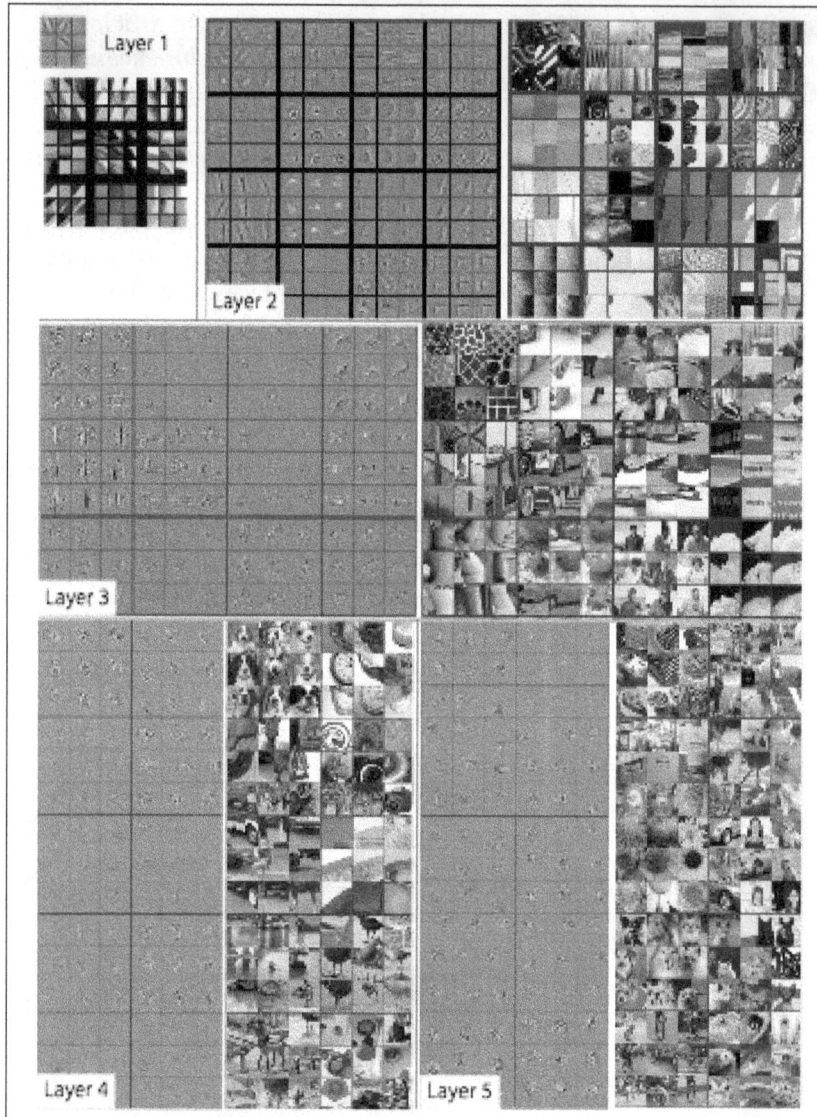

Image taken from M. Zeiler and R. Fergus, Visualizing and Understanding Convolutional Networks

Deep learning can also be used in unsupervised learning by using networks that incorporate RBMs and autoencoders. In an article by Q. Le, M. Ranzato, M. Devin, G. Corrado, K. Chen, J. Dean, and A. Ng, *Building high-level features using large scale unsupervised learning*, in Proceedings of International Conference on Machine Learning (ICML) (`http://static.googleusercontent.com/media/research.google.com/en//archive/unsupervised_icml2012.pdf`) the authors used a 9-layer network with autoencoders, with one billion connections trained on 10 million images downloaded from the Internet. The unsupervised feature learning allows the system to be trained to recognize faces without being told whether the image contains a face or not. In the article the authors state:

> *"It is possible to train neurons to be selective for high-level concepts using entirely unlabeled data ... neurons functions as detectors for faces, human bodies, and cat faces by training on random frames of YouTube videos ... starting from these representations we obtain 15.8% accuracy for object recognition on ImageNet with 20,000 categories, a significant leap of 70% relative improvement over the state-of-the-art."*

# GPU versus CPU

One of the reasons for the popularity of deep learning today is the drastically increased processing capacity of **GPUs (Graphical Processing Units)**. Architecturally, the **CPU (Central Processing Unit)** is composed of a few cores that can handle a few threads at a time, while GPUs are composed of hundreds of cores that can handle thousands of threads at the same time. A GPU is a highly parallelizable unit, compared to the CPU that is mainly a serial unit.

DNNs are composed of several layers, and each layer has neurons that behave in the same manner. Moreover, we have discussed how the activity value for each neuron is , or, if we express it in matrix form, we have $a = wx$, where $a$ and $x$ are vectors and $w$ a matrix. All activation values are calculated in the same way across the network. CPUs and GPUs have a different architecture, in particular they are optimized differently: CPUs are latency optimized and GPUs are bandwidth optimized. In a deep neural network with many layers and a large number of neurons, bandwidth becomes the bottleneck, not latency, and this is the reason why GPUs perform so much better. In addition, the L1 cache of the GPU is much faster than the L1 cache for the CPU and is also larger.

The L1 cache represents memory of information that the program is likely to use next, and storing this data can speed up the process. Much of the memory gets re-used in deep neural networks, which is why L1 cache memory is important. Using GPUs, you can get your program, go up to one order of magnitude faster than simply using CPUs, and use of this speed-up is also the reason behind much of the recent progress in speech and image processing using deep neural networks, an increase in computing power that was not available a decade ago.

$$a_j = \sum_i w_{ij} x_i$$

In addition to be faster for DNN *training*, GPUs are also more efficient to run the DNN *inference*. Inference is the post-training phase where we deploy our trained DNN. In a whitepaper published by GPU vendor Nvidia titled *GPU-Based Deep Learning Inference: A Performance and Power Analysis*, available online at http://www.nvidia.com/content/tegra/embedded-systems/pdf/jetson_tx1_whitepaper.pdf, an efficiency comparison is made between the use of GPUs and CPUs on the AlexNet network (a DNN with several convolutional layers) and the results are summarized in the following table:

| Network: AlexNet | Batch Size | Tegra X1 (FP32) | Tegra X1 (FP16) | Core i7 6700K (FP32) |
|---|---|---|---|---|
| Inference performance | | 47 img/sec | 67 img/sec | 62 img/sec |
| Power | 1 | 5.5 W | 5.1 W | 49.7 W |
| Performance/ Watt | | 8.6 img/sec/W | 13.1 img/sec/W | 1.3 img/sec/W |
| Inference performance | 128 (Tegra X1) | 155 img/sec | 258 img/sec | 242 img/sec |
| Power | 48 (Core i7) | 6.0 W | 5.7 W | 62.5 W |
| Performance/ Watt | | 25.8 img/sec/W | 45 img/sec/W | 3.9 img/sec/W |

The results show that inference on Tegra X1 can be up to an order of magnitude more energy-efficient that CPU-based inference while achieving comparable performance levels

Writing code to access the GPU directly instead of the CPU is not easy, but that is why most popular open source libraries like Theano or TensorFlow allow you to simply turn on a simple *switch* in your code to use the GPU rather than the CPU. Use of these libraries does not require writing specialized code, but the same code can run on both the CPU and the GPU, if available. The *switch* depends on the open source library, but typically it can be through setting up determined environment variables or by creating a specialized resource (`.rc`) file that is used by the particular open source library chosen.

# Popular open source libraries – an introduction

There are several Open Source libraries available that allow the creation of deep neural nets in Python without having to explicitly write the code from scratch. The most commonly used are: Keras, Theano, TensorFlow, Caffe, and Torch. In this book we will provide examples using the first three libraries, which can all be used in Python. The reason for this is that Torch is not based on Python, but on a different language, called Lua, while Caffe is mainly used for Image recognition only. For these libraries, we will quickly describe how to turn on the GPU *switch we discussed in the previous paragraph. Much of the code in this book can then be run on a CPU or a GPU, depending on the hardware available to the reader.*

# Theano

Theano (`http://deeplearning.net/software/theano/`) is an open source library written in Python that implements many features that make it easy to write code for neural networks. In addition, Theano makes it very easy to take advantage of GPU acceleration and performance. Without going into the details of how Theano works, Theano uses symbolic variables and functions. Among many features that are really appealing, Theano allows us to use back-propagation very easily by calculating all the derivatives for us.

As mentioned earlier, Theano also makes it very easily to utilize the GPU on your machine. There are many ways to do this, but the simplest is to create a resource file called `.theanorc` with the following lines:

```
[global]
device = gpu
floatX = float32
```

It is easy to check whether Theano is configured to use your GPU by simply typing:

```
print(theano.config.device)
```

We refer to the Theano documentation for learning the first steps on how to use Theano, and we will implement some test code examples using Theano for deep learning in this book.

# TensorFlow

TensorFlow (`https://www.tensorflow.org`) works very similarly to Theano, and in TensorFlow, computations are also represented as graphs. A TensorFlow graph is therefore a description of computations. In TensorFlow, you do not need to explicitly require the use of your GPU, rather, TensorFlow will automatically try to use your GPU if you have one, however if you have more than one GPU you must assign operations to each GPU explicitly, or only the first one will be used. To do this, you simply need to type the line:

```
with tensorflow.device("/gpu:1"):
```

Here, the following devices can be defined:

- `"/cpu:0"`: main CPU of your machine
- `"/gpu:0"`: first GPU of your machine, if one exists
- `"/gpu:1"`: second GPU of your machine, if it exists
- `"/gpu:2"`: third GPU of your machine, if it exists, and so on

Once again, we refer to the TensorFlow documentation for learning the first steps on how to use TensorFlow and test code examples using TensorFlow will be implemented in the book.

# Keras

Keras (`http://keras.io`) is a neural net Python library that can run on top of either Theano or TensorFlow, even though it will run by default using TensorFlow. Instructions online are provided at `http://keras.io/backend/`. Keras can run on a CPU or GPU and to do that, if you run it on top of Theano, you will need to set up a `.theanorc` file as described before. Keras allows different ways to create deep neural networks, and it makes it easy by using a *model* for the neural network. The main type of *model* is the `Sequential` model which creates a linear stack of layers. You can then add new layers by simply calling the `add` function. In the coming section, we will create a few examples using Keras. Keras can be easily installed with the following, simple command:

```
pip install Keras
```

It can also be installed by forking from its Git repository and then running setup on it:

```
git clone https://github.com/fchollet/keras.git
cd keras
python setup.py install
```

However, we refer the reader to the online documentation for further information.

# Sample deep neural net code using Keras

In this section, we will introduce some simple code to use Keras for the correct classification of digits using the popular dataset MNIST. MNIST is a dataset comprised of 70,000 examples of handwritten digits by many different people. The first 60,000 are typically used for training and the remaining 10,000 for testing.

Sample of digits taken from the MNIST dataset

One of the advantages of Keras is that it can import this dataset for you without the need to explicitly download it from the web (Keras will download it for you). This can be achieved by one simple line of code:

```
from keras.datasets import mnist
```

There are a few classes we need to import from Keras to use a classical deep neural net, and these are:

```
from keras.models import Sequential
from keras.layers.core import Dense, Activation
from keras.utils import np_utils
```

We are now ready to start writing our code to import the data, and we can do this with just one line:

```
(X_train, Y_train), (X_test, Y_test) = mnist.load_data()
```

This imports the training data and the testing data; in addition, both datasets are divided into two subsets: one that contains the actual images and the other that contains the labels. We need to slightly modify the data to be able to use it. The x_train and x_test data in fact is comprised of 60000 small (28,28)-pixels images, but we want to reshape each sample to be a 784-pixels long vector, rather than a (28,28) 2-dimensional matrix. This can be easily accomplished with these two lines:

```
X_train = X_train.reshape(60000, 784)
X_test = X_test.reshape(10000, 784)
```

Similarly, the labels are indicating the value of the digit depicted by the images, and we want to convert this into a 10-entry vector with all zeroes and just one 1 in the entry corresponding to the digit, so for example 4 is mapped to [0, 0, 0, 0, 1, 0, 0, 0, 0, 0].

```
classes = 10
Y_train = np_utils.to_categorical(Y_train, classes)
Y_test = np_utils.to_categorical(Y_test, classes)
```

Finally, before calling our main function, we just need to set the size of our input (the size of the mnist images), how many hidden neurons our hidden layer has, for how many epochs we want to try our network, and the batch size for our training:

```
input_size = 784
batch_size = 100
hidden_neurons = 100
epochs = 15
main(X_train, X_test, Y_train, Y_test)
```

We are now ready to write the code for our main function. Keras works by defining a model, and we will use the Sequential model, then add layers (in this case we will use regular *dense*, not sparse layers) specifying the number of input and output neurons. For each layer, we specify the activity function of its neurons:

```
model = Sequential()
model.add(Dense(hidden_neurons, input_dim=input_size))
model.add(Activation('sigmoid'))
model.add(Dense(classes, input_dim=hidden_neurons))
model.add(Activation('softmax'))
```

Keras now provides a simple way to specify the cost function (the `loss`) and its optimization (training rate, momentum, and so on). We are not going to modify the default values, so we can simply pass:

```
model.compile(loss='categorical_crossentropy', metrics=['accuracy'],
optimizer='sgd')
```

In this example, the optimizer is `sgd`, which stands for stochastic gradient descent. At this point, we need to train the network, and this, similarly to scikit-learn, is done calling a `fit` function. We will use the verbose parameter so that we can follow the process:

```
model.fit(X_train, Y_train, batch_size=batch_size, nb_epoch=epochs,
verbose=1)
```

All that is left to do is to add code to evaluate our network on the test data and print the accuracy result, which is done simply by:

```
score = model.evaluate(X_test, Y_test, verbose=1)
print('Test accuracy:', score[1])
```

And that's it. It is now enough to run. The test accuracy will be about 94%, which is not a great result, but this example runs in less than 30 seconds on a CPU and is an extremely simple implementation. There are simple improvements that could be made, for example selecting a larger number of hidden neurons or selecting a larger number of epochs, and we leave those simple changes to the reader to familiarize himself or herself with the code.

Keras allows us to also look at the weight matrix it creates. To do that, it is enough to type the following line:

```
weights = model.layers[0].get_weights()
```

By adding the following lines to our previous code, we can look at what the hidden neurons have learned:

```
import matplotlib.pyplot as plt
import matplotlib.cm as cm
w = weights[0].T
for neuron in range(hidden_neurons):
    plt.imshow(numpy.reshape(w[neuron], (28, 28)),
    cmap = cm.Greys_r)
    plt.show()
```

To get a clearer image, we have increased the number of epochs to 100 to get the following figure:

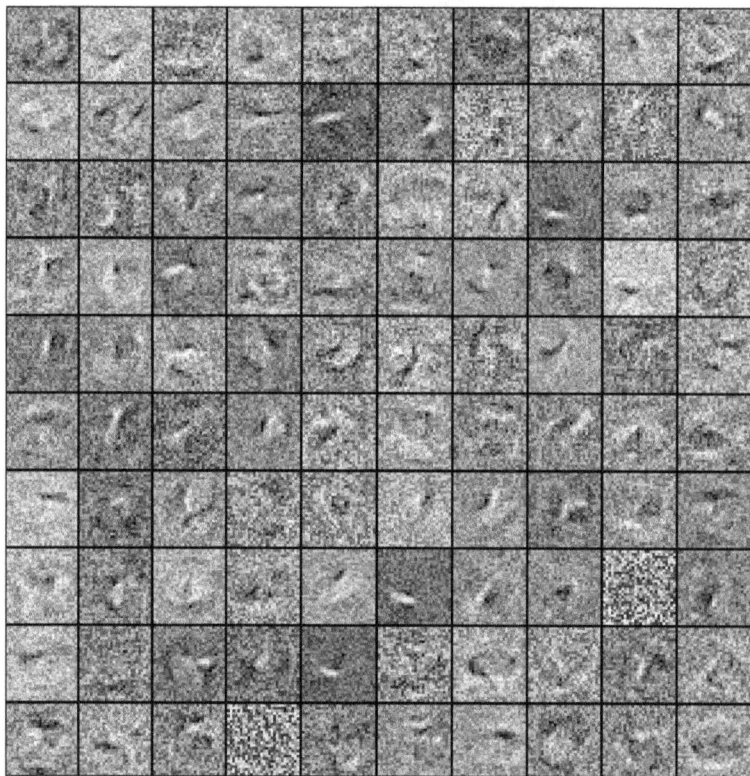

Composite figure with what was learned by all the hidden neurons

For simplicity, we have aggregated all the images for each neuron in a single figure that represents a composite for all the neurons. Clearly, since the initial images are very small and do not have lots of details (they are just digits), the features learned by the hidden neurons are not all that interesting, but it is already clear that each neuron is learning a different "shape".

The code for drawing above should be immediately clear; we just notice that the following line is importing `cm`:

```
import matplotlib.cm as cm
```

This simply allows for a grayscale representation of the neurons, and it is used inside the `imshow()` call by passing in the option `cmap = cm.Greys_r`. This is because the `mnist` images are not color images but gray scale images.

The beauty of Keras is that it is easy to create neural nets, but it is also easy to download test datasets. Let's try to use the `cifar10` dataset instead of the `mnist` dataset. Instead of digits, the `cifar10` dataset is comprised of 10 classes of objects: airplanes, automobiles, birds, cats, deers, dogs, frogs, horses, ships, and trucks. To use the `cifar10` dataset, it is enough to write:

```
from keras.datasets import cifar10
```

In place of the preceding code line:

```
from keras.datasets import mnist
```

Then, we need to make these changes to the code we wrote above:

```
(X_train, Y_train), (X_test, Y_test) = cifar10.load_data()
X_train = X_train.reshape(50000, 3072)
X_test = X_test.reshape(10000, 3072)
input_size = 3072
```

This is because there are only 50,000 training images (instead of 60,000) and because the images are colored (RGB) 32 x 32 pixel images, therefore their size is 3 x 32 x3 2. We can keep everything else as before for now, however, if we run this example, we can see that our performance is now very bad, just around 20%. This is due to the fact that the data is much more complex and it requires a more complex neural network. In fact, most neural networks implemented for classification of images use some basic convolutional layers, that will be discussed only in *Chapter 5, Image Recognition*, however, for now we could try raising the number of hidden neurons to 3,000, and adding a second hidden layer with 2,000 neurons. We are also going to use the ReLU activity function in the first hidden layer.

To do this we simply need to write the following lines defining the model, instead of what we had before:

```
model = Sequential()
model.add(Dense(3000, input_dim=input_size))
model.add(Activation('sigmoid'))
model.add(Dense(2000, input_dim=3000))
model.add(Activation('sigmoid'))
model.add(Dense(classes, input_dim=2000))
model.add(Activation('softmax'))
```

If we run this code, we will see that it will take much longer to train, however, at the end, we will have about a 60% accuracy rate for the training set, but only about a 50% accuracy for the test data. The much poorer accuracy rate, with respect to the much simpler mnist dataset, despite the larger network and the much longer training time, is due to the higher complexity of the data. In addition, by substituting the line where we fit the network with the following line:

```
model.fit(X_train, Y_train, batch_size=batch_size, nb_epoch=epochs,
validation_split=0.1, verbose=1)
```

We can also output during the process how the accuracy improves on a split 90/10 of the training data. This also shows that while the accuracy of the training keeps increasing during training, the accuracy of the validation set plateaus at some point, showing that the network starts to overfit and to saturate some parameters.

While this may seem like a failure of deep networks to deliver good accuracy on richer datasets, we will see that in fact, there are ways around this problem that will allow us to get better performances on even much more complex and larger datasets.

# Summary

In this chapter, we have walked the reader toward an understanding of what deep learning is and how it is related to deep neural networks. We have also discussed how many different implementations of deep neural networks exist, besides the classical feed-forward implementation, and have discussed the recent successes deep learning has had on many standard classification tasks. This chapter has been rich with concepts and ideas, developed through examples and historical remarks from the Jacquard loom to the Ising model. This is just the beginning, and we will work out many examples in which the ideas introduced in this chapter will be explained and developed more precisely.

We are going to start this process in the coming chapter, where we will finally introduce the readers to many of the concepts we have touched on in this one, like RBMs and auto-encoders, and it will be clear how we can create more powerful deep neural networks than simple feed-forward DNNs. In addition, it will also be clear how the concept of representations and features arise naturally in these particular neural networks. From the last example, using cifar10, it is clear that classical feed-forward DNNs are difficult to train on more complex datasets, and we need a better way to set the weight parameters. X. Glorot and Y. Bengio, *Understanding the difficulty of training deep feed-forward neural* networks, in Proceedings of the International Conference on Artificial Intelligence and Statistics (AISTATS'10), (2010) (`http://jmlr.org/proceedings/papers/v9/glorot10a/glorot10a.pdf`), treats the issue of poor performance of deep neural networks trained with gradient descent on random weight initialization. New algorithms that can be used to train deep neural networks successfully will be introduced and discussed in the next chapter.

# 4
# Unsupervised Feature Learning

One of the reasons why deep neural networks can succeed where other traditional machine learning techniques struggle is the capability of learning the right representations of entities in the data (features) without needing (much) human and domain knowledge.

Theoretically, neural networks are able to consume raw data directly as it is and map the input layers to the desired output via the hidden intermediate representations. Traditional machine learning techniques focus mainly on the final mapping and assume the task of "feature engineering" to have already been done.

Feature engineering is the process that uses the available domain knowledge to create smart representations of the data, so that it can be processed by the machine learning algorithm.

Andrew Yan-Tak Ng is a professor at Stanford University and one of the most renowned researchers in the field of machine learning and artificial intelligence. In his publications and talks, he describes the limitations of traditional machine learning when applied to solving real-world problems.

The hardest part of making a machine learning system work is to find the right feature representations:

> *Coming up with features is difficult, time-consuming, requires expert knowledge. When working applications of learning, we spend a lot of time tuning features.*

> *Anrew Ng, Machine Learning and AI via Brain simulations, Stanford University*

Let's assume we are classifying pictures into a few categories, such as animals versus vehicles. The raw data is a matrix of the pixels in the image. If we used those pixels directly in a logistic regression or a decision tree, we would create rules (or associating weights) for every single picture that might work for the given training samples, but that would be very hard to generalize enough to small variations of the same pictures. In other words, let's suppose that my decision tree finds that there are five important pixels whose brightness (supposing we are displaying only black and white tones) can determine where most of the training data get grouped into the two classes--animals and vehicles. The same pictures, if cropped, shifted, rotated, or re-colored, would not follow the same rules as before. Thus, the model would probably randomly classify them. The main reason is that the features we are considering are too weak and unstable. However, we could instead first preprocess the data such that we could extract features like these:

- Does the picture contain symmetric centric, shapes like wheels?
- Does it contain handlebars or a steering wheel?
- Does it contain legs or heads?
- Does it have a face with two eyes?

In such cases, the decision rules would be quite easy and robust, as follows:

$$wheels \lor handlebars \Rightarrow vehicle$$

$$eyes \lor legs \Rightarrow animal$$

How much effort is needed in order to extract those relevant features?

Since we don't have handlebar detectors, we could try to hand-design features to capture some statistical properties of the picture, for example, finding edges in different orientations in different picture quadrants. We need to find a better way to represent images than pixels.

Moreover, robust and significant features are generally made out of hierarchies of previously extracted features. We could start extracting edges in the first step, then take the generated "edges vector", and combine them to recognize object parts, such as an eye, a nose, a mouth, rather than a light, a mirror, or a spoiler. The resulting object parts can again be combined into object models; for example, two eyes, one nose, and one mouth form a face, or two wheels, a seat, and a handlebar form a motorcycle. The whole detection algorithm could be simplified in the following way:

$$pixel \Rightarrow edges \Rightarrow 2wheels + seat + handlebar \Rightarrow motorcycle \Rightarrow vehicle$$

$$pixel \Rightarrow edges \Rightarrow twoeyes + nose + mouth \Rightarrow face \Rightarrow animal$$

By recursively applying sparse features, we manage to get higher-level features. This is why you need deeper neural network architectures as opposed to the shallow algorithms. The single network can learn how to move from one representation to the following, but stacking them together will enable the whole end-to-end workflow.

The real power is not just in the hierarchical structures though. It is important to note that we have only used unlabeled data so far. We are learning the hidden structures by reverse-engineering the data itself instead of relying on manually labeled samples. The supervised learning represents only the final classification steps, where we need to assign to either the vehicle class or the animal class. All of the previous steps are performed in an unsupervised fashion.

We will see how the specific feature extraction for pictures is done in the following *Chapter 5, Image Recognition*. In this chapter, we will focus on the general approach of learning feature representations for any type of data (for example, time signals, text, or general attribute vectors).

For that purpose, we will cover two of the most powerful and quite used architectures for unsupervised feature learning: autoencoders and restricted Boltzmann machines.

# Autoencoders

Autoencoders are symmetric networks used for unsupervised learning, where output units are connected back to input units:

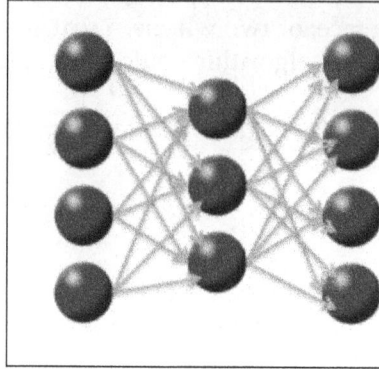

Autoencoder simple representation from H2O training book (https://github.com/h2oai/h2o-training-book/blob/master/hands-on_training/images/autoencoder.png)

The output layer has the same size of the input layer because its purpose is to reconstruct its own inputs rather than predicting a dependent target value.

The goal of those networks is to act as a compression filter via an encoding layer, $\phi$, that fits the input vector $X$ into a smaller latent representation (the code) $c$, and then a decoding layer, $\varphi$, tries to reconstruct it back to $X'$:

$$\phi : X \rightarrow c, \varphi : c \rightarrow X'$$

The loss function is the reconstruction error, which will force the network to find the most efficient compact representation of the training data with minimum information loss. For numerical input, the loss function can be the mean squared error:

$$L_{MSE} = \left\| X - X' \right\|^2$$

If the input data is not numerical but is represented as a vector of bits or multinomial distributions, we can use the cross-entropy of the reconstruction:

$$L_H = -\sum_{k=1}^{d} x_k \log\left(x_k'\right) + \left(1 - x_k\right)\log\left(1 - x_k'\right)$$

Here, *d* is the dimensionality of the input vectors.

The central layer (the code) of the network is the compressed representation of the data. We are effectively translating an n-dimensional array into a smaller m-dimensional array, where $m < n$. This process is very similar to dimensionality reduction using **Principal Component Analysis (PCA)**. PCA divides the input matrix into orthogonal axes (called components) in such, way that you can reconstruct an approximation of the original matrix by projecting the original points on those axes. By sorting them by their importance, we can extract the top *m* components that can be though as high-level features of the original data.

For example, in a multivariate Gaussian distribution, we could represent each point as a coordinate over the two orthogonal components that would describe the largest possible variance in the data:

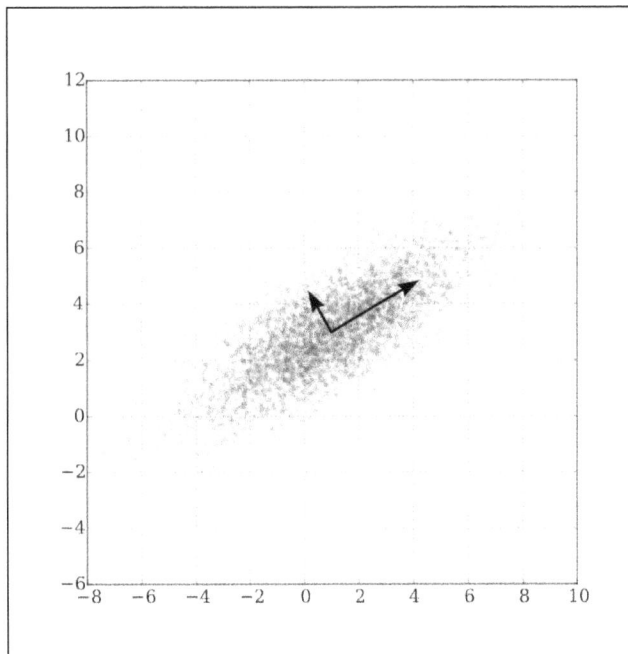

A scatter plot of samples that are distributed according a multivariate (bivariate) Gaussian distribution centered at (1,3) with a standard deviation of 3 in the (0.866, 0.5) direction and of 1 in the orthogonal direction. The directions represent the principal components (PC) associated with the sample. By Nicoguaro (own work) CC BY 4.0 (http://creativecommons.org/licenses/by/4.0), via Wikimedia Commons.

The limitation of PCA is that it allows only linear transformation of the data, which is not always enough.

Autoencoders have the advantage of being able to represent even non-linear representations using a non-linear activation function.

One famous example of an autoencoder was given by MITCHELL, T. M. in his book *Machine Learning*, wcb, 1997. In that example, we have a dataset with eight categorical objects encoded in binary with eight mutually exclusive labels with bits. The network will learn a compact representation with just three hidden nodes:

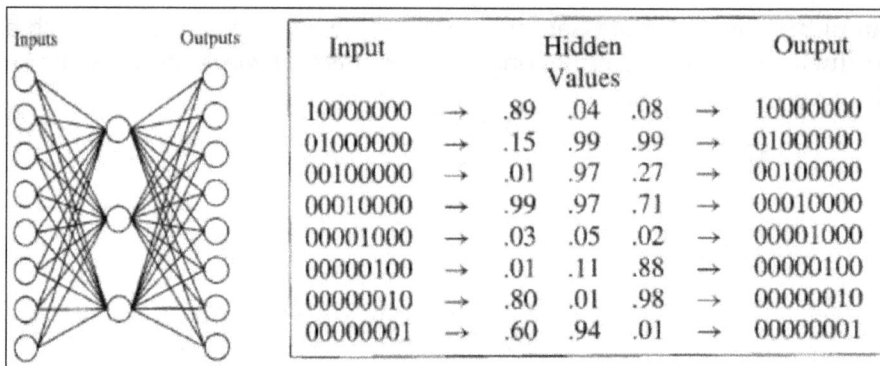

| Input | | Hidden Values | | | | Output |
|---|---|---|---|---|---|---|
| 10000000 | → | .89 | .04 | .08 | → | 10000000 |
| 01000000 | → | .15 | .99 | .99 | → | 01000000 |
| 00100000 | → | .01 | .97 | .27 | → | 00100000 |
| 00010000 | → | .99 | .97 | .71 | → | 00010000 |
| 00001000 | → | .03 | .05 | .02 | → | 00001000 |
| 00000100 | → | .01 | .11 | .88 | → | 00000100 |
| 00000010 | → | .80 | .01 | .98 | → | 00000010 |
| 00000001 | → | .60 | .94 | .01 | → | 00000001 |

Tom Mitchell's example of an autoencoder.

By applying the right activation function, the learn-compact representation corresponds exactly with the binary representation with three bits.

There are situations though where just the single hidden layer is not enough to represent the whole complexity and variance of the data. Deeper architecture can learn more complicated relationships between the input and hidden layers. The network is then able to learn latent features and use those to best represent the non-trivial informative components in the data.

A deep autoencoder is obtained by concatenating two symmetrical networks typically made of up to five shallow layers:

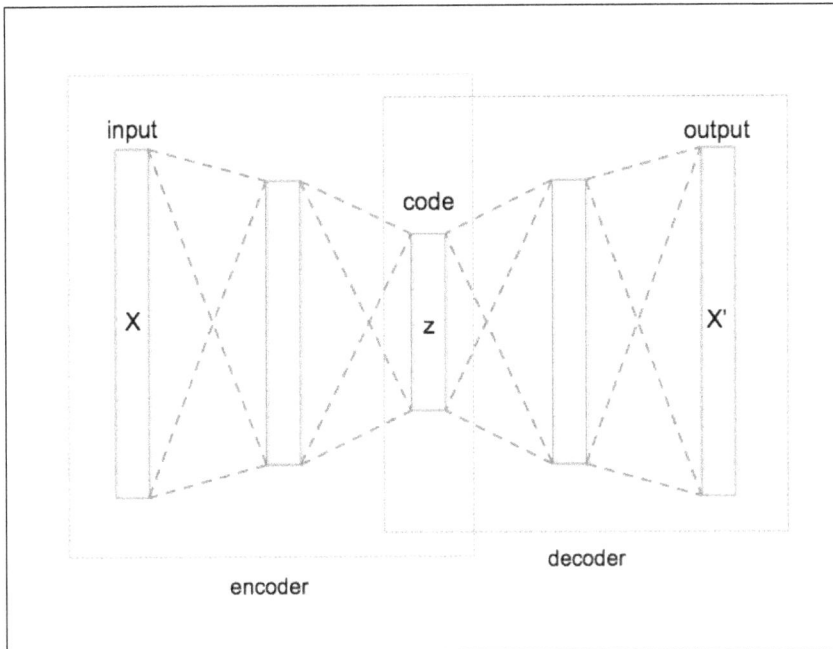

Schematic structure of an autoencoder with 3 fully-connected hidden layers (https://en.wikipedia.org/wiki/Autoencoder#/media/File:Autoencoder_structure.png)

Deep autoencoders can learn new latent representations, combining the previously learned ones so that each hidden level can be seen as some compressed hierarchical representation of the original data. We could then use the code or any other hidden layer of the encoding network as valid features describing the input vector.

# Network design

Probably the most common question when building a deep neural network is: how do we choose the number of hidden layers and the number of neurons for each layer? Furthermore, which activation and loss functions do we use?

There is no closed answer. The empirical approach consists of running a sequence of trial and error or a standard grid search, where the depth and the size of each layer are simply defined as tuning hyperparameters. We will look at a few design guidelines.

For autoencoders, the problem is slightly simplified. Since there are many variants of autoencoders, we will define the guidelines for the general use case. Please keep in mind that each variation will have its own rules to be considered. We can suggest the following:

- The output layer consists of exactly the same size of the input.

- The network is symmetric most of the time. Having an asymmetric network would mean having different complexities of the encoder and decoder functions. Unless you have a particular reason for doing so, there is generally no advantage in having asymmetric networks. However, you could decide to share the same weights or decide to have different weights in the encoding and decoding networks.

- During the encoding phase, the hidden layers are smaller than the input, in which case, we are talking about "undercomplete autoencoders". A multilayer encoder gradually decreases the representation size. The size of the hidden layer, generally, is at most half the size of the previous one. If the data input layer has 100 nodes, then a plausible architecture could be 100-40-20-40-100. Having bigger layers than the input would lead to no compression at all, which means no interesting patterns are learned. We will see in the *Regularization* section how this constraint is not necessary in case of sparse autoencoders.

- The middle layer (the code) covers an important role. In the case of feature reduction, we could keep it small and equal to 2, 3, or 4 in order to allow efficient data visualizations. In the case of stacked autoencoders, we should set it to be larger because it will represent the input layer of the next encoder.

- In the case of binary inputs, we want to use sigmoid as the output activation function and cross-entropy, or more precisely, the sum of Bernoulli cross-entropies, as the loss function.

- For real values, we can use a linear activation function (ReLU or softmax) as the output and the **mean squared error** (**MSE**) as the loss function.

- For different types of input data($x$)and output $u$, you can follow the general approach, which consists of the following steps:

  1. Finding the probability distribution of observing x, given $u$, $P(x/u)$

  2. Finding the relationship between $u$ and the hidden layer h(x)

  3. Using $\phi : X \rightarrow c, \varphi : c \rightarrow X'$

- In the case of deep networks (with more than one hidden layer), use the same activation function for all of them in order to not unbalance the complexity of the encoder and decoder.

- If we use a linear activation function throughout the whole network, we will approximate the behavior of PCA.

- It is convenient to Gaussian scale (0 mean and unit standard deviation) your data unless it is binary, and it is better to leave the input values to be either 0 or 1. Categorical data can be represented using one-hot-encoding with dummy variables.

- Activation functions are as follows:

  ○ ReLU is generally the default choice for majority of neural networks. Autoencoders, given their topology, may benefit from a symmetric activation function. Since ReLU tends to overfit more, it is preferred when combined with regularization techniques (such as dropout).

  ○ If your data is binary or can be scaled in the range of [0, 1], then you would probably use a sigmoid activation function. If you used one-hot-encoding for the input categorical data, then it's better use ReLU.

○ Hyperbolic tangent (*tanh*) is a good choice for computation optimization in case of gradient descent. Since data will be centered around 0, the derivatives will be higher. Another effect is reducing bias in the gradients as is well explained in the "Efficient BackProp" paper (`http://yann.lecun.com/exdb/publis/pdf/lecun-98b.pdf`).

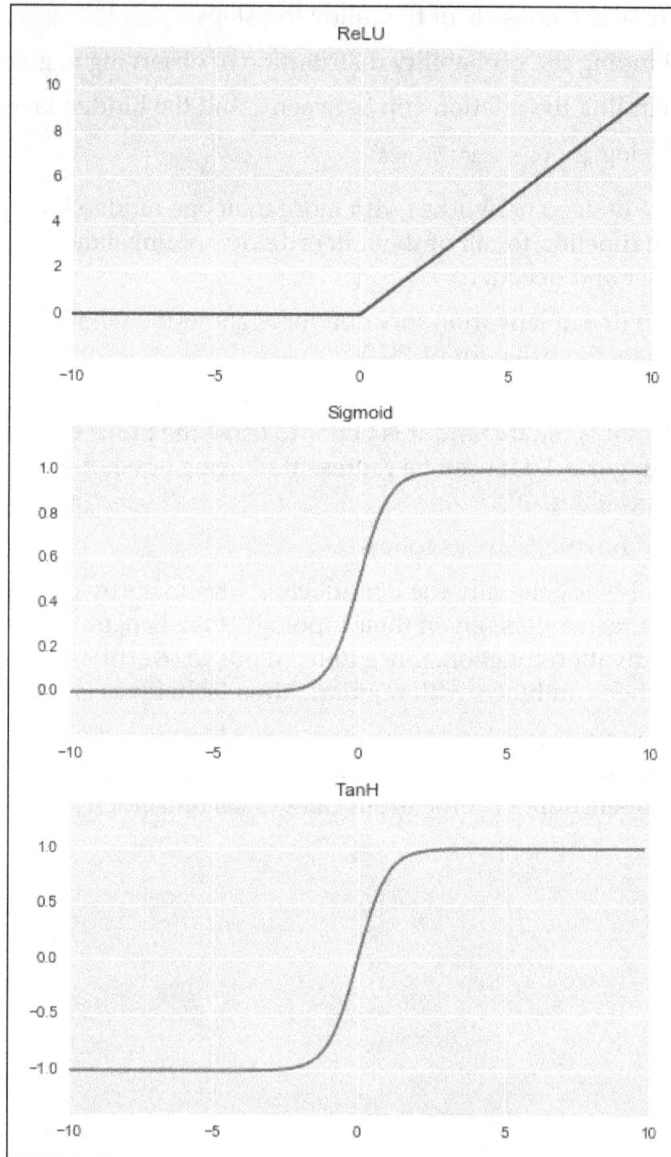

Different activation functions commonly used for deep neural networks

# Regularization techniques for autoencoders

In the previous chapters, we already saw different forms of regularizations, such as L1, L2, early stopping, and dropout. In this section, we will describe a few popular techniques specifically tailored for autoencoders.

So far, we have always described autoencoders as "undercomplete", which means the hidden layers are smaller than the input layer. This is because having a bigger layer would have no compression at all. The hidden units may just copy exactly the input and return an exact copy as the output.

On the other hand, having more hidden units would allow us to have more freedom on learning smarter representations.

We will see how we can address this problem with three approaches: denoising autoencoders, contractive autoencoders, and sparse autoencoders.

## Denoising autoencoders

The idea is that we want to train our model to learn how to reconstruct a noisy version of the input data.

We will use x to represent the original input, $\tilde{x}$, the noisy input, and $\hat{x}$, the reconstructed output.

The noisy input, $\tilde{x}$, is generated by randomly assigning a subset of the input $x$ to 0, with a given probability $p$, plus an additive isotropic Gaussian noise, with variance $v$ for numerical inputs.

We would then have two new hyper-parameters to tune $p$ and $v$, which represent the noise level.

We will use the noisy variant, $\tilde{x}$, as the input of the network, but the loss function will still be the error between the output $\hat{x}$ and the original noiseless input $x$. If the input dimensionality is $d$, the encoding function $f$, and the decoding function $g$, we will write the loss function $j$ as this:

$$x_i, g\left(f\left(x_i\right)\right)$$

$$J\ denoising = \sum_{i=1}^{d} L\left(x_i, \hat{x}_i\right)$$

Here, $L$ is the reconstruction error, typically either the MSE or the cross-entropy.

With this variant, if a hidden unit tries to exactly copy the input values, then the output layer cannot trust 100% because it knows that it could be the noise and not the original input. We are forcing the model to reconstruct based on the interrelationships between other input units, aka the meaningful structures of the data.

What we would expect is that the higher the added noise, the bigger the filters applied at each hidden unit. By filter, we mean the portion of the original input that is activated for that particular feature to be extracted. In case of no noise, hidden units tend to extract a tiny subset of the input data and propose it at the most untouched version to the next layer. By adding noise to the units, the error penalty on badly reconstructing $\hat{x}_i$ will force the network to keep more information in order to contextualize the features regardless of the possible presence of noise.

Please pay attention that just adding a small white noise could be equivalent to using weight decay regularization. Weight decay is a technique that consists of multiplying to a factor less than 1 the weights at each training epoch in order to limit the free parameters in our model. Although this is a popular technique to regularize neural networks, by setting inputs to 0 with probability $p$, we are effectively achieving a totally different result.

We don't want to obtain high-frequency filters that when put together give us a more generalized model. Our denoising approach generates filters that do represent unique features of the underlying data structures and have individual meanings.

## Contractive autoencoders

Contractive autoencoders aim to achieve a similar goal to that of the denoising approach by explicitly adding a term that penalizes when the model tries to learn uninteresting variations and promote only those variations that are observed in the training set.

In other words, the model may try to approximate the identity function by coming out with filters representing variations that are not necessarily present in the training data.

We can express this sensitivity as the sum of squares of all partial derivatives of the extracted features with respect to the input dimensions.

For an input $x$ of dimensionality $d_x$ mapped by the encoding function $f$ to the hidden representation $h$ of size $d_h$, the following quantity corresponds to the L2 norm (Frobenius) of the Jacobian matrix $J_f(x)$ of the encoder activations:

$$\left\| J_f(x) \right\|_F^2 = \sum_{i=1}^{d_x} \sum_{j=1}^{d_h} \left( \frac{\partial h_j(x)}{\partial x_i} \right)^2$$

The loss function will be modified as follows:

$$Jcontractive = J + \lambda \left\| J_f(x) \right\|_F^2$$

Here, $\lambda$ is the regularization factor. It is easy to see that the Frobenius norm of the Jacobian corresponds to L2 weight decay in the case of a linear encoder. The main difference is that for the linear case, the only way of achieving contraction would be by keeping weights very small. In case of a sigmoid non-linearity, we could also push the hidden units to their saturated regime.

Let's analyze the two terms.

The error $J$ (the MSE or cross-entropy) pushes toward keeping the most possible information to perfectly reconstruct the original value.

The penalty pushes toward getting rid of all of that information such that the derivatives of the hidden units with respect to $X$ are minimized. A large value means that the learned representation is too unstable with respect to input variations. We obtain a small value when we observe very little change to the hidden representations as we change the input values. In case of the limit of these derivatives being 0, we would only keep the information that is invariant with respect to the input $X$. We are effectively getting rid of all of the hidden features that are not stable enough and too sensitive to small perturbations.

Let's suppose we have as input a lot of variations of the same data. In the case of images, they could be small rotations or different exposures of the same subject. In case of network traffic, they could be an increase/decrease of the packet header of the same type of traffic, maybe because of a packing/unpacking protocol.

If we only look at this dimension, the model is likely to be very sensitive. The Jacobian term would penalize the high sensitivity, but it is compensated by the low reconstruction error.

In this scenario, we would have one unit that is very sensitive on the variation direction but not very useful for all other directions. For example, in the case of pictures, we still have the same subject; thus, all of the remaining input values are constant. If we don't observe variations on a given direction in the training data, we want to discard the feature.

H2O currently does not support contractive autoencoders; however, an open issue can be found at https://0xdata.atlassian.net/browse/PUBDEV-1265.

# Sparse autoencoders

Autoencoders, as we have seen them so far, always have the hidden layers smaller than the input.

The major reason is that otherwise, the network would have enough capability to just memorize exactly the input and reconstruct it perfectly as it is. Adding extra capacity to the network would just be redundant.

Reducing the capacity of the network forces to learn based on a compression version of the input. The algorithm will have to pick the most relevant features that help better reconstruct the training data.

There are situations though where compressing is not feasible. Let's consider the case where each input node is formed by independent random variables. If the variables are not correlated with each other, the only way of achieving compression is to get rid of some of them entirely. We are effectively emulating the behavior of PCA.

In order to solve this problem, we can set a **sparsity** constraint on the hidden units. We will try to push each neuron to be inactive most of the time that corresponds to having the output of the activation function close to 0 for sigmoid and ReLU, -1 for tanh.

If we call $a_j^{(l)}\left(x^{(i)}\right)$ the activation of hidden unit $j$ at layer $l$ when input is $x^{(i)}$, we can define the average activation of hidden unit $j$ as follows:

$$\hat{\rho}_j = \frac{1}{m}\sum_{i=1}^{m} a_j^{(l)}\left(x^{(i)}\right)$$

Here, $m$ is the size of our training dataset (or batch of training data).

The sparsity constraint consists of forcing $\hat{\rho}_j = \rho$, where $\rho$ is the **sparsity parameter** bounded in the interval [1,0] and ideally close enough to 0.

The original paper (http://web.stanford.edu/class/cs294a/sparseAutoencoder.pdf) recommends values near 0.05.

We model the average activation of each hidden unit as a Bernoulli random variable with mean $\hat{\rho}$, and we want to force all of them to converge to a Bernoulli distribution with mean $\rho$

In order to do so, we need to add an extra penalty that quantifies the divergence of those two distributions. We can define this penalty based on the **Kullback-Leibler** (**KL**) divergence between the real distribution $B(1,\hat{\rho})$ and the theoretical one $B(1,\rho)$ we would like to achieve.

In general, for discrete probability distributions $P$ and $Q$, the $KL$ divergence when information is measured in bits is defined as follows:

$$D_{KL}(P \vee Q) = \sum_x P(x) \log_2 \frac{P(x)}{Q(x)}$$

One requirement is that $P$ is absolutely continuous with respect to $Q$, that is, $Q(x) = 0 \Rightarrow P(x) = 0$ for any measurable value of $x$. This is also written as $P \ll Q$. Whenever $P(x) = 0$, the contribution of that term will be $0$ since that $\lim_{x \to 0} x \log x = 0$.

In our case, the KL divergence of unit $j$ would be as follows:

$$KL(\rho \vee \hat{\rho}_j) = \rho \log_2 \frac{\rho}{\hat{\rho}_j} + 1(1-\rho)\log_2 \frac{1-\rho}{1-\hat{\rho}_j}$$

This function has the property to be $0$ when the two means are equal and increase monotonically, otherwise until approaching $\infty$ when $\hat{\rho}_j$ is close to 0 or 1.

The final loss function with extra penalty term added will be this:

$$J_{sparse} = J + \beta \sum_{j=1}^{s} KL(\rho \vee \hat{\rho}_j)$$

Here, $J$ is the standard loss function (the RMSE), $s$ is the number of hidden units, and $\beta$ is a weight of the sparsity term.

This extra penalty will cause a small inefficiency to the backpropagation algorithm. In particular, the preceding formula will require an additional forward step over the whole training set to precompute the average activations $\hat{\rho}_j$ before computing the backpropagation on each example.

# Summary of autoencoders

Autoencoders are powerful unsupervised learning algorithms, which are getting popularity in fields such as anomaly detection or feature engineering, using the output of intermediate layers as features to train a supervised model instead of the raw input data.

Unsupervised means they do not require labels or ground truth to be specified during training. They just work with whatever data you put as input as long as the network has enough capability to learn and represent the intrinsic existing relationships. That means that we can set both the size of the code layer (the reduced dimensionality $m$) but obtain different results depending on the number and size of the hidden layers, if any.

If we are building an autoencoder network, we want to achieve robustness in order to avoid wrong representations but at the same time not limit the capacity of the network by compressing the information through smaller sequential layers.

Denoising, contractive, and autoencoders are all great techniques for solving those problems.

Adding noise is generally simpler and doesn't add complexity in the loss function, which results in less computation. On the other hand, the noisy input makes the gradient to be sampled and also discard part of the information in exchange for better features.

Contractive autoencoders are very good at making the model more stable to small deviations from the training distribution. Thus, it is a very good candidate for reducing false alarms. The drawback is a sort of countereffect that increases the reconstruction error in order to reduce the sensibility.

Sparse autoencoders are probably the most complete around solution. It is the most expensive to compute for large datasets, but since the gradient is deterministic, it can be useful in case of second-order optimizers and, in general, to provide a good trade-off between stability and low reconstruction error.

Regardless of what choice you make, adopting a regularization technique is strongly recommended. They both come with hyper-parameters to tune, which we will see how to optimize in the corresponding *Tuning* section.

In addition to the techniques described so far, it is worth mentioning variational autoencoders, which seem to be the ultimate solution for regularizing autoencoders. Variational autoencoders belong to the class of generative models. They don't just learn the structures that better describe the training data, they learn the parameters of a latent unit Gaussian distribution that can best regenerate the input data. The final loss function will be the sum of the reconstruction error and the KL divergence between the reconstructed latent variable and the Gaussian distribution. The encoder phase will generate a code consisting of a vector of means and a vector of standard deviations. From the code, we can characterize the latent distribution parameters and reconstruct the original input by sampling from that distribution.

# Restricted Boltzmann machines

- In the early 90s, neural networks had largely gone out of fashion. The bulk of machine learning research was around other techniques, such as random forests and support vector machines. Neural networks with only a single hidden layer were less performant than these other techniques, and it was thought that deeper neural networks were too difficult to train.

- The resurgence of interest in neural networks was spearheaded by Geoffrey Hinton, who, in 2004, led a team of researchers who proceeded to make a series of breakthroughs using restricted Boltzmann machines (RBM) and creating neural networks with many layers; they called this approach deep learning. Within 10 years, deep learning would go from being a niche technique to dominating every single AI competition. RBMs were part of the big breakthrough, allowing Hinton and others to get world record scores on a variety of image and speech recognition problems.

- In this section, we will look at the theory of how RBMs work, how to implement them, and how they can be combined into deep belief networks.

A restricted Boltzmann machine looks a lot like a single layer of a neural network. There are a set of input nodes that have connections to another set of output nodes:

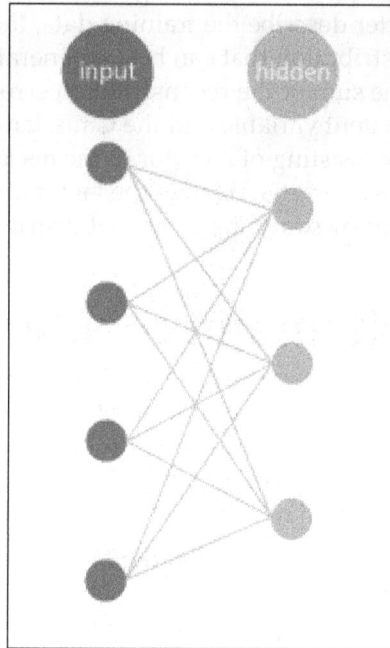

Figure 1. Restricted Boltzmann machine

The way these output nodes are activated is also identical to an autoencoder. There is a weight between each input node and output node, the activation of each input nodes multiplied by this matrix of weight mappings, and a bias vector is then applied, and the sum for each output node is then put through a sigmoid function.

What makes a restricted Boltzmann machine different is what the activations represent, how we think about them, and the way in which they are trained. To begin with, when talking about RBMs rather than talking about input and output layers, we refer to the layers as visible and hidden. This is because, when training, the visible nodes represent the known information we have. The hidden nodes will aim to represent some variables that generated the visible data. This contrasts with an autoencoder, where the output layer doesn't explicitly represent anything, is just a constrained space through which the information is passed.

The basis of learning the weights of a restricted Boltzmann machine comes from statistical physics and uses an **energy-based model (EBM)**. In these, every state is put through an energy function, which relates to the probability of a state occurring. If an energy function returns a high value, we expect this state to be unlikely, rarely occurring. Conversely, a low result from an energy function means a state that is more stable and will occur more frequently.

A good intuitive way of thinking about an energy function is to imagine a huge number of bouncy balls being thrown into a box. At first, all the balls have high energy and so will be bouncing very high. A state here would be a single snapshot in time of all the balls' positions and their associated velocities. These states, when the balls are bouncing, are going to be very transitory; they will only exist for moments and because of the range of movement of the balls, are very unlikely to reoccur. But as the balls start to settle, as the energy leaves the system, some of the balls will start to be increasingly stationary. These states are stable once it occurs once it never stops occurring. Eventually, once the balls have stopped bouncing and all become stationary, we have a completely stable state, which has high probability.

- To give an example that applies to restricted Boltzmann machines, consider the task of learning a group of images of butterflies. We train our RBM on these images, and we want it to assign a low energy value to any image of a butterflies. But when given an image from a different set, say cars, it will give it a high energy value. Related objects, such as moths, bats, or birds, may have a more medium energy value.

- If we have an energy function defined, the probability of a given state is then given as follows:

$$p(v) = \frac{e^{-E(v)}}{Z}$$

- Here, v is our state, E is our energy function, and Z is the partition function; the sum of all possible configurations of v is defined as follows:

$$Z = \sum_{v} e^{-E(v)}$$

# Hopfield networks and Boltzmann machines

- Before we go further into restricted Boltzmann machines, let's briefly talk about Hopfield networks; this should help in giving us a bit more of an understanding about how we get to restricted Boltzmann machines. Hopfield networks are also energy-based models, but unlike a restricted Boltzmann machine, it has only visible nodes, and they are all interconnected. The activation of each node will always be either -1 or +1.

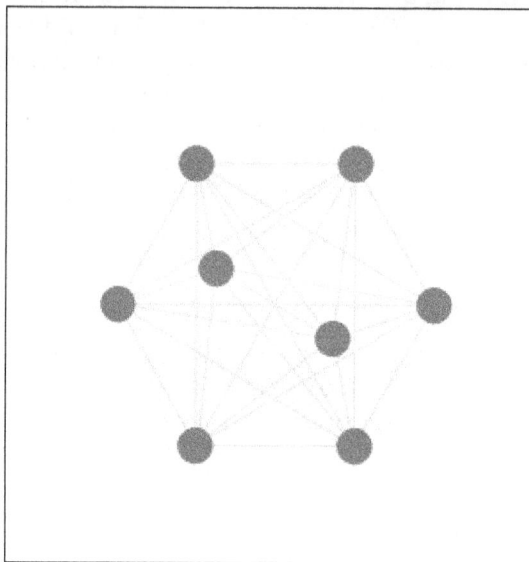

Figure 2. Hopfield network, all input nodes are interconnected

- When running a Hopfield network (or RBM), you have two options. The first option is that you can set the value of every visible node to the corresponding value of your data item you are triggering it on. Then you can trigger successive activations, where, at each activation, every node has its value updated based on the value of the other visible nodes it is connected to. The other option is to just initialize the visible nodes randomly and then trigger successive activations so it produces random examples of the data it has been trained on. This is often referred to as the network daydreaming.

- The activation of each of these visible nodes at the next time step is defined as follows:

$$a_i^{(t+1)} = \sum_j W_{ij} v_j^{(t)}$$

- Here, W is a matrix defining the connection strength between each node v at time step t. A thresholding rule is then applied to a to get a new state for v:

$$v_i = \begin{cases} 1 \ if a_i \geq 0 \\ -1 \ if a_i < 0 \end{cases}$$

- The weights W between nodes can be either positive or negative, which will lead nodes to attract or repel the other nodes in the network, when active. The Hopfield network also has a continuous variant, which simply involves replacing the thresholding function with the tanh function.

- The energy function for this network is as follows:

$$E(v) = \frac{-1}{2} \sum_{i,j} v_i W_{ij} v_j$$

- In matrix notation, it is as follows:

$$E(v) = \frac{-1}{2} v^T W v$$

- The $\frac{1}{2}$ in the equation is because we are going through every pair of i and j and so double-counting each connection (once when i=1 and j=2 then again when i=2 and j=1).

- The question that might arise here is: why have a model with only visible nodes? I will activate it with data I give it, then trigger some state updates. But what useful information does this new state give me? This is where the properties of energy-based models become interesting. Different configurations of W will vary the energy function associated with the states v. If we set the state of the network to something with a high energy function, that is an unstable state (think of the many bouncing balls); the network will over successive iterations move to a stable state.

- If we train a Hopefield network on a dataset to learn a W with low energy for each item in the dataset, we can then make a corrupted sample from the data, say, by randomly swapping a few of the inputs between their minus one and plus one states. The corrupted samples may be in a high-energy state now because the corruption has made it unlikely to be a member of the original dataset. If we activate the visible nodes of the network on the corrupted sample, run a few more iterations of the network until it has reached a low-energy state; there is a good chance that it will have reconstructed the original uncorrupted pattern.

- This leads to one use of the Hopfield networks being spelling correction; you can train it on a library of words, with the letters used in the words as inputs. Then if it is given a misspelled word, it may be able to find the correct original word. Another use of the Hopfield networks is as a content-addressable memory. One of the big differences between the computer memory and the human memory is that with computers, memories are stored with addresses. If a computer wants to retrieve a memory, it must know the exact place it stored it in. Human memory, on the other hand, can be given a partial section of that memory, the content of which can be used to recover the rest of it. For example, if I need to remember my pin number, I know the content I'm looking for and the properties of that content, a four digit number; my brain uses that to return the values.

- Hopfield networks allow you to store content-addressable memories, which have led some people to suggest (speculatively) that the human memory system may function like a Hopfield network, with human dreaming being the attempt to learn the weights.

- The last use of a Hopfield network is that it can be used to solve optimization tasks, such as the traveling salesman task. The energy function can be defined to represent the cost of the task to be optimized, and the nodes of the network to represent the choices being optimized. Again, all that needs to be done is to minimize the energy function with respect to the weights of the network.

# Boltzmann machine

- A Boltzmann machine is also known as a stochastic Hopfield network. In a Hopfield network, node activations are set based on the threshold; but in a Boltzmann machine, activation is stochastic. The value of a node in a Boltzmann machine is always set to either +1 or -1. The probability of the node being in the state +1 is defined as follows:

$$p(x_i = 1) = \frac{1}{1 + e^{-2a_i}}$$

- Here, $a_i$ is the activation for that node as defined for the Hopfield network.

To learn the weights of our Boltzmann machine or Hopfield network, we want to maximize the likelihood of the dataset, given the W, which is simply the product of the likelihood for each data item:

$$p(x \mid W) = \prod_{n=1}^{N} p\left(x^{(n)} \vee W\right)$$

Here, W is the weights matrix, and $x^{(n)}$ is the nth sample from the dataset x of size N. Let's now replace $p\left(x^{(n)} \vee W\right)$ with the actual likelihood from our Boltzmann machine:

$$p(x \mid W) = \prod_{n=1}^{N} \frac{e^{\frac{1}{2}x^{(n)T}Wx^{(n)}}}{Z}$$

Here, $Z$ is as shown in the following equation:

$$Z = \sum_{x' \in p(x \vee W)} e^{\frac{1}{2}x'^{T}Wx'}$$

If you look at the original definition of our energy function and Z, then $x'$ should be every possible configuration of $x$ based on the probability distribution $p(x)$. We now have W as part of our model, so the distribution will change to $p(x|W)$ . Unfortunately, $x' \in p(x \vee W)$ is, if not completely intractable, at the very least, far too computationally expensive to compute. We would need to take every possible configuration of x across all possible W.

One approach to computing an intractable probability distribution such as this is what's called Monte Carlo sampling. This involves taking lots of samples from the distribution and using the average of these samples to approximate the true value. The more samples we take from the distribution, the more accurate it will tend to be. A hypothetical infinite number of samples would be exactly the quantity we want, while 1 would be a very poor approximation.

Since the products of probabilities can get very small, we will instead use the log probability; also, let's also include the definition of Z:

$$ lnp(x|W) = \sum_{n=1}^{N} \left\{ \frac{1}{2} x^{(n)T} W x^{(n)} - \sum_{x' \in p(x \vee W)} \frac{1}{2} x'^{T} W x' \right\} $$

Here, x' is a sample of state of the network, as taken from the probability distribution $p(x|W)$ learned by the network. If we take the gradient of this with respect to a single weight between nodes i and j, it looks like this:

$$ \nabla_{w_{ij}} lnp(x) = \sum_{n=1}^{N} \left\{ x_i^{(n)} x_j^{(n)} - \sum_{x' \in p(x \vee W)} x_i'^{(n)} x_j'^{(n)} \right\} $$

Here, $x_i^{(n)} x_j^{(n)}$ across all N samples is simply the correlation between the nodes i and j. Another way to write this across all N samples, for each weight $i$ and $j$, would be this:

$$\nabla_{w_{ij}} lnp(x) = corr(x_i, x_j) - \frac{1}{N} \sum_{x' \in p(x \vee W)} corr(x_i', x_j') p(x \vee W)$$

This equation can be understood as being two phases of learning, known as positive and negative or, more poetically, waking and sleeping. In the positive phase, $corr(x_i, x_j)$ increases the weights based on the data we are given. In the negative phase, $\frac{-1}{N} \sum_{x' \in p(x|W)} corr(x_i', x_j') p(x|W)$, we draw samples from the model as per the weights we currently have, then move the weights away from that distribution. This can be thought of as reducing the probability of items generated by the model. We want our model to reflect the data as closely as possible, so we want to reduce the selection generated by our model. If our model was producing images exactly like the data, then the two terms would cancel each other out, and equilibrium would be reached.

Boltzmann machines and Hopfield networks can be useful for tasks such as optimization and recommendation systems. They are very computationally expensive. Correlation must be measured between every single node, and then a range of Monte Carlo samples must be generated from the model for every training step. Also, the kinds of patterns it can learn are limited. If we are training on images to learn shapes, it cannot learn position invariant information. A butterfly on the left-hand side of an image is a completely different beast to a butterfly on the right-hand side of an image. In *Chapter 5, Image Recognition*, we will take a look at convolutional neural networks, which offers a solution to this problem.

# Restricted Boltzmann machine

Restricted Boltzmann machines make two changes from the Boltzmann machines: the first is that we add in hidden nodes, each of which is connected to every visible node, but not to each other. The second is that we remove all connections between visible nodes. This has the effect of making each node in the visible layer conditionally independent of each other if we are given the hidden layer. Nodes in the hidden layer are also conditionally independent, given the visible layer. We will also now add bias terms to both the visible and hidden nodes. A Boltzmann machine can also be trained with a bias term for each node, but this was left out of the equations for ease of notation.

- Given that the data we have is only for the visible units, what we aim to do through training is find configurations of hidden units that lead to low-energy states when combined with the visible units. In our restricted Boltzmann machine, the state $x$ is now the full configuration of both visible and hidden nodes. So, we will parameterize our energy function as E(v, h). It now looks like this:

$$E(v,h) = -a^T v - b^T h - v^T W h$$

- Here, a is the bias vector for the visible nodes, b is the bias vector for the hidden nodes, and W is the matrix of weights between the visible and hidden nodes. Here, $a^T v$ is the dot product of the two vectors, equivalent to $\Sigma_i a_i v_i$. Now we need to take the gradients of our biases and weights with respect to this new energy function.

- Because of the conditional independence between layers, we now have this:

  ○  $p(h\,|\,v,W,b) = sigmoid(vW + b)$

  ○  $p(v\,|\,h,W,b) = sigmoid(hW^T + a)$

- These two definitions will be used in the normalization constant, Z. Since we longer have connections between visible nodes, our $lnp(v)$ has changed a lot:

$$lnp(v\,|\,W,a,b) = \sum_{n=1}^{N}\left\{\left(av + \sum_i \log \sum_j e^{h_j(b+W_i v)}\right) - Z\right\}$$

- Here, i is going through each visible node and j through each hidden node. If we take the gradient with respect to the different parameters, then what you eventually end up with is this:

$$\nabla_{w_{ij}} lnp(v) = corr\left(v_i^{(0)}, p\left(h^{(0)} \mid v^{(0)}\right)_j\right) - corr\left(p\left(v^{(1)} \mid h^{(0)}\right), p\left(h^{(1)} \vee v^{(1)}\right)\right)$$

$$\nabla_{a_i} lnp(v) = v_i^{(0)} - p\left(v^{(1)} \mid h^{(0)}\right)_i$$

$$\nabla_{b_i} lnp(v) = p\left(h^{(0)} \mid v^{(0)}\right)_i - p\left(h^{(1)} \vee v^{(1)}\right)_i$$

As before, $p\left(v^{(0)} \mid h^{(0)}\right)$ is approximated by taking the Monte Carlo samples from the distribution. These final three equations give us the complete way to iteratively train all the parameters for a given dataset. Training will be a case of updating our parameters by some learning rate by these gradients.

It is worth restating on a conceptual level what is going on here. v denotes the visible variables, the data from the world on which we are learning. h denotes the hidden variables, the variables we will train to generate visible variables. The hidden variables do not explicitly represent anything, but through training and minimizing the energy in the system, they should eventually find important components of the distribution we are looking at. For example, if the visible variables are a list of movies, with a value of 1 if a person likes the movie and 0 if they do not, the hidden variables may come to represent genres of movie, such as horror or comedy, because people may have genre preferences, so this is an efficient way to encode people's tastes.

If we generate random samples of hidden variables and then activate the visible variables based on this, it should give us a plausible looking set of human tastes in movies. Likewise, if we set the visible variables to a random selection of movies over successive activations of the hidden and visible nodes, it should move us to find a more plausible selection.

# Implementation in TensorFlow

Now that we have gone through the math, let's see what an implementation of it looks like. For this, we will use TensorFlow. TensorFlow is a Google open source mathematical graph library that is popular for deep learning. It does not have built-in neural network concepts, such as network layers and nodes, which a higher-level library such as Keres does; it is closer to a library such as Theano. It has been chosen here because being able to work directly on the mathematical symbols underlying the network allows the user to get a better understanding of what they are doing.

TensorFlow can be installed directly via `pip` using the command `pip install tensorflow` for the CPU version or `pip install tensorflow-gpu` if you have NVidea GPU-enabled machine.

We will build a small restricted Boltzmann machine and train it on the MNIST collection of handwritten digits. We will have a smaller number of hidden nodes than visible nodes, which will force the RBM to learn patterns in the input. The success of the training will be measured in the network's ability to reconstruct the image after putting it through the hidden layer; for this, we will use the mean squared error between the original and our reconstruction. The full code sample is in the GitHub repo `https://github.com/DanielSlater/PythonDeepLearningSamples` in the `restricted_boltzmann_machine.py` file.

Since the MNIST dataset is used so ubiquitously, TensorFlow has a nice built-in way to download and cache the MNIST dataset. It can be done by simply calling the following code:

```
from tensorflow.examples.tutorials.mnist import input_data
mnist = input_data.read_data_sets("MNIST_data/")
```

This will download all the MNIST data into `MNIST_data` into the `"MNIST_data/"` directory, if it is not already there. The `mnist` object has properties, `train` and `test`, which allow you to access the data in NumPy arrays. The `MNIST` images are all sized 28 by 28, which means 784 pixels per image. We will need one visible node in our RBM for each pixel:

```
input_placeholder = tf.placeholder("float", shape=(None, 784))
```

A placeholder object in TensorFlow represents values that will be passed in to the computational graph during usage. In this case, the `input_placeholder` object will hold the values of the `MNIST` images we give it. The `"float"` specifies the type of value we will be passing in, and the `shape` defines the dimensions. In this case, we want 784 values, one for each pixel, and the `None` dimension is for batching. Having a None dimension means that it can be of any size; so, this will allow us to send variable-sized batches of 784-length arrays:

```
weights = tf.Variable(tf.random_normal((784, 300), mean=0.0,
                                         stddev=1./784))
```

`tf.variable` represents a variable on the computational graph. This is the $W$ from our preceding equations. The argument passed to it is how the variable values should first be initialized. Here, we are initializing it from a normal distribution of size 784 by 300, the number of visible nodes to hidden nodes:

```
hidden_bias = tf.Variable(tf.zeros([300]))
visible_bias = tf.Variable(tf.zeros([784]))
```

These variables will be the a and b from our preceding equation; they are initialised to all start with a value of 0. Now we will program in the activations of our network:

```
hidden_activation = tf.nn.sigmoid(tf.matmul(input_placeholder,
weights) + hidden_bias)
```

This represents the activation of the hidden nodes, $p\left(h^{(0)} \mid v^{(0)}\right)$, in the preceding equations. After applying the `sigmoid` function, this activation could be put into a binomial distribution so that all values in the hidden layer go to 0 or 1, with the probability given; but it turns out an RBM trains just as well as the raw probabilities. So, there's no need to complicate the model by doing this:

```
visible_reconstruction = tf.nn.sigmoid(tf.matmul(hidden_activation,
tf.transpose(weights))
+ visible_bias)
```

Now we have the reconstruction of the visible layer, $p\left(v^{(1)} \mid h^{(0)}\right)$. As specified by the equation, we give it the `hidden_activation`, and from that, we get our sample from the visible layer:

```
final_hidden_activation =
tf.nn.sigmoid(tf.matmul(visible_reconstruction, weights) +
hidden_bias)
```

We now compute the final sample we need, the activation of the hidden nodes from our `visible_reconstruction`. This is equivalent to $p\left(h^{(1)}|v^{(1)}\right)$ in the equations. We could keep going with successive iterations of hidden and visual activation to get a much more unbiased sample from the model. But it doing just one rotation works fine for training:

```
Positive_phase = tf.matmul(tf.transpose(input_placeholder),
hidden_activation)
Negative_phase = tf.matmul(tf.transpose(visible_reconstruction),
final_hidden_activation)
```

Now we compute the positive and negative phases. The first phase is the correlation across samples from our mini-batch of the `input_placeholder`, $v^{(0)}$ and the first `hidden_activation`, $p\left(h^{(0)}|v^{(0)}\right)$. Then the negative phase gets the correlation between the `visible_reconstruction`, $p\left(v^{(1)}|h^{(0)}\right)$ and the `final_hidden_activation`, $p\left(h^{(1)}|v^{(1)}\right)$:

```
LEARING_RATE = 0.01
weight_update = weights.assign_add(LEARING_RATE *
(positive_phase - negative_phase))
```

Calling `assign_add` on our `weights` variable creates an operation that, when run, adds the given quantity to the variable. Here, 0.01 is our learning rate, and we scale the positive and negative phases by that:

```
visible_bias_update = visible_bias.assign_add(LEARING_RATE *
tf.reduce_mean(input_placeholder - visible_reconstruction, 0))
hidden_bias_update = hidden_bias.assign_add(LEARING_RATE *
tf.reduce_mean(hidden_activation - final_hidden_activation, 0))
```

Now we create the operations for scaling the hidden and visible biases. These are also scaled by our 0.01 learning rate:

```
train_op = tf.group(weight_update, visible_bias_update,
hidden_bias_update)
```

Calling `tf.group` creates a new operation than when called executes all the operation arguments together. We will always want to update all the weights in unison, so it makes sense to create a single operation for them:

```
loss_op = tf.reduce_sum(tf.square(input_placeholder -
visible_reconstruction))
```

This `loss_op` will give us feedback on how well we are training, using the MSE. Note that this is purely used for information; there is no backpropagation run against this signal. If we wanted to run this network as a pure autoencoder, we would create an optimizer here and activate it to minimize the `loss_op`:

```
session = tf.Session()
session.run(tf.initialize_all_variables())
```

Then we create a session object that will be used for running the computational graph. Calling `tf.initialize_all_variables()` is when everything gets initialized on to the graph. If you are running TensorFlow on the GPU, this is where the hardware is first interfaced with. Now that we have created every step for the RBM, let's put it through a few epochs of running against MNIST and see how well it learns:

```
current_epochs = 0

for i in range(10):
    total_loss = 0
    while mnist.train.epochs_completed == current_epochs:
        batch_inputs, batch_labels = mnist.train.next_batch(100)
        _, reconstruction_loss = session.run([train_op, loss_op],
        feed_dict={input_placeholder: batch_inputs})
        total_loss += reconstruction_loss

    print("epochs %s loss %s" % (current_epochs,
    reconstruction_loss))
    current_epochs = mnist.train.epochs_completed
```

Every time we call `mnist.train.next_batch(100)`, 100 images are retrieved from the `mnist` dataset. At the end of each epoch, the `mnist.train.epochs_completed` is incremented by 1, and all the training data is reshuffled. If you run this, you may see results something like this:

```
epochs 0 loss 1554.51
epochs 1 loss 792.673
epochs 2 loss 572.276
epochs 3 loss 479.739
epochs 4 loss 466.529
epochs 5 loss 415.357
epochs 6 loss 424.25
epochs 7 loss 406.821
epochs 8 loss 354.861
```

```
epochs 9 loss 410.387
epochs 10 loss 313.583
```

We can now see what an image reconstruction looks like by running the following command on the mnist data:

```
reconstruction = session.run(visible_reconstruction, feed_dict={input_
placeholder:[mnist.train.images[0]]})
```

Here are some examples of what the reconstructed images with 300 hidden nodes look like:

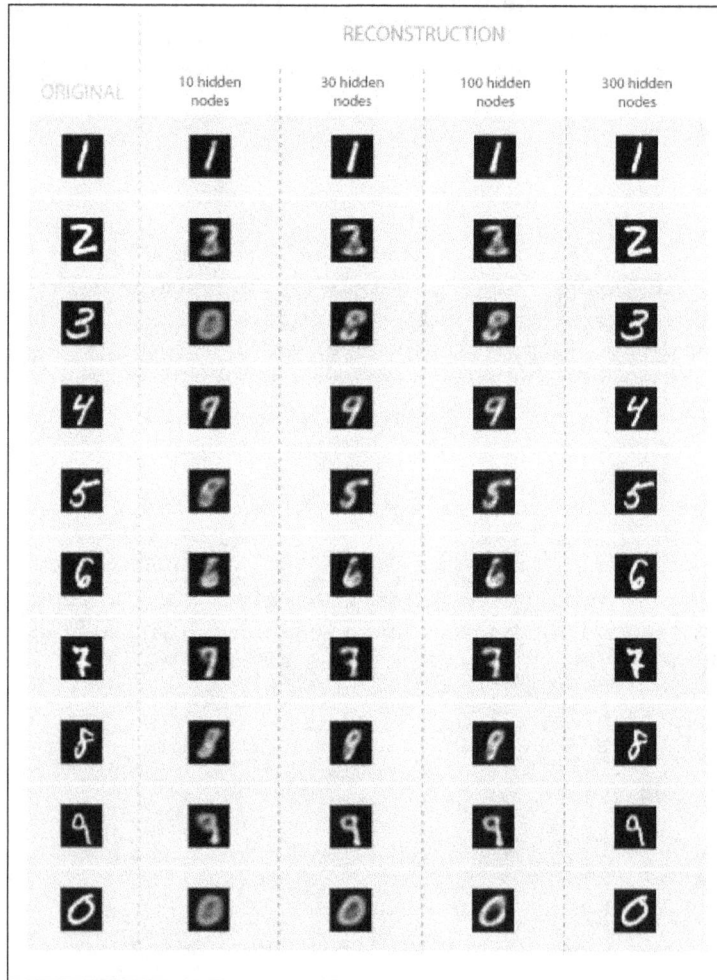

Figure 3. Reconstructions of digits using restricted Boltzmann machines
with different numbers of hidden nodes

As you can see, with 300 hidden nodes, less than half the number of pixels, it can still do an almost perfect reconstruction of the image, with only a little blurring around the edges. But as the number of hidden nodes decreases, so does the quality of the reconstruction. Going down to just 10 hidden nodes, the reconstructions can produce images that, to the human eye, look like the wrong digit, such as the 2 and 3 in Figure 3.

# Deep belief networks

If we imagine our RBM is learning a set of latent variables that generated our visible data and we were feeling inquisitive, we might wonder: can we then learn a second layer of latent variables that generated the latent variables for the hidden layer? The answer is yes, we can stack RBMs on top of previously trained RBMs to be able to learn second, third, fourth, and so on, order information about the visible data. These successive layers of RBMs allow the network to learn increasingly invariant representations of the underlying structure:

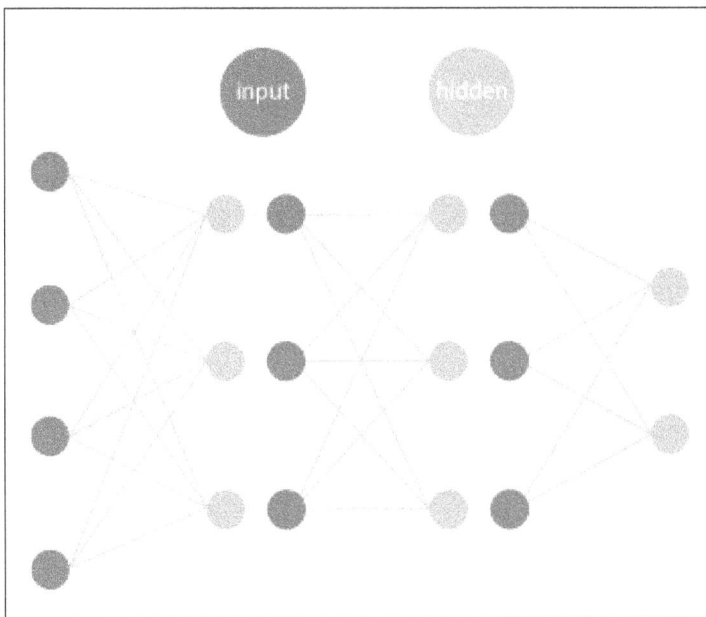

Figure 4 Deep belief network, containing many chained RBMs

These stacked RBMs are known as deep belief networks and were the deep networks used by Geoffrey Hinton in his 2002 paper *Training Products of Experts by Minimizing Contrastive Divergence*, to first produce the record-breaking results on MNIST. The exact technique he found useful was to train successive RBMs on data with only a slight reduction in the size of the layers. Once a layer was trained to the point where the reconstruction error was no longer improving, its weights were frozen, and a new RBM was stacked on top and again trained until error rate convergence. Once the full network was trained, a final supervised layer was put at the end in order to map the final RBM's hidden layer to the labels of the data. Then the weights of the whole network were used to construct a standard deep feed-forward neutral network, allowing those precalculated weights of the deep belief network to be updated by backpropagation.

At first, these had great results, but over time, the techniques for training standard feed-forward networks have improved, and RBMs are no longer considered the best for image or speech recognition. They also have the problem that because of their two-phase nature, they can be a lot slower to train. But they are still very popular for things such as recommender systems and pure unsupervised learning. Also, from a theoretical point of view, using the energy-based model to learn deep representations is a very interesting approach and leaves the door open for many extensions that can be built on top of this approach.

# Summary

We have seen in this chapter two of the most powerful techniques at the core of many practical deep learning implementations: autoencoders and restricted Boltzmann machines.

For both of them, we started with the shallow example of one hidden layer, and we explored how we can stack them together to form a deep neural network able to automatically learn high-level and hierarchical features without requiring explicit human knowledge.

They both serve similar purposes, but there is a little substantial difference.

Autoencoders can be seen as a compression filter that we use to compress the data in order to preserve only the most informative part of it and be able to deterministically reconstruct an approximation of the original data. Autoencoders are an elegant solution to dimensionality reduction and non-linear compression bypassing the limitations of the principal component analysis (PCA) technique. The advantages of autoencoders are that they can be used as preprocessing steps for further classification tasks, where the output of each hidden layer is one of the possible levels of informative representations of the data, or a denoised and recovered version of it. Another great advantage is to exploit the reconstruction error as a measure of dissimilarity of a single point from the rest of the group. Such a technique is widely used for anomaly detection problems, where the relationships from what we observe and the internal representations are constant and deterministic. In the case of time-variant relationships or depending upon an observable dimension, we could group and train different networks in order to be adaptive, but once trained, the network assumes those relationships to not be affected by random variations.

On the other hand, RBM uses a stochastic approach to sample and adjust weights to minimize the reconstruction error. The intuition could be that there might exist some visible random variables and some hidden latent attributes, and the goal is to find how the two sets are connected to each other. To give an example, in the case of movie rating, we can have some hidden attributes, such as film genre, and some random observations, such as the rating and/or review. In such topology, we can also see the bias term as a way of adjusting the different inherent popularities of each movie. If we asked our users to rate which movie they like from a set made of *Harry Potter*, *Avatar*, *Lord of The Ring*, *Gladiator*, and *Titanic*, we might get a resulting network where two of the latent units could represent science fiction movies and Oscar-winning movies:

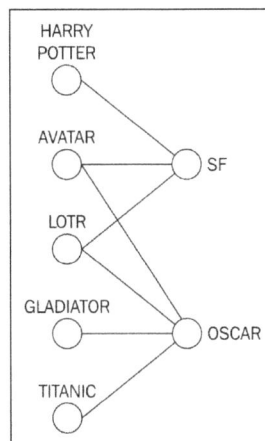

Example of possible RBM where only the links with a weight significantly different from 0 are drawn.

Although the attributes of SF and Oscar-winning are deterministic (effectively, they are attributes of the movie), the ratings of the users are influenced by that in a probabilistic way. The learned weights are the parameters that characterize the probability distribution of the movie rating (for example, Harry Potter with five stars), given that the user likes a particular genre (for example, science fiction).

In such a scenario, where the relationships are not deterministic, we want to prefer using RBM to using an autoencoder.

In conclusion, unsupervised features learning is a very powerful methodology to enrich feature engineering with the minimum required knowledge and human interaction.

Standing to a few benchmarks ([Lee, Pham and Ng, 2009] and [Le, Zhou and Ng, 2011]) performed in order to measure the accuracy of different feature learning techniques, it was proved that unsupervised feature learning improved accuracy with respect to the current state of the art.

There are a few open challenges though. If you do have some knowledge, it is always good not to discard it. We could embed that knowledge in the form of priors during the initialization step, where we might handcraft the network topology and initial state accordingly.

Moreover, since neural networks are already hard to explain and are mostly approached as black box, having an understanding of at least the input features could help. In our unsupervised feature learning, we want to consume raw data directly. Hence, understanding how the model works becomes even harder.

We will not address those issues in this book. We believe that it is too early to make some conclusions and that further evolutions of deep learning and the way people and businesses approach those applications will converge to a steady trustworthiness.

# Image Recognition

5

Vision is arguably the most important human sense. We rely on our vision to recognize our food, to run away from danger, to recognize our friends and family, and to find our way in familiar surroundings. We rely on our vision, in fact, to read this book and to recognize each and every letter and symbol printed in it. However, image recognition has (and in many ways still is) for the longest time been one of the most difficult problems in computer science. It is very hard to teach a computer programmatically how to recognize different objects, because it is difficult to explain to a machine what features make up a specified object. In deep learning, however, as we have seen, the neural network learns by itself, that is, it learns what features make up each object, and it is therefore well suited for a task such as image recognition.

In this chapter we will cover the following topics:

- Similarities between artificial and biological models
- Intuition and justification for CNN
- Convolutional layers
- Pooling layers
- Dropout
- Convolutional layers in deep learning

# Similarities between artificial and biological models

Human vision is a complex and heavily structured process. The visual system works by hierarchically understanding reality through the retina, the thalamus, the visual cortex, and the inferior temporal cortex. The input to the retina is a two-dimensional array of color intensities that is sent, through the optical nerve, to the thalamus. The thalamus receives sensory information from all of our senses with the exception of the olfactory system and then it forwards the visual information collected from the retina to the primary visual cortex, which is the striate cortex (called V1), which extracts basic information such as lines and movement directions. The information then moves to the V2 region that is responsible for color interpretation and color constancy under different lighting conditions, then to the V3 and V4 regions that improve color and form perception. Finally, the information goes down to the **Inferior Temporal** cortex (**IT**) for object and face recognition (in reality, the IT region is also further subdivided in three sub-regions, the posterior IT, central IT, and anterior IT). It is therefore clear that the brain processes visual information by hierarchically processing the information at different levels. Our brain then seemingly works by creating simple abstract representations of reality at different levels that can then be recombined together (see for reference: J. DiCarlo, D. Zoccolan, and N. Rust, *How does the brain solve visual object recognition?*, https://www.ncbi.nlm.nih.gov/pmc/articles/PMC3306444).

The Deep Learning neural networks we have seen so far work similarly by creating abstract representations, as we have seen in RBMs, for example, but there is another important piece to the puzzle for understanding sensory information: the information we extract from sensory inputs is often determined mostly by the information most closely related. Visually, we can assume that pixels that are close by are most closely related and their collective information is more relevant than what we can derive from pixels very far from each other. In understanding speech, as another example, we have discussed how the study of tri-phones is important, that is, the fact that the understanding of a sound is dependent on the sounds preceding and following it. To recognize letters or digits, we need to understand the dependency of pixels close by, since that is what determines the shape of the element to figure out the difference between, say, a 0 or a 1. Pixels that are very far from those making up a 0 hold, in general, little or no relevance for our understanding of the digit "0". Convolutional networks are built exactly to address this issue: how to make information pertaining to neurons that are closer more relevant than information coming from neurons that are farther apart. In visual problems, this translates into making neurons process information coming from pixels that are near, and ignoring information related to pixels that are far apart.

# Intuition and justification

We have already mentioned in *Chapter 3, Deep Learning Fundamentals*, the paper published in 2012 by Alex Krizhevsky, Ilya Sutskever, and Geoffrey Hinton titled: *ImageNet Classification with Deep Convolutional Neural Networks*. Though the genesis of convolutional may be traced back to the '80s, that was one of the first papers that highlighted the deep importance of convolutional networks in image processing and recognition, and currently almost no deep neural network used for image recognition can work without some convolutional layer.

An important problem that we have seen when working with classical feed-forward networks is that they may overfit, especially when working with medium to large images. This is often due to the fact that neural networks have a very large number of parameters, in fact in classical neural nets all neurons in a layer are connected to each and every neuron in the next. When the number of parameters is large, over-fitting is more likely. Let's look at the following images: we can fit the data by drawing a line that goes exactly through all the points, or better, a line that will not match exactly the data but is more likely to predict future examples.

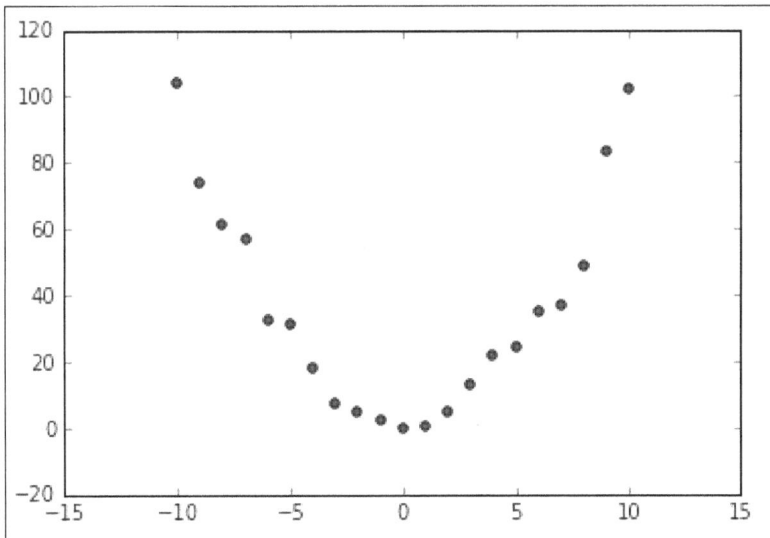

The points in the figure represent input data points. While they clearly follow the shape of a parabola, because of noise in the data, they may not be precisely plotted onto a parabola

In the first example of the two pictures represented, we overfit the data. In the second we have matched our prediction to the data in such a way that our prediction is more likely to better predict future data. In the first case, we just need three parameters to describe the curve: $y = ax^2 + bx + c$, while in the second case we would need many more than just three parameters to write the equation for that curve. This gives an intuitive explanation of why, sometimes, having too many parameters may not be a good thing and it may lead to over-fitting. A classical feed-forward network for an image as small as those in the `cifar10` examples (`cifar10` is an established computer-vision dataset consisting of 60000 32 x 32 images divided in to 10 classes, and we will see a couple of examples from this dataset in this chapter) has inputs of size 3 x 32 x 32, which is already about four times as large as a simple `mnist` digit image. Larger images, say 3 x 64 x 64, would have about as many as 16 times the number of input neurons multiplying the number of connection weights:

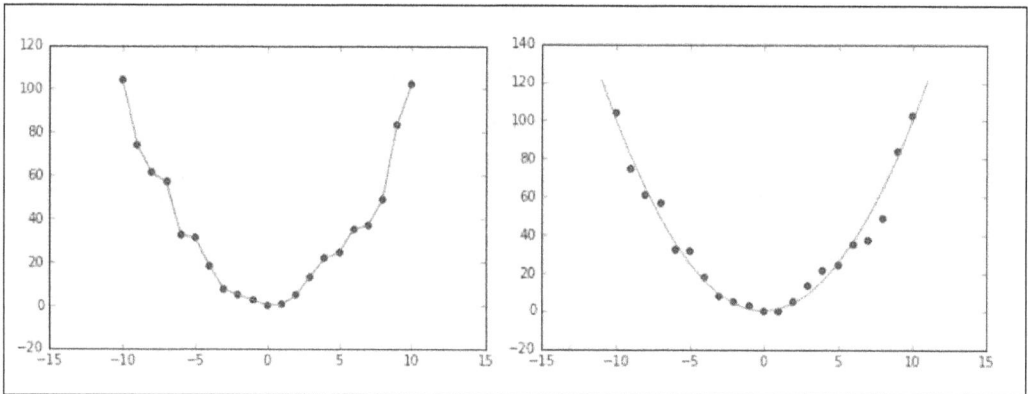

In the left figure we draw a line that matches the data exactly. In the second figure we draw a line that approximates the shape of the line connecting the data points, but that does not match exactly the data points. The second curve, though less precise on the current input, is more likely to predict future data points than the curve in the first figure.

Convolutional networks reduce the number of parameters needed, since they require neurons to only connect locally to neurons corresponding to neighboring pixels, and therefore help avoid overfitting. In addition, reducing the number of parameters also helps computationally. In the next section, will introduce some convolutional layer examples to help the intuition and then we will move to formally define them.

# Convolutional layers

A convolutional layer (sometimes referred to in the literature as "filter") is a particular type of neural network that manipulates the image to highlight certain features. Before we get into the details, let's introduce a convolutional filter using some code and some examples. This will make the intuition simpler and will make understanding the theory easier. To do this we can use the `keras` datasets, which makes it easy to load the data.

We will import `numpy`, then the `mnist` dataset, and `matplotlib` to show the data:

```
import numpy
from keras.datasets import mnist
import matplotlib.pyplot as plt
import matplotlib.cm as cm
```

Let's define our main function that takes in an integer, corresponding to the image in the `mnist` dataset, and a filter, in this case we will define the `blur` filter:

```
def main(image, im_filter):
    im = X_train[image]
```

Now we define a new image `imC`, of size (`im.width-2`, `im.height-2`):

```
width = im.shape[0]
height = im.shape[1]
imC = numpy.zeros((width-2, height-2))
```

At this point we do the convolution, which we will explain soon (as we will see, there are in fact several types of convolutions depending on different parameters, for now we will just explain the basic concept and get into the details later):

```
for row in range(1,width-1):
    for col in range(1,height-1):
        for i in range(len(im_filter[0])):
            for j in range(len(im_filter)):
                imC[row-1][col-1] += im[row-1+i]
                [col-1+j]*im_filter[i][j]
        if imC[row-1][col-1] > 255:
            imC[row-1][col-1] = 255
        elif imC[row-1][col-1] < 0:
            imC[row-1][col-1] = 0
```

Now we are ready to display the original image and the new image:

```
plt.imshow( im, cmap = cm.Greys_r )
plt.show()
plt.imshow( imC/255, cmap = cm.Greys_r )
plt.show()
```

Now we are ready to load the `mnist` dataset using Keras as we did in *Chapter 3, Deep Learning Fundamentals*. Also, let's define a filter. A filter is a small region (in this case 3 x 3) with each entry defining a real value. In this case we define a filter with the same value all over:

```
blur = [[1./9, 1./9, 1./9], [1./9, 1./9, 1./9],
[1./9, 1./9, 1./9]]
```

Since we have nine entries, we set the value to be 1/9 to normalize the values.

And we can call the `main` function on any image (expressed by an integer that indicates the position) in such a dataset:

```
if __name__ == '__main__':
    (X_train, Y_train), (X_test, Y_test) = mnist.load_data()
    blur = [[1./9, 1./9, 1./9], [1./9, 1./9, 1./9], [1./9, 1./9,
1./9]]
    main(3, blur)
```

Let's look at what we did. We multiplied each entry of the filter with an entry of the original image, and then we summed them all up to get a single value. Since the filter size is smaller than the image size, we moved the filter by 1 pixel and kept doing this process until we covered the whole image. Since the filter was composed by values that are all equal to 1/9, we have in fact averaged all input values with the values that are close to it, and this has the effect of blurring the image.

This is what we get:

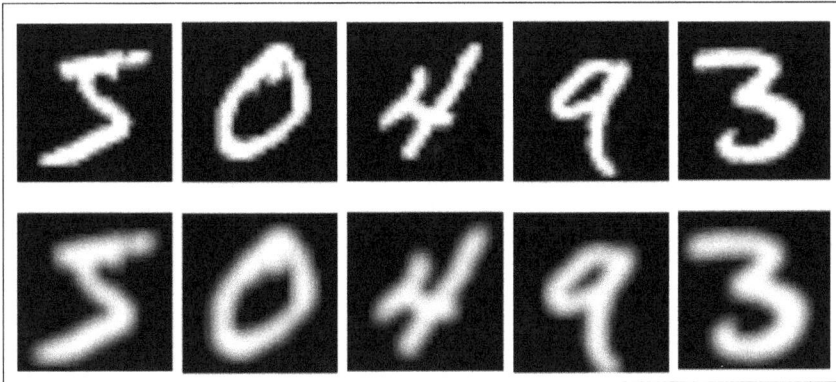

On top is the original mnist image, on the bottom is the new image after we applied the filter

In the choice of the filter we can use any value we want; in this case we have used values that are all the same. However, we can instead use different values, for example values that only look at the neighboring values of the input, add them up, and subtract the value of the center input. Let's define a new filter, and let's call it edges, in the following way:

```
edges = [[1, 1, 1], [1, -8, 1], [1, 1, 1]]
```

If we now apply this filter, instead of the filter `blur` defined earlier, we get the following images:

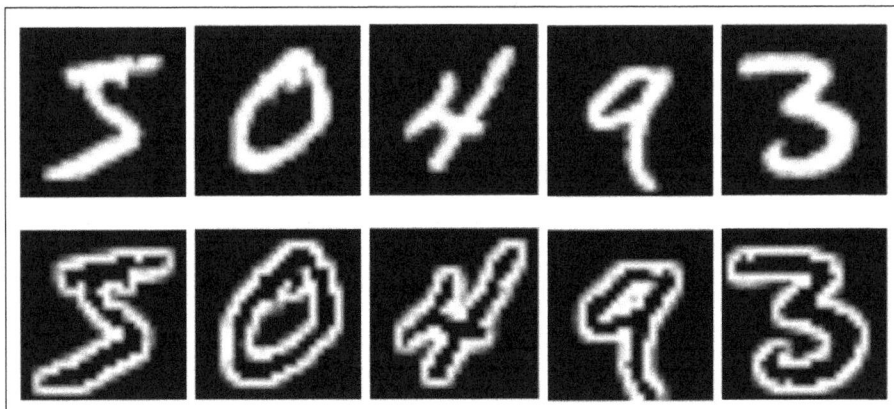

On top is the original mnist image, on the bottom is the new image after we applied the filter

It is clear, therefore, that filters can alter the images, and show "features" that can be useful to detect and classify images. For example, to classify digits, the color of the inside is not important, and a filter such as "edges" helps identify the general shape of the digit which is what is important for a correct classification.

We can think of filters in the same way we think about neural networks, and think that the filter we have defined is a set of weights, and that the final value represents the activation value of a neuron in the next layer (in fact, even though we chose particular weights to discuss these examples, we will see that the weights will be *learned* by the neural network using back-propagation):

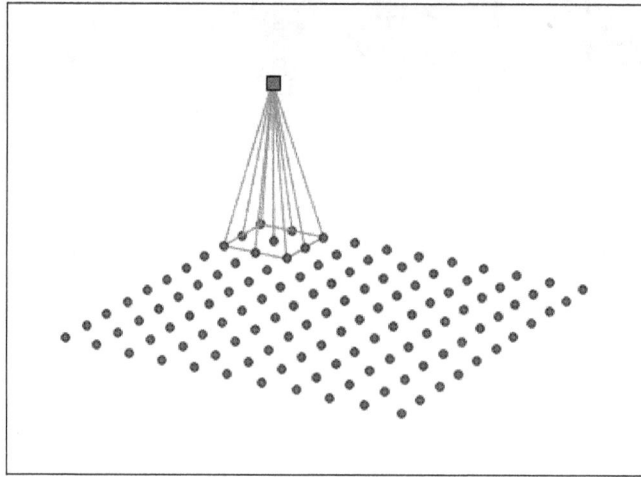

The filter covers a fixed region, and for each neuron in that region, it defines a connection weight to a neuron in the next layer. The neuron in the next layer will then have an input value equal to the regular activation value calculated by summing the contributions of all input neurons mediated by the corresponding connection weights.

We then keep the same weights and we slide the filter across, generating a new set of neurons, which correspond to the filtered image:

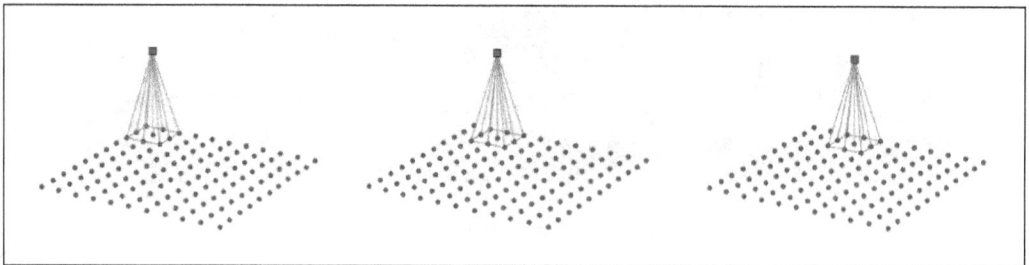

We can keep repeating the process until we have moved across the whole image, and we can repeat this process with as many filters as we like, creating a new set of images, each of which will have different features or characteristics highlighted. While we have not used a bias in our examples, it is also possible to add a bias to the filter, which will be added to the neural network, and we can also define different activity functions. In our code example you will notice that we have forced the value to be in the range (0, 255), which can be thought of as a simple threshold function:

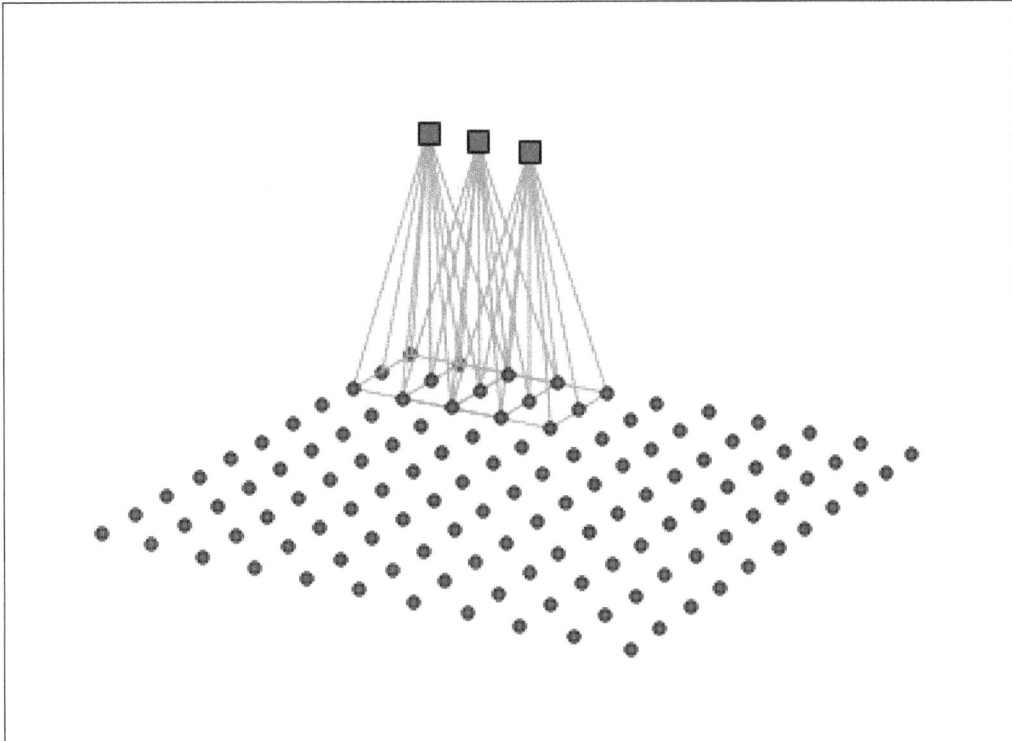

As the filter moves across the image, we define new activation values for the neurons in the output image.

Since one may define many filters, we should think of the output not as a single image, but as a set of images, one for each filter defined. If we used just the "edges" and the "blur" filter, the output layer would therefore have two images, one per filter chosen. The output will therefore have, besides a width and a height, also a depth equal to the number of filters chosen. In actuality, the input layer can also have a depth if we use color images as input; images are in fact usually comprised of three channels, which in computer graphics are represented by RGB, the red channel, the green channel, and the blue channel. In our example, the filter is represented by a two-dimensional matrix (for example the `blur` filter is a 3 x 3 matrix with all entries equal to 1/9. However, if the input is a color image, the filter will also have a depth (in this case equal to three, the number of color channels), and it will therefore be represented by three (number of color channels) 3 x 3 matrices. In general, the filter will therefore be represented by a three-dimensional array, with a width, a height, and a depth, which are sometimes called "volumes". In the preceding example, since the `mnist` images are gray-scale only, the filter had depth 1. A general filter of depth $d$ is therefore comprised of $d$ filters of the same width and height. Each of those $d$ filters are called a "slice" or a "leaf":

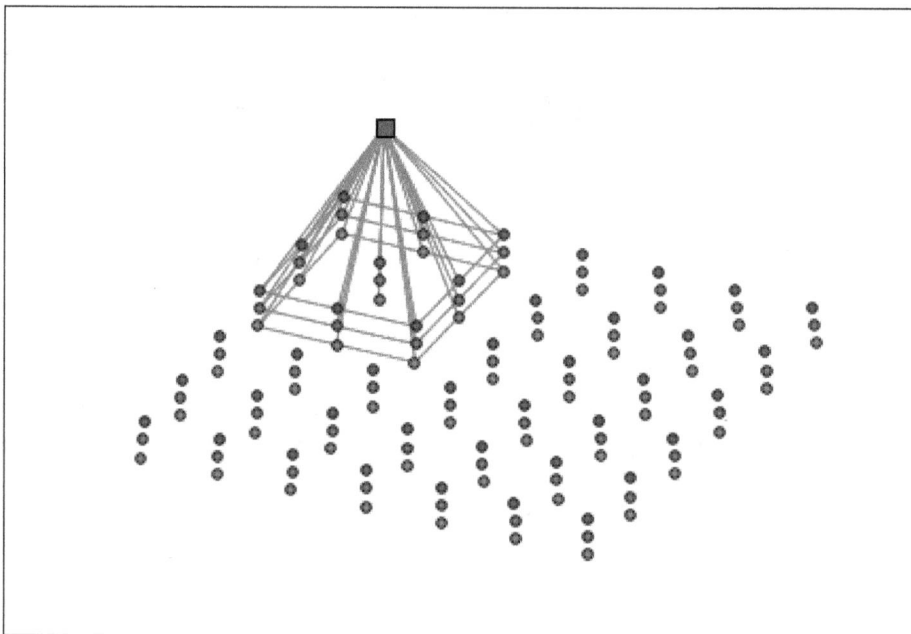

Similarly, as before, for each "leaf" or "slice", we connect each neuron in the small sub-region, as well as a bias, to a neuron and we calculate its activation value defined by the connection weights set in the filter, and we slide the filter across the whole area. Such a procedure, as it is easy to calculate, requires a number of parameters that are equal to the number of weights defined by the filter (in our example above, this would be 3 x 3=9), multiplied by the number of "leaves", that is, the depth of the layer, plus one bias. This defines a feature map, because it highlights specific features of the input. In our code above we defined two feature maps, a "blur" and an "edges". Therefore, we need to multiply the number of parameters by the number of feature maps. Note that the weights for each filter are fixed; when we slide the filter across the region we do not change weights. Therefore, if we start with a layer with size (width, height, depth), and a filter of dimension (`filter_w, filter_h`), the output layer after having applied the convolution is (`width - filter_w + 1, height - filter_h + 1`). The depth of the new layer depends on how many feature maps we want to create. In our `mnist` code example earlier, if we applied both the `blur` and `edges` filters, we would have an input layer of size (28 x 28 x 1), since there is only one channel because the digits are gray-scale images, and an output layer of dimension (26 x 26 x 2), since our filters had dimension (3 x 3) and we used two filters. The number of parameters is only 18 (3 x 3 x 2), or 20 (3 x 3 x 2+2) if we add a bias. This is way less than what we would need to have with classical feed-forward networks, whereas, since the input is 784 pixels, a simple hidden layer with just 50 neurons would need 784 x 50 = 39200 parameters, or 39250 if we add the bias:

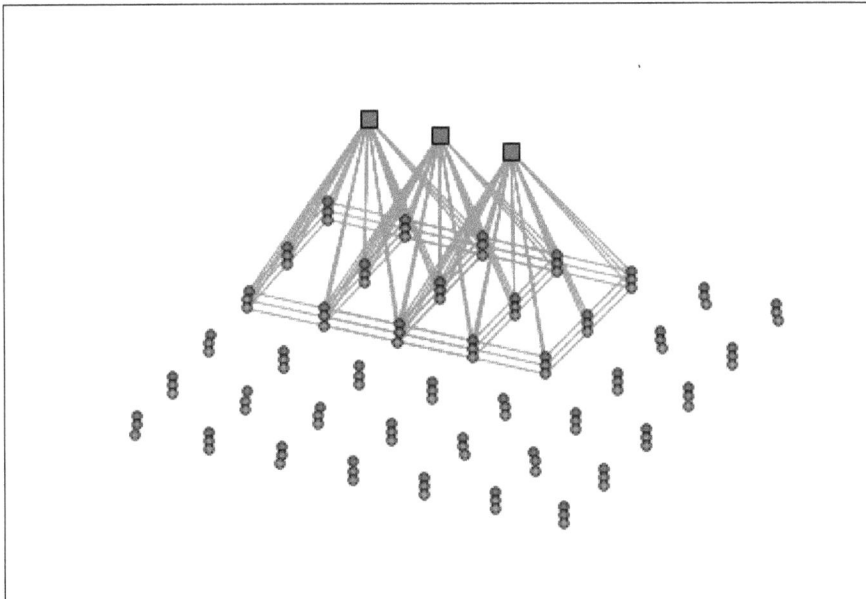

We slide the filter across the image over all the "leaves" comprising the layer.

Convolutional layers moreover can work better, since each neuron gets its input only from neighboring neurons, and does not care about collecting input from neurons that are distant from each other.

# Stride and padding in convolutional layers

The examples we have shown, aided by pictures, in fact only tell one particular application of filters (as we mentioned earlier, there are different types of convolutions, depending on the parameters chosen). In fact, the size of the filter may vary, as well as how it moves across the image and its behavior at the edges of the image. In our example, we moved the filter across the image 1 pixel at a time. How many pixels (neurons) we skip each time we move our filter is called the stride. In the above example, we used a stride of 1, but it is not unusual to use larger strides, of 2 or even more. In this case the output layer would have a smaller width and height:

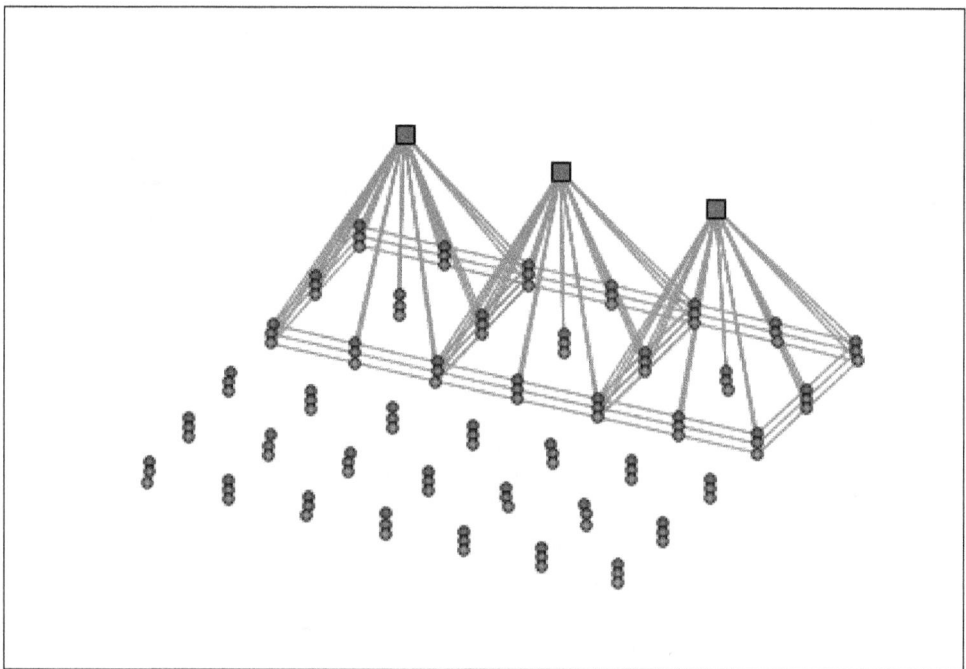

A filter applied with stride 2—the filter is moved by two pixels at a time.

In addition, we might also decide to apply the filter partially outside of the original picture. In that case, we would assume that the missing neurons would have value 0. This is called padding; that is, we add 0 value neurons outside the original image. This can be useful if, for example, we want the output image to be the same size as the input image. Above, we wrote the formula for the size of the new output image in case of zero padding, and that was (`width - filter_w + 1, height - filter_h + 1`) for an input of size (`width, height`) and a filter of dimensions (`filter_w, filter_h`). If we use a padding P all around the image, the output size will be (`width + 2P - filter_w + 1, height + 2P - filter_h + 1`). To summarize, in each dimension (either width or height), let the size of the input slice be called $I=(I_w, I_h)$, the size of the filter $F=(F_w, F_h)$, the size of the stride $S=(S_w, S_h)$, and the size of the padding $P=(P_w, P_h)$, then the size $O=(O_w, O_h)$ for the output slice is given by:

$$O_w = \frac{\left(I_w + 2P_w - F_w\right)}{S_w} + 1$$

$$O_h = \frac{\left(I_h + 2P_h - F_h\right)}{S_h} + 1$$

This of course identifies one of the constraints for $S$, that it must divide $(I + 2P - F)$ both in the width direction and the height direction. The dimension for the final volume is obtained by multiplying for the number of desired feature maps.

The number of parameters $W$ used, instead, is independent of the stride and padding, and it is just a function of the (square) size of the filter, the depth $D$ (number of slices) of the input, and the number of feature maps $M$ chosen:

$$W = \left(D * F_w F_h + 1\right) * M$$

The use of padding (also called zero-padding, as we are padding the image with zeros) is sometimes useful if we are seeking to make the output dimension the same as the input dimension. If we use a filter of dimension (2 x 2), it is in fact clear that by applying a padding of value 1 and a stride of 1, we have the dimension of the output slice the same as the size of the input slice.

# Pooling layers

In the previous section, we have derived the formula for the size for each slice in a convolutional layer. As we discussed, one of the advantages of convolutional layers is that they reduce the number of parameters needed, improving performance and reducing over-fitting. After a convolutional operation, another operation is often performed — pooling. The most classical example is called max-pooling, and this means creating (2 x 2) grids on each slice, and picking the neuron with the maximum activation value in each grid, discarding the rest. It is immediate that such an operation discards 75% of the neurons, keeping only the neurons that contribute the most in each cell.

There are two parameters for each pooling layer, similar to the stride and padding parameters found in convolutional layers, and they are the size of the cell and the stride. One typical choice is to choose a cell size of 2 and a stride of 2, though it is not uncommon to pick a cell size of 3 and a stride of 2, creating some overlap. It should be noted, however, that if the cell size is too large, the pooling layer may be discarding too much information and is not helpful. We can derive a formula for the output of a pooling layer, similar to the one we derived for convolutional layers. Let's call, like before, $I$ the size of the input slice, $F$ the size of the cell (also called the receptive field), $S$ the size of the stride, and $O$ the size of the output. Pooling layers typically do not use any padding. Then we obtain in each dimension:

$$O_w = \frac{\left(I_w - F_w\right)}{S_w} + 1$$

$$O_h = \frac{\left(I_h - F_h\right)}{S_h} + 1$$

Pooling layers do not change the depth of the volume of the layer, keeping the same number of slices, since the pooling operation is performed in each slice independently.

It should also be noted that, similar to how we can use different activation functions, we can also use different pooling operations. Taking the max is one of the most common operations, but it is not uncommon to take the average of all the values, or even an $L^2$ measure, which is the square root of the sum of all the squares. In practice, max-pooling often performs better, since it retains the most relevant structures in the image.

It should be noted, however, that while pooling layers are still very much used, one can sometimes achieve similar or better results by simply using convolutional layers with larger strides instead of pooling layers (see, for example, J. Springerberg, A. Dosovitskiy, T. Brox, and M. Riedmiller, *Striving for Simplicity: The All Convolutional Net*, (2015), https://arxiv.org/pdf/1412.6806.pdf).

However, if pooling layers are used, they are generally used in the middle of a sequence of a few convolutional layers, generally after every other convolutional operation.

It is also important to note that pooling layers add no new parameters, since they are simply extracting values (like the max) without needing additional weights or biases:

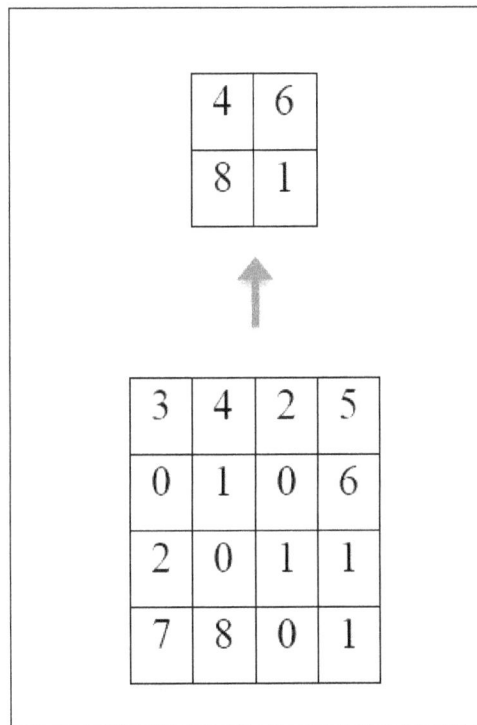

An example of a max-pool layer: the maximum from each 2x2 cell is calculated to generate a new layer.

# Dropout

Another important technique that can be applied after a pooling layer, but can also generally be applied to a fully connected layer, is to "drop" some neurons and their corresponding input and output connections randomly and periodically. In a dropout layer we specify a probability $p$ for neurons to "drop out" stochastically. During each training period, each neuron has probability $p$ to be dropped out from the network, and a probability *(1-p)* to be kept. This is to ensure that no neuron ends up relying too much on other neurons, and each neuron "learns" something useful for the network. This has two advantages: it speeds up the training, since we train a smaller network each time, and also helps in preventing over-fitting (see N. Srivastava, G. Hinton, A. Krizhevsky, I. Sutskever, and R. Salakhutdinov, *Dropout: A Simple Way to Prevent Neural Networks from Overfitting,* in *Journal of Machine Learning Research* 15 (2014), 1929-1958, `http://www.jmlr.org/papers/volume15/srivastava14a.old/source/srivastava14a.pdf`).

It is however, important to note that dropout layers are not strictly restricted to convolutional layers; in fact dropout layers find applications in different neural network architectures. Dropout layers should be regarded as a regularization technique for reducing overfitting, and we mention them since they will be explicitly used in our code example.

# Convolutional layers in deep learning

When we introduced the idea of deep learning, we discussed how the word "deep" refers not only to the fact that we use many layers in our neural net, but also to the fact that we have a "deeper" learning process. Part of this deeper learning process was the ability of the neural net to learn features autonomously. In the previous section, we defined specific filters to help the network learn specific characteristics. This is not necessarily what we want. As we discussed, the point of deep learning is that the system learns on its own, and if we had to teach the network what features or characteristics are important, or how to learn to recognize digits by applying layers such as the *edges* layer that highlights the general shape of a digit, we would be doing most of the work and possibly constraining the network to learn features that may be relevant to us but not to the network, degrading its performance. The point of Deep Learning is that the system needs to learn by itself.

In the *Chapter 2, Neural Networks*, we showed how the hidden layers in a neural net learn the weights by using back-propagation; the weights were not set by the operator. Similarly, it makes no sense for the operator to set the weights in the filters, rather we want the neural net to learn the weights in the filters, again by using back-propagation. All the operator needs to do is to set the size of the layer, the stride, and the padding, and decide how many feature maps we are asking the network to learn. By using supervised learning and back-propagation, the neural net will set the weights (and biases) for each filter autonomously.

We should also mention that, while it may be simpler to use the description of convolutional layers we have provided, convolutional layers could still be thought of as the regular fully connected layers we introduced in *Chapter 3, Deep Learning Fundamentals*. In fact, the two main characteristics of convolutional layers are the fact that each neuron only connects to a small region of the input layer, and the fact that different slices corresponding to the same small region share the same weights. These two properties can be rendered with a regular layer by creating a matrix of weights which is sparse, that is, with many zeros (due to the local connectivity of the convolutional network) and which has many weights repeated (due to the parameter sharing properties across slices). Understanding this point makes it clear why convolutional layers have much fewer parameters than fully connected layers; in convolutional layers the matrix of weights is comprised mostly of zeros entries. In practice, however, it helps the intuition to think of convolutional layers as they have been described in this chapter, since one can better appreciate how convolutional layers can highlight features of the original image, as we have shown graphically by blurring the image or highlighting the contours of the digits in our examples.

One more important point to make is that convolutional networks should generally have a depth equal to a number which is iteratively divisible by 2, such as 32, 64, 96, 128, and so on. This is important when using pooling layers, such as the max-pool layer, since the pooling layer (if it has size (2,2)) will divide the size of the input layer, similarly to how we should define "stride" and "padding" so that the output image will have integer dimensions. In addition, padding can be added to ensure that the output image size is the same as the input.

# Convolutional layers in Theano

Now that we have the intuition of how convolutional layers work, we are going to implement a simple example of a convolutional layer using Theano.

Let us start by importing the modules that are needed:

```
import numpy
import theano
import matplotlib.pyplot as plt
import theano.tensor as T
from theano.tensor.nnet import conv
import skimage.data
import matplotlib.cm as cm
```

Theano works by first creating a symbolic representation of the operations we define. We will later have another example using Keras, that, while it provides a nice interface to make creating neural networks easier, it lacks some of the flexibility one can have by using Theano (or TensorFlow) directly.

We define the variables needed and the neural network operations, by defining the number of feature maps (the depth of the convolutional layer) and the size of the filter, then we symbolically define the input using the Theano tensor class. Theano treats the image channels as a separate dimension, so we define the input as a tensor4. Next we initialize the weights using a random distribution between -0.2 and 0.2. We are now ready to call the Theano convolution operation and then apply the logistic sigmoid function on the output. Finally, we define the function f that takes an input and defines an output using the operations used:

```
depth = 4
filter_shape = (3, 3)

input = T.tensor4(name='input')

w_shape = (depth, 3, filter_shape[0], filter_shape[1])
dist = numpy.random.uniform(-0.2, 0.2, size=w_shape)
W = theano.shared(numpy.asarray(dist, dtype=input.dtype),
name = 'W')
conv_output = conv.conv2d(input, W)
output = T.nnet.sigmoid(conv_output)
f = theano.function([input], output)
```

The `skimage` module we imported can be used to load an image, we will import an image called `lena`, then after having reshaped the image to be passed in to the Theano function we defined, we can call the Theano function on it:

```
astronaut = skimage.data.astronaut()
img = numpy.asarray(astronaut, dtype='float32') / 255
filtered_img = f(img.transpose(2, 0, 1).reshape(1, 3, 512, 512))
```

This is it. We can now print out the original image and the filtered images by using this simple code:

```
plt.axis('off')
plt.imshow(img)
plt.show()
for img in range(depth):
    fig = plt.figure()
    plt.axis( 'off')
    plt.imshow(filtered_img[0, img, :, :, ], cmap = cm.gray)
    plt.show()
    filename = "astro" + str(img)
    fig.savefig(filename, bbox_inches='tight')
```

If the reader were interested in visualizing the weights used, in Theano, it is possible to print out the values by using `print W.get_value()`.

The output from this code is as follows: (since we have not fixed a random seed, and since the weights are initialized randomly, the reader may get slightly different images):

The original and filtered images.

# A convolutional layer example with Keras to recognize digits

In the third chapter, we introduced a simple neural network to classify digits using Keras and we got 94%. In this chapter, we will work to improve that value above 99% using convolutional networks. Actual values may vary slightly due to variability in initialization.

First of all, we can start by improving the neural network we had defined by using 400 hidden neurons and run it for 30 epochs; that should get us already up to around 96.5% accuracy:

```
hidden_neurons = 400
epochs = 30
```

Next we could try scaling the input. Images are comprised of pixels, and each pixel has an integer value between 0 and 255. We could make that value a float and scale it between 0 and 1 by adding these four lines of code right after we define our input:

```
X_train = X_train.astype('float32')
X_test = X_test.astype('float32')
X_train /= 255
X_test /= 255
```

If we run our network now, we get a poorer accuracy, just above 92%, but we need not worry. By rescaling, we have in fact changed the values of the gradient of our function, which therefore will converge much more slowly, but there is an easy work-around. In our code, inside the model.compile function, we defined an optimizer equal to "sgd". That is the standard stochastic gradient descent, which uses the gradient to converge to a minimum. However, Keras allows other choices, in particular "adadelta", which automatically uses momentum and adjusts the learning rate depending on the gradient, making it larger or smaller in an inversely proportional way to the gradient, so that the network does not learn too slowly and it does not skip minima by taking too large a step. By using adadelta, we dynamically adjust the parameters with time (see also: Matthew D. Zeiler, *Adadelta: An Adaptive Learning Rate Method*, arXiv:1212.5701v1 (https://arxiv.org/pdf/1212.5701v1.pdf)).

Inside the main function, we are now going to change our compile function and use:

```
model.compile(loss='categorical_crossentropy',
              metrics=['accuracy'], optimizer='adadelta')
```

If we run our algorithm again, we are now at about 98.25% accuracy. Finally, let's modify our first dense (fully connected) layer and use the `relu` activation function instead of the `sigmoid`:

```
model.add(Activation('relu'))
```

This will now give around 98.4% accuracy. The problem is that now it becomes increasingly difficult to improve our results using a classical feed-forward architecture, due to over-fitting, and increasing the number of epochs or modifying the number of hidden neurons will not bring any added benefit, as the network will simply learn to over-fit the data, rather than learn to generalize better. We are therefore now going to introduce convolutional networks in the example.

To do this, we keep our input scaled between 0 and 1. However, we reshape the data to a volume of size (28, 28, 1) = (width of image, height of image, number of channels) in order to be used by a convolutional layer, and we bring the number of hidden neurons down to 200, but we now add a simple convolutional layer at the beginning, with a 3 x 3 filter, no padding, and stride 1, followed by a max-pooling layer of stride 2 and size 2. In order to be able to then pass the output to the dense layer, we need to flatten the volume (convolutional layers are volumes) to pass it to the regular dense layer with 100 hidden neurons by using the following code:

```
from keras.layers import Convolution2D, MaxPooling2D, Flatten
hidden_neurons = 200
X_train = X_train.reshape(60000, 28, 28, 1)
X_test = X_test.reshape(10000, 28, 28, 1)
model.add(Convolution2D(32, (3, 3), input_shape=(28, 28, 1)))
model.add(Activation('relu'))
model.add(MaxPooling2D(pool_size=(2, 2)))
model.add(Flatten())
```

We can also reduce the number of epochs down to just 8, and we will get an accuracy of around 98.55%. Often it is common to use pairs of convolutional layers, so we add a second one similar to the first one, (before the pooling layer):

```
model.add(Convolution2D(32, (3, 3)))
model.add(Activation('relu'))
```

And we will now be at 98.9%.

In order to get to 99%, we add a dropout layer as we have discussed. This does not add any new parameters, but helps prevent overfitting, and we add it right before the flatten layer:

```
from keras.layers import Dropout
model.add(Dropout(0.25))
```

In this example we use a dropout rate of about 25%, so each neuron is randomly dropped once every four times.

This will take us above 99%. If we want to improve more (accuracy may vary due to differences in initializations), we can also add more dropout layers, for example, after the hidden layer and increase the number of epochs. This would force the neurons on the final dense layer, prone to overfit, to be dropped randomly. Our final code looks like this:

```python
import numpy as np
np.random.seed(0)  #for reproducibility
from keras.datasets import mnist
from keras.models import Sequential
from keras.layers import Dense, Activation, Convolution2D,
MaxPooling2D, Flatten, Dropout
from keras.utils import np_utils

input_size = 784
batch_size = 100
hidden_neurons = 200
classes = 10
epochs = 8

(X_train, Y_train), (X_test, Y_test) = mnist.load_data()
X_train = X_train.reshape(60000, 28, 28, 1)
X_test = X_test.reshape(10000, 28, 28, 1)
X_train = X_train.astype('float32')
X_test = X_test.astype('float32')
X_train /= 255
X_test /= 255
Y_train = np_utils.to_categorical(Y_train, classes)
Y_test = np_utils.to_categorical(Y_test, classes)
model = Sequential()
model.add(Convolution2D(32, (3, 3), input_shape=(28, 28, 1)))
model.add(Activation('relu'))
model.add(Convolution2D(32, (3, 3)))
model.add(Activation('relu'))
model.add(MaxPooling2D(pool_size=(2, 2)))
model.add(Dropout(0.25))
model.add(Flatten())
model.add(Dense(hidden_neurons))
model.add(Activation('relu'))
model.add(Dense(classes))
model.add(Activation('softmax'))
```

```
model.compile(loss='categorical_crossentropy',
            metrics=['accuracy'], optimizer='adadelta')
model.fit(X_train, Y_train, batch_size=batch_size,
        epochs=epochs, validation_split = 0.1, verbose=1)
score = model.evaluate(X_train, Y_train, verbose=1)
print('Train accuracy:', score[1])
score = model.evaluate(X_test, Y_test, verbose=1)
print('Test accuracy:', score[1])
```

It is possible to further optimize this network, but the point here is not to get an award-winning score, but to understand the process, and understand how each step we have taken has improved performance. It is also important to understand that by using the convolutional layer, we have in fact also avoided overfitting our network, by utilizing fewer parameters.

# A convolutional layer example with Keras for cifar10

We can now try to use the same network on the `cifar10` dataset. In *Chapter 3*, *Deep Learning Fundamentals*, we were getting a low 50% accuracy on test data, and to test the new network we have just used for the `mnist` dataset, we need to just make a couple of small changes to our code: we need to load the `cifar10` dataset (without doing any re-shaping, those lines will be deleted):

```
(X_train, Y_train), (X_test, Y_test) = cifar10.load_data()
```

And then change the input values for the first convolutional layer:

```
model.add(Convolution2D(32, (3, 3), input_shape=(32, 32, 3)))
```

Running this network for 5 epochs will give us around 60% accuracy (up from about 50%) and 66% accuracy after 10 epochs, but then the network starts to overfit and stops improving performance.

Of course the `cifar10` images have 32 x 32 x 3 = 3072 pixels, instead of 28 x 28=784 pixels, so we may need to add a couple more convolutional layers, after the first two:

```
model.add(Convolution2D(64, (3, 3)))
model.add(Activation('relu'))
model.add(Convolution2D(64, (3, 3)))
model.add(Activation('relu'))
model.add(MaxPooling2D(pool_size=(2, 2)))
model.add(Dropout(0.25))
```

In general, it is better to split large convolutional layers into smaller-sized convolutional layers. For example, if we have two consecutive (3 x 3) convolutional layers, the first layer will have a (3 x 3) view of the input image, and the second layer will have a (5 x 5) view of the input image for each pixel. However, each layer will have non-linear features that will stack up, creating more complex and interesting features of the input than we would get by simply creating a single (5 x 5) filter.

If we run this network for 3 epochs, we are also getting around 60%, but after 20 epochs we are up to 75% accuracy by using a simple network. The state-of-the-art convolutional networks can get around 90% accuracy, but require longer training and are more complicated. We will graphically present the architecture of one important convolutional neural network, called VGG-16, in the next paragraph so that the user can try to implement it using Keras or any other language he or she is comfortable with, such as Theano or TensorFlow (the network was originally created using Caffe, an important deep learning framework developed at Berkeley, see: http://caffe.berkeleyvision.org).

When working with neural networks, it is important to be able to "see" the weights the network has learned. This allows the user to understand what features the network is learning and to allow for better tuning. This simple code will output all the weights for each layer:

```
index = 0
numpy.set_printoptions(threshold='nan')
for layer in model.layers:
    filename = "conv_layer_" + str(index)
    f1 = open(filename, 'w+')
    f1.write(repr(layer.get_weights()))
    f1.close()
    print (filename + " has been opened and closed")
    index = index+1
```

If, for example, we are interested in the weights for layer 0, the first convolutional layer, we can apply them to the image to see what features the network is highlighting. If we apply these filters to the image lena, we get:

We can see how each filter is highlighting different features.

# Pre-training

As we have seen, neural networks, and convolutional networks in particular, work by tuning the weights of the network as if they were coefficients of a large equation in order to get the correct output given a specific input. The tuning happens through back-propagation to move the weights towards the best solution given the chosen neural net architecture. One of the problems is therefore finding the best initialization values for the weights in the neural network. Libraries such as Keras can automatically take care of that. However, this topic is important enough to be worth discussing this point.

Restricted Boltzmann machines have been used to pre-train the network by using the input as the desired output to make the network automatically learn representations of the input and tune its weights accordingly, and this topic has already been discussed in *Chapter 4, Unsupervised Feature Learning*.

In addition, there exists many pre-trained networks that offer good results. As we have mentioned, many people have been working on convolutional neural networks and have been getting impressive results, and one can often save time by reutilizing the weights learnt by these networks and applying them to other projects.

The VGG-16 model used in K. Simonyan, A. Zisserman, *Very Deep Convolutional Networks for Large-Scale Image Recognition* arXiv:1409.1556, `http://arxiv.org/pdf/1409.1556v6.pdf`, is an important model for image recognition. In this model, the input is a fixed 224 x 224 RGB-valued image where the only pre-processing is subtracting the mean RGB-value computed on the training set. We outline the architecture for this network in the attached diagram, and the user can try to implement by himself or herself such a network, but also keep in mind the computationally intensive nature of running such a network. In this network the architecture is as follows:

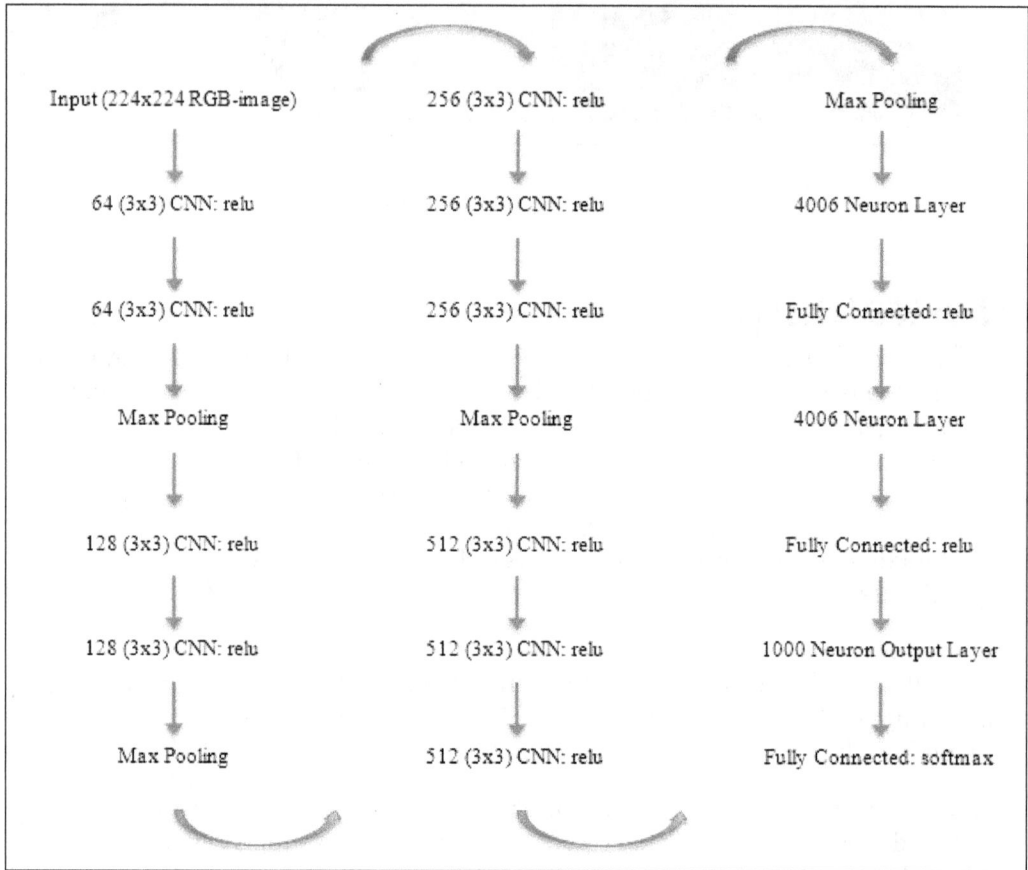

VGG-16 convolutional neural network architecture by Simonyan and Zisserman.

We also refer the interested reader to another noteworthy example, the AlexNet network, contained in Alex Krizhevsky, Ilya Sutskeve, Geoffrey Hinton, *ImageNet Classification with Deep Convolutional Networks*, in Advances in Neural Information Processing Systems 25 (NIPS 2012), `https://papers.nips.cc/paper/4824-imagenet-classification-with-deep-convolutional-neural-networks.pdf`, that we will not be discussing this here for the sake of brevity, but we invite the interested reader to look at it. We also invite the interested reader to look at `https://github.com/fchollet/deep-learning-models` for code examples of the VGG-16 and other networks.

# Summary

It should be noted, as it may have become clear, that there is no general architecture for a convolutional neural network. However, there are general guidelines. Normally, pooling layers follow convolutional layers, and often it is customary to stack two or more successive convolutional layers to detect more complex features, as it is done in the VGG-16 neural net example shown earlier. Convolutional networks are very powerful. However, they can be quite resource-heavy (the VGG-16 example above, for example, is relatively complex), and usually require a long training time, which is why the use of GPU can help speed up performance. Their strength comes from the fact that they do not focus on the entire image, rather they focus on smaller sub-regions to find interesting features that make up the image in order to be able to find discriminating elements between different inputs. Since convolutional layers are very resource-heavy, we have introduced pooling layers that help reduce the number of parameters without adding complexity, while the use of dropout layers helps insure that no neuron will rely too heavily on other neurons, and therefore each element in the neural net will contribute to learning.

In this chapter, starting from drawing an analogy with how our visual cortex works, we have introduced convolutional layers and followed up with a descriptive intuition of why they work. We have introduced filters, we have also covered how filters can be of different sizes and can have different padding, and we have looked at how setting zero-padding can ensure that the resulting image has the same size as the original image. As mentioned above, pooling layers can help reduce the complexity, while dropout layers can make the neural network much more effective at recognizing patterns and features, and in particular can be quite effective at reducing the risk of over-fitting.

In general, in the examples given, and in the `mnist` example in particular, we have shown how convolutional layers in neural networks can achieve much better accuracy than regular deep neural networks when dealing with images, reaching over 99% accuracy in digit recognition, without overfitting the model, by limiting the use of parameters. In the next chapters, we will look at speech recognition and then start looking at examples of models that use reinforcement learning, rather than supervised or unsupervised learning, by introducing deep learning for board games and deep learning for video games.

# 6
# Recurrent Neural Networks and Language Models

The neural network architectures we discussed in the previous chapters take in fixed sized input and provide fixed sized output. Even the convolutional networks used in image recognition (*Chapter 5, Image Recognition*) are flattened into a fixed output vector. This chapter will lift us from this constraint by introducing **Recurrent Neural Networks** (**RNNs**). RNNs help us deal with sequences of variable length by defining a recurrence relation over these sequences, hence the name.

The ability to process arbitrary sequences of input makes RNNs applicable for tasks such as language modeling (see section on *Language Modelling*) or speech recognition (see section on *Speech Recognition*). In fact, in theory, RNNs can be applied to any problem since it has been proven that they are Turing-Complete [1]. This means that theoretically, they can simulate any program that a regular computer would not be able to compute. As an example of this, Google DeepMind has proposed a model named "Neural Turing Machines", which can learn how to execute simple algorithms, such as sorting [2].

In this chapter, we will cover the following topics:

- How to build and train a simple RNN, based on a toy problem
- The problem of vanishing and exploding gradients in RNN training and how to solve them
- The LSTM model for long-term memory learning
- Language modeling and how RNNs can be applied to this problem
- A brief introduction to applying deep learning to speech recognition

# Recurrent neural networks

RNNs get their name because they recurrently apply the same function over a sequence. An RNN can be written as a recurrence relation defined by this function:

$$S_t = f(S_{t-1}, X_t)$$

Here $S_t$ — the state at step $t$ — is computed by the function $f$ from the state in the previous step, that is $t-1$, and an input $X_t$ at the current step. This recurrence relation defines how the state evolves step by step over the sequence via a feedback loop over previous states, as illustrated in the following figure:

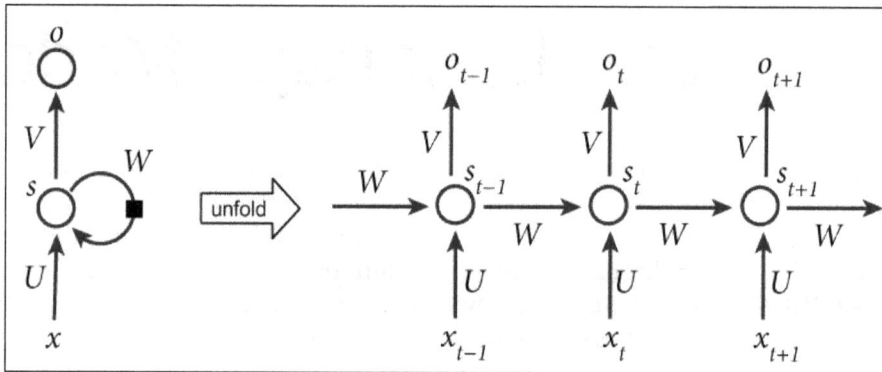

Figure from [3]

Left: Visual illustration of the RNN recurrence relation: $S_t = S_{t-1} * W + X_t * U$. The final output will be $o_t = V*S_t$

Right: RNN states recurrently unfolded over the sequence $t-1$, $t$, $t+1$. Note that the parameters U, V, and W are shared between all the steps.

Here $f$ can be any differentiable function. For example, a basic RNN is defined by the following recurrence relation:

$$S_t = tanh(S_{t-1} * W + X_t * U)$$

Here $W$ defines a linear transformation from state to state, and $U$ is a linear transformation from input to state. The *tanh* function can be replaced by other transformations, such as logit, tanh, or ReLU. This relation is illustrated in the following figure where $O_t$ is the output generated by the network.

For example, in word-level language modeling, the input X will be a sequence of words encoded in input vectors $(X_1 \ldots X_t \ldots)$. The state S will be a sequence of state vectors $(S_1 \ldots S_t \ldots)$. And the output O will be a sequence of probability vectors $(O_1 \ldots O_t \ldots)$ of the next words in the sequence.

Notice that in an RNN, each state is dependent on all previous computations via this recurrence relation. An important implication of this is that RNNs have memory over time because the states $S$ contain information based on the previous steps. In theory, RNNs can remember information for an arbitrarily long period of time, but in practice, they are limited to look back only a few steps. We will address this issue in more detail in section on *Vanishing and exploding gradients*.

Because RNNs are not limited to processing input of fixed size, they really expand the possibilities of what we can compute with neural networks, such as sequences of different lengths or images of varied sizes. The next figure visually illustrates some combinations of sequences we can make. Here's a brief note on these combinations:

- **One-to-one**: This is non-sequential processing, such as feedforward neural networks and convolutional neural networks. Note that there isn't much difference between a feedforward network and applying an RNN to a single time step. An example of one-to-one processing is the image classification from chapter (See *Chapter 5, Image Recognition*).

- **One-to-many**: This generates a sequence based on a single input, for example, caption generation from an image [4].

- **Many-to-one**: This outputs a single result based on a sequence, for example, sentiment classification from text.

- **Many-to-many indirect**: A sequence is encoded into a state vector, after which this state vector is decoded into a new sequence, for example, language translation [5], [6].

- **Many-to-many direct**: This outputs a result for each input step, for example, frame phoneme labeling in speech recognition (see the *Speech recognition* section).

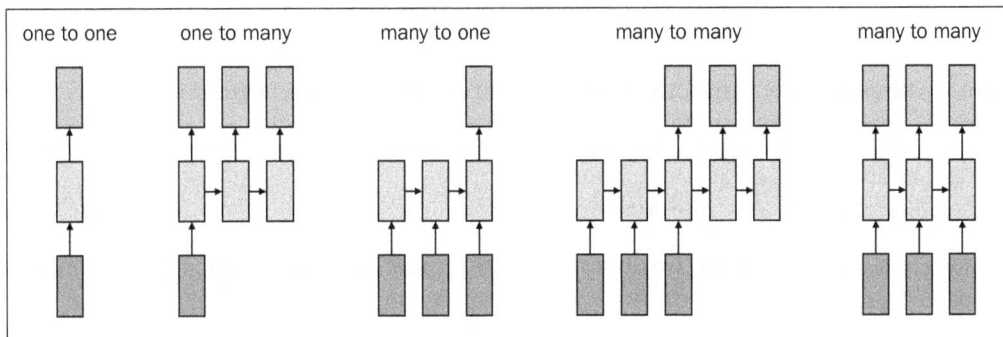

Image from [7]

RNNs expand the possibilities of what we can compute with neural networks—Red: input X, Green: states S, Blue: outputs O.

# RNN — how to implement and train

In the previous section, we briefly discussed what RNNs are and what problems they can solve. Let's dive into the details of an RNN and how to train it with the help of a very simple toy example: counting ones in a sequence.

In this problem, we will teach the most basic RNN how to count the number of ones in the input and output the result at the end of the sequence. We will show an implementation of this network in Python and NumPy. An example of input and output is as follows:

```
In:    (0, 0, 0, 0, 1, 0, 1, 0, 1, 0)
Out:   3
```

The network we are going to train is a very basic one and is illustrated in the following figure:

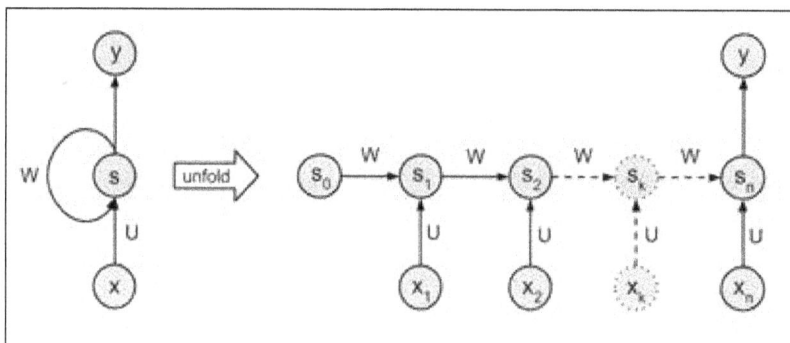

Basic RNN for counting ones in the input

The network will have only two parameters: an input weight $U$ and a recurrence weight $W$. The output weight $V$ is set to 1 so we just read out the last state as the output $y$. The recurrence relation defined by this network is $S_t = S_{t-1} * W + X_t * U$. Note that this is a linear model since we don't apply a nonlinear function in this formula. This function can be defined in terms of code as follows:

```
def step(s, x, U, W):
    return x * U + s * W
```

Because 3 is the number we want to output and there are three ones, a good solution to this is to just get the sum of the input across the sequence. If we set $U=1$, then whenever an input is received, we will get its full value. If we set $W=1$, then the value we would accumulate will never decay. So for this example, we would get the desired output: 3.

Nevertheless, the training and implementation of this neural network will be interesting, as we will see in the rest of this section. So let's see how we could get this result through backpropagation.

# Backpropagation through time

The backpropagation through time algorithm is the typical algorithm we use to train recurrent networks [8]. The name already implies that it is based on the backpropagation algorithm we discussed in *Chapter 2, Neural Networks*.

If you understand regular back-propagation, then backpropagation through time is not too difficult to understand. The main difference is that the recurrent network needs to be unfolded through time for a certain number of time steps. This unfolding is illustrated in the preceding figure (*Basic RNN for counting ones in the input*). Once the unfolding is complete, we end up with a model that is quite similar to a regular multilayer feedforward network. The only differences are that each layer has multiple input (the previous state, which is $S_{t-1}$), and the current input ($X_t$) and the parameters (here $U$ and $W$) are shared between each layer.

The forward pass unwraps the RNN along the sequence and builds up a stack of activities for each step. The forward step with a batch of input sequences $X$ can be implemented as follows:

```
def forward(X, U, W):
    # Initialize the state activation for each sample along the
    sequence
    S = np.zeros((number_of_samples, sequence_length+1))
    # Update the states over the sequence
    for t in range(0, sequence_length):
        S[:,t+1] = step(S[:,t], X[:,t], U, W)   # step function
    return S
```

After this forward step, we have the resulting activations, represented by $S$, for each step and each sample in the batch. Because we want to output more or less continuous output (sum of all ones), we use the mean squared error cost function to define our output cost with respect to the targets and output y, as follows:

```
cost = np.sum((targets - y)**2)
```

Now that we have our forward step and cost function, we can define how the gradient is propagated backward. First, we need to get the gradient of the output y with respect to the cost function ($\partial \xi / \partial y$).

Once we have this gradient, we can propagate it backward through the stack of activities we built during the forward step. This backward pass pops activities off the stack to accumulate the error derivatives at each time step. The recurrence relation to propagate this gradient through the network can be written as follows:

$$\frac{\partial \xi}{\partial S_{t-1}} = \frac{\partial \xi}{\partial S_t}\frac{\partial S_t}{\partial S_{t-1}} = \frac{\partial \xi}{\partial S_t}W$$

The gradients of the parameters are accumulated with this:

$$\frac{\partial \xi}{\partial U} = \sum_{t=0}^{n}\frac{\partial \xi}{\partial S_t}x_t$$

$$\frac{\partial \xi}{\partial W} = \sum_{t=1}^{n}\frac{\partial \xi}{\partial S_t}S_{t-1}$$

In the following implementation, the gradients for U and W are accumulated during gU and gW, respectively, during the backward step:

```
def backward(X, S, targets, W):
    # Compute gradient of output
    y = S[:,-1]  # Output `y` is last activation of sequence
    # Gradient w.r.t. cost function at final state
    gS = 2.0 * (y - targets)
    # Accumulate gradients backwards
    gU, gW = 0, 0  # Set the gradient accumulations to 0
    for k in range(sequence_len, 0, -1):
        # Compute the parameter gradients and accumulate the
        results.
        gU += np.sum(gS * X[:,k-1])
        gW += np.sum(gS * S[:,k-1])
        # Compute the gradient at the output of the previous layer
        gS = gS * W
    return gU, gW
```

We can now try to use gradient descent to optimize our network:

```
learning_rate = 0.0005
# Set initial parameters
parameters = (-2, 0)   # (U, W)
# Perform iterative gradient descent
for i in range(number_iterations):
    # Perform forward and backward pass to get the gradients
    S = forward(X, parameters(0), parameters(1))
    gradients = backward(X, S, targets, parameters(1))
    # Update each parameter `p` by p = p - (gradient *
    learning_rate).
    # `gp` is the gradient of parameter `p`
    parameters = ((p - gp * learning_rate)
                  for p, gp in zip(parameters, gradients))
```

There is an issue though. Notice that if you try to run this code, the final parameters *U* and *W* tend to end up as **Not a Number (NaN)**. Let's try to investigate what happened by plotting the parameter updates over an error surface, as shown in the following figure. Notice that the parameters slowly move toward the optimum *(U=W=1)* until it overshoots and hits approximately *(U=W=1.5)*. At this point, the gradient values just blow up and make the parameter values jump outside the plot. This problem is known as exploding gradients. The next section will explain why this happens in detail and how to prevent it.

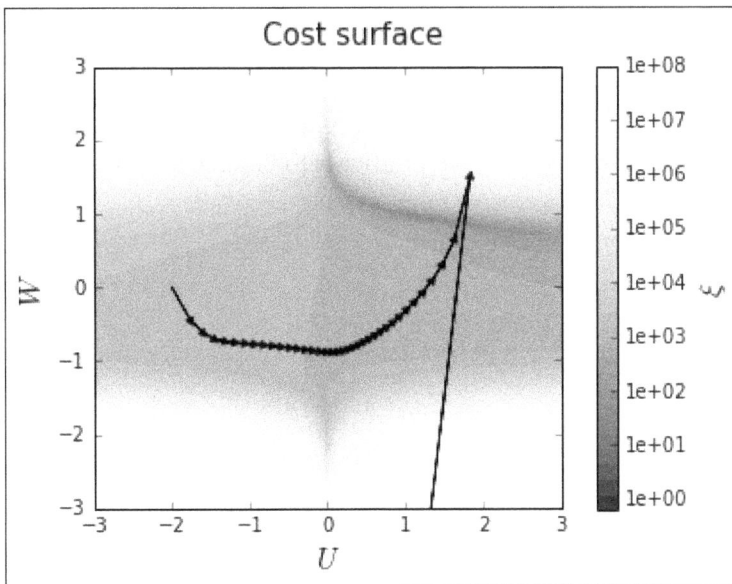

Parameter updates plotted on an error surface via a gradient descent. The error surface is plotted on a logarithmic color scale

# Vanishing and exploding gradients

RNNs can be harder to train than feedforward or convolutional networks. Some difficulties arise due to the recurrent nature of the RNN where the same weight matrix is used to compute all the state updates [9], [10].

The end of the last section, the preceding figure, illustrated the exploding gradient, which brings RNN training to an unstable state due to the blowing up of long-term components. Besides the exploding gradient problem, there is also the vanishing gradient problem where the opposite happens. Long-term components go to zero exponentially fast, and the model is unable to learn from temporally distant events. In this section, we will explain both the problems in detail and also how to deal with them.

Both exploding and vanishing gradients arise from the fact that the recurrence relation that propagates the gradient backward through time forms a geometric sequence:

$$\frac{\partial S_t}{\partial S_{t-m}} = \frac{\frac{\partial S_t}{\partial S_{t-1}} * \ldots * \partial S_{t-m+1}}{\partial S_{t-m}} = W^m$$

In our simple linear RNN, the gradient grows exponentially if $|W| > 1$. This is known as the exploding gradient (for example, 50 time steps over W=1.5 is $W_{50}$ = $1.5^{50} \approx 6 * 10^8$ ). The gradient shrinks exponentially if $|W| < 1$; this is known as the vanishing gradient (for example, 20 time steps over W=0.6 is $W_{20}$ = $0.6^{20} \approx 3*10^{-5}$ ). If the weight parameter $W$ is a matrix instead of a scalar, this exploding or vanishing gradient is related to the largest eigenvalue ($\rho$) of $W$ (also known as a spectral radius). It is sufficient for $\rho < 1$ for the gradients to vanish, and it is necessary for $\rho > 1$ for them to explode.

The following figure visually illustrates the concept of exploding gradients. What happens is that the cost surface we are training on is highly unstable. Using small steps, we might move to a stable part of the cost function, where the gradient is low, and suddenly hit upon a jump in cost and a corresponding huge gradient. Because this gradient is so huge, it will have a big effect on our parameters. They will end up in a place on the cost surface that is far from where they originally were. This makes gradient descent learning unstable and even impossible in some cases.

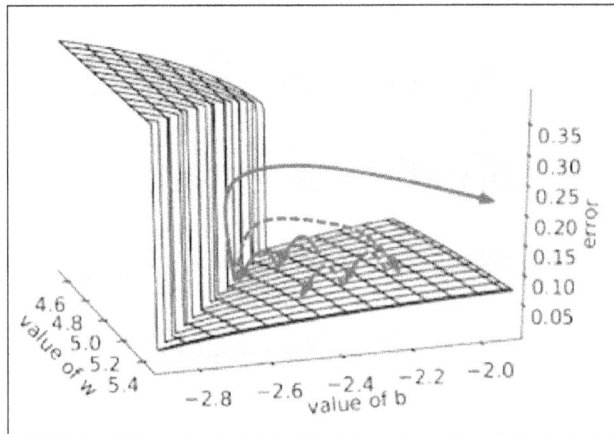

Illustration of an exploding gradient [11]

We can counter the effects of exploding gradients by controlling the size our gradients can grow to. Some examples of solutions are:

- Gradient clipping, where we threshold the maximum value a gradient can get [11].

- Second order optimization (Newton's method), where we model the curvature of the cost function. Modeling the curvature allows us to take big steps in low-curvature scenarios and small steps in high-curvature scenarios. For computational reasons, typically only an approximation of the second order gradient is used [12].

- Optimization methods, such as momentum [13] or RmsProp that rely less on the local gradient [14].

For example, we can retrain our network that wasn't able to converge (refer the preceding figure of *Illustration of an exploding gradient*) with the help of Rprop [15]. Rprop is a momentum-like method that only uses the sign of the gradient to update the momentum parameters, and it is thus not affected by exploding gradients. If we run Rprop optimization, we can see that the training converges in the following figure. Notice that while the training starts in a high gradient region ($U$=-1.5, $W$=2), it converges fast until it finds the optimum at ($U$=$W$=1).

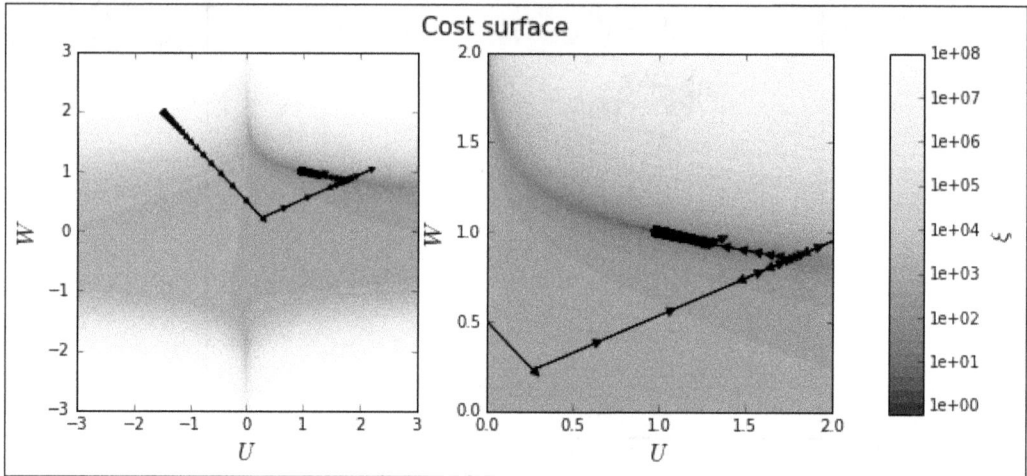

Parameter updates via Rprop plotted on an error surface. Error surface is plotted on a logarithmic scale.

The vanishing gradient problem is the inverse of the exploding gradient problem. The gradient decays exponentially over the number of steps. This means that the gradients in earlier states become extremely small, and the ability to retain the history of these states vanishes. The small gradients from earlier time steps are outcompeted by the larger gradients from more recent time steps. Hochreiter and Schmidhuber [16] describe this as follows: *Backpropagation through time is too sensitive to recent distractions.*

This problem is more difficult to detect because the network will still learn and output something (unlike in the exploding gradients case). It just won't be able to learn long-term dependencies. People have tried to tackle this problem with solutions similar to the ones we have for exploding gradients, such as second order optimization or momentum. These solutions are far from perfect, and learning long-term dependencies with simple RNNs is still very difficult. Thankfully, there is a clever solution to the vanishing gradient problem that uses a special architecture made up of memory cells. We will discuss this architecture in detail in the next section.

# Long short term memory

In theory, simple RNNs are capable of learning long-term dependencies, but in practice, due to the vanishing gradient problem, they only seem to limit themselves to learning short-term dependencies. Hochreiter and Schmidhuber studied this problem extensively and came up with a solution called **Long Short Term Memory (LSTM)** [16]. LSTMs can handle long-term dependencies due to a specially crafted memory cell. They work so well that most of the current accomplishments in training RNNs on a variety of problems are due to the use of LSTMs. In this section, we will explore how this memory cell works and how it solves the vanishing gradient issue.

The key idea of LSTM is the cell state, of which the information can only be explicitly written in or removed so that the cell state stays constant if there is no outside interference. This cell state for time t is illustrated as $c_t$ in the next figure.

The LSTM cell state can only be altered by specific gates, which are a way to let information pass through. These gates are composed of a logistic sigmoid function and element-wise multiplication. Because the logistic function only outputs values between 0 and 1, the multiplication can only reduce the value running through the gate. A typical LSTM is composed of three gates: a forget gate, input gate, and output gate. These are all illustrated as $f$, $i$, and $o$, in the following figure. Note that the cell state, input, and output are all vectors, so the LSTM can hold a combination of different information blocks at each time step. Next, we will describe the workings of each gate in more detail.

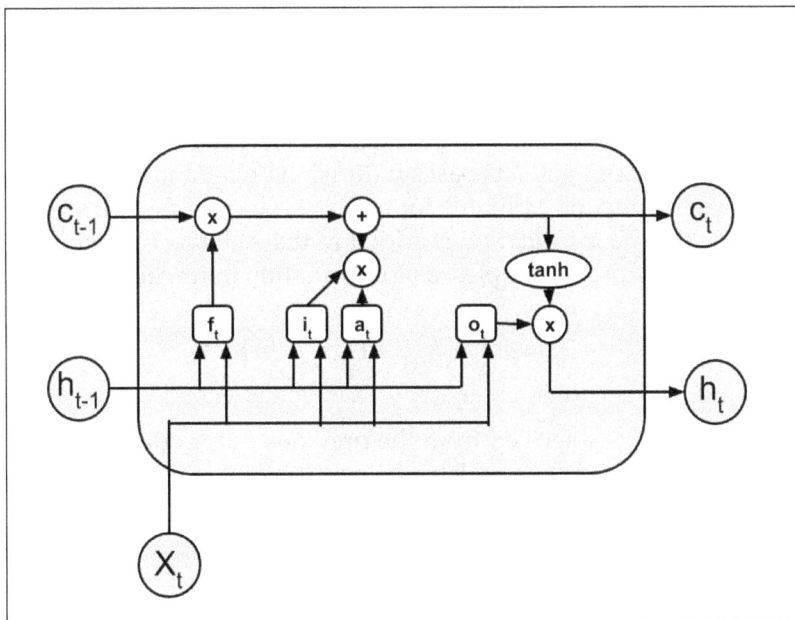

$$f_t = \sigma\left(W_f h_{t-1} + U_f x_t + b_f\right)$$
$$i_t = \sigma\left(W_i h_{t-1} + U_i x_t + b_i\right)$$
$$a_t = \tanh\left(W_c h_{t-1} + U_c x_t + b_c\right)$$
$$o_t = \sigma\left(W_o h_{t-1} + U_o x_t + b_o\right)$$
$$c_t = f_t * c_{t-1} + i_t * a_t$$
$$h_t = o_t * \tanh\left(c_t\right)$$

LSTM cell

$x_t, c_t, h_t$ are the input, cell state, and LSTM output at time $t$, respectively.

The first gate in LSTM is the forget gate; it is called so because it decides whether we want to erase the cell state or not. This gate was not in the original LSTM proposed by Hochreiter; it was proposed by Gers and others [17]. The forget gate bases its decision on the previous output $h_{t-1}$ and current input $x_t$. It combines this information and squashes them by a logistic function so that it outputs a number between 0 and 1 for each block of the cell's vector. Because of the element-wise multiplication with the cell, an output of 0 erases a specific cell block completely and an output of 1 leaves all of the information in that cell blocked. This means that the LSTM can get rid of irrelevant information in its cell state vector.

$$f_t = \sigma\left(W_f h_{t-1} + U_f x_t + b_f\right)$$

The next gate decides what new information is going to be added to the memory cell. This is done in two parts. The first part decides whether information is going to be added. As in the input gate, its bases it decision on $h_{t-1}$ and $x_t$ and outputs 0 or 1 through the logistic function available for each cell block of the cell's vector. An output of 0 means that no information is added to that cell block's memory. As a result, the LSTM can store specific pieces of information in its cell state vector:

$$i_t = \sigma\left(W_i h_{t-1} + U_i x_t + b_i\right)$$

The input to be added, $a_t$, is derived from the previous output ($h_{t-1}$) and the current input ($x_t$) and is transformed via a *tanh* function:

$$a_t = \tanh\left(W_c h_{t-1} + U_c x_t + b_c\right)$$

The forget and input gates completely decide the new cell by adding the old cell state with the new information to add:

$$c_t = f_t * c_{t-1} + i_t * a_t$$

The last gate decides what the output is going to be. The output gate takes $h_{t-1}$ and $x_t$ as input and outputs 0 or 1 through the logistic function available for each cell block's memory. An output of 0 means that the cell block doesn't output any information, while an output of 1 means that the full cell block's memory is transferred to the output of the cell. The LSTM can thus output specific blocks of information from its cell state vector:

$$o_t = \sigma \left( W_o h_{t-1} + U_o x_t + b_o \right)$$

The final value outputted is the cell's memory transferred by a *tanh* function:

$$h_t = o_t * \tanh \left( c_t \right)$$

Because all these formulas are derivable, we can chain LSTM cells together just like we chain simple RNN states together and train the network via backpropagation through time.

Now how does the LSTM protect us from vanishing gradients? Notice that the cell state is copied identically from step to step if the forget gate is 1 and the input gate is 0. Only the forget gate can completely erase the cell's memory. As a result, memory can remain unchanged over a long period of time. Also, notice that the input is a tanh activation added to the current cell's memory; this means that the cell memory doesn't blow up and is quite stable.

How the LSTM is unrolled in practice is illustrated in the following figure.

Initially, the value of 4.2 is given to the network as input; the input gate is set to 1 so the complete value is stored. Then for the next two time steps, the forget gate is set to 1. So the entire information is kept throughout these steps and no new information is being added because the input gates are set to 0. Finally, the output gate is set to 1, and 4.2 is outputted and remains unchanged.

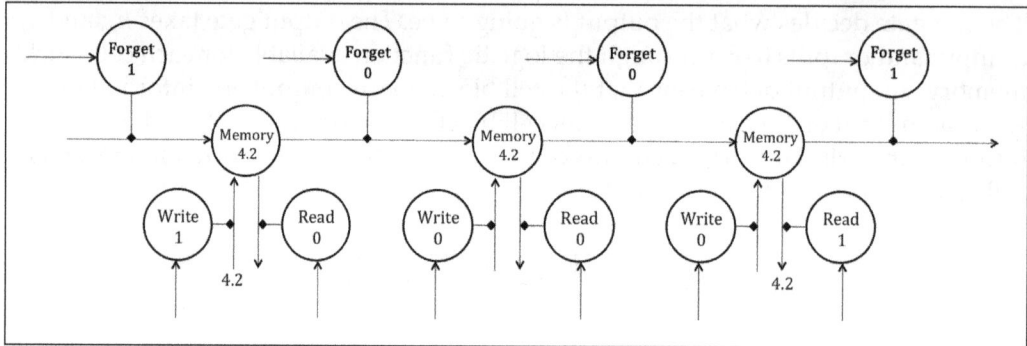

Unrolling LSTM through time [18]

While the LSTM network described in the preceding diagram is a typical LSTM version used in most applications, there are many variants of LSTM networks that combine different gates in different orders [19]. Getting into all these different architectures is out of the scope of this book.

# Language modeling

The goal of language models is to compute a probability of a sequence of words. They are crucial to a lot of different applications, such as speech recognition, optical character recognition, machine translation, and spelling correction. For example, in American English, the two phrases *wreck a nice beach* and *recognize speech* are almost identical in pronunciation, but their respective meanings are completely different from each other. A good language model can distinguish which phrase is most likely correct, based on the context of the conversation. This section will provide an overview of word- and character-level language models and how RNNs can be used to build them.

# Word-based models

A word-based language model defines a probability distribution over sequences of words. Given a sequence of words of length $m$, it assigns a probability $P(w_1, \dots, w_m)$ to the full sequence of words. The application of these probabilities are two-fold. We can use them to estimate the likelihood of different phrases in natural language processing applications. Or, we can use them generatively to generate new text.

# N-grams

The inference of the probability of a long sequence, say $w_1$, ..., $w_m$, is typically infeasible. Calculating the joint probability of $P(w_1, ... , w_m)$ would be done by applying the following chain rule:

$$P(w_1,\ldots,w_m) = P(w_1)P(w_2 \mid w_1)P(w_3 \mid w_2, w_1) \cdot \ldots \cdot P(w_m \mid w_1,\ldots, w_{m-1})$$

Especially the probability of the later words given the earlier words would be difficult to estimate from the data. This is why this joint probability is typically approximated by an independence assumption that the $i^{th}$ word is only dependent on the $n$-1 previous words. We only model the joint probabilities of $n$ sequential words called n-grams. Note that n-grams can be used to refer to other sequences of length $n$, such as $n$ characters.

The inference of the joint distribution is approximated via n-gram models that split up the joint distribution in multiple independent parts. Note that n-grams are combinations of multiple sequential words, where $n$ is the number of sequential words. For example, in the phrase *the quick brown fox*, we have the following n-grams:

- **1-gram**: "The," "quick," "brown," and "fox" (also known as unigram)
- **2-grams**: "The quick," "quick brown," and "brown fox" (also known as bigram)
- **3-grams**: "The quick brown" and "quick brown fox" (also known as trigram)
- **4-grams**: "The quick brown fox"

Now if we have a huge corpus of text, we can find all the n-grams up until a certain $n$ (typically 2 to 4) and count the occurrence of each n-gram in that corpus. From these counts, we can estimate the probabilities of the last word of each n-gram, given the previous $n$-1 words:

- **1-gram**: $P(word) = \dfrac{count(word)}{total\ number\ of\ words\ in\ corpus}$

- **2-gram**: $P(w_i \mid w_{i-1}) = \dfrac{count(w_{i-1}, w_i)}{count(w_{i-1})}$

- **n-gram**: $P(w_{n+i} \mid w_n, \ldots w_{n+i-1}) = \dfrac{count(w_n, \ldots w_{n+i-1}, w_{n+i})}{count(w_n, \ldots w_{n+i-1})}$

The independence assumption that the $i^{th}$ word is only dependent on the previous *n-1* words can now be used to approximate the joint distribution.

For example, for a unigram, we can approximate the joint distribution by:

$$P(w_1,\ldots,w_m) = P(w_1)P(w_2)P(w_3)\cdot\ldots\cdot P(w_m)$$

For a trigram, we can approximate the joint distribution by:

$$P(w_1,\ldots,w_m) = P(w_1)P(w_2\mid w_1)P(w_3\mid w_2,w_1)\cdot\ldots\cdot P(w_m\mid w_{m-2},w_{m-1})$$

We can see that based on the vocabulary size, the number of n-grams grows exponentially with *n*. For example, if a small vocabulary contains 100 words, then the number of possible 5-grams would be *$100^5$ = 10,000,000,000* different 5-grams. In comparison, the entire works of Shakespeare contain around *30,000* different words, illustrating the infeasibility of using n-grams with a large *n*. Not only is there the issue of storing all the probabilities, we would also need a very large text corpus to create decent n-gram probability estimations for larger values of *n*. This problem is what is known as the curse of dimensionality. When the number of possible input variables (words) increases, the number of different combinations of these input values increases exponentially. This curse of dimensionality arises when the learning algorithm needs at least one example per relevant combination of values, which is the case in n-gram modeling. The larger our *n*, the better we can approximate the original distribution and the more data we would need to make good estimations of the n-gram probabilities.

## Neural language models

In the previous section, we illustrated the curse of dimensionality when modeling text with n-grams. The number of n-grams we need to count grows exponentially with *n* and with the number of words in the vocabulary. One way to overcome this curse is by learning a lower dimensional, distributed representation of the words [20]. This distributed representation is created by learning an embedding function that transforms the space of words into a lower dimensional space of word embeddings, as follows:

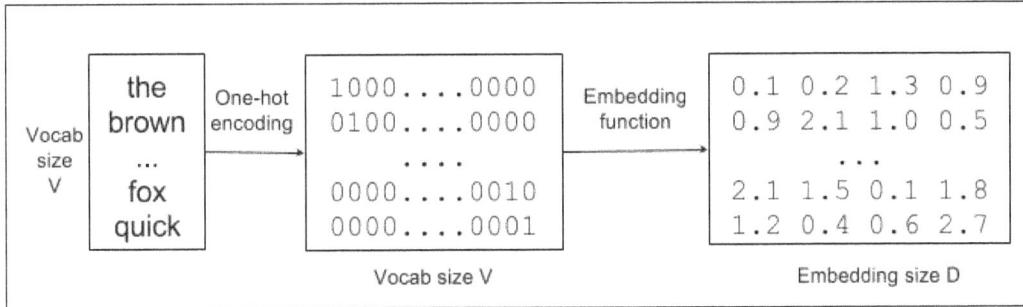

V-words from the vocabulary are transformed into one-hot encoding vectors of size V
(each word is encoded uniquely). The embedding function then transforms this V-dimensional
space into a distributed representation of size D (here D=4).

The idea is that the learned embedding function learns semantic information about the words. It associates each word in the vocabulary with a continuous-valued vector representation, the word embedding. Each word corresponds to a point in this embedding space where different dimensions correspond to the grammatical or semantic properties of these words. The goal is to ensure that the words close to each other in this embedding space should have similar meanings. This way, the information that some words are semantically similar can be exploited by the language model. For example, it might learn that "fox" and "cat" are semantically related and that both "the quick brown fox" and "the quick brown cat" are valid phrases. A sequence of words can then be transformed into a sequence of embedding vectors that capture the characteristics of these words.

It is possible to model the language model via a neural network and learn this embedding function implicitly. We can learn a neural network that given a sequence of $n-1$ words ($w_{t-n+1}$, ..., $w_{t-1}$) tries to output the probability distribution of the next word, that is, $w_t$. The network is made up of different parts.

The embedding layer takes the one-hot representation of the word $w_i$ and converts it into its embedding by multiplying it with the embedding matrix C. This computation can be efficiently implemented by a table lookup. The embedding matrix C is shared over all the words, so all words use the same embedding function. C is represented by a $V * D$ matrix, where V is the size of the vocabulary and D the size of the embedding. The resulting embeddings are concatenated into a hidden layer; after this, a bias b and a nonlinear function, such as *tanh*, can be applied. The output of the hidden layer is thus represented by the function $z = tanh(concat(w_{t-n+1}, ..., w_{t-1}) + b)$. From the hidden layer, we can now output the probability distribution of the next word $w_t$ by multiplying the hidden layer with U. This maps the hidden layer to the word space, adding a bias b and applying the softmax function to get a probability distribution. The final layer computes $softmax(z*U +b)$. This network is illustrated in the following figure:

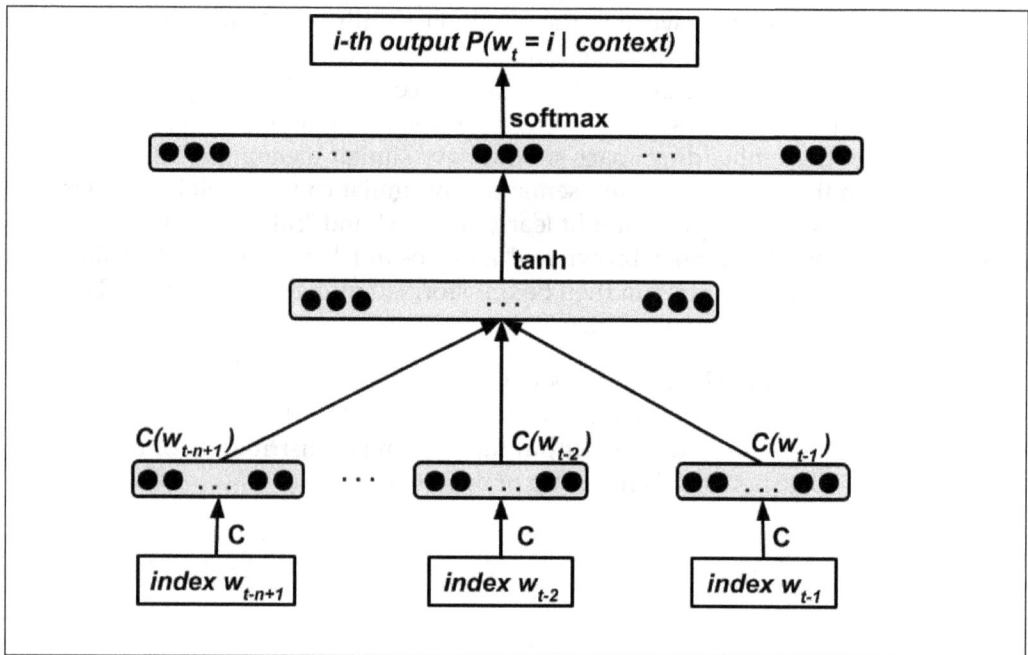

A neural network language model that outputs the probability distribution of the word $w_t$, given the words $w_{t-1}$ ... $w_{t-n+1}$. C is the embedding matrix.

This model simultaneously learns an embedding of all the words in the vocabulary and a model of the probability function for sequences of words. It is able to generalize this probability function to sequences of words not seen during training, thanks to these distributed representations. A specific combination of words in the test set might not be seen in the training set, but a sequence with similar embedding features is much more likely to be seen during training.

A 2D projection of some word embeddings is illustrated in the following figure. It can be seen that words that are semantically close are also close to each other in the embedding space.

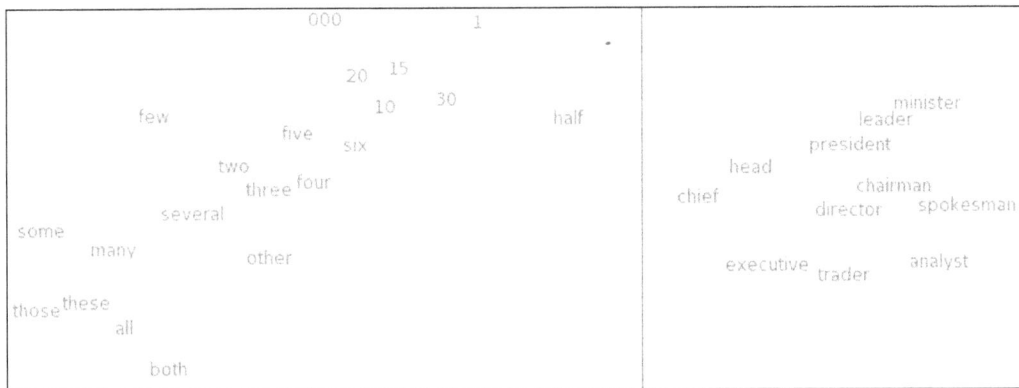

Related words in a 2D embedding space are close to each other in this space [21]

Word embeddings can be trained unsupervised on a large corpus of text data. This way, they are able to capture general semantic information between words. The resulting embeddings can now be used to improve the performance of other tasks where there might not be a lot of labeled data available. For example, a classifier trying to classify the sentiment of an article might be trained on using previously learned word embeddings, instead of one-hot encoding vectors. This way, the semantic information of the words becomes readily available for the sentiment classifier. Because of this, a lot of research has gone into creating better word embeddings without focusing on learning a probability function over sequences of words. For example, a popular word embedding model is word2vec [22], [23].

A surprising result is that these word embeddings can capture analogies between words as differences. It might, for example, capture that the difference between the embedding of "woman" and "man" encodes the gender and that this difference is the same in other gender-related words such as "queen" and "king."

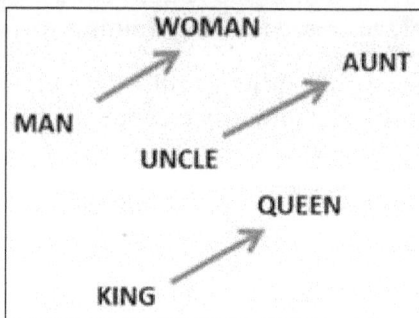

Word embeddings can capture semantic differences between words [24]

embed(woman) - embed(man) ≃ embed(aunt) - embed(uncle)

embed(woman) - embed(man) ≃ embed(queen) - embed(king)

While the previous feedforward network language model can overcome the curse of dimensionality of modeling a large vocabulary input, it is still limited to only modeling fixed length word sequences. To overcome this issue, we can use RNNs to build an RNN language model that is not limited by fixed length word sequences [25]. These RNN-based models can then not only cluster similar words in the input embedding, but can also cluster similar histories in the recurrent state vector.

One issue with these word-based models is computing the output probabilities, $P(w_i \mid context)$, of each word in the vocabulary. We get these output probabilities by using a softmax over all word activations. For a small vocabulary $V$ of *50,000* words, this would need a $|S| * |V|$ output matrix, where $|V|$ is the size of the vocabulary and $|S|$ the size of the state vector. This matrix is huge and would grow even more when we increase our vocabulary. And because softmax normalizes the activation of a single word by a combination of all other activations, we need to compute each activation to get the probability of a single word. Both illustrate the difficulty of computing the softmax over a large vocabulary; a lot of parameters are needed to model the linear transformation before the softmax, and the softmax itself is computationally intensive.

There are ways to overcome this issue, for example, by modeling the softmax function as a binary tree, essentially only needing $log(|V|)$ computations the calculate to final output probability of a single word [26].

Instead of going into these workarounds in detail, let's check out another variant of language modeling that is not affected by these large vocabulary issues.

# Character-based model

In most cases, language modeling is performed at the word level, where the distribution is over a fixed vocabulary of $|V|$ words. Vocabularies in realistic tasks, such as the language models used in speech recognition, often exceed *100,000* words. This huge dimensionality makes modeling the output distribution very challenging. Furthermore, these word level models are quite limited when it comes to modeling text data that contains non-word strings, such as multidigit numbers or words that were never part of the training data (out-of-vocabulary words).

A class of models that can overcome these issues is called a character-level language model [27]. These models model the distribution over sequences of characters instead of words, thus allowing you to compute probabilities over a much smaller vocabulary. The vocabulary here comprises all the possible characters in our text corpus. There is a downside to these models, though. By modeling the sequence of characters instead of words, we need to model much longer sequences to capture the same information over time. To capture these long-term dependencies, let's use an LSTM RNN language model.

The following part of this section will go into detail on how to implement a character-level LSTM in Tensorflow and how to train it on Leo Tolstoy's *War and Peace*. This LSTM will model the probability of the next character, given the previously seen characters: $P(c_t \mid c_{t-1} \ldots c_{t-n})$.

Because the full text is too long to train a network with **back-propagation through time (BPTT)**, we will use a batched variant called truncated BPTT. In this method, we will divide the training data into batches of fixed sequence length and train the network batch by batch. Because the batches will follow up with each other, we can use the final state of the last batch as the initial state in the next batch. This way, we can exploit the information stored in the state without having to do a full backpropagation through the full input text. Next, we will describe how to read these batches and feed them into the network.

# Preprocessing and reading data

To train a good language model, we need a lot of data. For our example, we will learn about a model based on the English translation of Leo Tolstoy's "War and peace." This book contains more than *500,000* words, making it the perfect candidate for our small example. Since it's in the public domain, "War and peace" can be downloaded as plain text for free from Project Gutenberg. As part of preprocessing, we will remove the Gutenberg license, book information, and table of contents. Next, we will strip out newlines in the middle of sentences and reduce the maximum number of consecutive newlines allowed to two.

To feed the data into the network, we will have to convert it into a numerical format. Each character will be associated with an integer. In our example, we will extract a total of 98 different characters from the text corpus. Next, we will extract input and targets. For each input character, we will predict the next character. Because we are training with truncated BPTT, we will make all the batches follow up on each other to exploit the continuity of the sequence. The process of converting the text into a list of indices and splitting it up in to batches of input and targets is illustrated in the following figure:

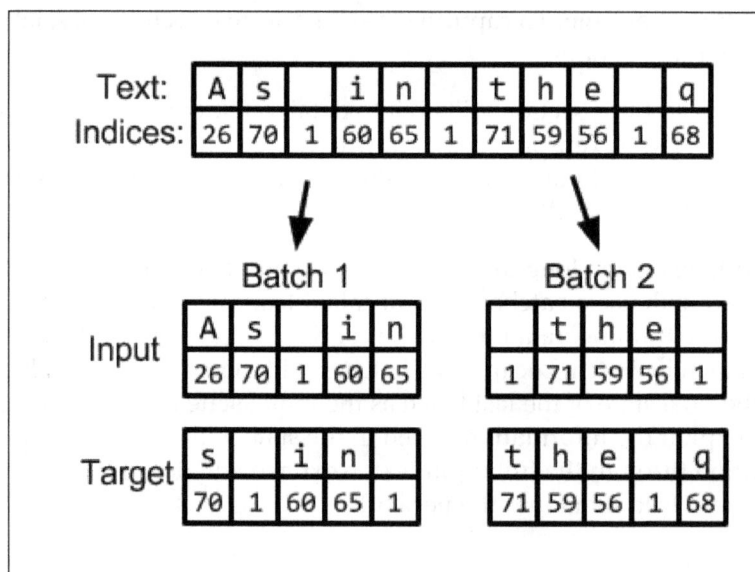

Converting text into input and target batches of integer labels with length 5.
Note that batches follow on to each other.

# LSTM network

The network we will train will be a two-layer LSTM network with 512 cells in each layer. We will train this network with truncated BPTT, so we will need to store the state between batches.

First, we need to define placeholders for our input and targets. The first dimension of both the input and targets is the batch size, the number of examples processed in parallel. The second dimension will be the dimension along the text sequence. Both these placeholders take batches of sequences where the characters are represented by their index:

```
inputs = tf.placeholder(tf.int32, (batch_size, sequence_length))
targets = tf.placeholder(tf.int32, (batch_size, sequence_length))
```

To feed the characters to the network, we need to transform them into a vector. We will transform them into one-hot encoding, which means that each character is going to be transformed into a vector with length equal to the size of the number of different characters in the dataset. This vector will be all zeros, except the cell that corresponds to its index, which will be set to 1. This can be done easily in TensorFlow with the following line of code:

```
one_hot_inputs = tf.one_hot(inputs, depth=number_of_characters)
```

Next, we will define our multilayer LSTM architecture. First we need to define the LSTM cells for each layer (`lstm_sizes` is a list of sizes for each layer, for example (512, 512), in our case):

```
cell_list = (tf.nn.rnn_cell.LSTMCell(lstm_size) for lstm_size in lstm_sizes)
```

Then, we wrap these cells in a single multilayer RNN cell using this:

```
multi_cell_lstm = tf.nn.rnn_cell.MultiRNNCell(cell_list)
```

To store the state between the batches, we need to get the initial state of the network and wrap it in the variable to be stored. Note that for computational reasons, TensorFlow stores LSTM states in a tuple of two separate tensors (c and h from the *Long Short Term Memory* section ). We can flatten this nested data structure with the `flatten` method, wrap each tensor in a variable, and repack it as the original structure with the `pack_sequence_as` method:

```
initial_state = self.multi_cell_lstm.zero_state(batch_size, tf.float32)
# Convert to variables so that the state can be stored between batches
```

```
state_variables = tf.python.util.nest.pack_sequence_as(
    self.initial_state,
    (tf.Variable(var, trainable=False)
     for var in tf.python.util.nest.flatten(initial_state)))
```

Now that we have the initial state defined as a variable, we can start unrolling the network through time. TensorFlow provides the `dynamic_rnn` method that does this unrolling dynamically as per the sequence length of the input. This method will return a tuple consisting of a tensor representing the LSTM output and the final state:

```
lstm_output, final_state = tf.nn.dynamic_rnn(
    cell=multi_cell_lstm, inputs=one_hot_inputs,
    initial_state=state_variable)
```

Next, we need to store the final state as the initial state for the next batch. We use the variable `assign` method to store each final state in the right initial state variable. The `control_dependencies` method is used to force that the state update to run before we return the LSTM output:

```
store_states = (
    state_variable.assign(new_state)
    for (state_variable, new_state) in zip(
        tf.python.util.nest.flatten(self.state_variables),
        tf.python.util.nest.flatten(final_state)))
with tf.control_dependencies(store_states):
    lstm_output = tf.identity(lstm_output)
```

To get the logit output from the final LSTM output, we need to apply a linear transformation to the output so it can have *batch size * sequence length * number of symbols* as its dimensions. Before we apply this linear transformation, we need to flatten the output to a matrix of the size number of *outputs * number of output features*:

```
output_flat = tf.reshape(lstm_output, (-1, lstm_sizes(-1)))
```

We can then define and apply the linear transformation with a weight matrix $W$ and bias $b$ to get the logits, apply the softmax function, and reshape it to a tensor of the size *batch size * sequence length * number of characters*:

```
# Define output layer
logit_weights = tf.Variable(
    tf.truncated_normal((lstm_sizes(-1), number_of_characters),
stddev=0.01))
logit_bias = tf.Variable(tf.zeros((number_of_characters)))
# Apply last layer transformation
logits_flat = tf.matmul(output_flat, self.logit_weights) + self.logit_
bias
```

```
probabilities_flat = tf.nn.softmax(logits_flat)
# Reshape to original batch and sequence length
probabilities = tf.reshape(
    probabilities_flat, (batch_size, -1, number_of_characters))
```

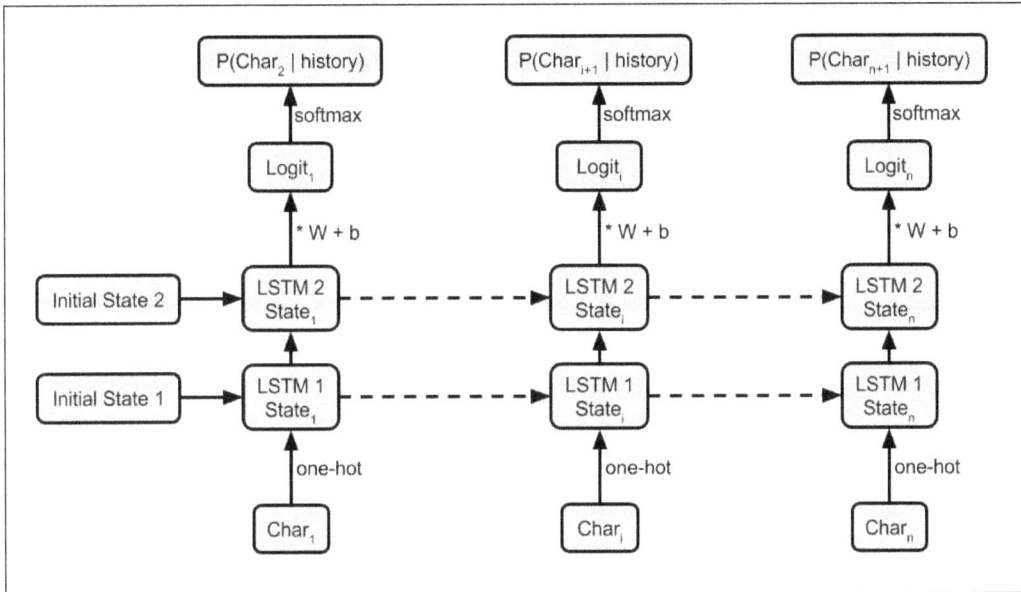

LSTM character language model unfolded

# Training

Now that we have defined the input, targets, and architecture of our network, let's define how to train it. The first step in training is defining a loss function that we want to minimize. This loss function describes the cost of outputting a wrong sequence of characters, given the input and targets. Because we are predicting the next character considering the previous characters, it is a classification problem and we will use cross-entropy loss. We do this by using the sparse_softmax_cross_entropy_with_logits TensorFlow function. This function takes the logit output of the network as input (before the softmax) and targets as class labels and computes the cross-entropy loss of each output with respect to its target. To reduce the loss over the full sequence and all the batches, we take the mean value of all of them.

Note that we flatten the targets to a one-dimensional vector first to make them compatible with the flattened logit output from our network:

```
# Flatten the targets to be compatible with the flattened logits
targets_flat = tf.reshape(targets, (-1, ))
# Get the loss over all outputs
loss = tf.nn.sparse_softmax_cross_entropy_with_logits(
    logits_flat, targets_flat)
# Reduce the loss to single value over all outputs
loss = tf.reduce_mean(loss)
```

Now that we have this loss function defined, it is possible to define the training operation in TensorFlow that will optimize our network of input and target batches. To execute the optimization, we will use the Adam optimizer; this helps stabilize gradient updates. The Adam optimizer is just a specific way of performing gradient descent in a more controlled way [28]. We will also clip the gradients to prevent exploding gradients:

```
# Get all variables that need to be optimised
trainable_variables = tf.trainable_variables()
# Compute and clip the gradients
gradients = tf.gradients(loss, trainable_variables)
gradients, _ = tf.clip_by_global_norm(gradients, 5)
# Apply the gradients to those variables with the Adam optimisation
algorithm.
optimizer = tf.train.AdamOptimizer(learning_rate=2e-3)
train_op = optimizer.apply_gradients(zip(gradients, trainable_
variables))
```

Having defined all the TensorFlow operations required for training, we can now start with the optimization in mini batches. If `data_feeder` is a generator that returns consecutive batches of input and targets, then we can train these batches by iteratively feeding in the input and target batches. We reset the initial state every 100 mini batches so that the network learns how to deal with the initial states in the beginning of sequences. You can save the model with a TensorFlow saver to reload it for sampling later:

```
with tf.Session() as session:
    session.run(tf.initialize_all_variables())
    for i in range(minibatch_iterations):
        input_batch, target_batch = next(data_feeder)
        loss, _ = sess.run(
            (loss, train_op),
            feed_dict={ inputs: input_batch,targets:
            target_batch})
```

```
    # Reset initial state every 100 minibatches
        if i % 100 == 0 and i != 0:
            for state in tf.python.util.nest.flatten(
                    state_variables):
                session.run(state.initializer)
```

# Sampling

Once our model is trained, we might want to sample the sequences from this model to generate text. We can initialize our sampling architecture with the same code we used for training the model, but we'd need to set `batch_size` to 1 and `sequence_length` to None. This way, we can generate a single string and sample sequences of different lengths. We can then initialize the parameters of the model with the parameters saved after training. To start with the sampling, we feed in an initial string (`prime_string`) to prime the state of the network. After this string is fed in, we can sample the next character based on the output distribution of the softmax function. We can then feed in this sampled character and get the output distribution for the next one. This process can be continued for a number of steps until a string of a specified size is generated:

```
    # Initialize state with priming string
    for character in prime_string:
        character_idx = label_map(character)
        # Get output distribution of next character
        output_distribution = session.run(
            probabilities,
            feed_dict={inputs: np.asarray(((character_idx)))})
    # Start sampling for sample_length steps
    for _ in range(sample_length):
        # Sample next character according to output distribution
        sample_label = np.random.choice(
            labels, size=(1), p=output_distribution(0, 0))
        output_sample += sample_label
        # Get output distribution of next character
        output_distribution = session.run(
            probabilities,
            feed_dict={inputs: np.asarray((label_map(character))))})
```

# Example training

Now that we have our code for training and sampling, we can train the network on Leo Tolstoy's *War and Peace* and sample what the network has learned every couple of batch iterations. Let's prime the network with the phrase "*She was born in the year*" and see how it completes it during training.

After 500 batches, we get this result: *She was born in the year sive but us eret tuke Tofflin e feale shoud pille saky doctonas laft the comssing hinder to gam the droved at ay vime.* The network has already picked up some distribution of characters and has come up with things that look like words.

After 5,000 batches, the network picks up a lot of different words and names: "*She was born in the year he had meaningly many of Seffer Zsites. Now in his crownchy-destruction, eccention, was formed a wolf of Veakov one also because he was congrary, that he suddenly had first did not reply.*" It still invents plausible looking words likes "congrary" and "eccention".

After 50,000 batches, the network outputs the following text: *She was born in the year 1813. At last the sky may behave the Moscow house there was a splendid chance that had to be passed the Rostóvs', all the times: sat retiring, showed them to confure the sovereigns.*" The network seems to have figured out that a year number is a very plausible words to follow up our prime string. Short strings of words seem to make sense, but the sentences on their own don't make sense yet.

After 500,000 batches, we stop the training and the network outputs this: "*She was born in the year 1806, when he entered his thought on the words of his name. The commune would not sacrifice him: "What is this?" asked Natásha. "Do you remember?""*. We can see that the network is now trying to make sentences, but the sentences are not coherent with each other. What is remarkable is that it models small conversations in full sentences at the end, including quotes and punctuation.

While not perfect, it is remarkable how the RNN language model is able to generate coherent phrases of text. We would like to encourage you at this point to experiment with different architectures, increase the size of the LSTM layers, put a third LSTM layer in the network, download more text data from the Internet, and see how much you can improve the current model.

The language models we have discussed so far are used in many different applications, ranging from speech recognition to creating intelligent chat bots that are able to build a conversation with a user. In the next section, we will briefly discuss deep learning speech recognition models in which language models play an important part.

# Speech recognition

In the previous sections, we saw how RNNs can be used to learn patterns of many different time sequences. In this section, we will look at how these models can be used for the problem of recognizing and understanding speech. We will give a brief overview of the speech recognition pipeline and provide a high-level view of how we can use neural networks in each part of the pipeline. In order to know more about the methods discussed in this section, we would like you to refer to the references.

## Speech recognition pipeline

Speech recognition tries to find a transcription of the most probable word sequence considering the acoustic observations provided; this is represented by the following:

*transcription = argmax(P(words | audio features))*

This probability function is typically modeled in different parts (note that the normalizing term P (audio features) is usually ignored):

$$P \ (words \mid audio \ features) = P \ (audio \ features \mid words) * P \ (words)$$

$$= P \ (audio \ features \mid phonemes) * P \ (phonemes \mid words) * P \ (words)$$

**What are phonemes?**

Phonemes are a basic unit of sound that define the pronunciation of words. For example, the word "bat" is composed of three phonemes /b/, /ae/, and /t/. Each phoneme is tied to a specific sound. Spoken English consists of around 44 phonemes.

Each of these probability functions will be modeled by different parts of the recognition system. A typical speech recognition pipeline takes in an audio signal and performs preprocessing and feature extraction. The features are then used in an acoustic model that tries to learn how to distinguish between different sounds and phonemes: *P (audio features | phonemes)*. These phonemes are then matched to characters or words with the help of pronunciation dictionaries: *P(phonemes | words)*. The probabilities of the words extracted from the audio signal are then combined with the probabilities of a language model, *P(words)*. The most likely sequence is then found via a decoding search step that searches for the most likely sequence(see *Decoding* section). A high-level overview of this speech recognition pipeline is described in the following figure:

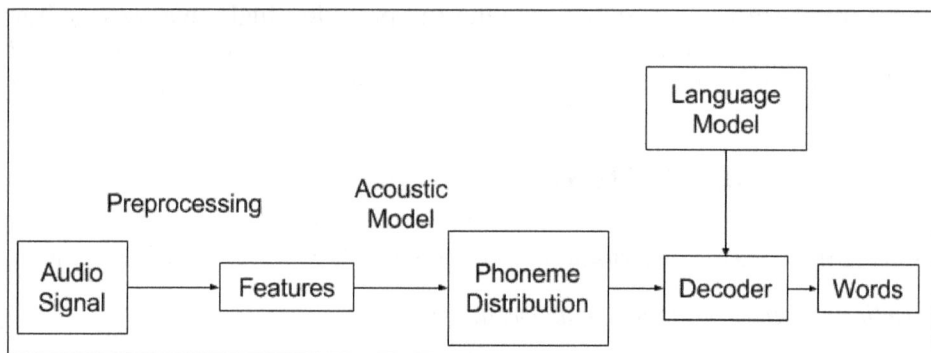

Overview of a typical speech recognition pipeline

Large, real-world vocabulary speech recognition pipelines are based on this same pipeline; however, they use a lot of tricks and heuristics in each step to make the problem tractable. While these details are out of the scope of this section, there is open source software available—Kaldi [29]—that allows you to train a speech recognition system with advanced pipelines.

In the next sections, we will briefly describe each of the steps in this standard pipeline and how deep learning can help improve these steps.

# Speech as input data

Speech is a type of sound that typically conveys information. It is a vibration that propagates through a medium, such as air. If these vibrations are between 20 Hz and 20 kHz, they are audible to humans. These vibrations can be captured and converted into a digital signal so that they can be used in audio signal processing on computers. They are typically captured by a microphone after which the continuous signal is sampled at discrete samples. A typical sample rate is 44.1 kHz, which means that the amplitude of the incoming audio signal is measured 44,100 times per second. Note that this is around twice the maximum human hearing frequency. A sampled recording of someone saying "hello world" is plotted in the following figure:

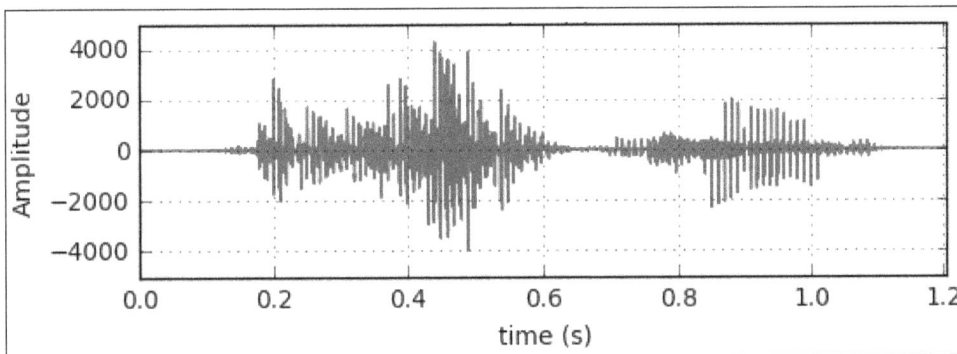

Speech signal of someone saying "hello world" in the time domain

# Preprocessing

The recording of the audio signal in the preceding figure is recorded over 1.2 seconds. To digitize the audio, it is sampled 44,100 times per second (44.1 kHz). This means that roughly 50,000 amplitude samples were taken for this 1.2-second audio signal.

For only a small example, these are a lot of points over the time dimension. To reduce the size of the input data, these audio signals are typically preprocessed to reduce the number of time steps before feeding them into speech recognition algorithms. A typical transformation transforms a signal to a spectrogram, which is a representation of how the frequencies in the signal change over time, see the next figure.

This spectral transformation is done by dividing the time signal in overlapping windows and taking the Fourier transform of each of these windows. The Fourier transform decomposes a signal over time into frequencies that make up the signal [30]. The resulting frequencies responses are compressed into fixed frequency bins. This array of frequency bins is also known as a filter banks. A filter bank is a collection of filters that separate out the signal in multiple frequency bands.

Say the previous "hello world" recording is divided into overlapping windows of 25 ms with a stride of 10 ms. The resulting windows are then transformed into a frequency space with the help of a windowed Fourier transform. This means that the amplitude information for each time step is transformed into amplitude information for each frequency. The final frequencies are mapped to 40 frequency bins according to a logarithmic scale, also known as the Mel scale. The resulting filter bank spectrogram is shown in the following figure . This transformation resulted in reducing the time dimension from 50,000 to 118 samples, where each sample is a vector of size 40.

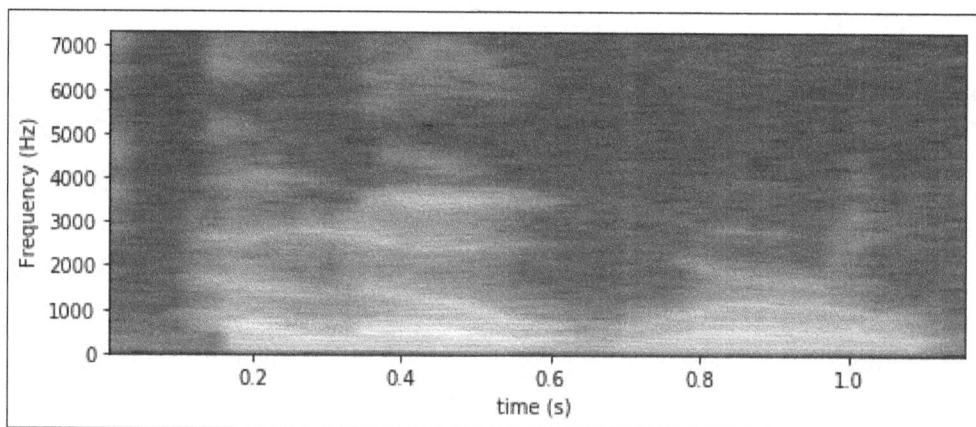

Mel spectrum of speech signal from the previous figure

Especially in older speech recognition systems, these Mel-scale filter banks are even more processed by decorrelation to remove linear dependencies. Typically, this is done by taking a **discrete cosine transform** (**DCT**) of the logarithm of the filter banks. This DCT is a variant of the Fourier transform. This signal transformation is also known as **Mel Frequency Cepstral Coefficients** (**MFCC**).

More recently, deep learning methods, such as convolutional neural networks, have learned some of these preprocessing steps [31], [32].

# Acoustic model

In speech recognition, we want to output the words being spoken as text. This can be done by learning a time-dependent model that takes in a sequence of audio features, as described in the previous section, and outputs a sequential distribution of possible words being spoken. This model is called the acoustic model.

The acoustic model tries to model the likelihood that a sequence of audio features was generated by a sequence of words or phonemes: *P (audio features | words) = P (audio features | phonemes) * P (phonemes | words)*.

A typical speech recognition acoustic model, before deep learning became popular, would use **hidden Markov models (HMMs)** to model the temporal variability of speech signals [33], [34]. Each HMM state emits a mixture of Gaussians to model the spectral features of the audio signal. The emitted Gaussians form a **Gaussian mixture model (GMM)**, and they determine how well each HMM state fits in a short window of acoustic features. HMMs are used to model the sequential structure of data, while GMMs model the local structure of the signal.

The HMM assumes that successive frames are independent given the hidden state of the HMM. Because of this strong conditional independence assumption, the acoustic features are typically decorrelated.

# Deep belief networks

The first step in using deep learning in speech recognition is to replace GMMs with **deep neural networks (DNN)** [35]. DNNs take a window of feature vectors as input and output the posterior probabilities of the HMM states: *P (HMM state | audio features)*.

The networks used in this step are typically pretrained as a general model on a window of spectral features. Usually, **deep belief networks (DBN)** are used to pretrain these networks. The generative pretraining creates many layers of feature detectors of increased complexity. Once generative pretraining is finished, the network is discriminatively fine-tuned to classify the correct HMM states, based on the spectral features. HMMs in these hybrid models are used to align the segment classifications provided by the DNNs to a temporal classification of the full label sequence. These DNN-HMM models have been shown to achieve better phone recognition than GMM-HMM models [36].

# Recurrent neural networks

This section describes how RNNs can be used to model sequential data. The problem with the straightforward application of RNNs on speech recognition is that the labels of the training data need to be perfectly aligned with the input. If the data isn't aligned well, then the input to output mapping will contain too much of noise for the network to learn anything. Some early attempts tried to model the sequential context of the acoustic features by using hybrid RNN-HMM models, where the RNNs would model the emission probabilities of the HMM models, much in the same way that DBNs are used [37].

Later experiments tried to train LSTMs (see section on *Long Short Term Memory*) to output the posterior probability of the phonemes at a given frame [38].

The next step in speech recognition would be to get rid of the necessity of having aligned labeled data and removing the need for hybrid HMM models.

# CTC

Standard RNN objective functions are defined independently for each sequence step, each step outputs its own independent label classification. This means that training data must be perfectly aligned with the target labels. However, a global objective function that maximizes the probability of a full correct labeling can be devised. The idea is to interpret the network outputs as a conditional probability distribution over all possible labeling sequences, given the full input sequence. The network can then be used as a classifier by searching for the most probable labeling given the input sequence.

**Connectionist Temporal Classification** (CTC) is an objective function that defines a distribution over all the alignments with all the output sequences [39]. It tries to optimize the overall edit distance between the output sequence and the target sequence. This edit distance is the minimum number of insertions, substitutions, and deletions required to change the output labeling to target labeling.

A CTC network has a softmax output layer for each step. This softmax function outputs label distributions for each possible label plus an extra blank symbol (Ø). This extra blank symbol represents that there is no relevant label at that time step. The CTC network will thus output label predictions at any point in the input sequence. The output is then translated into a sequence labeling by removing all the blanks and repeated labels from the paths. This corresponds to outputting a new label when the network switches from predicting no label to predicting a label or from predicting one label to another. For example, "ØaaØabØØ" gets translated into "aab". This has as effect that only the overall sequence of labels has to be correct, thus removing the need for aligned data.

Doing this reduction means that multiple output sequences can be reduced to the same output labeling. To find the most likely output labeling, we have to add all the paths that correspond to that labeling. The task of searching for this most probable output labeling is known as decoding (see the *Decoding* section).

An example of such a labeling in speech recognition could be outputting a sequence of phonemes, given a sequence of acoustic features. The CTC objective's function, built on top of an LSTM, has been to give state-of-the-art results on acoustic modeling and to remove the need of using HMMs to model temporal variability [40], [41].

# Attention-based models

An alternative to using the CTC sequence to sequence a model is an attention-based model [42]. These attention models have the ability to dynamically pay attention to parts of the input sequence. This allows them to automatically search for relevant parts of the input signal to predict the right phoneme, without having to have an explicit segmentation of the parts.

These attention-based sequence models are made up of an RNN that decodes a representation of the input into a sequence of labels, which are phonemes in this case. In practice, the input representation will be generated by a model that encodes the input sequence into a suitable representation. The first network is called the decoder network, while the latter is called the encoder network [43].

The decoder is guided by an attention model that focuses each step of the decoder on an attention window over encoded input. The attention model can be driven by a combination of context (what it is focusing on) or location-based information (where it is focusing on). The decoder can then use the previous information and the information from the attention window to output the next label (phoneme).

# Decoding

Once we model the phoneme distribution with the acoustic model and train a language model (see the *Language Modelling* section), we can combine them together with a pronunciation dictionary to get a probability function of words over audio features:

*P (words | audio features) = P (audio features | phonemes) * P (phonemes | words) * P (words)*

This probability function doesn't give us the final transcript yet; we still need to perform a search over the distribution of the word sequence to find the most likely transcription. This search process is called decoding. All possible paths of decoding can be illustrated in a lattice data structure:

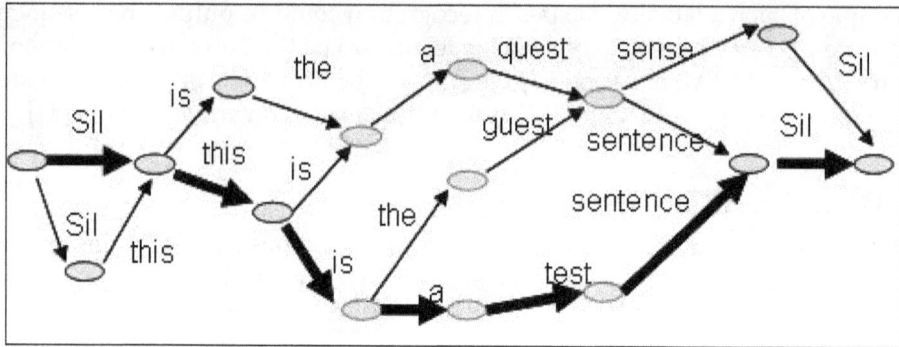

A pruned word lattice [44]

The most likely word sequence, given a sequence of audio features, is found by searching through all the possible word sequences [33]. A popular search algorithm based on dynamic programming that guarantees it could find the most likely sequence is the Viterbi algorithm [45]. This algorithm is a breadth-first search algorithm that is mostly associated with finding the most likely sequence of states in an HMM.

For large vocabulary speech recognition, the Viterbi algorithm becomes intractable for practical use. So in practice, heuristic search algorithms, such as beam search, are used to try and find the most likely sequence. The beam search heuristic only keeps the n-best solutions during the search and assumes that all the rest don't lead to the most likely sequence.

Many different decoding algorithms exist [46] and the problem of finding the best transcription from the probability function is mostly seen as unsolved.

# End-to-end models

We want to conclude this chapter by mentioning end-to-end techniques. Deep learning methods, such as CTC [47], [48] and attention based models [49], have allowed us to learn the full speech recognition pipeline in an end-to-end fashion. They do so without modeling phonemes explicitly. This means that these end-to-end models will learn acoustic and language models in one single model and directly output a distribution over words. These models illustrate the power of deep learning by combining everything in one model; with this, the model becomes conceptually easier to understand. We speculate that this will lead to speech recognition being recognized as a solved problem in the next few years.

# Summary

In the beginning of this chapter, we learned what RNNs are, how to train them, what problems might occur during training, and how to solve these problems. In the second part, we described the problem of language modeling and how RNNs help us solve some of the difficulties in modeling languages. The third section brought this information together in the form of a practical example on how to train a character-level language model to generate text based on Leo Tolstoy's *War and Peace*. The last section gave a brief overview of how deep learning, and especially RNNs, can be applied to the problem of speech recognition.

The RNNs discussed in this chapter are very powerful methods that have been very promising when it comes to a lot of tasks, such as language modeling and speech recognition. They are especially suited for modeling sequential problems where they could discover patterns over sequences.

# Bibliography

- [1] Siegelmann, H.T. (1995). "Computation Beyond the Turing Limit". Science. 238 (28): 632–637. URL: http://binds.cs.umass.edu/papers/1995_Siegelmann_Science.pdf

- [2] Alex Graves and Greg Wayne and Ivo Danihelka (2014). "Neural Turing Machines". CoRR URL: https://arxiv.org/pdf/1410.5401v2.pdf

- [3] Yann LeCun, Yoshua Bengio & Geoffrey Hinton (2015). "Deep Learning". Nature 521. URL: http://www.nature.com/nature/journal/v521/n7553/full/nature14539.html

- [4] Oriol Vinyals and Alexander Toshev and Samy Bengio and Dumitru Erhan (2014). "Show and Tell: {A} Neural Image Caption Generator". CoRR. URL: https://arxiv.org/pdf/1411.4555v2.pdf

- [5] Kyunghyun Cho et al. (2014). "Learning Phrase Representations using RNN Encoder-Decoder for Statistical Machine Translation". CoRR. URL: https://arxiv.org/pdf/1406.1078v3.pdf

- [6] Ilya Sutskever et al. (2014). "Sequence to Sequence Learning with Neural Networks". NIPS'14. URL: http://papers.nips.cc/paper/5346-sequence-to-sequence-learning-with-neural-networks.pdf

- [7] Andrej Karpathy (2015). "The Unreasonable Effectiveness of Recurrent Neural Networks". URL: http://karpathy.github.io/2015/05/21/rnn-effectiveness/

- [8] Paul J. Werbos (1990). "Backpropagation Through Time: What It Does and How to Do It" Proceedings of the IEEE. URL: `http://axon.cs.byu.edu/~martinez/classes/678/Papers/Werbos_BPTT.pdf`

- [9] Razvan Pascanu and Tomas Mikolov and Yoshua Bengio. (2012). "Understanding the exploding gradient problem". URL: `http://proceedings.mlr.press/v28/pascanu13.pdf`

- [10] Yoshua Bengio et al. (1994). "Learning long-term dependencies with gradient descent is difficult". URL: `http://proceedings.mlr.press/v28/pascanu13.pdf`

- [11] Razvan Pascanu and Tomas Mikolov and Yoshua Bengio. (2012). "Understanding the exploding gradient problem". URL: `http://proceedings.mlr.press/v28/pascanu13.pdf`

- [12] James Martens, Ilya Sutskever. (2011). "Learning Recurrent Neural Networks with Hessian-Free Optimization". URL: `http://www.icml-2011.org/papers/532_icmlpaper.pdf`

- [13] Ilya Sutskever et al. (2013). "On the importance of initialization and momentum in deep learning". URL: `http://proceedings.mlr.press/v28/sutskever13.pdf`

- [14] Geoffrey Hinton & Tijmen Tieleman. (2014) "Neural Networks for Machine Learning - Lecture 6a - Overview of mini-batch gradient descent". URL: `http://www.cs.toronto.edu/~tijmen/csc321/slides/lecture_slides_lec6.pdf`

- [15] Martin Riedmiller und Heinrich Braun (1992). "Rprop - A Fast Adaptive Learning Algorithm" URL: `http://axon.cs.byu.edu/~martinez/classes/678/Papers/riedmiller92rprop.pdf`

- [16] Sepp Hochreiter and Jurgen Schmidhuber (1997). "Long Short-Term Memory". URL: `http://www.bioinf.jku.at/publications/older/2604.pdf`

- [17] Gers et al. (2000) "Learning to Forget: Continual Prediction with LSTM" URL: `https://pdfs.semanticscholar.org/1154/0131eae85b2e11d53df7f1360eeb6476e7f4.pdf`

- [18] Nikhil Buduma (2015) "A Deep Dive into Recurrent Neural Nets" URL: `http://nikhilbuduma.com/2015/01/11/a-deep-dive-into-recurrent-neural-networks/`

- [19] Klaus Greff et al. (2015). "LSTM: A Search Space Odyssey". URL: `https://arxiv.org/pdf/1503.04069v1.pdf`

- [20] Yoshua Bengio et al. (2003). "A Neural Probabilistic Language Model". URL: `https://papers.nips.cc/paper/1839-a-neural-probabilistic-language-model.pdf`

- [21] Christopher Olah (2014) "Deep Learning, NLP, and Representations". URL: `http://colah.github.io/posts/2014-07-NLP-RNNs-Representations/`

- [22] Tomas Mikolov et al. (2013) "Distributed Representations of Words and Phrases and their Compositionality". URL: `http://papers.nips.cc/paper/5021-distributedrepresentations-of-words-and-phrases-and-theircompositionality.pdf`

- [23] Tomas Mikolov et al. (2013). "Efficient Estimation of Word Representations in Vector Space". URL: `https://arxiv.org/pdf/1301.3781.pdf`

- [24] Tomas Mikolov et al. (2013). "Linguistic Regularities in Continuous Space Word Representations". URL: `https://www.microsoft.com/en-us/research/wp-content/uploads/2016/02/rvecs.pdf`

- [25] Thomas Mikolov et al. (2010) "Recurrent neural network based language model". URL: `http://www.fit.vutbr.cz/research/groups/speech/publi/2010/mikolov_interspeech2010_IS100722.pdf`

- [26] Frederic Morin and Yoshua Bengio (2005). "Hierarchical probabilistic neural network language model". URL: `http://www.iro.umontreal.ca/~lisa/pointeurs/hierarchical-nnlm-aistats05.pdf`

- [27] Alex Graves (2013). "Generating Sequences With Recurrent Neural Networks". URL: `https://arxiv.org/pdf/1308.0850.pdf`

- [28] Diederik P. Kingma and Jimmy Ba (2014). "Adam: A Method for Stochastic Optimization". URL: `https://arxiv.org/pdf/1412.6980.pdf`

- [29] Daniel Povey et al. (2011) "The Kaldi Speech Recognition Toolkit". URL: `http://kaldi-asr.org/`

- [30] Hagit Shatkay. (1995). "The Fourier Transform - A Primer". URL: `https://pdfs.semanticscholar.org/fe79/085198a13f7bd7ee95393dcb82e715537add.pdf`

- [31] Dimitri Palaz et al. (2015). "Analysis of CNN-based Speech Recognition System using Raw Speech as Input". URL: `https://ronan.collobert.com/pub/matos/2015_cnnspeech_interspeech`

- [32] Yedid Hoshen et al. (2015) "Speech Acoustic Modeling from Raw Multichannel Waveforms". URL: `https://static.googleusercontent.com/media/research.google.com/en//pubs/archive/43290.pdf`

- [33] Mark Gales and Steve Young. (2007). "The Application of Hidden Markov Models in Speech Recognition". URL: `http://mi.eng.cam.ac.uk/~mjfg/mjfg_NOW.pdf`

- [34] L.R. Rabiner. (1989). "A tutorial on hidden Markov models and selected applications in speech recognition". URL: `http://www.cs.ubc.ca/~murphyk/Bayes/rabiner.pdf`

- [35] Abdel-rahman Mohamed et al. (2011). "Acoustic Modeling Using Deep Belief Networks". URL: `http://www.cs.toronto.edu/~asamir/papers/speechDBN_jrnl.pdf`

- [36] Geoffrey Hinton et al. (2012) "Deep Neural Networks for Acoustic Modeling in Speech Recognition". URL: `https://www.microsoft.com/en-us/research/wp-content/uploads/2016/02/HintonDengYuEtAl-SPM2012.pdf`

- [37] Tony Robinson et al. (1996) "The Use of Recurrent Neural Networks in Continuous Speech Recognition". URL: `http://www.cstr.ed.ac.uk/downloads/publications/1996/rnn4csr96.pdf`

- [38] Graves A, Schmidhuber J. (2005) "Framewise phoneme classification with bidirectional LSTM and other neural network architectures.". URL: `https://www.cs.toronto.edu/~graves/nn_2005.pdf`

- [39] Alex Graves et al. (2006). "Connectionist Temporal Classification: Labelling Unsegmented Sequence Data with Recurrent Neural Networks". URL: `http://www.cs.toronto.edu/~graves/icml_2006.pdf`

- [40] Alex Graves et al. (2013) "Speech Recognition with Deep Recurrent Neural Networks". URL: `https://arxiv.org/pdf/1303.5778.pdf`

- [41] Dario Amodei et al. (2015). "Deep Speech 2: End-to-End Speech Recognition in English and Mandarin". URL: `https://arxiv.org/pdf/1512.02595.pdf`

- [42] Jan Chorowski et al. (2015). "Attention-Based Models for Speech Recognition", URL: `https://arxiv.org/pdf/1506.07503.pdf`

- [43] Dzmitry Bahdanau et al. (2015) "Neural Machine Translation by Jointly Learning to Align and Translate" URL: `https://arxiv.org/pdf/1409.0473.pdf`

- [44] The Institute for Signal and Information Processing. "Lattice tools". URL: `https://www.isip.piconepress.com/projects/speech/software/legacy/lattice_tools/`

- [45] G.D. Forney. (1973). "The viterbi algorithm". URL: `http://www.systems.caltech.edu/EE/Courses/EE127/EE127A/handout/ForneyViterbi.pdf`

- [46] Xavier L. Aubert (2002). "An overview of decoding techniques for large vocabulary continuous speech recognition". URL: `http://www.cs.cmu.edu/afs/cs/user/tbergkir/www/11711fa16/aubert_asr_decoding.pdf`

- [47] Alex Graves and Navdeep Jaitly. (2014). "Towards End-To-End Speech Recognition with Recurrent Neural Networks" URL: `http://proceedings.mlr.press/v32/graves14.pdf`

- [48] Awni Hannun. (2014) "Deep Speech: Scaling up end-to-end speech recognition". URL: `https://arxiv.org/pdf/1412.5567.pdf`

- [49] William Chan (2015). "Listen, Attend and Spell" URL: `https://arxiv.org/pdf/1508.01211.pdf`

# 7
# Deep Learning for Board Games

You may have read sci-fi novels from the 50's and 60's; they are full of visions of what life in the 21st century would look like. They imagined a world of people with personal jet packs, underwater cities, intergalactic travel, flying cars, and truly intelligent robots capable of independent thought. The 21st century has arrived now; sadly, we are not going to get those flying cars, but thanks to deep learning, we may get that robot.

What does this have to do with deep learning for board games? In the next two chapters, including the current one, we will look at how to build **Artificial Intelligence (AI)** that can learn game environments. Reality has a vast space of possibilities. Doing even simple human tasks, such as getting a robot arm to pick up objects, requires analyzing huge amounts of sensory data and controlling many continuous response variables for the movement of the arms.

Games act as a great playing field for testing general purpose learning algorithms. They give you an environment of large, but manageable possibilities. Also, when it comes to computer games, we know that humans can learn to play a game just from the pixels visible on the screen and the most minor of instructions. If we input the same pixels plus an objective into a computer agent, we know we have a solvable problem, given the right algorithm. In fact, for the computer, the problem is easier because a human being identifies that the things they seeing in their field of vision are actually game pixels, as opposed to the area around the screen. This is why so many researchers are looking at games as a great place to start developing true AI's—self-learning machines that can operate independently from us. Also, if you like games, it's lots of fun.

In this chapter, we will cover the different tools used for solving board games, such as checkers and chess. Eventually, we'll build up enough knowledge to be able to understand and implement the kind of deep learning solution that was used to build AlphaGo, the AI that defeated the greatest human Go player. We'll use a variety of deep learning techniques to accomplish this. The next chapter will build on this knowledge and cover how deep learning can be used to learn how to play computer games, such as Pong and Breakout.

The full list of concepts that we will cover across both the chapters is as follows:

- The min-max algorithm
- Monte-Carlo Tree Search
- Reinforcement learning
- Policy gradients
- Q-learning
- Actor-Critic
- Model-based approaches

We will use a few different terms to describe tasks and their solutions. The following are some of the definitions. They all use the example of a basic maze game as it is a good, simple example of a reinforcement learning environment. In a maze game, there are a set of locations with paths between them. There is an agent in this maze that can use the paths to move between the different locations. Some locations have a reward associated with them. The agent's objective is to navigate their way through the maze to get the best possible reward.

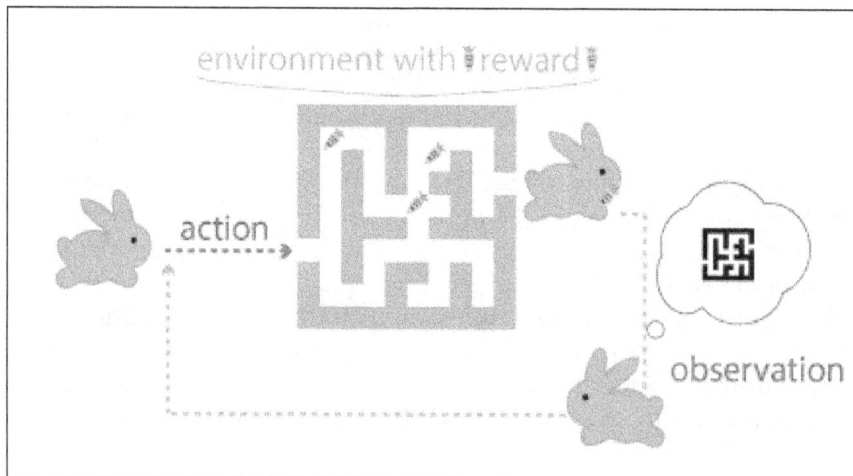

Figure 1

- **Agent** is the entity for which we are trying to learn actions. In the game, this is the player that will try to find its way through the maze.

- **Environment** is a world/level/game in which the agent operates, that is, the maze itself.

- **Reward** is the feedback that the agent gets within the environment. In the case of this example maze game, it might be the exit square or the carrots in the image that the agent is trying to collect. Some mazes may also have traps that give a negative reward, which the agent should try to avoid.

- **State** refers to all of the information available to the agent about its current environment. In a maze, the state is simply the agent's position.

- **Action** is a possible response, or set of responses, that an agent can make. In a maze, this is a potential path that an agent can take from one state to another.

- **Control policy** determines what actions the agent will take. In the context of deep learning, this is the neural network that we will train. Other policies might be selecting actions at random or selecting actions based on the code that the programmer has written.

A lot of this chapter is code-heavy, so as an alternative to copying all the samples from the book, you can find the full code in a GitHub repository at `https://github.com/DanielSlater/PythonDeepLearningSamples`. All the examples in the chapters are presented using TensorFlow, but the concepts could be translated into other deep learning frameworks.

# Early game playing AI

Building AI's to play games started in the 50's with researchers building programs that played checkers and chess. These two games have a few properties in common:

- They are zero-sum games. Any reward that one player receives is a corresponding loss to the other player and vice versa. When one player wins, the other loses. There is no possibility of cooperation. For example, consider a game such as the prisoner's dilemma; here, the two players can agree to cooperate and both receive a smaller reward.

- They are both games of perfect information. The entire state of the game is always known to both the players unlike a game such as poker, where the exact cards that your opponents are holding is unknown. This fact reduces the complexity that the AI must handle. It also means that a decision about what the best move can be made is based on just the current state. In poker, the hypothetical optimal decision about how to play would require information that is not just on your current hand and how much money is available to each player, but also about the playing styles of the opponents and what they had bid in the previous positions they were in.

- Both games are deterministic. If a given move is made by either player, then that will result in an exact next state. In some games, the play may be based on a dice roll or random drawing of a card from a deck; in these cases, there would be many possible next states to consider.

The combination of perfect information and determinism in chess and checkers means that given the current state, we can exactly know what state we will be in if the current player takes an action. This property also chains if we have a state, then takes an action leading to a new state. We can again take an action in this new state to keep playing as far into the future as we want.

To experiment with some of the approaches of mastering board games, we will give examples using a Python implementation of the game called *Tic-Tac-Toe*. Also known as *noughts and crosses,* this is a simple game where players take turns making marks on a 3 by 3 grid. The first player to get three marks in a row wins. *Tic-Tac-Toe* is another deterministic, zero sum, perfect information game and is chosen here because a Python implementation of it is a lot simpler than chess. In fact, the whole game can be done in less than a page of code, which will be shown later in this chapter.

# Using the min-max algorithm to value game states

Say we want to work out the best move in a zero sum, deterministic, perfect information game. How can we do this? Well, first off, given that we have perfect information, we know exactly what moves are available to us. Given that the game is deterministic, we know exactly what state the game will change to due to each of those moves. The same is then true for the opponent's move as well; we know exactly what possible moves they have and how the state would look as a result of each of those moves.

One approach for finding the best move would be to construct a full tree of every possible move for each player at each state until we reach a state where the game is over. This end state of the game is also known as the terminal state. We can assign a value to this terminal state; a win could carry the value 1, a draw 0, and a loss -1. These values reflect the states' desirability to us. We would prefer a win than a draw and a draw to a loss. *Figure 2* shows an example of this:

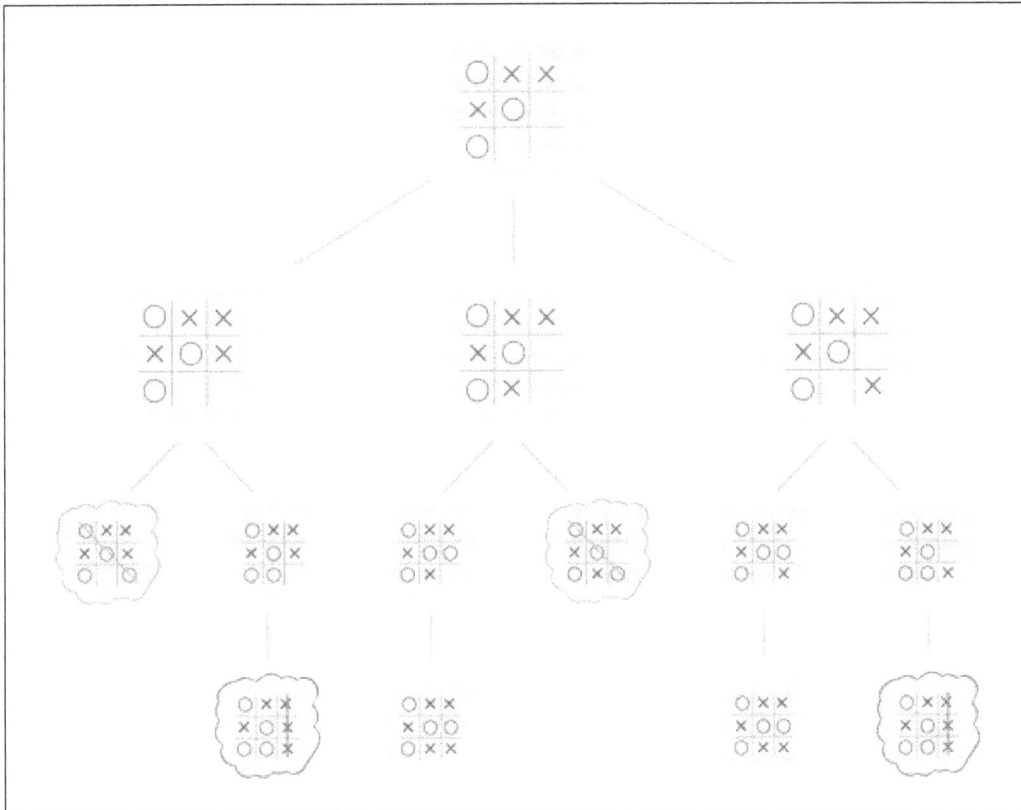

Figure 2: Tree of all the states of tic-tac-toe

In a terminal state, we can go back to the state where the player chose the move that led to the terminal state. That player, whose objective is to find the best possible move, can determine exactly what value they will get from the actions they would take, which is the terminal state that they eventually led the game to. They will obviously want to select the move that would lead to the best possible value for themselves. If they have a choice of actions that would either lead to winning the terminal state or losing it, they will select the one that leads to a winning state.

The value of the state where terminal states are selected can then be marked with the value of the best possible action that the player could make. This gives us the value to that player of being in this state. But we are playing a two-player game here, so if we go back a state, we would be in a state where the other player is due to make a move. We now on our graph have the value that this opponent will get from their actions in this state.

This being a zero sum game, we want our opponent to do as badly as possible, so we will select the move that leads to the lowest value state for them. If we keep going back through the graph of states, marking all the states with the value of the best state that any action could lead to, we can determine exactly what is the best action in the current state.

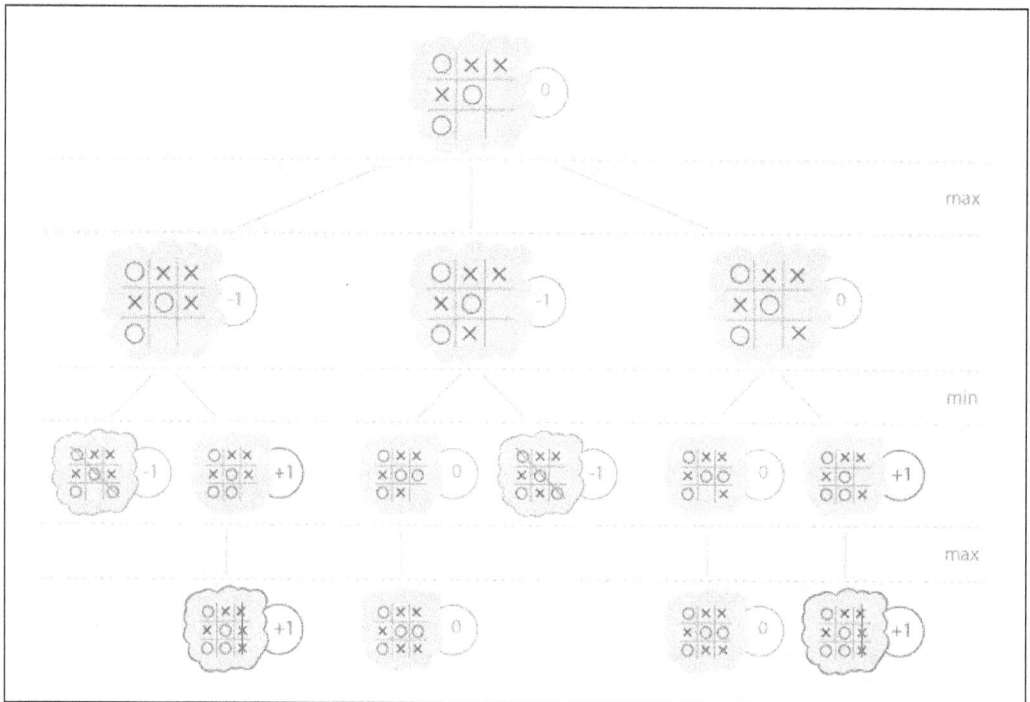

Figure 3. Min-max algorithm

In this way, a complete tree of the game can be constructed, showing us the best move that we can make in the current state. This approach is called the min-max algorithm and is what the early researchers used for their chess and checkers games.

Though this approach tells us the exact best move for any zero sum, deterministic, perfect information game, it unfortunately has a major problem. Chess has on average about 30 possible moves per turn and games last on average 40 turns. So to build a graph from the first state in chess to all the terminal states would require approximately $30^{40}$ states. Many orders of magnitude larger than this is possible on the world's best hardware. When talking about games, the number of moves a player can take per turn is referred to as the **breadth** and the number of moves the game takes per turn as the **depth**.

To make chess tractable with the Min-Max algorithm, we need to massively reduce the depth of our search. Rather than calculate the whole tree through to the end of the game, we can construct our tree down to a fixed depth, say six moves on from the current state. At each leaf that is not an actual terminal state, we can use an evaluation function to estimate how likely the player is to win in that state.

For chess, a good evaluation function is to do a weighted count of the number of pieces available with each player. So, one point for a pawn, three for a bishop or knight, five for a rook, and eight for a queen. If I have three pawns and a knight, I have six points; similarly, if you have two pawns and a rook, you have seven points. Therefore, you are one point ahead. A player with more pieces left generally tends to win in chess. However, as any keen chess player who has played against a good exchange sacrifice will know, this evaluation function has its limits.

# Implementing a Python Tic-Tac-Toe game

Let's build a basic implementation of *Tic-Tac-Toe* so we can see what an implementation of the min-max algorithm looks like. If you do not feel like copying all of this, you can find the full code in the GitHub repository `https://github.com/DanielSlater/PythonDeepLearningSamples` in the `tic_tac_toe.py` file.

In the game board, we will be represented by a 3 x 3 tuple of integers. Tuples are used instead of lists so that later on, we can get equality between matching board states. In this case, **0** represents a square that has not been played in. The two players will be marked **1** and **-1**. If player one makes a move in a square, that square will be marked with their number. So here we go:

```
def new_board():
    return ((0,0,0),
            (0,0,0),
            (0,0,0))
```

The `new_board` method will be called before the play for a fresh board, ready for the players to make their moves on:

```
def apply_move(board_state, move, side):
    move_x, move_y = move
    state_list = list(list(s) for s in board_state)
    state_list[move_x][move_y] = side
    return tuple(tuple(s) for s in state_list)
```

The `apply_move` method takes one of the 3 x 3 tuples for `board_state` and returns a new `board_state` with the move by the given side applied. A move will be a tuple of length 2, containing the coordinate of the space that we want to move to as two integers. Side will an integer representing the player who is playing the move, either 1 or -1:

```
import itertools

def available_moves(board_state):
    for x, y in itertools.product(range(3), range(3)):
        if board_state[x][y] == 0:
            yield (x, y)
```

This method gives us the list of legal moves for a given 3 x 3 `board_state`, which is simply all the non-zero squares. Now we just need a method to determine whether a player has the three winning marks in a row:

```
def has_3_in_a_line(line):
    return all(x==-1 for x in line) | all(x==1 for x in line)
```

The `has_3_in_a_line` takes a sequence of three squares from the board. If all are either 1 or -1, it means one of the players has gotten three in a row and has won. We then need to run this method against each possible line on the Tic-Tac-Toe board to determine whether a player has won:

```
def has_winner(board_state):
    # check rows
    for x in range(3):
        if has_3_in_a_line(board_state[x]):
            return board_state[x][0]
    # check columns
    for y in range(3):
        if has_3_in_a_line([i[y] for i in board_state]):
            return board_state[0][y]
    # check diagonals
    if has_3_in_a_line([board_state[i][i] for i in range(3)]):
        return board_state[0][0]
```

```
        if has_3_in_a_line([board_state[2 - i][i] for i in range(3)]):
            return board_state[0][2]
    return 0 # no one has won
```

With just these few functions, you can now play a game of *Tic-Tac-Toe*. Simply start by getting a new board, then have the players successively choose moves and apply those moves to board_state. If we find that there are no available moves left, the game is a draw. Otherwise, if has_winner returns either 1 or -1, it means one of the players has won. Let's write a simple function for running a Tic-Tac-Toe game with the moves decided by methods that we pass in, which will be the control policies of the different AI players that we will try out:

```
def play_game(plus_player_func, minus_player_func):
    board_state = new_board()
    player_turn = 1
```

We declare the method and take it to the function that will choose the action for each player. Each player_func will take two arguments: the first being the current board_state and the second being the side that the player is playing, 1 or -1. The player_turn variable will keep track of this for us:

```
    while True:
        _available_moves = list(available_moves(board_state))
        if len(_available_moves) == 0:
            print("no moves left, game ended a draw")
            return 0.
```

This is the main loop of the game. First we have to check whether there are any available moves left on board_state; if there are, the game is not over and it is a draw:

```
        if player_turn > 0:
            move = plus_player_func(board_state, 1)
        else:
            move = minus_player_func(board_state, -1)
```

Run the function associated with whichever player's turn it is to decide a move:

```
        if move not in _avialable_moves:
            # if a player makes an invalid move the other player
            wins
            print("illegal move ", move)
            return -player_turn
```

If either player makes an illegal move, that is an automatic loss. Agents should know better:

```
board_state = apply_move(board_state, move, player_turn)
print(board_state)

winner = has_winner(board_state)
if winner != 0:
    print("we have a winner, side: %s" % player_turn)
    return winner
player_turn = -player_turn
```

Apply the move to `board_state` and check whether we have a winner. If we do, end the game; if we don't, switch `player_turn` to the other player and loop back around.

Here is how we could write a method for a control policy that would choose actions completely at random out of the available legal moves:

```
def random_player(board_state, side):
    moves = list(available_moves(board_state))
    return random.choice(moves)
```

Let's run two random players against each other and check whether the output might look something like this:

```
play_game(random_player, random_player)


((0, 0, 0), (0, 0, 0), [1, 0, 0])
([0, -1, 0], (0, 0, 0), [1, 0, 0])
([0, -1, 0], [0, 1, 0], [1, 0, 0])
([0, -1, 0], [0, 1, 0], [1, -1, 0])
([0, -1, 0], [0, 1, 1], [1, -1, 0])
([0, -1, 0], [0, 1, 1], [1, -1, -1])
([0, -1, 1], [0, 1, 1], [1, -1, -1])
we have a winner, side: 1
```

Now we have a good way of trying out different control policies on a board game, so let's go about writing something a bit better. We can start with a min-max function that should play at a much higher standard than our current random players. The full code for the min-max function is also available in the GitHub repo in the `min_max.py` file.

Tic-tac-toe is a game with a small space of possibilities, so we could simply run a min-max for the whole game from the board's starting position until we have gone through every possible move for every player. But it is good practice to still use an evaluation function, as for most other games we might play, this will not be the case. The evaluation function here will give us one point for getting two in a line if the third space is empty; it'll be the opposite if our opponent achieves this. First, we will need a method for scoring each individual line that we might make. The `score_line` will take sequences of length 3 and score them:

```
def score_line(line):
    minus_count = line.count(-1)
    plus_count = line.count(1)
    if plus_count == 2 and minus_count == 0:
        return 1
    elif minus_count == 2 and plus_count == 0:
        return -1
    return 0
```

Then the `evaluate` method simply runs through each possible line on the tic-tac-toe board and sums them up:

```
def evaluate(board_state):
    score = 0
    for x in range(3):
        score += score_line(board_state[x])
    for y in range(3):
        score += score_line([i[y] for i in board_state])
    #diagonals
    score += score_line([board_state[i][i] for i in range(3)])
    score += score_line([board_state[2-i][i] for i in range(3)])

    return score
```

Then, we come to the actual `min_max` algorithm method:

```
def min_max(board_state, side, max_depth):
    best_score = None
    best_score_move = None
```

The first two arguments to the method, which we are already familiar with, are
`board_state` and `side`; however, `max_depth` is new. Min-max is a recursive
algorithm, and `max_depth` will be the maximum number of recursive calls we will
make before we stop going down the tree and just evaluate it to get the result. Each
time we call `min_max` recursively, we will reduce `max_depth` by 1, stopping to
evaluate when we hit 0:

```
moves = list(available_moves(board_state))
if not moves:
    return 0, None
```

If there are no moves to make, then there is no need to evaluate anything; it is a
draw, so let's return with a score of 0:

```
for move in moves:
    new_board_state = apply_move(board_state, move, side)
```

Now we will run through each legal move and create a `new_board_state` with that
move applied:

```
winner = has_winner(new_board_state)
if winner != 0:
    return winner * 10000, move
```

Check whether the game is already won in this `new_board_state`. There is no
need to do any more recursive calling if the game is already won. Here, we are
multiplying the winner's score by 1,000; this is just an arbitrary large number so that
an actual win or loss is always considered better/worse than the most extreme result
we might get from a call to `evaluate`:

```
else:
    if max_depth <= 1:
        score = evaluate(new_board_state)
    else:
        score, _ = min_max(new_board_state, -side, max_depth -
1)
```

If you don't already have a winning position, then the real meat of the algorithm starts. If you have reached `max_depth`, then now is the time to evaluate the current `board_state` to get our heuristic for how favorable the current position is to the first player. If you haven't reached `max_depth`, then recursively call `min_max` with a lower `max_depth` until you hit the bottom:

```
if side > 0:
    if best_score is None or score > best_score:
        best_score = score
        best_score_move = move
else:
    if best_score is None or score < best_score:
        best_score = score
        best_score_move = move
return best_score, best_score_move
```

Now that we have our evaluation for the score in `new_board_state`, we want either the best or worst scoring position depending on which side we are. We keep track of which move leads to this in the `best_score_move` variable, which we return to with the score at the end of the method.

A `min_max_player` method can now be created to go to our earlier `play_game` method:

```
def min_max_player(board_state, side):
    return min_max(board_state, side, 5)[1]
```

Now if we run a series of games with `random_player` against a `min_max` player, we will find that the min_max player wins almost every time.

The min max algorithm, though important to understand, is never used in practice because there is a better version of it: min max with alpha beta pruning. This takes advantage of the fact that certain branches of the tree can be ignored or pruned, without needing to be fully evaluated. Alpha beta pruning will produce the same result as min max but with, on average, half as much search time.

To explain the idea behind alpha beta pruning, let's consider that while building our min-max tree, half of the nodes are trying to make decisions to maximize the score and the other half to minimize it. As we start evaluating some of the leaves, we get results that are good for both min and max decisions. If taking a certain path through the tree scores, say -6, the min branch knows it can get this score by following the branch. The thing that stops it from using this score is that max decisions has to make the decisions, and it cannot choose a leaf favorable to the min node.

But as more leaves are evaluated, another might be good for the max node, with a score of +5. The max node will never choose a worse outcome than this. But now that we have a score for both min and max, we know if we start going down a branch where the best score for min is worse than -6 and the best score for max is worse than +5, then neither min nor max will choose this branch, and we can save on the evaluation of that whole branch.

The alpha in alpha beta pruning stores the best result that the max decisions can achieve. The beta stores the best result (lowest score) that the min decisions can achieve. If alpha is ever greater than or equal to beta, we know we can skip further evaluation of the current branch we are on. This is because both the decisions already have better options.

*Figure 4* gives an example of this. Here see that from the very first leaf itself, we can set an alpha value of 0. This is because once the max player has found a score of 0 in a branch, they need never choose a lower score. Next, in the third leaf across, the score is 0 again, so the min player can set their beta score to 0. The branch that reads *branch ignored* no longer needs to be evaluated because both alpha and beta are 0.

To understand this, consider all the possible results that we could get from evaluating the branch. If it were to result in a score of +1, then the min player would simply choose an already existing branch where it had scored 0. In this case, the branch to the ignored branches left. If the score results in -1, then the max player would simply choose the left most branch in the image where they can get 0. Finally, if it results in a score of 0, it means no one has improved, so the evaluation of our position remains unchanged. You will never get a result where evaluating a branch would change the overall evaluation of the position. Here is an example of the min max method modified to use alpha beta pruning:

```
import sys

def
```

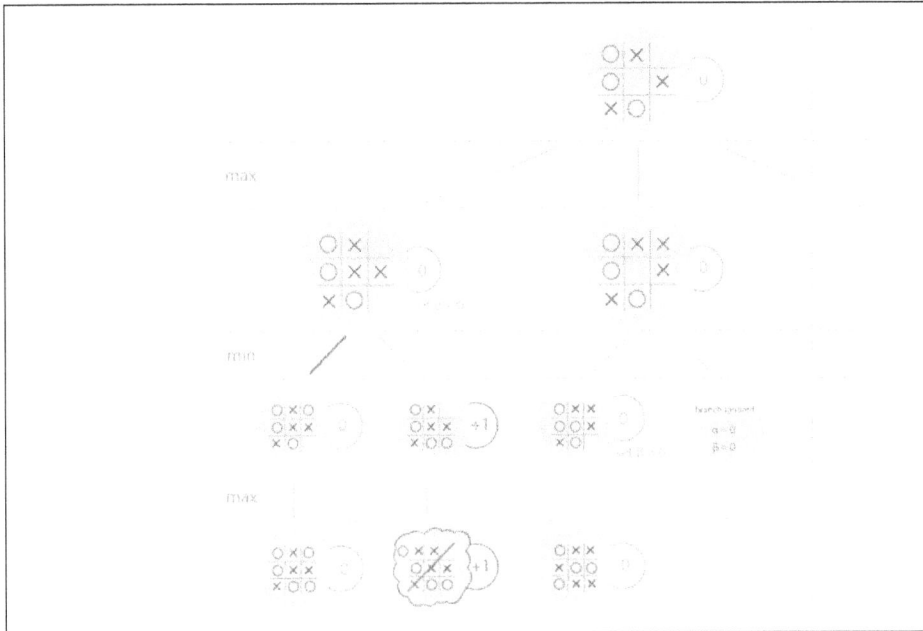

Figure 4: Min max method with alpha beta pruning

```
min_max_alpha_beta(board_state, side, max_depth,
                   alpha=-sys.float_info.max,
                   beta=sys.float_info.max):
```

We now pass in both `alpha` and `beta` as parameters; we stop searching through the branches that are either less than alpha or more than beta:

```
best_score_move = None
moves = list(available_moves(board_state))
if not moves:
    return 0, None

for move in moves:
    new_board_state = apply_move(board_state, move, side)
    winner = has_winner(new_board_state)
    if winner != 0:
        return winner * 10000, move
    else:
        if max_depth <= 1:
            score = evaluate(new_board_state)
        else:
            score, _ = min_max_alpha_beta(new_board_state,
            -side, max_depth - 1, alpha, beta)
```

Now when we recursively call `min_max_alpha_beta`, we pass in our new alpha and beta values that may have been updated as part of the search:

```
if side > 0:
    if score > alpha:
        alpha = score
        best_score_move = move
```

The `side > 0` expression means that we are looking to maximize our score, so we will store the score in the alpha variable if it's better than our current alpha:

```
else:
    if score < beta:
        beta = score
        best_score_move = move
```

If `side` is < 0 we are minimizing, so store the lowest scores in the beta variable:

```
if alpha >= beta:
    break
```

If alpha is greater than beta, then this branch cannot improve the current score, so we stop searching it:

```
return alpha if side > 0 else beta, best_score_move
```

In 1997, IBM created a chess program called *Deep Blue*. It was the first to beat the reigning world chess champion Garry Kasparov. While an amazing achievement, it would be hard to call *Deep Blue* intelligent. Though, it has huge computational power, and its underlying algorithm is just the same min-max algorithm from the 50's. The only major difference is that *Deep Blue* took advantage of the opening theory in chess.

The opening theory comprises of a sequences of moves that are from the starting position and are known to lead to favorable or unfavorable positions. For example, if white starts with the move pawn e4 (the pawn in front of the king moved forward by two spaces), then black responds with pawn c5; this is known as the Sicilian defense, and there are many books written on the sequences of play that could follow from this position. Deep Blue was programmed to simply follow the best moves recommended from these opening books and only start calculating the best min-max move once the opening line of play reaches its end. In this way, it saves on computational time, but it also takes advantage of the vast human research that has gone into the working out of the best positions in the opening stages of chess.

# Learning a value function

Let's get a bit more details on exactly how much computation the min max algorithm has to do. If we have a game of breadth $b$ and depth $d$, then evaluating a complete game with min-max would require the construction of a tree with eventual $d^b$ leaves. If we use a max depth of $n$ with an evaluation function, it would reduce our tree size to $n^b$. But this is an exponential equation, and even though $n$ is as small as 4 and $b$ as 20, you still have 1,099,511,627,776 possibilities to evaluate. The tradeoff here is that as $n$ gets lower, our evaluation function is called at a shallower level, where it may be a lot less good than the estimated quality of the position. Again, think of chess where our evaluation function is simply counting the number of pieces left on the board. Stopping at a shallow point may miss the fact that the last move put the queen in a position where it could be taken in the following move. Greater depth always equals greater accuracy of evaluation.

# Training AI to master Go

The number of possibilities in chess, though vast, is not so vast that with a powerful computer, you can't defeat the world's greatest human player. Go, an ancient Chinese game whose origin goes back to more than 5,500 years, is far more complex. In Go, a piece can be placed anywhere on the 19 x 19 board. To begin with, there are 361 possible moves. So to search forward $k$ moves, you must consider $361^k$ possibilities. To make things even more difficult, in chess, you can evaluate how good a position is fairly accurately by counting the number of pieces on each side, but in Go, no such simple evaluation function has been found. To know the value of a position, you must calculate through to the end of the game, some 200+ moves later. This makes the game impossible to play to a good standard using min-max.

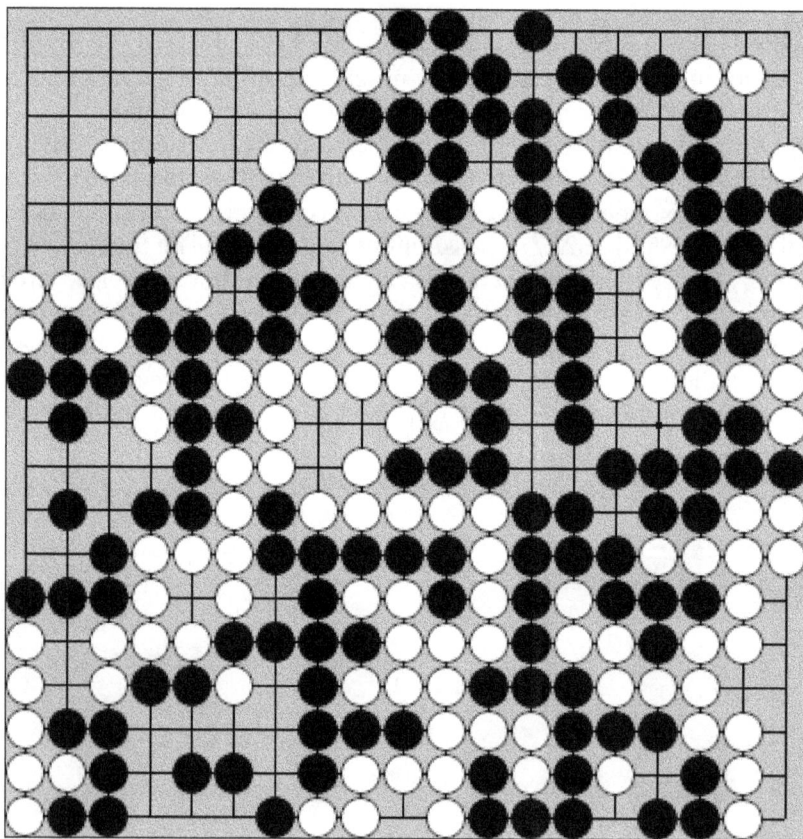

Figure 5

To get a good feel of the complexity of Go, it is worth thinking about how humans learn to play Go versus Chess. When beginners starts learning Chess, they make a series of moves in the direction of their opponent's side of the board. At some point, they make a move that leaves one of their pieces open for capture. So the opponent obliges and takes the piece. It is then that the beginner player immediately understands that their last move was bad, and if they want to improve, they cannot make the same mistake again. It is very easy for the player to identify what they did wrong, though correcting yourselves consistently may require a lot of practice.

Alternatively, when a beginner learns Go, it looks like a series of almost random moves across the board. At a certain point, both players run out of their moves and the position is counted up to see who won. The beginner finds out he has lost and stares at the mass of pieces in different positions and scratches his head wondering exactly what happened. For humans, Go is incredibly difficult and takes a high degree of experience and skill to be able to understand where players are going wrong.

Also, Go doesn't have anything like the opening theory books that Chess has. Go's opening theory rather than being sequences of moves that a computer could follow is lots of general principles instead, such as good shapes to aim for or ways to take corners of the board. There is something called *Joseki* in Go, which are studied sequences of moves known to lead to different advantages. But all of these must be applied to that context when a player recognizes a particular arrangement is possible; they are not actions that can be blindly followed.

One approach for games such as Go, where evaluation is so difficult, is **Monte Carlo Tree Search** (**MCTS**). If you have studied Bayesian probability, you will have heard of Monte Carlo sampling. This involves sampling from a probability distribution to obtain an approximation for an intractable value. MCTS is similar. A single sample involves randomly selecting actions for each player until you reach a terminal state. We maintain statistics for each sample so that after we are done, we can select the action from the current state with the highest mean success rate. Here is an example of MCTS for the tic tac toe game we spoke about. The complete code can also be found in the GitHub repo in the `monte_carlo.py` file:

```
import collections


def monte_carlo_sample(board_state, side):
    result = has_winner(board_state)
    if result != 0:
        return result, None
    moves = list(available_moves(board_state))
    if not moves:
        return 0, None
```

The `monte_carlo_sample` method here generates a single sample from a given position. Again, we have a method that has `board_state` and `side` as arguments. This method will be called recursively until we reach a terminal state, so either a draw because no new move can be played or a win for one player or another:

```
# select a random move
move = random.choice(moves)
result, next_move = monte_carlo_sample(apply_move(board_state,
move, side), -side)
return result, move
```

A move will be selected randomly from the legal moves in the position, and we will recursively call the sample method:

```
def monte_carlo_tree_search(board_state, side, number_of_samples):
    results_per_move = collections.defaultdict(lambda: [0, 0])
    for _ in range(number_of_samples):
        result, move = monte_carlo_sample(board_state, side)
        results_per_move[move][0] += result
        results_per_move[move][1] += 1
```

Take monte carlo samples from this board state and update our results based on them:

```
move = max(results_per_move,
    key=lambda x: results_per_move.get(x)[0] /
            results_per_move[move][1])
```

Get the move with the best average result:

```
return results_per_move[move][0] / results_per_move[move][1],
move
```

This is the method that brings it all together. We will call the `monte_carlo_smaple` method `number_of_samples` times, keeping track of the result of each call. We then return the move with the best average performance.

It is good to think about how different the results obtained from MCTS will be of those that involve min-max. If we go back to chess as an example, in the position illustrated, white has a winning move, putting the rook on the back rank, c8, to give mate. Using min-max, this position would be evaluated as a winning position for white. But using MCTS, given that all other moves here lead to a probable victory for black, this position will be rated as favorable to black. This is why MCTS is very poor at chess and should give you a feel of why MCTS should only be used when Min-Max is not viable. In Go, which falls into the other category, the best AI performance was traditionally found using MCTS.

Figure 6: A Chess position that is badly evaluated by Monte Carlo sampling. If white is to move, they have a winning move; however, if the samples randomly move, black has an opportunity to win

# Upper confidence bounds applied to trees

To recap, Min-Max gives us the actual best move in a position, given perfect information; however, MCTS only gives an average value; though it allows us to work with much larger state spaces that cannot be evaluated with Min-Max. Is there a way that we could improve MCTS so it could converge to the Min-Max algorithm if enough evaluations are given? Yes, Monte Carlo Tree Search with Confidence bounds applied to Trees (UCT) does exactly this. The idea behind it is to treat MCTS like a multiarmed bandit problem. The multiarmed bandit problem is that we have a group of slot machines—one armed bandits—each of which has an undetermined payout and average amount of money received per play. The payout for each machine is random, but the mean payout may vary significantly. How should we determine which slot machines to play?

There are two factors that need to be considered when choosing a slot machine. The first is the obvious one, an exploitative value, which is the expected return that the given slot machine will output. To maximize the payout, we would need to always play the machine with the highest expected payout. The second is the explorative value, where we want our playing machine to increase the information we have about the payoffs of different machines.

If we play machine *A* thrice, you get a payoff of 13, 10, and 7 for an average payoff of 10. We also have machine *B*; we have played it once and have gotten a payoff of 9. In this case, it might be preferable to play machine *B* because though the average payoff is lower, 9 versus 10. The fact that we have only played it once means the lower payout may have just been bad luck. If we play it again and get a payout of 13, our average for machine B would be 11. Therefore, we should switch to playing that machine for the best payout.

The multiarmed bandit problem has been widely studied within mathematics. If we can reframe our MCTS evaluation to look like a multiarmed bandit problem, we can take advantage of these well-developed theories. One way of thinking about it is rather than seeing the problem as one with maximizing reward, think of it as a problem with minimizing regret. Regret here is defined as the difference between the reward we get for the machine we play and the maximum possible reward we would get if we knew the best machine from the beginning. If we follow a policy, $\pi(a)$ chooses an action that gives a reward at each time step. The regret for *t* number of plays, given $r^*$ as the reward of the best possible action, is as follows:

$$regret_t = E\left[\sum_{t-1}^{t} r - \pi(a)\right]$$

If we were to choose a policy of always picking the machine with the highest reward, it may not be the true best machine. Therefore, our regret will increase linearly with each play. Similarly, if we take a policy of always trying to explore for finding the best machine, our regret will also increase linearly. What we want is a policy for $\pi(a)$ that increases in sublinear time.

The best theoretical solution is to perform the search based on confidence intervals. A confidence interval is the range within which we expect the true mean, with some probability. We want to be optimistic in the face of uncertainty. If we don't know something, we want to find it out. The confidence interval represents our uncertainty about the true mean of a given random variable. Select something based on your sample mean plus the confidence interval; it will encourage you to explore the space of possibilities while also exploiting it at the same time.

For an i.i.d random variable $x$, in the range of 0 to 1, over n samples, the probability that the true mean is greater than the sample mean $-\overline{x}_n$ plus constant $u$ – is given by Hoeffding's inequality: Hoeffding, Wassily (1963). *Probability inequalities for sums of bounded random variables*. Journal of the American Statistical Association:

$$P\left[E\{x\} > \overline{x}_n + u\right] \le e^{-2nu^2}$$

We want to use this equation to find the upper bound confidence for each machine. $E\{x\}, x$, and $n$ are all part of statistics we have already. We need to solve it to use it for the purpose of finding a value for $u$. In order to do this, reduce the left side of the equation to p and find where it equals the right side:

$$p = e^{-2nu^2}$$

We can rearrange it to make $u$ defined in terms of $n$ and $p$:

$$lnp = -2nu^2$$

$$\frac{-lnp}{2n} = u^2$$

$$u = \sqrt{\frac{-lnp}{2n}}$$

Now we want to choose a value for $p$ so that our precision increases over time. If we set $p = n^{-4}$, then as n approaches infinity, our regret will tend toward 0. Substitute that in and we can simplify it down to:

$$u = \sqrt{\frac{-2lnn}{n}}$$

The mean plus u is our upper confidence bounds, so we can use it to give us the **UCB1 (Upper Confidence Bounds)** algorithm. We can substitute our values with the values in the multiarmed bandit problem we saw earlier, where $r_i$ is the sum of the reward received from the machine $i$, $n_i$ is the number of plays of machine $i$, and $n$ is the sum of plays across all machines:

$$\frac{r_i}{n_i} + \sqrt{\frac{2lnn}{n_i}}$$

We will always want to choose the machine that will give us the highest score for this equation. If we do so, our regret will scale logarithmically with the number of plays, which is the theoretical best we can do. Using this equation for our action choice has the behavior that we will try a range of machines early on, but the more we try a single machine, the more it will encourage us to eventually try a different machine.

It's also good to remember that an assumption at the beginning of this series of equations was that the range, for x in early equations, and r for when we apply it to the multiarmed bandit problem was that values were in the range of 0 to 1. So if we are not working in this range, we need to scale our input. We have not made any assumptions about the nature of the distribution though; it could be Gaussian, binomial, and so on.

Now we have an optimal solution to the problem of sampling from a set of unknown distributions; how do you apply it to MCTS? The simplest way to do this is to only treat the first moves from the current board state as bandits or slot machines. Though this would improve the estimation at the top level a little, every move beneath that would be completely random, meaning the $r_i$ estimation would be very inaccurate.

Alternatively, we could treat every move at every branch of the tree as a multiarmed bandit problem. The issue with this is that if our tree is very deep, as our evaluation goes deeper, we will reach positions we have never encountered before so we would have no samples for the range of moves we need to choose between. We would be keeping a huge number of statistics for a huge range of positions, most of which will never be used.

The compromise solution, known as Upper Confidence for Trees, is to do what we discuss next. We will do successive rollouts from the current board state. At each branch of the tree, where we have a range of actions to choose from, if we have previous sample statistics for each potential move, we will use the UCB1 algorithm to choose which action to choose for the rollout. If we do not have sample statistics for every move, we will choose the move randomly.

How do we decide which sample statistics to keep? For each rollout, we keep new statistics for the first position we encounter that we do not have previous statistics for. After the rollout is complete, we update the statistics for every position we are keeping track of. This way, we ignore all the positions deeper down the rollout. After $x$ evaluations, we should have exactly $x$ nodes of our tree, growing by one with each rollout. What's more, the nodes we keep track of are likely to be around the paths we are using the most, allowing us to increase our top-level evaluation accuracy by increasing the accuracy of the moves we evaluate further down the tree.

The steps are as follows:

1. Start a rollout from the current board state. When you select a move, do the following:

    1. If you have statistics for every move from the current position, use the UCB1 algorithm to choose the move.

    2. Otherwise, choose the move randomly. If this is the first randomly chosen position, add it to the list of positions we are keeping statistics for.

2. Run the rollout until you hit a terminal state, which will give you the result of this rollout.

3. Update the statistics for every position you are keeping statistics for, indicating what you went through in the rollout.

4. Repeat until you get to the maximum number of rollouts. Upper confidence bounds applied to Trees, the statistics for each position, are shown in the square boxes:

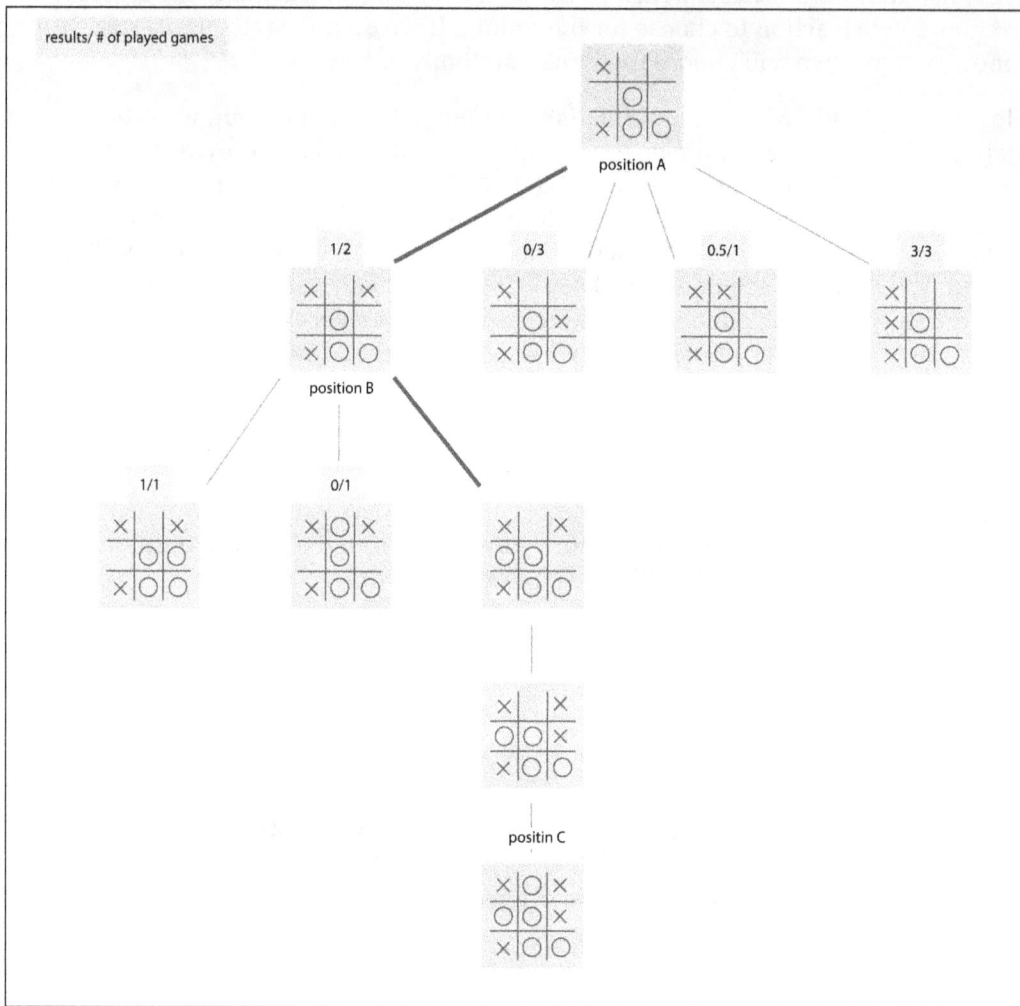

5.  The preceding diagram illustrates how this happens. In position A, there is statistics collected for all four possible moves. Because of this, the UCB1 algorithm can be used to select the best move, balancing exploitative for exploitative value. In the preceding diagram, the leftmost move is chosen. This leads us to **position B**; here only two out of the three possible moves have statistics collected on them. Because of this, the move you need to make for this rollout is selected randomly. By chance, the rightmost move is selected; the remaining moves are selected randomly until you reach the final **position C**, where the noughts were to win. This information is then applied to a graph, as shown in the following diagram:

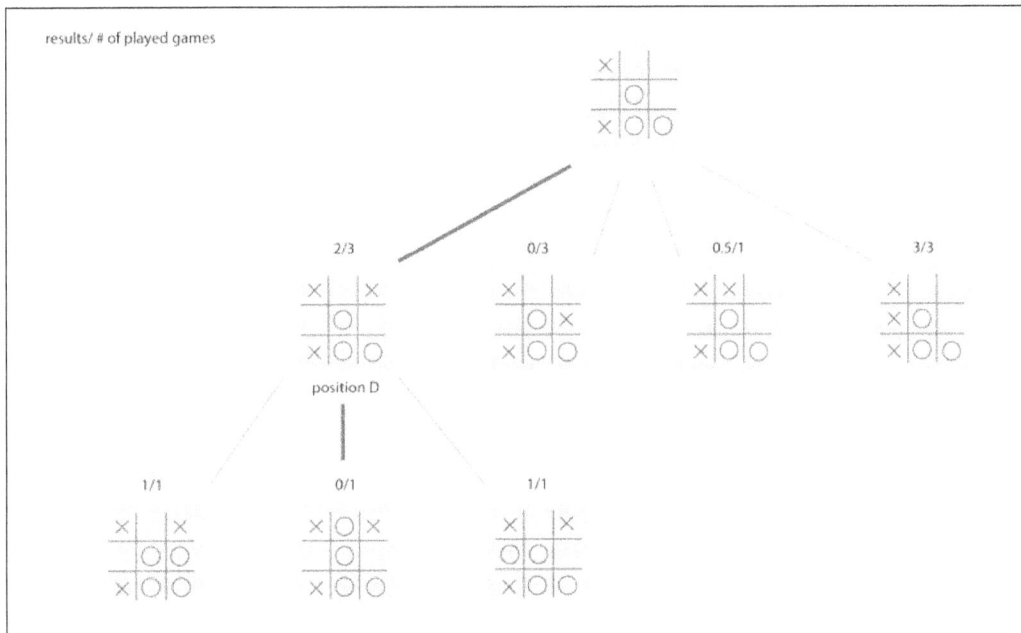

6.  We add statistics for any position that we passed through that already has statistics, so 1/2 in the first diagram now becomes 2/3. We also add statistics for the first position we encounter with no stats. Here, it is the rightmost position in the second row; it now has a score of 1/1 because the nought player won. If this branch is selected again and you get to position D, use the UCB1 algorithm to select the move, not just make a random selection as before.

7. Here is what this looks like in Python for our *Tic-Tac-Toe* game:

```
def upper_confidence_bounds(payout, samples_for_this_machine, log_
total_samples):
    return payout / samples_for_this_machine
        + math.sqrt((2 * log_total_samples)
                / samples_for_this_machine)
```

First, we need a method that calculates UCB1; this is the UCB1 equation in Python. The one difference is here we are using `log_total_samples` as input because it allows us to do a small optimization later on:

```
def monte_carlo_tree_search_uct(board_state, side, number_of_
rollouts):
    state_results = collections.defaultdict(float)
    state_samples = collections.defaultdict(float)
```

Declare the method and the two dictionaries, namely `state_results` and `state_samples`. They will keep track of our statistics for the different board states we will encounter during the rollouts:

```
    for _ in range(number_of_rollouts):
        current_side = side
        current_board_state = board_state
        first_unvisited_node = True
        rollout_path = []
        result = 0
```

The main loop is what we go through for each rollout. At the beginning of the rollout, we need to initialize the variables that will track our progress within the rollout. `first_unvisited_node` will keep track of whether we have created a new statistics tracking node for this rollout. On encountering the first state for which we have no statistics, we create the new statistics node, adding it to `state_results` and `state_samples` dictionaries and then setting the variable to `False`. `rollout_path` will keep track of each node we visit in this rollout that we are keeping statistics nodes for. Once we obtain the result at the end of the rollout, we will update the statistics of all the states along the path:

```
        while result == 0:
            move_states = {move: apply_move(current_board_state,
            move, current_side)
                        for move in
                        available_moves(current_board_state)}

            if not move_states:
                result = 0
                break
```

The `while result == 0` puts us into the loop for a rollout; this will run until one side or the other wins. In each loop of the rollout, we first construct a dictionary, `move_states`, mapping each available move to the state that move will put us into. If there are no moves to make, we are in a terminal state, it is a draw. So you need to record that as `result` and break out of the rollout loop:

```
if all((state in state_samples) for _, state in
move_states):
    log_total_samples = math.log(sum(state_samples[s]
    for s in move_states.values()))
    move, state = max(move_states, key=lambda _, s:
    upper_confidence_bounds(state_results[s],
    state_samples[s], log_total_samples))
else:
    move = random.choice(list(move_states.keys()))
```

Now we need to choose which move we are going to take at this step of the rollout. As specified by the MCTS-UCT algorithm, if we have statistics for every possible move, we choose the move with the best `upper_confidence_bounds` score; otherwise, we make the selection randomly:

```
current_board_state = move_states[move]
```

Now that we have selected our move, we can update `current_board_state` to the state that the move puts us in:

```
if first_unvisited_node:
    rollout_path.append((current_board_state,
    current_side))
    if current_board_state not in state_samples:
        first_unvisited_node = False
```

Now we need to check whether we have hit the end of our MCTS-UCT tree. We will add every node we visit up to the first previously unvisited node to `rollout_path`. We will update the statistics of all these nodes once we get our result from this rollout:

```
current_side = -current_side
result = has_winner(current_board_state)
```

We are at the end of our rollout loop, so switch the sides for the next iteration and check whether anyone has won in the current state. If so, it will cause us to break out of the rollout loop when we pop back to the `while result == 0` statement:

```
for path_board_state, path_side in rollout_path:
    state_samples[path_board_state] += 1.
    result = result*path_side/2.+.5
    state_results[path_board_state] += result
```

Now we have completed a single rollout and thus left the rollout loop. We now need to update our statistics with the result. `rollout_path` contains `path_board_state` and `path_side` for each node we want to update, so we need to go through every entry in there. The last two points to make are that the results from our game are between -1 and 1. But the UCB1 algorithm expects its payouts between 0 and 1; the line `result *path_side/2.+.5` does this. Second, we also need to switch the results to represent the side they are for. A good move for my opponent is the opposite of a good move for me:

```
move_states = {move: apply_move(board_state, move, side) for
move in available_moves(board_state)}

move = max(move_states, key=lambda x:
state_results[move_states[x]] / state_samples[move_states[x]])

return state_results[move_states[move]] /
state_samples[move_states[move]], move
```

Finally, once we have done the required number of rollouts, we can choose the best move from the current state based on the best expected payout. There is no longer any need to use UCB1 to choose the best move. It's because this being the final decision, there is no value in doing any extra exploration; the best move is simply the best mean payout.

This is the MCTS-UCT algorithm. There are many different variants to it with different advantages in specific situations, but they all have this as core logic. MCTS-UCT gives us a general way to judge moves for games, such as Go, with vast search spaces. Also, it isn't limited to games of perfect information; it can often perform well in games with partially observed states, such as poker. Or, even more generally, any problem we might encounter that we can reconfigure to fit it, for example, it was used as a basis for an automated theorem proving machine.

# Deep learning in Monte Carlo Tree Search

Even with MCTS-UCT, computers could still not even come close to beating the best Go players; however, in 2016, a team from *Google Deep Mind* developed an AI they called AlphaGo. It defeated Lee Sedol, the world's top Go player, over a five game series, winning 4-1. The way they did this was using three improvements over the standard MCTS UCT approach.

If we were to think about why MCTS is so inaccurate, an intuitive answer that might arise is that the moves used in the evaluation are selected randomly when we know that some moves are much more likelier than others. In Go, when there is a battle for control of a corner, the moves around that area are much better candidates for selection, as opposed to moves on the opposite side of the board. If we had a good way of selecting which moves are likely to be played, we would have massively reduced the breadth of our search, and by extension, increased the accuracy of our MCTS evaluations. If we go back to the preceding chess position, although every legal move can potentially be played, if you are playing against someone who without any chess skill will only play the winning move, evaluation of the other moves is simply wasted CPU cycles.

This is where deep learning can help us. We can use the pattern recognition qualities of a neural network to give us a rough estimate of the probability of a move being played in the game, given a position. For AlphaGo, a 13-layer convolutional network with relu activation functions was used. The input to the network was the 19 x 19 board state and its output, another 19 x 19 softmax layer representing the probability of a move being played in each square of the board. It was then trained on a large database of expert-level human Go games. The network would be given a single position as input and the move that was played from that position as a target. The loss function is the mean squared error between network activation and the human move made. Given plenty of training, the network learned to predict human moves with 57 percent accuracy against a test set. The use of a test set here is particularly important because overfitting is a big worry. Unless the network can generalize its understanding of a position to a previously unseen position, it is useless.

If we wanted to implement something similar in our preceding Tic-tac-toe example, we would simply replace the `move = random.choice(moves)` line with the `monte_carlo_sample` method or the UCT version with a move chosen by a trained neural network. This technique will work for any discrete game if you have a large training set of example games.

If you do not have a database of example games, there is another approach you can use. If you have an agent that plays with a tiny degree of skill, you can even use that agent to generate the initial collection of example games. A good approach, for instance, is to generate example positions and moves using the min-max or MCTS UCT algorithms. A network can then be trained to play moves from that collection. This is a good way to get a network to learn how to play a game at a good enough standard so that it can at least explore the space of the game with the plausible moves, as opposed to completely random moves.

If we implement such a neural network, use it to select which moves to use in a Monte-Carlo rollout, with this, our evaluation will be much more accurate, but we will still suffer from the problem that our MCTS will be evaluating averages when we still care about the best outcome for us from the moves we make. This is where reinforcement learning can be introduced to improve our agent.

# Quick recap on reinforcement learning

We first encountered reinforcement learning in *Chapter 1, Machine Learning – An Introduction*, when we looked at the three different types of learning processes: supervised, unsupervised, and reinforcement. In reinforcement learning, an agent receives rewards within an environment. For example, the agent might be a mouse in a maze and the reward might be some food somewhere in that maze. Reinforcement learning can sometimes feel a bit like a supervised recurrent network problem. A network is given a series of data and must learn a response.

The key distinction that makes a task a reinforcement learning problem is that the responses the agent gives changes the data it receives in future time steps. If the mouse turns left instead of right at a $T$ section of the maze, it changes what its next state would be. In contrast, supervised recurrent networks simply predict a series. The predictions they make do not influence the future values in the series.

The AlphaGo network has already been through supervised training, but now the problem can be reformatted as a reinforcement learning task to improve the agent further. For AlphaGo, a new network was created that shares the structure and weights with the supervised network. Its training is then continued using reinforcement learning and by specifically using an approach called policy gradients.

# Policy gradients for learning policy functions

The problem policy gradients aims to solve is a more general version of the problem of reinforcement learning, which is how you can use backpropagation on a task that has no gradient, from the reward to the output of our parameters. To give a more concrete example, we have a neural network that produces the probability of taking an action $a$, given a state $s$ and some parameters $\theta$, which are the weights of our neural network:

$$p(a|s,\theta)$$

We also have our reward signal $R$. The actions affect the reward signal we take, but there is no gradient between them and the parameters. There is no equation in which we can plug $R$; it is just a value we obtain from our environment in response to $a$.

However, given that we know there is a link between the $a$ we choose and $R$, there are a few things we could try. We could create a range of values for our $\theta$ from a Gaussian distribution and run them in the environment. We could then select a percentage of the most successful group and get their mean and variance. We then create a new population of $\theta$ using the new mean and variance in our Gaussian distribution. We can keep doing this iteratively until we stop seeing improvements in $R$ and then use our final mean as the best choice for our parameters. This method is known as the **Cross Entropy Method**.

Though it can be quite successful, it is a hill-climbing method, which does not do a good job of exploring the space of possibilities. It is very likely to get stuck in local optima, which is very common in reinforcement learning. Also, it still does not take advantage of gradient information.

To use gradients, we can take advantage of the fact that although there is no mathematical relationship between $a$ and $R$, there is a probabilistic one. Certain $a$ taken in certain $s$ will tend to receive more $R$ than others. We can write the problem of getting the gradients of $\theta$ with respect to $R$ as follows:

$$\nabla_\theta E_t \{R\} = \nabla_\theta \sum_t P(a \mid s, \theta) r_t$$

Here, $r_t$ is the reward at time step $t$. This can be rearranged into:

$$\nabla_\theta E_t \{R\} = \sum_t \nabla_\theta P(a \mid s, \theta) r_t$$

If we multiply and divide it by $P(a \mid s, \theta)$, we have the following:

$$\nabla_\theta E_t \{R\} = \sum_t P(a \mid s, \theta) \frac{\nabla_\theta P(a \mid s, \theta)}{P(a \mid s, \theta)} r_t$$

Use the fact $\nabla_x \log(f(x)) = \dfrac{\nabla_x f(x)}{f(x)}$ and simplify it to the following:

$$\nabla_\theta E_t \{R\} = \sum_t P(a \mid s, \theta) \nabla_\theta \log(P(a \mid s, \theta)) r_t$$

What this amounts to is if we nudge our parameters along the log of the direction of the gradient of the reward at each time step, we tend to move towards the gradient of the reward across all time steps. To implement this in Python, we will need to take the following steps:

1. Create a neural network whose output is the probability of taking different actions, given an input state. In terms of the preceding equations, it will represent $P(a|s,\theta)$.

2. Run a batch of episodes with our agent running in its environment. Select its actions randomly according to the probability distribution output of the network. At every time step, record the input state, reward received, and the action you actually took.

3. At the end of each episode of training, assign rewards to each step using the sum of rewards in the episode from that point on. In the case of a game such as Go, this will just be 1, 0, or -1 representing the final result applied to each step. This will represent $r_t$ in the equations. For more dynamic games, discounted rewards can be used; discounted rewards will be explained in detail in the next chapter.

4. Once we have stored a set number of states running our episodes, we train them by updating our network parameters based on the log of our network output times the actual move that was taken, times the reward. This is used as a loss function of our neural network. We do this for each time step as a single batch update.

5. This is then repeated from step 2 until we hit a stopping point, either at some number of iterations or some score within the environment.

The effect of this loop is that if an action is associated with positive rewards, we increase the parameters that lead to this action in that state. If the reward is negative, we decrease the parameters leading to the action. Note that for this to work, it requires us to have some negative valued rewards; otherwise, over time, all actions are simply pulled up. The best option if this does not occur naturally is to normalize our rewards in each batch.

The policy gradient approach has been shown to be successful at learning a range of complex tasks, although it can take a very long time to train well and is very sensitive to the learning rate. Too high the learning rate and the behavior will oscillate wildly, never becoming stable enough to learn anything of note. Too low and it will never converge. This is why in the following example, we use RMSProp as the optimizer. Standard gradient descent with a fixed learning rate is often a lot less successful. Also, although the example shown here is for board games, policy gradients also work very well for learning more dynamic games, such as Pong.

Now let's create `player_func` for our tic-tac-toe's `play_game` method; it uses policy gradients to learn the optimal play. We will set up the neural network that will take the nine squares of the board as input. The number 1 will be a mark for the player, -1 for the opponent, and 0 an unmarked square. Here the network will be set up with three hidden layers, each with 100 hidden nodes and relu activation functions. The output layer will also contain nine nodes, one for each board square. Because we want our final output to be the *probability* of a move being the best one, we want the output of all the nodes in the final layer to sum to 1. This means using a softmax activation function is a natural choice. The softmax activation function looks as follows:

$$y_i = \frac{c^{x_i}}{\sum_j c^{x_j}}$$

Here, $x$ and $y$ are vectors with equal dimensions.

Here is the code for creating the network in TensorFlow. The full code can also be found in the GitHub repo in `policy_gradients.py`:

```
import numpy as np
import tensorflow as tf

HIDDEN_NODES = (100, 100, 100)
INPUT_NODES = 3 * 3
LEARN_RATE = 1e-4
OUTPUT_NODES = INPUT_NODES
```

First, we import NumPy and TensorFlow, which will be used for the network, and create a few constant variables, which will be used later. The 3 * 3 input nodes is the size of the board:

```
input_placeholder = tf.placeholder("float", shape=(None, INPUT_NODES))
```

The `input_placeholder` variable is the placeholder that holds the input to the neural network. In TensorFlow, placeholder objects are used for all values provided to the network. When running the network, it will be set to `board_state` of the game. Also, the first dimension of `input_placeholder` is None. This is because, as mentioned a few times in this book, training mini-batching is much faster. The None will adjust to become the size of our mini-batch of samples come training time:

```
hidden_weights_1 = tf.Variable(tf.truncated_normal((INPUT_NODES,
HIDDEN_NODES[0]), stddev=1. / np.sqrt(INPUT_NODES)))
hidden_weights_2 = tf.Variable(
tf.truncated_normal((HIDDEN_NODES[0], HIDDEN_NODES[1]), stddev=1. /
np.sqrt(HIDDEN_NODES[0])))
```

```
hidden_weights_3 = tf.Variable(
tf.truncated_normal((HIDDEN_NODES[1], HIDDEN_NODES[2]), stddev=1. /
np.sqrt(HIDDEN_NODES[1])))
output_weights = tf.Variable(tf.truncated_normal((HIDDEN_NODES[-1],
OUTPUT_NODES), stddev=1. / np.sqrt(OUTPUT_NODES)))
```

Here we create the weights we will need for the three layers of our network. They will all be created with a random Xavier initialization; more on this in chapter:

```
hidden_layer_1 = tf.nn.relu(
    tf.matmul(input_placeholder, hidden_weights_1) +
    tf.Variable(tf.constant(0.01, shape=(HIDDEN_NODES[0],))))
```

Create the first hidden layer, our `hidden_weights_1` 2d tensor, and matrix multiply it by `input_placeholder`. Then add the bias variable, `tf.Variable(tf. constant(0.01, shape=(HIDDEN_NODES[0],)))`, which gives the network a bit more flexibility in learning patterns. The output is then put through a relu activation function: `tf.nn.relu`. This is how we write the basic equation for a layer of a neural network in TensorFlow. The other thing to note is 0.01. When using the `relu` function, it is good practice to add a small amount of positive bias. This is because the relu function is the maximum value and is 0. This means that values below 0 will have no gradient and so will not be adjusted during learning. If node activation is always below zero, because of bad luck with weight initialization, then it is considered a dead node and will never have an impact on the network and will simply take up GPU/CPU cycles. A small amount of positive bias greatly reduces the chance of having completely dead nodes in the network:

```
hidden_layer_2 = tf.nn.relu(
tf.matmul(hidden_layer_1, hidden_weights_2) +
tf.Variable(tf.truncated_normal((HIDDEN_NODES[1],),
stddev=0.001)))
hidden_layer_3 = tf.nn.relu(
tf.matmul(hidden_layer_2, hidden_weights_3) +
tf.Variable(tf.truncated_normal((HIDDEN_NODES[2],),
stddev=0.001)))
output_layer = tf.nn.softmax(tf.matmul(hidden_layer_3,
output_weights) + tf.Variable(tf.truncated_normal((OUTPUT_NODES,),
stddev=0.001)))
```

The next few layers are created in the same way:

```
reward_placeholder = tf.placeholder("float", shape=(None,))
actual_move_placeholder = tf.placeholder("float", shape=(None,
OUTPUT_NODES))
```

For the `loss` function, we need two additional placeholders. One of them is for the reward we receive from the environment, in this case, the result of our game of tic-tac-toe. The other is meant for the actual action we will take at each time step. Remember, we will choose our moves according to a stochastic policy based on the output of our network. When we adjust our parameters, we need to know the actual move we took so we can move the parameters towards it if we have a positive reward and away from it if the reward is negative:

```
policy_gradient = tf.reduce_sum(
    tf.reshape(reward_placeholder, (-1, 1)) *
    actual_move_placeholder * output_layer)

train_step = tf.train.RMSPropOptimizer(LEARN_RATE).minimize(-policy_
gradient)
```

The `actual_move_placeholder` when activated will be a one hot vector, for example, `[0, 0, 0, 0, 1, 0, 0, 0, 0]`, with 1 being the square in which the actual move was played. This will act as a mask across `output_layer`, so that only the gradients of that move are adjusted. Success or failure in moving to the first square tells us nothing about the success or failure of moving to the second square. Multiplying it by `reward_placeholder` tells us whether we want to increase the weights leading to this move or reduce them. We then put `policy_gradient` into our optimizer; we want to maximize our reward, which means minimizing the inverse of it.

One final point is that here we are using `RMSPropOptimizer`. As mentioned before, policy gradients are very sensitive to the learning rate and type used. `RMSProp` has been shown to work well.

Within TensorFlow, variables also need to be initialized within a session; this session will then be used to run our calculations:

```
sess = tf.Session()
sess.run(tf.initialize_all_variables())
```

Now we need a method for running our network to choose the actions that will be passed in to the `play_game` method that we created previously:

```
board_states, actual_moves, rewards = [], [], []

def make_move(board_state):
    board_state_flat = np.ravel(board_state)
    board_states.append(board_state_flat)
    probability_of_actions = sess.run(output_layer,
    feed_dict={input_placeholder: [board_state_flat]})[0]
```

In the `make_move` method, we do a few different things. First, we flatten `board_state`, which starts as the second array in a one-dimensional array that we need to use as input for the network. We then append that state to our `board_states` list so we can later use it for training, once we have the reward for the episode. We then run the network using our TensorFlow session: `probability_of_actions`. There will now be an array with nine numbers that will sum up to one; these are the numbers that the network will learn to have the probability where it can set each move as the current most favorable:

```
try:
        move = np.random.multinomial(1, probability_of_actions)
except ValueError:
        move = np.random.multinomial(1, probability_of_actions /
        (sum(probability_of_actions) + 1e-7))
```

We now use `probability_of_actions` as the input to a multinomial distribution. The `np.random.multinomial` returns a series of values from the distribution you pass. Because we gave 1 for the first argument, only a single value will be generated; this is the move we will make. The `try...catch` around the multinomial call exists because owing to the small rounding errors, `probability_of_actions` sometimes sums up to be greater than 1. This only happens roughly once every 10,000 calls, so we will be *pythonic*; if it fails, simply adjust it by some small epsilon and try again:

```
actual_moves.append(move)

move_index = move.argmax()
return move_index / 3, move_index % 3
```

The last bit of the `make_move` method is that we need to store the move we actually used later in training. Then return the move to the format that our Tic-Tac-Toe game expects it in, which is as a tuple of two integers: one for the $x$ position and one for the $y$ position.

The final step before training is that once we have a complete batch to train on, we need to normalize the rewards from the batch. There are a few advantages to this. First, during early training, when it is losing or winning almost all games, we want to encourage the network to move towards better examples. Normalizing will allow us to have that extra weight applied to the rare examples that are more significant. Also, batch normalization tends to speed up training because it reduces the variance in targets:

```
BATCH_SIZE = 100
episode_number = 1
```

We define a constant for how big our `BATCH_SIZE` is. This defines how many examples go into our mini-batches for training. Many different values of this work well; 100 is one of these. `episode_number` will keep track of how many game loops we have done. This will track when we need to kick off a mini-batch training:

```
while True:
    reward = play_game(make_move, random_player)
```

`while True` puts us into the main loop. The first step we need to make here is to run a game using our old friend, the `play_game` method from earlier in the chapter. For simplicity's sake, we will always have the policy gradient player, using the `make_move` method as the first player and `random_player` as the second player. It would not be too difficult to change it to alternate the order of moves:

```
last_game_length = len(board_states) - len(rewards)

# we scale here
reward /= float(last_game_length)
rewards += ([reward] * last_game_length)
```

Get the length of the game we just played and append the reward we received for it to the `rewards` array so that each board state gets the same final reward we received. In reality, some moves may have had more or less impact on the final reward than others, but we cannot know that here. We will hope that through training, with similar good states showing up with positive rewards more often, the network will learn this over time. We also scale the reward by `last_game_length`, so winning quickly is better than winning slowly and losing slowly is better than losing quickly. Another point to note is if we were running a game with a more unevenly distributed reward—such as Pong, where most frames would have 0 reward with the occasional one—this is where we might apply future discounting across the time steps of the episode:

```
episode_number += 1

if episode_number % BATCH_SIZE == 0:
    normalized_rewards = rewards - np.mean(rewards)
    normalized_rewards /= np.std(normalized_rewards)

    sess.run(train_step, feed_dict={input_placeholder:
    board_states, reward_placeholder: normalized_rewards,
    actual_move_placeholder: actual_moves})
```

Increment `episode_number`, and if we have a `BATCH_SIZE` set of samples, jump into the training code. We start this by doing batch normalization on our rewards. This is not always necessary, but it is almost always advisable because it has many benefits. It tends to improve training time by reducing variance across training. If we have issues with all rewards being positive/negative, this solves them without you having to give it a second thought. Finally, kick off the training by running the `train_step` operation through the TensorFlow session object:

```
del board_states[:]
del actual_moves[:]
del rewards[:]
```

Finally, clear the current mini-batch to make way for the next one. Now let's see how policy gradients perform:

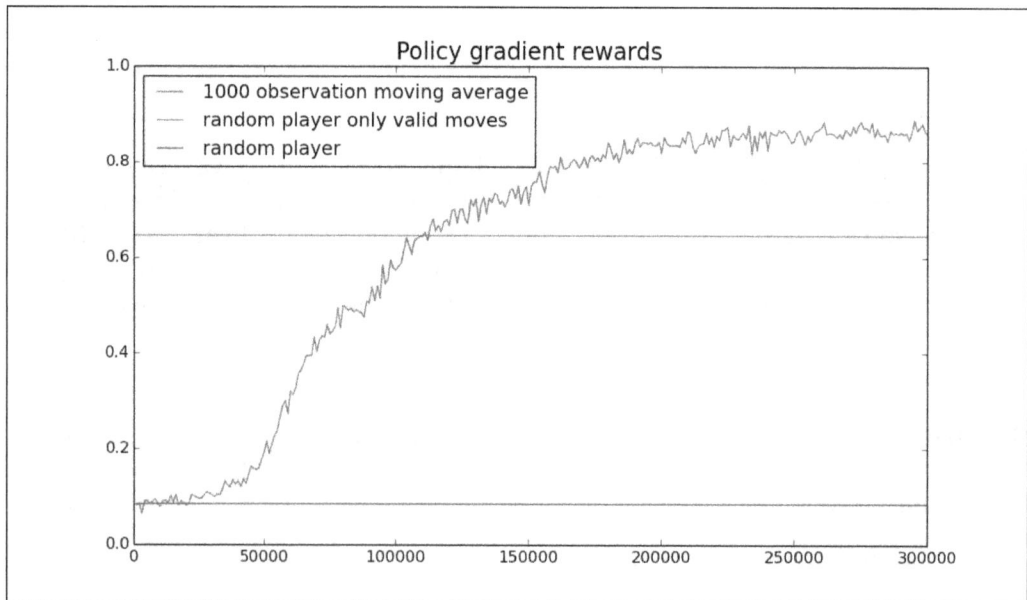

As you can see, it eventually achieves a respectable 85 percent winning rate. With more time and tuning of hyper-parameters, it could do even better. Also, note the reason that indicates why a random player who only chooses valid moves has a greater than 50 percent winning rate. This is because here, the observed player always goes first.

# Policy gradients in AlphaGo

For AlphaGo using policy gradients, the network was set up to play games against itself. It did so with a reward of 0 for every time step until the final one where the game is either won or lost, giving a reward of 1 or -1. This final reward is then applied to every time step in the network, and the network is trained using policy gradients in the same way as our Tic-tac-toe example. To prevent overfitting, games were played against a randomly selected previous version of the network. If the network constantly plays against itself, the risk is it could end up with some very niche strategies, which would not work against varied opponents, a local minima of sorts.

Building the initial supervised learning network that predicted the most likely moves by human players allowed AlphaGo to massively reduce the breadth of the search it needs to perform in MCTS. This allowed them to get much more accurate evaluation per rollout. The problem is that running a large many-layered neural network is very slow, compared to just selecting a random action. In our Monte-Carlo rollout, we need to select 100 moves on average and we want to do this in the order of hundreds of thousands of rollouts to evaluate a position. This makes using the network this way impractical. We need to find a way to reduce our computation time.

If we use the best moves selected by our network instead of manually selecting a move with the probability of our output, then our network is deterministic. Given a position on the board, the result achieved by the board will also be deterministic. When evaluated using the best moves from the network, the position is either a winning one for white or black or a draw. This result is the value of the position under the network's optimal policy. Because the result is deterministic, we can train a new deep neural network to learn the value of this position. If it performs well, a position can be evaluated accurately using just one pass of the neural network, rather than one for each move.

A final supervised network is created using the same structure as the previous networks, except this time the final output, rather than being a probability of actions across the board, is just a single node representing the expected result of the game: win for white, win for black, or draw.

The loss function for this network is the mean squared error between its output and the result achieved by the reinforcement learning network. It was found after training that the value network could achieve a mean squared error of just 0.226 and 0.234 on the training and test sets, respectively. This indicated that it could learn the result with good accuracy.

To recap, at this point, Alpha Go has three differently trained deep neural networks:

- **SL**: This is a network trained using supervised learning to predict the probability of a human move from a board position.

- **RL**: This is a network trained that initially used the weights from the SL network, but was then further trained using reinforcement learning to choose the best move from a given position.

- **V**: This is a network again trained with supervised learning to learn the expected result of the position when played using the RL network. It provides the value of the state.

For a real game against Lee Sedol, Alpha Go used a variant on the MCTS-UCT that we introduced earlier. When the rollout was simulated from the MCTS leaves, rather than selecting moves randomly, they were selected using another, much smaller, single layer network. This network called the fast rollout policy and used a softmax classifier across all possible moves, where the input was the 3 x 3 color pattern around the action and a collection of handcrafted features, such as the liberty count. This is, in our example, the following line:

```
move = random.choice(list(move_states.keys()))
```

This could be replaced with something like this:

```
probability_of_move = fast_rollout_policy.run(board_state)
move = np.random.binomial(1, probability_of_move)
```

This small network was used to run the Monte-Carlo rollout. The SL network would almost certainly have been better, but would have been prohibitively slow.

When evaluating the success value of a rollout from a leaf, the score was determined using a combination of the result from the fast rollout policy and the score as given by the V-network. A mixing parameter $\gamma$ was used to determine the relative weights of these:

$$(1-\gamma)V(s)+\gamma f(s)$$

Here, $s$ is the state of the leaf and $f$ is the result of the rollout using the fast rollout policy. After experimenting with a wide range of the values for $\gamma$, it was found that 0.5 yielded the best results, suggesting that both methods of evaluation are complementary.

The five-game series between Lee Sedol and Alpha Go started on March 9, 2016, in front of a large audience with a $1,000,000 prize for the winner. Lee Sedol was very confident in the buildup, declaring, "I have heard that Google DeepMind's AI is surprisingly strong and getting stronger, but I am confident that I can win at least this time." Sadly, for him, Alpha Go proceeded to win the first three games, each forcing a resignation. At this point, with the competition decided, he came back to win the fourth, but lost the fifth, leaving the series at 4-1.

This was very significant progress on the part of AI, marking the first time that an AI had come even close to beating a top human player at such a complex game. It raises all kinds of questions such as in which other domains, it might be possible to develop AI that can outperform the best humans. The match's full significance on humanity remains to be seen.

# Summary

We have covered a lot in this chapter and looked at a lot of Python code. We talked a bit about the theory of discrete state and zero sum games. We showed how min-max can be used to evaluate the best moves in positions. We also showed that evaluation functions can be used to allow min-max to operate on games where the state space of possible moves and positions are too vast.

For games where no good evaluation function exists, we showed how Monte-Carlo Tree Search can be used to evaluate the positions and then how Monte-Carlo Tree Search with Upper Confidence bounds for Trees can allow the performance of MCTS to coverage toward what you would get from Min-max. This took us to the UCB1 algorithm. Apart from allowing us to compute MCTS-UCT, it is also a great general purpose method for choosing between collections of unknown outcomes.

We then looked at how reinforcement learning can be integrated into these approaches. We also saw how the policy gradient can be used to train deep networks to learn complex patterns and find advantages in games with difficult-to-evaluate states. Finally, we looked at how these techniques were applied in AlphaGo to beat the reigning human world champion.

If you are interested in getting more involved in deep learning for board games, the Alpha Toe project (`https://github.com/DanielSlater/AlphaToe`) has examples of running deep learning on a wider range of games, including Connect Four and Tic-Tac-Toe on a 5 x 5 board.

Though these techniques have been introduced for board games, their application runs a lot wider. Many problems that we encounter can be formulated, such as like discrete state games, for example, optimizing routes for delivery companies, investing in financial markets, and planning strategies for businesses. We've only just started exploring all the possibilities.

In the next chapter, we will look at using deep learning for learning computer games. This will build on our knowledge of policy gradients from this chapter and introduce new techniques for dealing with the dynamic environments of computer games.

# 8
# Deep Learning for Computer Games

The last chapter focused on solving board games. In this chapter, we will look at the more complex problem of training AI to play computer games. Unlike with board games, the rules of the game are not known ahead of time. The AI cannot tell what will happen if it takes an action. It can't simulate a range of button presses and their effect on the state of the game to see which receive the best scores. It must instead learn the rules and constraints of the game purely from watching, playing, and experimenting.

In this chapter, we will cover the following topics:

- Q-learning
- Experience replay
- Actor-critic
- Model-based approaches

## A supervised learning approach to games

The challenge in reinforcement learning is working out a good target for our network. We saw one approach to this in the last chapter, policy gradients. If we can ever turn a reinforcement learning task into a supervised task problem, it becomes a lot easier. So, if our aim is to build an AI agent that plays computer games, one thing we might try is to look at how humans play and get our agent to learn from them. We can make a recording of an expert human player playing a game, keeping track of both the screen image and the buttons the player is pressing.

As we saw in the chapter on computer vision, deep neural networks can identify patterns from images, so we can train a network that has the screen as input and the buttons the human pressed in each frame as the targets. This is similar to how AlphaGo was pretrained in the last chapter. This was tried on a range of complex 3D games, such as Super Smash Bros and Mario Tennis. Convolutional networks were used for their image recognition qualities, and LTSMs were used to handle the long-term dependencies between frames. Using this approach, a trained network for Super Smash Bros could defeat the in-game AI on the hardest difficulty setting:

Learning from humans is a good starting point, but our aim in doing reinforcement learning should be to achieve super-human performance. Also, agents trained in this way will always be limited in what they can do, and what we really want are agents that can truly learn for themselves. In the rest of this chapter, we'll look at approaches that aim to go further than replicating human levels.

# Applying genetic algorithms to playing games

For a long time, the best results and the bulk of the research in AI's playing in video game environments were around genetic algorithms. This approach involves creating a set of modules that take parameters to control the behavior of the AI. The range of parameter values are then set by a selection of genes. A group of agents would then be created using different combinations of these genes, which would be run on the game. The most successful set of agent's genes would be selected, then a new generation of agents would be created using combinations of the successful agent's genes. Those would again be run on the game and so on until a stopping criteria is reached, normally either a maximum number of iterations or a level of performance in the game. Occasionally, when creating a new generation, some of the genes can be mutated to create new genes. A good example of this is *MarI/O*, an AI that learnt to play the classic SNES game *Super Mario World* using neural network genetic evolution:

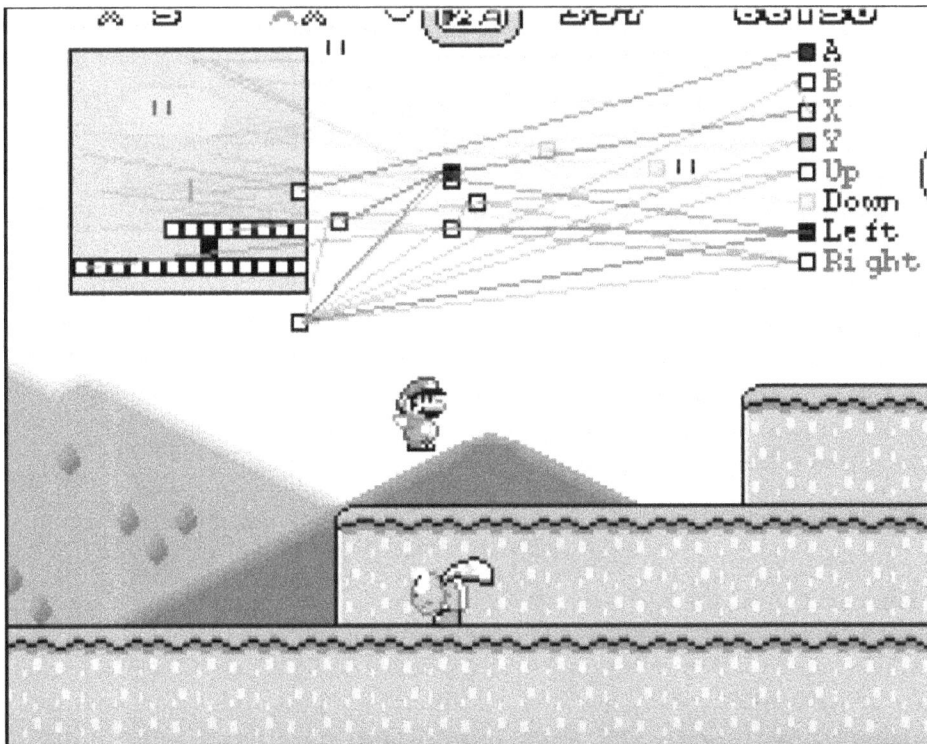

Figure 1: Learning Mario using genetic algorithms (https://www.youtube.com/watch?v=qv6UVOQ0F44)

The big downside of these approaches is that they require a lot of time and computational power to simulate all the variations of parameters. Each member of every generation must run through the whole game until the termination point. The technique also does not take advantage of any of the rich information in the game that a human can use. Whenever a reward or punishment is received, there is contextual information around the state and the actions taken, but Genetic algorithms only use the final result of a run to determine fitness. They are not so much learning as doing trial and error. In recent years, better techniques have been found, which take advantage of backpropagation to allow the agent to really learn as it plays. Like the last chapter, this one is quite code heavy; so if you don't want to spend your time copying text from the pages, you can find all the code in a GitHub repository here: `https://github.com/DanielSlater/PythonDeepLearningSamples`.

# Q-Learning

Imagine that we have an agent who will be moving through a maze environment, somewhere in which is a reward. The task we have is to find the best path for getting to the reward as quickly as possible. To help us think about this, let's start with a very simple maze environment:

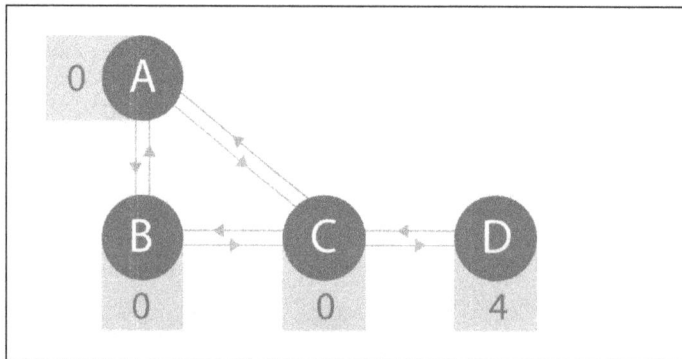

Figure 2: A simple maze, the agent can move along the lines to go from one state to another. A reward of 4 is received if the agent gets to state D.

In the maze pictured, the agent can move between any of the nodes, in both directions, by following the lines. The node the agent is in is its state; moving along a line to a different node is an action. There is a reward of **4** if the agent gets to the goal in state **D**. We want to come up with the optimum path through the maze from any starting node.

Let's think about this problem for a moment. If moving along a line puts us in state **D**, then that will always be the path we want to take as that will give us the **4** reward in the next time step. Then going back a step, we know that if we get to state **C**, which has a direct route to **D**, we can get that 4 reward.

To pick the best action, we need a function that can give us the reward we could expect for the state that action would put us in. The name for this function in reinforcement learning is the Q-function:

```
state, action => expected reward
```

As stated before, the reward for getting to state **D** is **4**. What should be the reward for getting to state **C**? From state **C**, a single action can be taken to move to state **D** and get a reward of **4**, so perhaps we could set the reward for **C** as **4**. But if we take a series of random actions in our maze pictured, we will always eventually reach state **D**, which would mean each action gives equal reward because from any state, we will eventually reach the reward of **4** in state **D**.

We want our expected reward to factor in the number of actions it will take to get a future reward. We will like this expectation to create the effect that when in state **A**, we go to state **C** directly rather than via state **B**, which will result in it taking longer to get to **D**. What is needed is an equation that factors in a future reward, but at a discount compared with reward gained sooner.

Another way of thinking about this is to think of human behavior towards money, which is good proxy for human behavior towards reward, in general. If given a choice between receiving $1 one week from now and $1 10 weeks from now, people will generally choose receiving the $1 sooner. Living in an uncertain environment, we place greater value on rewards we get with less uncertainty. Every moment we delay getting our reward is more time when the uncertainty of the world might remove our reward.

To apply this to our agent, we will use the temporal difference equation for valuing reward; it looks as follows:

$$V = r_t + \sum_{i=1}^{\infty} g^i r_{(t+i)}$$

In this equation, $V$ is the reward for a sequence of actions taken, $r_t$ is the reward received at time $t$ in this sequence, and $g$ is a constant, where $0 < g < 1$, which will mean rewards further in the future are less valuable than rewards achieved sooner; this is often referred to as the discount factor. If we go back to our maze, this function will give a better reward to actions that get to the reward in one move versus those that get to the reward in two or more moves. If a value of 1 is used for $g$, the equation becomes simply the sum of reward over time. This is rarely used in practice for Q-learning; it can result in the agent not converging.

# Q-function

Now that we can evaluate a path for our agent moving through the maze, how do we find the optimal policy? The simple answer for our maze problem is that given a choice of actions, we simply want the one leading to the max reward; this is not just for the current action but also the max action for the state that we would get into after the current action.

The name for this function is the Q-function. This function gives us the optimal action in any state if we have perfect information; it looks as follows:

$$Q(s,a) = reward(s,a) + g * \max\big(Q(s',a') \; for \; s',a' \in actions(s,a)\big)$$

Here, $s$ is a state, $a$ is an action that can be taken in that state, and $0 < g < 1$ is the discount factor. *rewards* is a function that returns the reward for taking an action in a state. *actions* is a function that returns the state $s'$ and that you transition into after taking actions $a$ in state $s$ and all the actions $a'$ available in that state.

Let's see how the maze looks if we apply the Q-function to the maze with discount factor $g=0.5$:

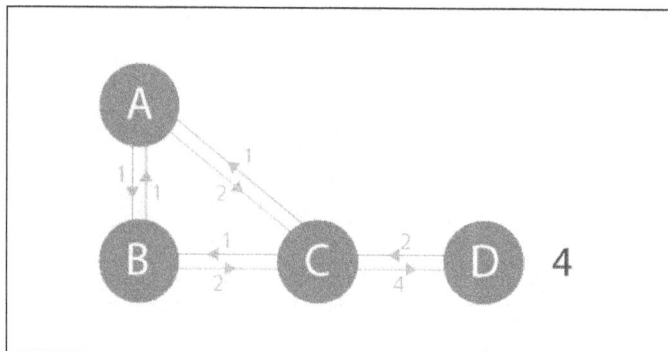

Figure 3: Simple maze, now with Q-values. the arrows show the expected reward for moving between the two states at each end

You will notice that the Q-function as shown is infinitely recursive. It is a hypothetical perfect Q-function, so not something we could apply in code. To use it in code, one approach is to simply have a maximum number of actions to look ahead; then it might look like this:

```
def q(state, action, reward_func, apply_action_func,
actions_for_state_func, max_actions_look_ahead,
discount_factor=0.9):
    new_state = apply_action_func(state, action)
    if max_actions_look_ahead > 0:
        return reward_func(new_state) + discount_factor \ *
        max(q(new_state, new_action, reward_func,
        apply_action_func, actions_for_state_func,
        max_actions_look_ahead-1)
for new_action in actions_for_state_func(new_state))
    else:
        return reward_func(new_state)
```

Here, `state` is some object that defines the state of the environment. `action` is some object that defines a valid action that can be taken in a state. `reward_func` is a function that returns the float value reward, given a state. `apply_action_func` returns a new state that is the result of applying a given action to a given state. `actions_for_state_func` is a function that returns all valid actions given a state.

The aforementioned will give good results if we don't have to worry about rewards far in the future and our state space is small. It also requires that we can accurately simulate forward from the current state to future states as we could for board games. But if we want to train an agent to play a dynamic computer game, none of these constraints is true. When presented with an image from a computer game, we do not know until we try what the image will be after pressing a given button or what reward we will receive.

# Q-learning in action

A game may have in the region of 16-60 frames per second, and often rewards will be received based on actions taken many seconds ago. Also, the state space is vast. In computer games, the state contains all the pixels on the screen used as input to the game. If we imagine a screen downsampled to say 80 x 80 pixels, all of which are single color and binary, black or white, that is still a $2^{6400}$ state. This makes a direct map from state to reward impractical.

What we will need to do is learn an approximation of the Q-function. This is where neural networks can be used for their universal function approximation ability. To train our Q-function approximation, we will store all the game states, rewards, and actions our agent took as it plays through the game. The loss function for our network will be the square of the difference between its approximation of the reward in the previous state and the actual reward it got in the current state, plus its approximation of the reward for the current state it reached in the game, times the discount factor:

$$Loss = \left\{ \left[ reward\left(s,a\right) + g * \max \left( Q\left(s',a'\right) \, for \, s',a' \in actions\left(s,a\right) \right) \right] - Q\left(,a\right) \right\}^2$$

*s* is the previous state, *a* is the action that was taken in that state, and $0 < g < 1$ is the discount factor. *rewards* is a function that returns the reward for taking an action in a state. *actions* is a function that returns the s' state and that you transition into after taking actions *a* in state *s* and all the actions a' available in that state. *Q* is the Q-function presented earlier.

By training successive iterations in this manner, our Q-function approximator will slowly converge towards the true Q-function.

Let's start by training the Q-function for the worlds simplest game. The environment is a one-dimensional map of states. A hypothetical agent must navigate the maze by moving either left or right to maximize its reward. We will set up the rewards for each state as follows:

```
rewards = [0, 0, 0, 0, 1, 0, 0, 0, 0]
```

If we were to visualize it, it might look something like this:

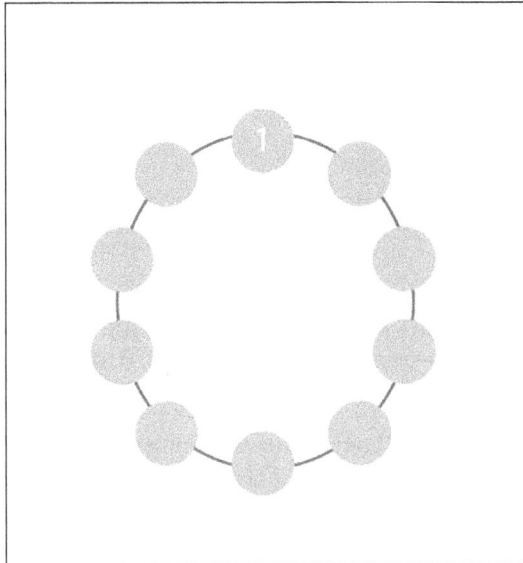

Figure 4: Simple maze game, agent can move between connected nodes and can get a reward of 1 in the top node.

If we were to put our agent into a space in this "maze" in position 1, he would have the option of moving to either position 0 or 2. We want to build a network that learns the value of each state and, by extension, the value of taking an action that moves to that state. The first pass of training our network will learn just the innate rewards of each state. But on the second pass, it will use the information gained from the first pass to improve its estimation of the rewards. What we expect to see at the end of training is a pyramid shape, with the most value in the 1 reward space and then decreasing value on either side as we move away from the center to spaces where you would have to travel further, and thus apply more future discounting to get the reward. Here is how this looks in code (the full sample is in `q_learning_1d.py` in the Git repo):

```python
import tensorflow as tf
import numpy as np

states = [0.0, 0.0, 0.0, 1.0, 0.0, 0.0, 0.0, 0.0, 0.0]
NUM_STATES = len(states)
```

We create a list of `states`; the value of each item in the list is the reward the agent will get for moving to that position. In this example, it gets a reward for getting to the 5th position:

```
NUM_ACTIONS = 2
DISCOUNT_FACTOR = 0.5

def one_hot_state(index):
    array = np.zeros(NUM_STATES)
    array[index] = 1.
    return array
```

This method will take a number and change it into a one-hot encoding for the space of our states, for example, 3 becomes [0, 0, 0, 1, 0, 0, 0, 0, 0, 0]:

```
session = tf.Session()
state = tf.placeholder("float", [None, NUM_STATES])
targets = tf.placeholder("float", [None, NUM_ACTIONS])
```

We create a TensorFlow `session` and placeholders for our input and targets; the `None` in the arrays is for the mini-batch dimension:

```
weights = tf.Variable(tf.constant(0., shape=[NUM_STATES,
NUM_ACTIONS]))
output = tf.matmul(state, weights)
```

For this simple example, we can accurately value everything just using a linear relationship between the state and the action reward, so we will only create an `output` layer that is a matrix multiplication of the `weights`. There's no need for a hidden layer or any kind of non-linearity function:

```
loss = tf.reduce_mean(tf.square(output - targets))
train_operation = tf.train.GradientDescentOptimizer(0.05).
minimize(loss)
session.run(tf.initialize_all_variables())
```

We use the MSE for the loss and standard gradient descent training. What makes this Q-learning is what we will eventually use as the value for the targets:

```
for _ in range(1000):
    state_batch = []
    rewards_batch = []

    for state_index in range(NUM_STATES):
        state_batch.append(one_hot_state(state_index))
```

We create a `state_batch`, each item of which is each of the states in the game, encoded in one hot form. For example, [1, 0, 0, 0, 0, 0, 0, 0, 0], [0, 1, 0, 0, 0, 0, 0, 0, 0], and so on. We will then train the network to approximate the value for each state:

```
minus_action_index = (state_index - 1) % NUM_STATES
plus_action_index = (state_index + 1) % NUM_STATES
```

For each state, we now get the position we would be in if we took each possible action from that state. Note for the example that the states wrap around, so moving -1 from position 0 puts you in position 8:

```
minus_action_state_reward = session.run(output,
    feed_dict={state: [one_hot_state(minus_action_index)]})
plus_action_state_reward = session.run(output,
    feed_dict={state: [one_hot_state(plus_action_index)]})
```

We use our network, which is our q-function approximator to get the reward it thinks we will get if we were to take each of the actions, `minus_action_index` and `plus_action_index`, which is the reward the network thinks we would get in the states it puts us into:

```
minus_action_q_value = states[minus_action_index] +
DISCOUNT_FACTOR * np.max(minus_action_state_reward)

plus_action_q_value = states[plus_action_index] +
DISCOUNT_FACTOR * np.max(plus_action_state_reward)]
```

Here, we have the Python version of the now familiar Q-function equation. We take the initial reward for moving into a state and add to it the `DISCOUNT_FACTOR` times the max reward we could receive for our actions taken in that state:

```
action_rewards = [minus_action_q_value, plus_action_q_value]
rewards_batch.append(action_rewards)
```

We add these to the `rewards_batch`, which will be used as targets for the training operation:

```
session.run(train_operation, feed_dict={
        state: state_batch,
        targets: rewards_batch})

print([states[x] + np.max(session.run(output,
feed_dict={state: [one_hot_state(x)]}))
    for x in range(NUM_STATES)])
```

We then run the actual train step once we have the full set of rewards for each state. If we run this script and look at the output, we can get a sense of how the algorithm iteratively updates. After the first training run, we see this:

```
[0.0, 0.0, 0.0, 0.05, 1.0, 0.05, 0.0, 0.0, 0.0, 0.0]
```

Everything is 0, except the items on either side of the rewarding state. These two states now get a reward on the basis that you could move from them to the reward square. Go forward a few more steps and you see that the reward has started to spread out across the states:

```
[0.0, 0.0, 0.013, 0.172, 1.013, 0.172, 0.013, 0.0, 0.0, 0.0]
```

The eventual output for this program will look something like this:

```
[0.053, 0.131, 0.295, 0.628, 1.295, 0.628, 0.295, 0.131, 0.053, 0.02]
```

As you can see, the highest reward is in the fifth spot in the array, the position we originally set up to have the reward. But the reward we gave was only 1; so why is the reward here higher than that? This is because `1.295` is the sum of the reward gained for being in the current space plus the reward we can get in the future for moving away from this space and coming back again repeatedly, with these future rewards reduced by our discount factor, 0.5.

Learning this kind of future reward to infinity is good, but rewards are often learned in the process of doing a task that has a fixed end. For example, the task might be stacking objects on a shelf that ends when either the stack collapses or all objects are stacked. To add this concept into our simple 1-D game, we need to add in terminal states. These will be states where, once reached, the task ends; so in contrast to every other state, when evaluating the Q-function for it, we would not train by adding a future reward. To make this change, first we need an array to define which states are terminal:

```
terminal = [False, False, False, False, True, False, False, False,
False, False]
```

This will be set in the fifth state, the one we get the reward from to be terminal. Then all we need is to modify our training code to take into account this terminal state:

```
if terminal[minus_action_index]:
    minus_action_q_value = DISCOUNT_FACTOR *
    states[minus_action_index]
else:
    minus_action_state_reward = session.run(output,
    feed_dict={state:
    [one_hot_state(minus_action_index)]})
```

```
    minus_action_q_value = DISCOUNT_FACTOR
    *(states[minus_action_index] +
    np.max(minus_action_state_reward))

if terminal[plus_action_index]:
    plus_action_q_value = DISCOUNT_FACTOR *
    states[plus_action_index]
else:
    plus_action_state_reward = session.run(output,
    feed_dict={state: [one_hot_state(plus_action_index)]})
    plus_action_q_value = DISCOUNT_FACTOR *
    (states[plus_action_index] +
    np.max(plus_action_state_reward))
```

If we run the code again now, the output will settle to this:

```
[0.049, 0.111, 0.242, 0.497, 1.0, 0.497, 0.242, 0.111, 0.0469, 0.018]
```

# Dynamic games

Now that we have learned the world's simplest game, let's try learning something a bit more dynamic. The cart pole task is a classic reinforcement learning problem. The agent must control a cart, on which is balanced a pole, attached to the cart via a joint. At every step, the agent can choose to move the cart left or right, and it receives a reward of 1 every time step that the pole is balanced. If the pole ever deviates by more than 15 degrees from upright, then the game ends:

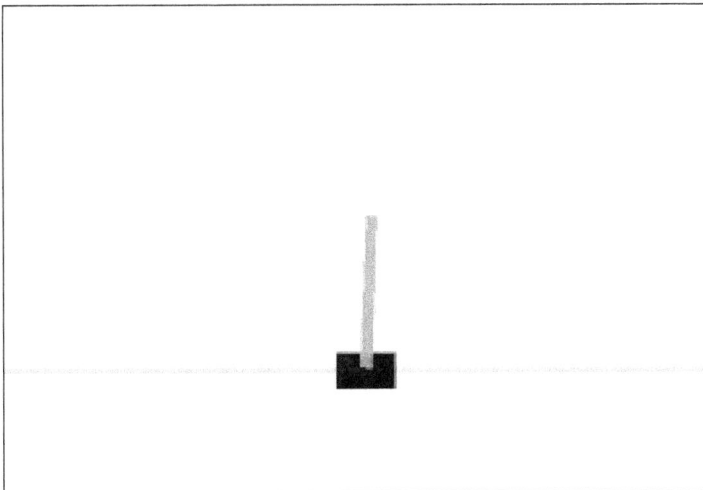

Figure 5: The cart pole task

To run the cart pole task, we will use OpenAIGym, an open source project set up in 2015, which gives a way to run reinforcement learning agents against a range of environments in a consistent way. At the time of writing, OpenAIGym has support for running a whole range of Atari games and even some more complex games, such as doom, with minimum setup. It can be installed using `pip` by running this:

```
pip install gym[all]
```

Running cart pole in Python can be done as follows:

```
import gym

env = gym.make('CartPole-v0')
current_state = env.reset()
```

The `gym.make` method creates the environment that our agent will run in. Passing in the `"CartPole-v0"` string tells OpenAIGym that we want this to be the cart pole task. The returned `env` object is used to interact with the cart pole game. The `env.reset()` method puts the environment into its initial state, returning an array that describes it. Calling `env.render()` will display the current state visually, and subsequent calls to `env.step(action)` allow us to interact with the environment, returning the new states in response to the actions we call it with.

In what ways will we need to modify our simple 1-D game code in order to learn the cart-pole challenge? We no longer have access to a well-defined position; instead, the cart pole environment gives us as input an array of four floating point values that describe the position and angle of the cart and pole. These will be the input into our neural network, which will consist of one hidden layer with 20 nodes and a `tanh` activation function, leading to an output layer with two nodes. One output node will learn the expected reward for a move left in the current state, the other the expected reward for a move right. Here is what that code looks like (the full code sample is in `deep_q_cart_pole.py` in the git repo):

```
feed_forward_weights_1 = tf.Variable(tf.truncated_normal([4,20],
stddev=0.01))
feed_forward_bias_1 = tf.Variable(tf.constant(0.0, shape=[20]))

feed_forward_weights_2 = tf.Variable(tf.truncated_normal([20,2],
stddev=0.01))
feed_forward_bias_2 = tf.Variable(tf.constant(0.0, shape=[2]))

input_placeholder = tf.placeholder("float", [None, 4])
hidden_layer = tf.nn.tanh(tf.matmul(input_placeholder,
feed_forward_weights_1) + feed_forward_bias_1)
output_layer = tf.matmul(hidden_layer, feed_forward_weights_2) +
feed_forward_bias_2
```

Why one hidden layer with 20 nodes? Why use a `tanh` activation function? Picking hyperparameters is a dark art; the best answer I can give is that when tried, these values worked well. But knowing that they worked well in practice and knowing something about what kind of level of complexity is needed to solve the cart pole problem, we can make a guess about why that may guide us in picking hyperparameters for other networks and tasks.

One rule of thumb for the number of hidden nodes in supervised learning is that it should be somewhere in between the number of input nodes and the number of output nodes. Often two-thirds of the number of inputs is a good region to look at. Here, however, we have chosen 20, five times larger than the number of input nodes. In general, there are two reasons for favoring fewer hidden nodes: the first is computation time, fewer units means our network is quicker to run and train. The second is to reduce overfitting and improve generalization. You will have learned from the previous chapters about overfitting and how the risk of having too complex a model is that it learns the training data exactly, but has no ability to generalize to new data points.

In reinforcement learning, neither of these issues is as important. Though we care about computation time, often a lot of the bottleneck is time spent running the game; so a few extra nodes is of less concern. For the second issue, when it comes to generalization, we don't have a division of test set and training set, we just have an environment in which an agent gets a reward. So overfitting is not something we have to worry about (until we start to train agents that can operate across multiple environments). This is also why you often won't see reinforcement learning agents use regularizers. The caveat to this is that over the course of training, the distribution of our training set may change significantly as our agent changes over the course of training. There is always the risk that the agent may overfit to the early samples we got from our environment and cause learning to become more difficult later.

Given these issues, it makes sense to choose an arbitrary large number of nodes in the hidden layers in order to give the maximum chances of learning complex interactions between inputs. But the only true way to know is testing. *Figure 6* shows the results of running a neural network with three hidden nodes against the cart pole task. As you can see, though it is able to learn eventually, it performs a lot worse than with 20 hidden nodes as shown in *Figure 7*:

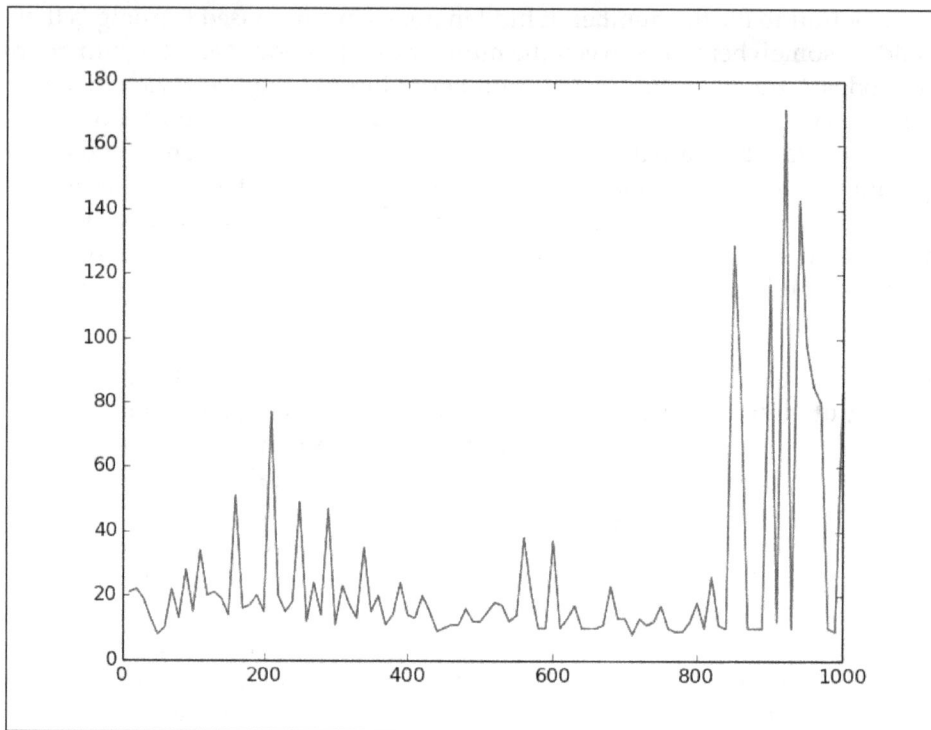

Figure 6: Cart pole with three hidden nodes, y = average reward of last 10 games, x = games played

Why only one hidden layer? The complexity of the task can help us estimate this. If we think about the cart pole task, we know that we care about the inter-relationship of input parameters. The position of the pole may be good or bad depending on the position of the cart. This level of interaction means that a purely linear combination of weights may not be enough. This guess can be confirmed by a quick run, which will show that though a network with no hidden layers can learn this task better than random, it performs a lot less well than a single hidden layer network.

Would a deeper network be better? Maybe, but for tasks that only have this kind of slight complexity, more layers tend not to improve things. Running the network will confirm extra hidden layers appear to make little difference. One hidden layer gives us the capacity we need to learn the things we want in this task.

As for the choice of *tanh*, there are a few factors to think about. The reason relu activation functions have been popular for deep networks is because of saturation. When running a many-layered network with activation functions bounded to a narrow range, for example the 0 to 1 of a logistic function, lots of nodes will learn to activate at close to the maximum of 1. They saturate at 1. But we often want something to signal to a greater degree when it has a more extreme input. This is why relu has been so popular—it gives non-linearity to a layer while not bounding its maximum activation. This is especially important in many layered networks because early layers may get extreme activations that it is useful to signal forward to future layers.

With only one layer, this is not a concern, so a sigmoid function makes sense. The output layer will be able to learn to scale the values from our hidden layer to what they need to be. Is there any reason to favor `tanh` over the logistic function? We know that our target will sometimes be negative, and that for some combinations of parameters can be either good or bad depending on their relative values. That would suggest that the range of -1 to 1 provided by the `tanh` function might be preferable to the logistic function, where to judge negative associations, the bias would first have to be learned. This is a lot of conjecture and reasoning after the fact; the best answer is ultimately that this combination works very well on this task, but hopefully, it should give some feeling for where to start guessing at the best hyperparameters when presented with other similar problems.

To get back to the code, here is what our loss and train functions will look like for our cart pole task:

```
action_placeholder = tf.placeholder("float", [None, 2])
target_placeholder = tf.placeholder("float", [None])

q_value_for_state_action = tf.reduce_sum(tf.mul(output_layer,
action_placeholder),reduction_indices=1)
```

The `q_value_for_state_action` variable will be the `q-value` that the network predicts for a given state and action. Multiplying `output_layer` by the `action_placeholder` vector, which will be 0 for everything except for a 1 for the action we took, and then summing across that means that our output will be our neural networks approximation for the expected value for just that action:

```
cost = tf.reduce_mean(tf.square(target_placeholder -
                      q_value_for_state_action))
train_operation = tf.train.RMSPropOptimizer(0.001).minimize(cost)
```

Our cost is the difference between what we think is the expected return of the state and action and what it should be as defined by the `target_placeholder`.

One of the downsides to the policy gradient approach described in *Chapter 7, Deep Learning for Board Games*, is that all training must be done against the environment. A set of policy parameters can only be evaluated by seeing its effect on the environments reward. With Q-learning, we are instead trying to learn how to value a state and action. As our ability to value specific states improves, we can use that new information to better value the previous states we have experienced. So, rather than always training on the currently experienced state, we can have our network store a history of states and train against those. This is known as **experience replay**.

## Experience replay

Every time we take an action and get into a new state, we store a tuple of `previous_state`, `action_taken`, `next_reward`, `next_state`, and `next_terminal`. These five pieces of information are all we need to run a q-learning training step. As we play the game, we will store this as a list of observations.

Another difficulty that experience replay helps solve is that in reinforcement learning, it can be very hard for training to converge. Part of the reason for this is that the data we train on is very heavily correlated. A series of states experienced by a learning agent will be closely related; a time series of states and actions leading to a reward if trained on together will have a large impact on the weights of the network and can undo a lot of the previous training. One of the assumptions of neural networks is that the training samples are all independent samples from a distribution. Experience replay helps with this problem because we can have our training mini-batches be randomly sampled from our memory, making it unlikely that samples are correlated.

A learning algorithm that learns from memories is called an off-line learning algorithm. The other approach is on-line learning, in which we are only able to adjust the parameters based on direct play of the game. Policy gradients, genetic algorithms, and cross-entropy methods are all examples of this.

Here is what the code for running cart pole with experience replay looks like:

```
from collections import deque
observations = deque(maxlen=20000)
last_action = np.zeros(2)
last_action[0] = 1
last_state = env.reset()
```

We start with our `observations` collection. A deque in Python is a queue that once hits capacity will start removing items from the beginning of the queue. Making the deque here has a maxlen of 20,000, which means we will only store the last 20,000 observations. We also create the last action, `np.array`, which will store the action we decided on from the previous main loop. It will be a one-hot vector:

```
while True:
    env.render()
    last_action = choose_next_action(last_state)
    current_state, reward, terminal, _ =
    env.step(np.argmax(last_action))
```

This is the main loop. We will first render the environment, then decide on an action to take based on the `last_state` we were in, then take that action so as to get the next state:

```
if terminal:
    reward = -1
```

The cart pole task in OpenAIGym always gives a reward of 1 for every time step. We will force giving a negative reward when we hit the terminal state so the agent has a signal to learn to avoid it:

```
observations.append((last_state, last_action, reward,
current_state, terminal))
if len(observations) > 10000:
    train()
```

We store the information for this transition in our observations array. We can also start training if we have enough observations stored. It is important to only begin training once we have a good number of samples, otherwise a few early observations could heavily bias training:

```
if terminal:
    last_state = env.reset()
else:
    last_state = current_state
```

If we are in a terminal state, we need to `reset` our `env` so as to give us a fresh state of the game. Otherwise, we can just set `last_state` to be the `current_state` for the next training loop. We also now need to decide what action to take based on the state. Then here is the actual `train` method, using the same steps as our earlier 1-D example, but changed to use samples from our observations:

```
def _train():
    mini_batch = random.sample(observations, 100)
```

Take 100 random items from our observations; these will be the `mini_batch` to train on:

```
previous_states = [d[0] for d in mini_batch]
actions = [d[1] for d in mini_batch]
rewards = [d[2] for d in mini_batch]
current_states = [d[3] for d in mini_batch]
```

Unpack the `mini_batch` tuples into separate lists for each type of data. This is the format we need to feed into our neural network:

```
agents_reward_per_action = session.run(_output_layer,
feed_dict={input_layer: current_states})
```

Get the reward for each `current_state` as predicted by our neural network. Output here will be an array of the size of the `mini_batch`, where each item is an array with two elements, the estimate of the Q-value for taking the action move left, and the estimate for taking the action move right. We take the max of these to get the estimated Q-value for the state. Successive training loops will improve this estimate towards the true Q-value:

```
agents_expected_reward = []
for i in range(len(mini_batch)):
    if mini_batch[i][4]:
        # this was a terminal frame so there is no future
        reward...
        agents_expected_reward.append(rewards[i])
    else:
        agents_expected_reward.append(rewards[i] +
        FUTURE_REWARD_DISCOUNT *
        np.max(agents_reward_per_action[i]))
```

Augment the rewards we actually got with the rewards our network predicts if it's a non-terminal state:

```
session.run(_train_operation, feed_dict={
    input_layer: previous_states,
    action: actions,
    target: agents_expected_reward})
```

Finally, run the training operation on the network.

# Epsilon greedy

Another issue Q-learning has is that initially, the network will be very poor at estimating the rewards of actions. But these poor action estimations are the things that determine the states we move into. Our early estimates may be so bad that we may never get into a reward state from which we would be able to learn. Imagine if in the cart pole the network weights are initialized so the agent always picks to go left and hence fails after a few time steps. Because we only have samples of moving left, we will never start to adjust our weights for moving right and so will never be able to find a state with better rewards.

There are a few different solutions to this, such as giving the network a reward for getting into novel situations, known as novelty search, or using some kind of modification to seek out the actions with the greatest uncertainty.

The simplest solution and one that has been shown to work well is to start by choosing actions randomly so as to explore the space, and then over time as the network estimations get better and better, replace those random choices with actions chosen by the network. This is known as the epsilon greedy strategy and it can be used as an easy way to implement exploration for a range of algorithms. The epsilon here refers to the variable that is used for choosing whether a random action is used, greedy refers to taking the maximum action if not acting randomly. In the cart pole example, we will call this epsilon variable `probability_of_random_action`. It will start at 1, meaning 0 chance of a random action, and then at each training step, we will reduce it by some small amount until it hits 0:

```
if probability_of_random_action > 0.and len(_observations) >
OBSERVATION_STEPS:
    probability_of_random_action -= 1. / 10000
```

In the final step, we need the method that changes our neural network output into the action of the agent:

```
def choose_next_action():
    if random.random() <= probability_of_random_action:
        action_index = random.randrange(2)
```

Choose an action randomly if a random value comes up less than `probability_of_random_action`; otherwise choose the max output of our neural network:

```
    else:
        readout_t = session.run(output_layer,
        feed_dict={input_layer: [last_state]})[0]
        action_index = np.argmax(readout_t)
    new_action = np.zeros([2])
    new_action[action_index] = 1
    return new_action
```

Here is a graph of training progress against the cart pole task:

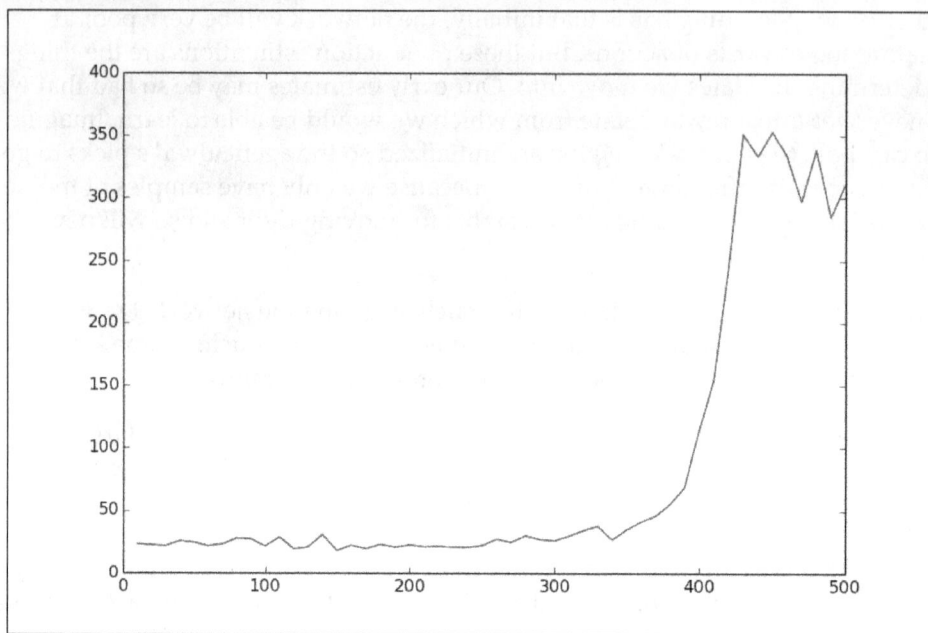

Figure 7: Cart pole task, y = average length of game over last 10 games x = number of games played

This looks good. Success for the cart pole task is defined as being able to last over 200 turns. After 400 games, we beat that comfortably averaging well over 300 turns per game. Because we set this learning task up using OpenAIGym, it is now easy to set up against other games. All we need to do is change the `gym.make` line to take a new input game string as input and then adjust the number of inputs and outputs to our network to fit that game. There are a few other interesting control tasks in OpenAIGym, such as the pendulum and acrobat, which q-learning should also do well on, but as a challenge, let's look at playing some Atari games.

# Atari Breakout

Breakout is a classic Atari game originally released in 1976. The player controls a paddle and must use it to bounce a ball into the colored blocks at the top of the screen. Points are scored whenever a block is hit. If the ball travels down past the paddle off the bottom of the screen, the player loses a life. The game ends either when the all the blocks have been destroyed or if the player loses all three lives that he starts with:

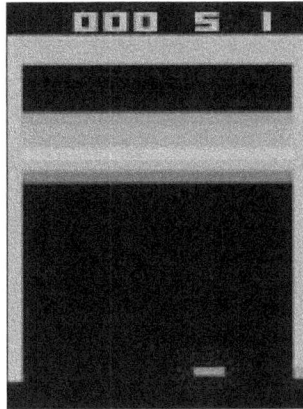

Figure 8: Atari Breakout

Think about how much harder learning a game like Breakout is compared to the cart pole task we just looked at. For cart pole, if a bad move is made that leads to the pole tipping over, we will normally receive feedback within a couple of moves. In Breakout, such feedback is much rarer. If we position our paddle wrong, that can be because of 20 or more moves that went into positioning.

# Atari Breakout random benchmark

Before we go any further, let's create an agent that will play Breakout by selecting moves randomly. That way we will have a benchmark against which to judge out a new agent:

```
from collections import deque

import random
import gym
import numpy as np

env = gym.make("Breakout-v0")
observation = env.reset()
reward_per_game = 0
scores = dequeu(maxlen=1000)

while True:
    env.render()

    next_action = random.randint(1, 3)
    observation, reward, terminal, info = env.step(next_action)
    reward_per_game += reward
```

We select our move randomly; in Breakout, the moves are as follows:

- 1: Move left
- 2: Stay still
- 3: Move right

```
if terminal:
    scores.append(reward_per_game)
    reward_per_game = 0
    print(np.mean(scores))
    env.reset()
```

If we've come to the end of our game, then we store our score, print it, and call `env.reset()` to keep playing. If we let this run for a few hundred games, we can see that random breakout tends to score around 1.4 points per game. Let's see how much better we can do with Q-learning.

The first issue we must deal with adapting from our cart pole task is that the state space is so much larger. Where the cart pole input was a set of four numbers for Breakout, it is the full screen of 210 by 160 pixels, with each pixel containing three floats, one for each color. To understand the game, those pixels must be related to blocks, paddles, and balls, and then the interaction between those things must be on some level computed. To make things even more difficult, a single image of the screen is not enough to understand what is going on in the game. The ball is moving over time with velocity; to understand the best move, you cannot just rely on the current screen image.

There are three approaches to dealing with this: one is to use a recurrent neural network that will judge the current state based on the previous output. This approach can work, but it is a lot more difficult to train. Another approach is to supply the screen input as a delta between the current frame and the last. In *Figure 9*, you will see an example of this. Both frames have been converted to grayscale because the color is providing us no information in Pong. The image of the previous frame has been subtracted from the image of the current frame. This allows you to see the path of the ball and the direction in which both paddles are moving:

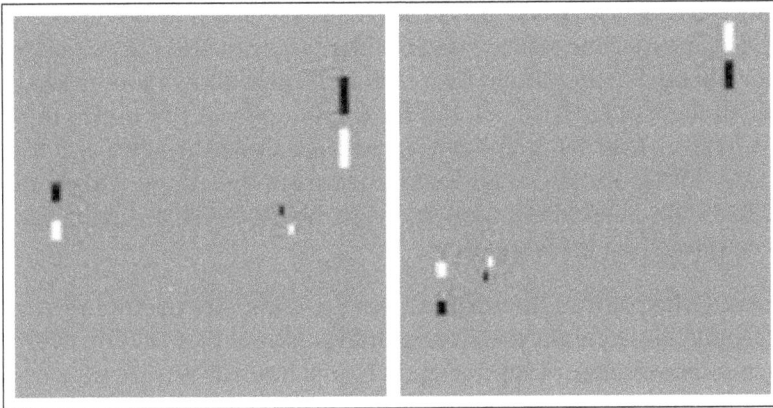

Figure 9: Pong delta images

This approach can work well for games such as Pong, which are only composed of moving elements, but for a game such as Breakout, where blocks are in fixed positions, we would be losing important information about the state of the world. Indeed, we would only ever be able to see a block for a brief flash when it was hit, while blocks we had not yet hit would remain invisible.

The third approach that we will take for Breakout is to set the current state to be the image of the last $n$ states of the game, where $n$ is 2 or more. This allows the neural network to have all the information it needs to make a good judgment about the state of the game. Using an $n$ of 4 is a good default value for most games; but for Breakout, $n$ of 2 has been found to be sufficient. It is good to use as low a value for $n$ as possible because this reduces the number of parameters that our network will need.

# Preprocessing the screen

The full code for this is in `deep_q_breakout.py` in the Git repo. But we will go through a few of the important modifications from the cart pole example here. The first is the type of neural network. For the cart pole, a network with a single hidden layer sufficed. But that involved four values being mapped to just two actions. Now we are working with `screen_width * screen_height * color_channels * number_of_frames_of_state = 201600` being mapped to three actions, a much higher level of complexity.

The first thing we can do to make life easier for ourselves is to resize the screen to a smaller size. From experimentation, we find that you can still play Breakout with a much smaller screen. Scaling down by a factor of 2 still allows you to see the ball, the paddles, and all the blocks. Also, a lot of the image space is not useful information for the agent. The score at the top, the gray patches along the sides and top, and the black space at the bottom can all be cropped from the image. This allows us to reduce the 210 * 160 screen into a more manageable 72 by 84, reducing the number of parameters by more than three quarters.

Also in Breakout, the color of the pixels doesn't contain any useful information, so we can replace the three colors with just a single color, which is only ever black or white, reducing the number of inputs again to just a third. We are now down to 72 by 84 = 6048 bits, and we need two frames of the game to be able to learn from. Let's write a method that does this processing of the Breakout screen:

```
def pre_process(screen_image):
```

The `screen_image` argument will be the Numpy array that we get from the `env.reset` or `env.next_step` operations on OpenAIGym. It will have shape 210 by 160 by 3, with each item being an `int` between 0 and 255 representing the value for that color:

```
screen_image = screen_image[32:-10, 8:-8]
```

This operation on the Numpy array crops the image, so we remove the scores at the top, black space at the bottom, and gray areas on either side:

```
screen_image = screen_image[::2, ::2, 0]
```

The `::2` argument to a Python array means we take every second item, which conveniently Numpy also supports. The 0 at the end means we just take the red color channel, which is fine because we are about to turn it into just black and white anyway. `screen_image` will now be of size 72 by 84 by 1:

```
screen_image[screen_image != 0] = 1
```

This sets everything that isn't completely black in the image to 1. This may not work for some games where you need precise contrast, but it works fine for Breakout:

```
return screen_image.astype(np.float)
```

Finally, this returns the `screen_image` from the method making sure that the type is converted to float. This will save time later when we want to put our values into TensorFlow. *Figure 10* shows how the screen looks before and after preprocessing. After processing, though it is a lot less pretty, the image still contains all the elements you would need to play the game:

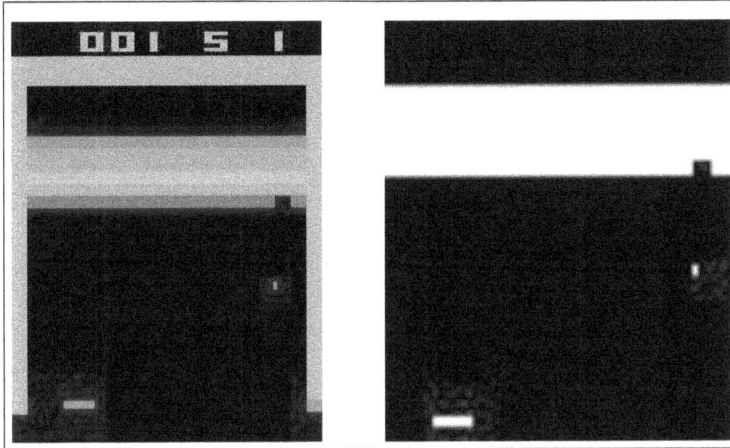

Figure 10: Breakout before and after processing

This leaves our state as 72*84*2 = 12800 bits, meaning we have $2^{12800}$ possible states that we need to map our three actions to. This sounds like a lot, but the problem is made simpler by the fact that though that is the full range of states possible in Breakout, only a quite small and predictable set of the states will occur. The paddles move horizontally across a fixed area; a single pixel will be active for the ball, and some number of blocks will exist across the central area. One could easily imagine that there are a small set of features that could be extracted from the image that might better relate to the actions we want to take — features such as the relative position of our paddle from the ball, the velocity of the ball, and so on — the kind of features deep neural networks can pick up.

# Creating a deep convolutional network

Let's next replace the single hidden layer network from the cart pole example with a deep convolutional network. Convolutional networks were first introduced in *Chapter 4, Unsupervised Feature Learning*. A convolutional network makes sense because we are dealing with image data. The network we create will have three convolutional layers leading to a single flat layer, leading to our output. Having four hidden layers makes some intuitive sense because we know we are going to need to detect very abstract invariant representations from the pixels, but it has also been shown to work successfully for a range of architectures. Because this is a deep network, relu activation functions make sense. *Figure 11* shows what the network will look like:

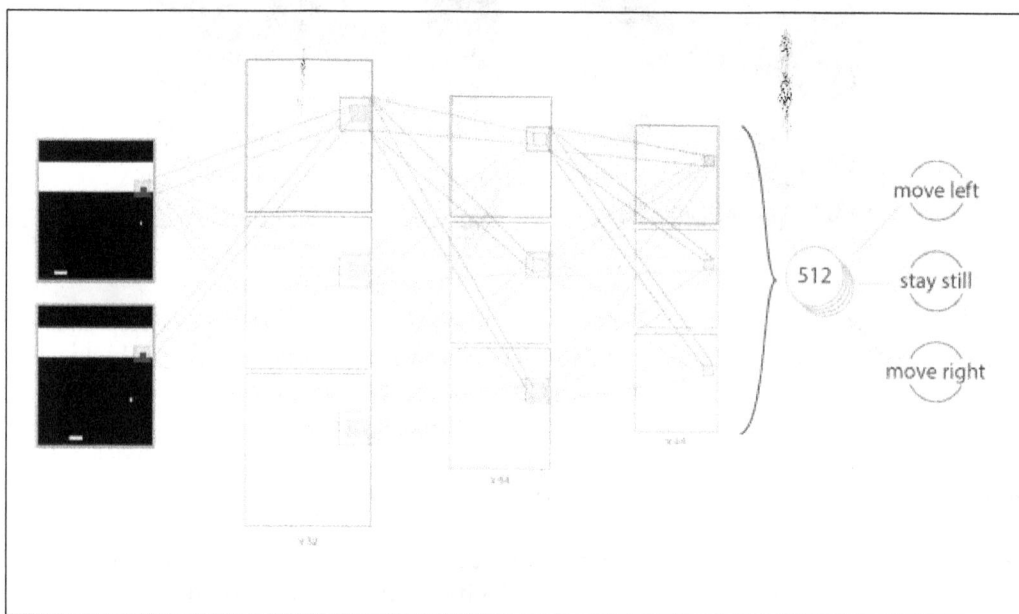

Figure 11: Architecture for our network that will learn to play breakout.

Here is the code for creating our deep convolutional network:

```
SCREEN_HEIGHT = 84
SCREEN_WIDTH = 74
STATE_FRAMES = 2

CONVOLUTIONS_LAYER_1 = 32
CONVOLUTIONS_LAYER_2 = 64
CONVOLUTIONS_LAYER_3 = 64
FLAT_HIDDEN_NODES = 512
```

These constants will be used throughout our `create_network` method:

```
def create_network():
    input_layer = tf.placeholder("float", [None, SCREEN_HEIGHT,
    SCREEN_WIDTH, STATE_FRAMES])
```

We define our input to be a product of the height, the width, and the state frames; the none dimension will be for batches of states:

```
convolution_weights_1 = tf.Variable(tf.truncated_normal([8, 8,
STATE_FRAMES, CONVOLUTIONS_LAYER_1], stddev=0.01))
    convolution_bias_1 = tf.Variable(tf.constant(0.01,
    shape=[CONVOLUTIONS_LAYER_1]))
```

The first convolutional layer will be an 8 by 8 widow across the width and height, taking in both the state frames. So it will get data on both the current 8 by 8 section of what the image looks like and what that 8 by 8 patch looked like in the previous frame. Each patch will map to 32 convolutions that will be the input to the next layer. We give the bias a very slight positive value; this can be good for layers with relu activations to reduce the number of dead neurons caused by the relu function:

```
    hidden_convolutional_layer_1 = tf.nn.relu(
        tf.nn.conv2d(input_layer, convolution_weights_1,
        strides=[1, 4, 4, 1], padding="SAME") +
        convolution_bias_1)
```

We put the weight and bias variables into the convolutional layer. This is created by the `tf.nn.conv2d` method. Setting `strides=[1, 4, 4, 1]` means the 8 by 8 convolutional window will be applied every four pixels across the width and height of the image. All the convolutional layers will go through the relu activation function:

```
        convolution_weights_2 = tf.Variable(tf.truncated_normal([4, 4,
        CONVOLUTIONS_LAYER_1, CONVOLUTIONS_LAYER_2], stddev=0.01))
        convolution_bias_2 = tf.Variable(tf.constant(0.01,
        shape=[CONVOLUTIONS_LAYER_2]))

        hidden_convolutional_layer_2 = tf.nn.relu(
            tf.nn.conv2d(hidden_convolutional_layer_1,
            convolution_weights_2, strides=[1, 2, 2, 1],
            padding="SAME") + convolution_bias_2)
        convolution_weights_3 = tf.Variable(tf.truncated_normal([3, 3,
        CONVOLUTIONS_LAYER_2, CONVOLUTIONS_LAYER_3], stddev=0.01))
        convolution_bias_3 = tf.Variable(tf.constant(0.01,
        shape=[CONVOLUTIONS_LAYER_2]))
        hidden_convolutional_layer_3 = tf.nn.relu(
```

```
tf.nn.conv2d(hidden_convolutional_layer_2,
convolution_weights_3, strides=[1, 1, 1, 1],
 padding="SAME") + convolution_bias_3)
```

Creating the next two convolutional layers proceeds in the same way. Our final convolutional layer, `hidden_convolutional_layer_3`, must now be connected to a flat layer:

```
hidden_convolutional_layer_3_flat =
tf.reshape(hidden_convolutional_layer_3, [-1,
9*11*CONVOLUTIONAL_LAYER_3])
```

This reshapes our convolutional layer, which is of dimensions none, 9, 11, 64 into a single flat layer:

```
feed_forward_weights_1 =
tf.Variable(tf.truncated_normal([FLAT_SIZE,
FLAT_HIDDEN_NODES], stddev=0.01))
feed_forward_bias_1 = tf.Variable(tf.constant(0.01,
shape=[FLAT_HIDDEN_NODES]))

final_hidden_activations = tf.nn.relu(
    tf.matmul(hidden_convolutional_layer_3_flat,
    feed_forward_weights_1) + feed_forward_bias_1)

feed_forward_weights_2 =
tf.Variable(tf.truncated_normal([FLAT_HIDDEN_NODES,
ACTIONS_COUNT], stddev=0.01))
feed_forward_bias_2 = tf.Variable(tf.constant(0.01,
shape=[ACTIONS_COUNT]))

output_layer = tf.matmul(final_hidden_activations,
feed_forward_weights_2) + feed_forward_bias_2

return input_layer, output_layer
```

We then create the last two flat layers in the standard way. Note that there is no activation function on the final layer because we are learning the value of an action in a given state here, and that has an unbounded range.

Our main loop will now need the following code added so that the current state is the combination of multiple frames, for breakout STATE_FRAMES is set to 2, but higher numbers will also work:

```
screen_binary = preprocess(observation)

if last_state is None:
last_state = np.stack(tuple(screen_binary for _ in
range(STATE_FRAMES)), axis=2)
```

If we have no last_state, then we construct a new Numpy array that is just the current screen_binary stacked as many times as we want STATE_FRAMES:

```
else:
    screen_binary = np.reshape(screen_binary, (SCREEN_HEIGHT,
    SCREEN_WIDTH, 1))
    current_state = np.append(last_state[:, :, 1:], screen_binary,
    axis=2)
```

Otherwise, we append our new screen_binary into the first position in our last_state to create the new current_state. Then we just need to remember to re-assign our last_state to equal our current state at the end of the main loop:

```
last_state = current_state
```

One issue we may now run into is that our state space is now a 84*74*2 array, and we want to be storing in the order of 1,000,000 of these as our list of past observations from which to train. Unless your computer is quite a beast, you may start to run into memory issues. Fortunately, a lot of these arrays will be very sparse and only contain two states, so one simple solution to this is to use in memory compression. This will sacrifice a bit of CPU time to save on memory; so before using this, consider which one is more important to you. Implementing it in Python is only a few lines:

```
import zlib
import pickle

observations.append(zlib.compress(
pickle.dumps((last_state, last_action, reward, current_state,
terminal), 2), 2))
```

Here, we compress the data before adding it to our list of observations:

```
mini_batch_compressed = random.sample(_observations,
MINI_BATCH_SIZE)
mini_batch = [pickle.loads(zlib.decompress(comp_item)) for
comp_item in mini_batch_compressed]
```

Then when sampling from the list, we decompress only our mini batch sample as we use it.

Another issue we may run into is that while the cart pole is trained in as little as a couple of minutes, for Breakout, training will be measured in days. To guard against something going wrong, such as a power failure shutting off the computer, we will want to start saving our network weights as we go. In Tensorflow, this are only a couple of lines:

```
CHECKPOINT_PATH = "breakout"

saver = tf.train.Saver()

if not os.path.exists(CHECKPOINT_PATH):
    os.mkdir(CHECKPOINT_PATH)

checkpoint = tf.train.get_checkpoint_state(CHECKPOINT_PATH)
if checkpoint:
    saver.restore(session, checkpoint.model_checkpoint_path)
```

This can be put at the beginning of the file, just the `session.run( tf.initialize_all_variables())` line. Then we just need to run the following command:

```
saver.save(_session, CHECKPOINT_PATH + '/network')
```

This means every couple of thousand training iterations are to have regular backups of our network created. Now let's see what training looks like:

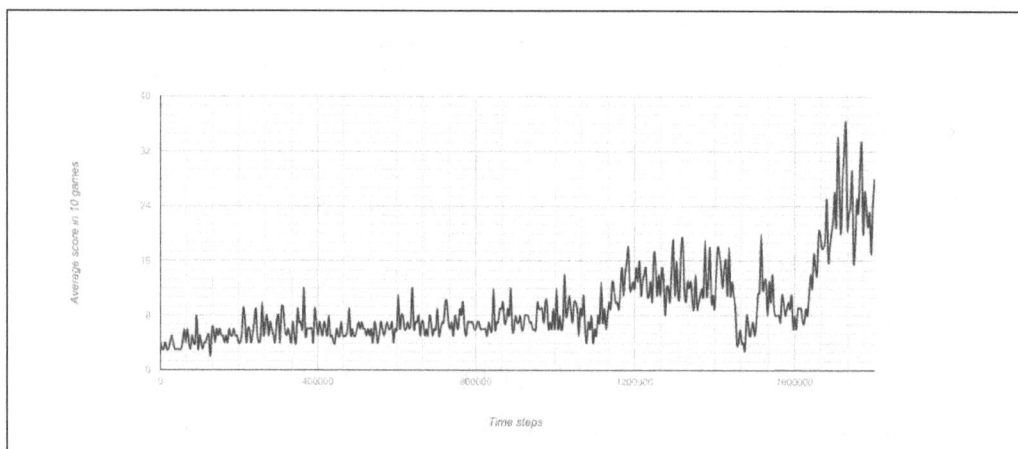

As we can see after 1.7 million iterations, we are playing at a level well above random. This same Q-learning algorithm has been tried on a wide range of Atari games, and with good hyper parameter, tuning was able to achieve human level or higher performance in, among others, Pong, Space Invaders, and Q*bert.

# Convergence issues in Q-learning

But it's not all plane sailing. Let's see how agent training is continued after the end of the preceding sequence:

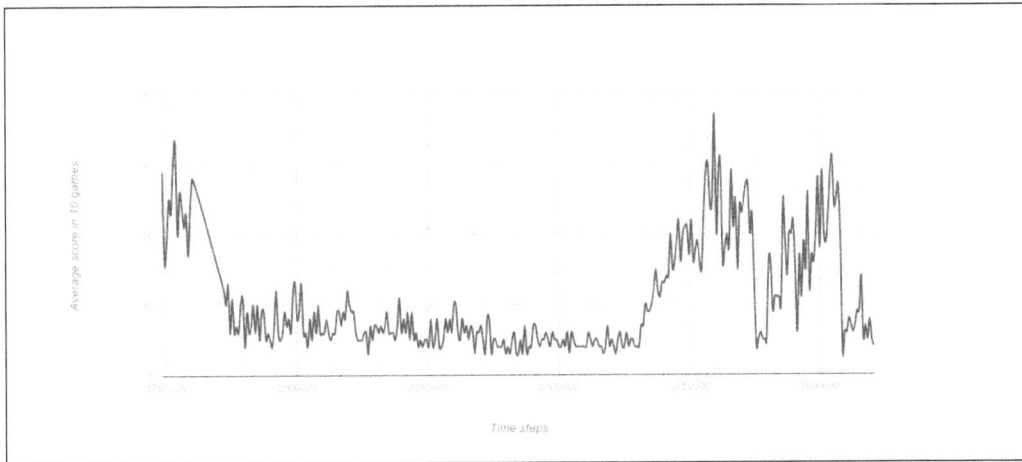

As you can see, at a certain point the agent's ability took a massive and prolonged drop off before returning to a similar level. The likely reason for this (as much as we can ever know the exact reasons) is one of the problems with Q-learning.

Q-learning is training against its own expectation of how good it thinks a state action pair will be. This is a moving target because every time you run a training step, the targets change. We hope that they are moving towards a more accurate estimation of the reward. But as they head there, small changes in parameters can result in quite extreme oscillations.

Once we end up in a space where we are doing worse than our previous estimations of ability, every single state action evaluation must adjust to this new reality. If we're getting an average of 30 points a game and with our new policy, we are down to just 20, the whole network must adjust to this.

Target network freezing (Minh et al 2015 Human-level control through deep reinforcement learning — Nature) can help reduce this. A second neural network, referred to as the target network, is created as a copy of the main training network. During training, we use the target network to generate the target values used to train the main neural network. In this way, the main network is learning against a more fixed point. The target networks weight frozen, but once a set number of iterations have passed, or a convergence criterion is reached, the target network is updated with the values from the main network. This process has been shown to significantly speed up training.

Another issue that a lot of reinforcement learning can struggle with pertains to games that have quite extreme rewards. Pac-Man, for example, has a very high reward for taking the power pill and then eating the ghosts. These extreme rewards received can cause problems with the gradients and lead to sub-optimal learning. The very easy but unsatisfactory way to fix this is called reward clipping, which just involves clipping the rewards received from the environment in some range (-1 and +1 are commonly used). For very little effort, this works, but it has the problem that the agent has lost the information about these larger rewards.

Another approach is what's called a normalized deep q network (**Hasselt et al — learning values across many orders of magnitude, 2016**). This involves setting up the neural network to output the expected reward of the state and action in the -1 to 1 range. Put the output into this range; it is put through the following equation:

$$Q(s,a) = \sigma U(s,a) + \mu$$

Here, $U(s, a)$ is the output of the neural network. The parameters $\sigma$ and $\mu$ can be worked out by making sure that the scaled output is constant between the target and main network, as described in target network freezing:

$$\sigma_1 U_{main}(s,a) + \mu_1 = \sigma_2 U_{target}(s,a) + \mu_2$$

Using this approach, the neural network gradients will be directed more towards learning the relative values of states and actions as opposed to expending energy simply learning the scale of the Q-value.

# Policy gradients versus Q-learning

Though we gave an example using policy gradients for learning a board game and Q-learning for a computer game, neither technique is limited to that type. Originally, Q-learning was considered the better technique overall, but over time and with better hyperparameters, tuning policy gradients have often been shown to perform better. The world's best performance in backgammon was achieved in 1991 using a neural network and Q-learning, and latest research suggests that policy gradients are best for most Atari games. So when should you use policy gradients versus Q-learning?

One constraint is that Q-learning can only work for discrete action tasks, whereas policy gradients can learn continuous action tasks. Also Q-learning is a deterministic algorithm, and for some tasks, the optimum behavior involves having some degree of randomness. For example, rock, paper, scissors, where any behavior that deviates from purely random can be exploited by an opponent.

There is also the online versus offline aspect. For many tasks, especially robot-control tasks, online learning may be very expensive. The ability to learn from memory is needed, so Q-learning is the best option. Unfortunately, the success of both Q-learning and policy gradients can vary a lot depending on the task and choice of hyperparameters; so when determining the best for a new task, experimentation appears to be the best approach.

Policy gradients also have a greater tendency to get stuck in local minima. Q-learning has a better chance of finding the global optima, but the cost of this is that it is not proven to converge, and performance may oscillate wildly or fail completely on its way there.

But there is also another approach that takes some of the best aspects of both. These are known as actor-critic methods.

# Actor-critic methods

Approaches to reinforcement learning can be divided into three broad categories:

- **Value-based learning**: This tries to learn the expected reward/value for being in a state. The desirability of getting into different states can then be evaluated based on their relative value. Q-learning in an example of value-based learning.

- **Policy-based learning**: In this, no attempt is made to evaluate the state, but different control policies are tried out and evaluated based on the actual reward from the environment. Policy gradients are an example of that.

- **Model-based learning**: In this approach, which will be discussed in more detail later in the chapter, the agent attempts to model the behavior of the environment and choose an action based on its ability to simulate the result of actions it might take by evaluating its model.

Actor-critic methods all revolve around the idea of using two neural networks for training. The first, the critic, uses value-based learning to learn a value function for a given state, the expected reward achieved by the agent. Then the actor network uses policy-based learning to maximize the value function from the critic. The actor is learning using policy gradients, but now its target has changed. Rather than being the actual reward received by playing, it is using the critic's estimate of that reward.

One of the big problems with Q-learning is that in complex cases, it can be very hard for the algorithm to ever converge. As re-evaluations of the Q-function change what actions are selected, the actual value rewards received can vary massively. For example, imagine a simple maze-walking robot. At the first T-junction it encounters in the maze, it initially moves left. Successive iterations of Q-learning eventually lead to it determining that right is the preferable way to move. But now because its path is completely different, every other state evaluation must now be recalculated; the previously learned knowledge is now of little value. Q-learning suffers from high variance because small shifts in policy can have huge impacts on reward.

In actor-critic, what the critic is doing is very similar to Q-learning, but there is a key difference: instead of learning the hypothetical best action for a given state, it is learning the expected reward based on the most likely sub-optimal policy that the actor is currently following.

Conversely, policy gradients have the inverse high variance problem. As policy gradients are exploring a maze stochastically, certain moves may be selected, which are, in fact, quite good but end up being evaluated as bad because of other bad moves being selected in the same rollout. It suffers because though the policy is more stable, it has high variance related to evaluating the policy.

This is where actor critic aims to mutually solve these two problems. The value-based learning now has lower variance because the policy is now more stable and predictable, while the policy gradient learning is also more stable because it now has a much lower variance value function from which to get its gradients.

# Baseline for variance reduction

There are a few different variants of actor-critic methods: the first one we will look at is the baseline actor critic. Here, the critic tries to learn the average performance of the agent from a given position, so its loss function would be this:

$$\left[ b\left(s_t\right) - r_t \right]^2$$

Here, $b\left(s_t\right)$ is the output of the critic network for the state at time step $t$, and $r_t$ is the cumulative discounted reward from time step $t$. The actor can then be trained using the target:

$$b\left(s_t\right) - r_t$$

Because the baseline is the average performance from this state, this has the effect of massively reducing the variance of training. If we run the cart pole task once using policy gradients and once using baselines, where we do not use batch normalization, we can see that baselines perform much better. But if we add in batch normalization, the result is not much different. For more complex tasks than cart pole, where the reward may vary a lot more with the state, the baselines approach may improve things a lot more. An example of this can be found at `actor_critic_baseline_cart_pole.py`.

# Generalized advantage estimator

The baselines approach does a great job at reducing variance, but it is not a true actor-critic approach because the actor is not learning the gradient of the critic, simply using it to normalize the reward. Generalized advantage estimator goes a step further and incorporates the critics gradients into the actor's objective.

In order to do this, we need to learn not just the value of the states the agent is in, but also of the state action pairs it takes. If $V(s_t)$ is the value of the state, and $Q(s_t, a_t)$ is the value of the state action pair, we can define an advantage function like this:

$$A\left(s_t, a_t\right) = Q\left(s_t, a_t\right) - V\left(s_t\right)$$

This will give us the difference between how well the action $a_t$ did in state $s_t$ and the average action the agent takes in this position. Moving towards the gradient of this function should lead to us maximizing our reward. Also, we don't need another network to estimate $Q(s_t, a_t)$ because we can use the fact that we have the value function for the state we reached at $s_{t+1}$, and the definition of a Q-function is as follows:

$$Q\left(s_t, a_t\right) = r_t + \gamma V\left(s_{t+1}\right)$$

Here, $r_t$ is now the reward for that time step, not the cumulative reward as in the baseline equation, and $\gamma$ is the future reward discount factor. We can now substitute that in to give us our advantage function purely in terms in $V$:

$$A\left(s_t, a_t\right) = r_t + \gamma V\left(s_{t+1}\right) - V\left(s_t\right)$$

Again, this gives us a measure of whether the critic thinks a given action improved or hurt the value of the position. We replace the cumulative reward in our actor's loss function with the result of the advantage function. The full code for this is in `actor_critic_advantage_cart_pole.py`. This approach used on the cart-pole challenge can complete it, but it may take longer than simply using policy gradients with batch normalization. But for more complex tasks such as learning computer games, advantage actor-critic can perform the best.

# Asynchronous methods

We have seen a lot of interesting methods in this chapter, but they all suffer from the constraint of being very slow to train. This isn't such a problem when we are running on basic control problems, such as the cart-pole task. But for learning Atari games, or the even more complex human tasks that we might want to learn in the future, the days to weeks of training time are far too long.

A big part of the time constraint, for both policy gradients and actor-critic, is that when learning online, we can only ever evaluate one policy at a time. We can get significant speed improvements by using more powerful GPUs and bigger and bigger processors; the speed of evaluating the policy online will always act as a hard limit on performance.

This is the problem that asynchronous methods aim to solve. The idea is to train multiple copies of the same neural networks across multiple threads. Each neural network trains online against a separate instance of the environment running on its thread. Instead of updating each neural network per training step, the updates are stored across multiple training steps. Every $x$ training steps the accumulated batch updates from each thread are summed together and applied to all the networks. This means network weights are being updated with the average change in parameter values across all the network updates.

This approach has been shown to work for policy gradients, actor-critic, and Q-learning. It results in a big improvement to training time and even improved performance. The best version of asynchronous methods was found to be asynchronous advantage actor-critic, which, at the time of writing , is said to be the most successful generalized game learning algorithm.

# Model-based approaches

The approaches we've so far shown can do a good job of learning all kinds of tasks, but an agent trained in these ways can still suffer from significant limitations:

- It trains very slowly; a human can learn a game like Pong from a couple of plays, while for Q-learning, it may take millions of playthroughs to get to a similar level.

- For games that require long-term planning, all the techniques perform very badly. Imagine a platform game where a player must retrieve a key from one side of a room to open a door on the other side. There will rarely be a passage of play where this occurs, and even then, the chance of learning that it was the key that lead to the extra reward from the door is miniscule.

- It cannot formulate a strategy or in any way adapt to a novel opponent. It may do well against an opponent it trains against, but when presented with an opponent showing some novelty in play, it will take a long time to learn to adapt to this.

- If given a new goal within an environment, it would require retraining. If we are training to play Pong as the left paddle and then we're recast as the right paddle, we would struggle to reuse the previously learned information. A human can do this without even thinking about it.

All these points could be said to relate to a central problem. Q-learning and policy gradients optimize parameters for a reward in a game very successfully, but they do not learn to understand a game. Human learning feels different from Q-learning in many ways, but one significant one is that when humans learn an environment, they are, on some level, learning a model of that environment. They can then use that model to make predictions or imagine hypothetical things that would happen if they made different actions within the environment.

Think of a player learning chess: he can think through what would happen if he were to make a certain move. He can imagine what the board would look like after this move, what options he would then have in that new position. He might even be able to factor his opponent into his model, what kind of personality this player has, what kinds of moves he favors, what his mood is.

This is what model-based approaches to reinforcement learning aim to do. A model-based approach to Pong would aim to build a simulation of the result of different actions it might take and try and get that simulation as close to reality as possible. Once a good model of an environment has been built up, learning the best action becomes a lot simpler as the agent can just treat the current state as the root of a Markov chain and use some of the techniques from *Chapter 7, Deep Learning for Board Games*, such as MCTS-UCT, to sample from its model to see which actions have the best results. It could even go further and use Q-learning or policy gradients trained on its own model, rather than the environment.

Model-based approaches also have the advantage that they might allow the AI to adapt much easier to change. If we have learned a model of an environment but want to change our goal within it, we can reuse the same model and simply adjust our policy within the model. If we are talking about robots, or other AI that operate in the physical world, learning using policy gradient by playing millions of episodes is completely impractical, especially when you consider that every experiment in the real world carries a cost in terms of time, energy, and the risk of damage through misadventure. Model-based approaches mitigate a lot of these issues.

Building a model raises all kinds of questions. If you were building a model-based agent to learn Pong, you know that it takes place in a 2D environment with two paddles and a ball and very basic physics. You would want all these elements in your model for it to be successful. But if you hand craft these, then there is no longer much learning going on, and your agent is very far from a generalized learning algorithm. What is the right *prior* for a model? How can we build a model that is flexible enough to learn the myriad things that can be encountered in the world while still being able to successfully learn specifics?

In more formal terms, learning the model can be seen as learning a function that gives the next state given the current state and action pair:

$$s_{t+1} = f\left(s_t, a_t\right)$$

If the environment is stochastic, the function might even return a probability distribution of possible next states. A deep neural network would naturally be a good choice for the function, and then learning would take the following steps:

1. Build a network where the input is the current state, and an action and output are the next state and the reward.

2. Gather a collection of state action transitions from the environment following an explorative policy. Simply making moves at random might be a good initial choice.

3. Use the collection of state action transitions to train the network in a supervised manner using the next states and state rewards as the targets.

4. Use the trained network transitions to determine the best move using MCTS, policy gradients, or Q-learning.

If we use the cart pole task as an example, using the MSE as our loss function, we can find that it is easy to train a deep neural network to accurately predict all the state transitions for this environment, including when a new state will be terminal. A code sample for this is in the Git repo.

It is even possible to learn models for more complex Atari games, using convolutional and recurrent layers. Here is an example of the architecture of the network:

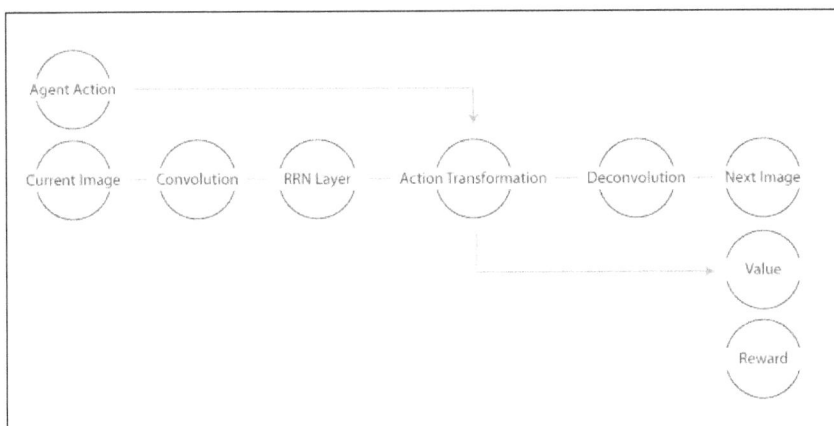

Source: http://cs231n.stanford.edu/reports2016/116_Report.pdf

A network like this was trained using two convolutional/deconvolutional layers and 128 node RNN to learn to predict next frames in Pong. It could do a good job of successfully predicting blurry versions of next frames, but the model was found to not be robust enough to run an MCTS to predict events beyond a frame or two in the future.

A modified version of this approach worked a lot better. In this, instead of trying to do a deconvolution to predict the next image, the network just tries to predict what the input to the RNN will be in the next frame, thus removing the need for the deconvolution. This network could learn to play Pong to a high enough standard to beat the in-game AI, winning by an average of 2.9 points per game after training. This is a long way short of the 20.0, which can be achieved by a fully trained Deep Q Network, but it is still a promising result for a very new approach. Similar results were also achieved on Breakout.

# Summary

In this chapter, we looked at building computer game playing agents using reinforcement learning. We went through the three main approaches: policy gradients, Q-learning, and model-based learning, and we saw how deep learning can be used with these approaches to achieve human or greater level performance. We would hope that the reader would come out of this chapter with enough knowledge to be able to use these techniques in other games or problems that they may want to solve. Reinforcement learning is an incredibly exciting area of research at the moment. Companies such as Google, Deepmind, OpenAI, and Microsoft are all investing heavily to unlock this future.

In the next chapter, we will take a look at anomaly detection and how the deep learning method can be applied to detect instances of fraud in financial transaction data.

# 9
# Anomaly Detection

In *Chapter 4, Unsupervised Feature Learning*, we saw the mechanisms of feature learning and in particular the use of auto-encoders as an unsupervised pre-training step for supervised learning tasks.

In this chapter, we are going to apply similar concepts, but for a different use case, anomaly detection.

One of the determinants for a good anomaly detector is finding smart data representations that can easily evince deviations from the normal distribution. Deep auto-encoders work very well in learning high-level abstractions and non-linear relationships of the underlying data. We will show how deep learning is a great fit for anomaly detection.

In this chapter, we will start by explaining the differences and communalities of concepts between outlier detection and anomaly detection. The reader will be guided through an imaginary fraud case study followed by examples showing the danger of having anomalies in real-world applications and the importance of automated and fast detection systems.

Before to move onto the deep learning implementations, we will cover a few families of techniques widely used in traditional machine learning and their current limits.

We will apply the architectures of deep auto-encoders seen in *Chapter 4, Unsupervised Feature Learning*, but for a particular kind of semi-supervised learning, also known as novelty detection. We will propose two powerful approaches: one based on reconstruction errors and another based on low-dimensional feature compression.

We will introduce H2O, one of the most demanded open source frameworks for building simple, but scalable feed-forward multi-layer neural networks.

Lastly, we will code a couple of examples of anomaly detection using the Python API of the H2O auto-encoder model.

The first example will reuse the MNIST digit dataset that you have seen *Chapter 3, Deep Learning Fundamentals* and *Chapter 4, Unsupervised Feature Learning*, but for detecting badly written digits. A second example will show how to detect anomalous pulsations in electrocardiogram time series.

To summarize, this chapter will cover the following topics:

- What is anomaly and outlier detection?
- Real-world applications of anomaly detection
- Popular shallow machine learning techniques
- Anomaly detection using deep auto-encoders
- H2O overview
- Code examples:
    - MNIST digit anomaly recognition
    - Electrocardiogram pulse detection

# What is anomaly and outlier detection?

Anomaly detection, often related to outlier detection and novelty detection, is the identification of items, events, or observations that deviate considerably from an expected pattern observed in a homogeneous dataset.

Anomaly detection is about predicting the unknown.

Whenever we find a discordant observation in the data, we could call it an anomaly or outlier. Although the two words are often used interchangeably, they actual refer to two different concepts, as Ravi Parikh describes in one of his blog posts (http://data.heapanalytics.com/garbage-in-garbage-out-how-anomalies-can-wreck-your-data):

> *"An outlier is a legitimate data point that's far away from the mean or median in a distribution. It may be unusual, like a 9.6-second 100-meter dash, but still within the realm of reality. An anomaly is an illegitimate data point that's generated by a different process than whatever generated the rest of the data."*

Let's try to explain the difference using a simple example of fraud detection.

In a log of transactions, we observe that a particular customer spends an average of $10 for their lunch every weekday. Suddenly, one day they spend $120. This is certainly an outlier, but perhaps that day they decided to pay the whole bill with their credit card. If a few of those transactions are orders of magnitude higher than their expected amount, then we could identify an anomaly. An anomaly is when the singular rare event justification does not hold anymore, for instance, transactions of $120 or higher over three consecutive orders. In this scenario, we are talking of anomalies because a pattern of repeated and linked outliers have been generated from a different process, possibly credit card fraud, with respect to the usual behavior.

While threshold rules can solve many detection problems, discovering complicated anomalies requires more advanced techniques.

What if a cloned credit card makes a lot of micro-payments of the amount of 10$? The rule-based detector would probably fail.

By simply looking at the measures over each dimension independently, the anomaly generation process could still be hidden within the average distribution. A single dimension signal would not trigger any alert. Let's see what happens if we add a few extra dimensions to the credit card fraud example: the geo-location, the time of the day in the local time zone, and the day of the week.

Let's analyze the same fraud example in more detail. Our customer is a full-time employee based in Milan, but resident in Rome. Every Monday morning, he takes the train, goes to work, and comes back to Rome on Saturday morning to see his friends and family. He loves cooking at home; he only goes out for dinner a few times during the week. In Rome, he lives near to his relatives, so he never has to prepare lunch during weekends, but he often enjoys spending the night out with friends. The distributions of the expected behavior would be as follows:

- **Amount**: Between $5 and $40
- **Location**: Milan 70% and Rome 30%
- **Time of the day**: 70% between noon and 2 P.M. and 30% between 9 P.M. and 11 P.M.
- **Day of the week**: Uniform over the week

One day, his credit card is cloned. The fraudulent person lives near his workplace and in order not to get caught, they systematically make small payments of $25 every night around 10 P.M. in an accomplice's corner shop.

If we look at the single dimensions, the fraudulent transactions would be just slightly outside the expected distribution, but still acceptable. The effect on the distributions of the amount and the day of the week would stay more or less the same while the location and time of the day would slightly increase toward Milan at evening time.

Even if systematically repeated, a little change in his lifestyle would be a reasonable explanation. The fraudulent activity would soon turn into the newer expected behavior, the normality.

Let's consider the joint distribution instead:

- 70% amount around 10$ in Milan over lunch time only on weekdays
- 30% amount around 30$ in Rome at dinner time only at weekends

In this scenario, the fraudulent activity would immediately be flagged as an outlier at its first occurrence since transactions in Milan at night above $20 are very rare.

Given the preceding example, we might think that considering more dimensions together makes our anomaly detection smarter. Just like any other machine learning algorithm, you need to find a trade-off between complexity and generalization.

Having too many dimensions would project all of the observations in a space where all of them are equally distant from each other. As a consequence, everything would be an "outlier", which, in the way we defined an outlier, intrinsically makes the whole dataset "normal". In other words, if every point looks just the same then you can't distinguish between the two cases. Having too few dimensions would not allow the model to spot an outlier from the haystack and may let it hide in the mass distribution for longer or maybe forever.

Nevertheless, only identifying outliers is not enough. Outliers can happen due to rare events, errors in data collection, or noise. Data is always dirty and full of inconsistencies. The first rule is "never assume your data is clean and correct". Finding outliers is just a standard routine. What would be surprising, instead, is finding contingent and unexplainable repeated behaviors:

> *"Data scientists realize that their best days coincide with discovery of truly odd features in the data."*

> *Haystacks and Needles: Anomaly Detection By: Gerhard Pilcher & Kenny Darrell, Data Mining Analyst, Elder Research, Inc.*

The persistence of a given outlier pattern is the signal that something has changed in the system we are monitoring. The real anomaly detection happens when observing systematic deviations in the underlying data generation process.

This also has an implication in the data preprocessing step. Contrary to what you would do for many machine learning problems, in anomaly detection you can't just filter out all of the outliers! Nevertheless, you should be careful in distinguishing between the nature of those. You do want to filter out wrong data entries, remove the noise, and normalize the remaining. Ultimately, you want to detect novelties in your cleaned dataset.

# Real-world applications of anomaly detection

Anomalies can happen in any system. Technically, you can always find a never-seen-before event that could not be found in the system's historical data. The implications of detecting those observations in some contexts can have a great impact (positive and negative).

In the field of law enforcement, anomaly detection could be used to reveal criminal activities (supposing you are in an area where the average person is honest enough to identify criminals standing out of the distribution).

In a network system, anomaly detection can help at finding external intrusions or suspicious activities of users, for instance, an employee who is accidentally or intentionally leaking large amounts of data outside the company intranet. Or maybe a hacker opening connections on non-common ports and/or protocols. In the specific case of Internet security, anomaly detection could be used for stopping new malware from spreading out by simply looking at spikes of visitors on non-trusted domains. And even if cyber security is not your core business, you should protect your network with data-driven solutions that can monitor and alert you in case of unrecognized activities.

Another similar example is authentication systems for many major social networks. Dedicated security teams have developed solutions that can measure each single activity, or sequence of them, and how distant those are from the median behavior of other users. Every time the algorithm marks an activity as suspicious, the system will prompt you with additional verifications. Those techniques can dramatically reduce identity theft and offer greater privacy protection. Likewise, the same concept can be applied to financial fraud, as we have seen in the previous example.

Anomalies generated by human behavior are among the most popular applications, but also the toughest. It is like a chess game. On one side, you have subject matter experts, data scientists, and engineers developing advanced detection systems. On the other side, you have hackers, aware of the game, studying their opponent's moves. That's why those kinds of systems require a lot of domain knowledge and should be designed to be reactive and dynamic.

Not all of the anomalies are originated from the "bad guys". In marketing, anomalies can represent isolated, but highly profitable customers who can be targeted with tailored offers. Their different and particular interests and/or profitable profile can be used to detect the outlying customers. For example, during an economy recession period, finding a few potential customers who are increasing their profit despite the mass trend could be an idea for adapting your product and redesigning your business strategy.

Other applications are medical diagnosis, hardware fault detection, predictive maintenance, and many more. Those applications also require agility.

Business opportunities, just like new malware, can rise every day and their life cycle could be very short, from hours to a few weeks. If your system is slow to react, you could be too late and will never catch up to your competitors.

Human detection systems are not able to scale and generally suffer from generalization. Deviations from normal behavior are not always obvious and it could be hard for an analyst to remember the whole history to compare to, which is the core requirement for anomaly detection. The situation complicates if the anomaly pattern is hidden inside abstract and non-linear relationships of entities in your data. The need for intelligent and fully automated systems that can learn complex interactions and provide real-time and accurate monitoring is the next frontier of innovation in the field.

# Popular shallow machine learning techniques

Anomaly detection is not new and many techniques have been well studied. The modeling can be divided and combined into two phases: data modeling and detection modeling.

# Data modeling

Data modeling generally consists of grouping available data in the granularity of observations we would like to detect such that it contains all of the necessary information we would like the detection model to consider.

We can identify three major types of data modeling techniques:

**Point anomaly**: This is similar to singular outlier detection. Each row in our dataset corresponds to an independent observation. The goal is to classify each observation as "normal" or "anomaly" or, better, to provide a numerical anomaly score.

**Contextual anomaly**: Each point is enriched with additional context information. A typical example is finding anomalies in a time series, where time itself represents the context. A spike of ice cream sales in January is not the same as in July. The context must be encapsulated into additional features. The time context could be a categorical calendar variable representing the month, quarter, day of month, day of week, or Boolean flags such as *is it a public holiday?*

**Collective anomaly**: Patterns of observations that represent the potential anomaly cause. The collective measures should be smartly aggregated into new features. An example is the fraud detection example described earlier. Transactions should be slotted into sessions or intervals and statistics should be extracted from the sequence such as standard deviation of payment amount, frequency, average interval between two consecutive transactions, spending trend, and so on.

The same problem could be addressed with multiple hybrid approaches defining data points at different granularities. For example, you could initially detect individual anomalous transactions independently, then link them chronologically, encapsulate the time context, and repeat the detection over the slotted sequence.

# Detection modeling

Regardless of the data type, the general input of the detection model consists of points in a multi-dimensional space (the feature space). Thus, with a bit of feature engineering, we can turn any anomaly representation into a single vector of features.

For this reason, we can see anomaly detection as a special case of outlier detection where the single point also encapsulates the context and any other information that can represent a pattern.

As any other machine learning technique, we have both supervised and unsupervised approaches. In addition, we also propose a semi-supervised schema:

- **Supervised**: Anomaly detection in a supervised manner can also be referred to as anomaly classification, for example, spam detection. In anomaly classification, we label each observation as anomaly (spam) or non-anomaly (ham) and then use a binary classifier to assign each point to the corresponding class. Any standard machine learning algorithm can be used, such as SVM, random forests, logistic regression, and of course neural networks even though it is not the focus of this chapter.

  One of the main problems with this approach is the skewness of the data. By definition, anomalies only represent a small percentage of the population. The absence of enough counter-examples during the training phase would lead to poor results. Moreover, some anomalies may have never been seen previously and it would be very hard to build a model that generalizes enough to correctly classify them.

- **Unsupervised**: A purely unsupervised approach means having no ground truth (no golden reference) of what constitutes an anomaly or not. We know there might be anomalies in the data, but no historical information is available about them.

  In these scenarios, the detection can also be seen as a clustering problem where the goal is not just grouping similar observations together, but also identifying all of the remaining isolated points. As such, it brings all of the issues and considerations of clustering problems. Data modeling and distance metrics should be carefully selected in order to be able to rank each point as close or far from one of the existing "normal behavior" clusters.

  Typical algorithms are k-means or density-based clustering. The major difficulties with clustering are the high sensitivity to noise and the well-known curse of dimensionality.

- **Semi-supervised**: Also known as novelty detection, semi-supervised learning might be a new term for you. It can be seen as both unsupervised learning (data is not labeled) and one-class supervised learning (all under the same label). The semi-supervision comes from the assumption that the training dataset belongs entirely to a single label: "the expected behavior". Instead of learning the rules for predicting whether it is "expected" or "anomalous", we learn the rules for predicting whether the observed point was generated from the same source that generated the training data or not. This is quite a strong assumption and it is what makes anomaly detection one of the hardest problems to solve in practice.

Popular techniques are SVM one-class classifier and statistical distribution models such as Multivariate Gaussian Distribution.

More information on Multivariate Gaussian Distribution for anomaly detection can be found in this tutorial: `http://dnene.bitbucket.org/docs/mlclass-notes/lecture16.html`. The following figure shows the classic identification of outliers from the main distribution visualized in a two-dimensional space:

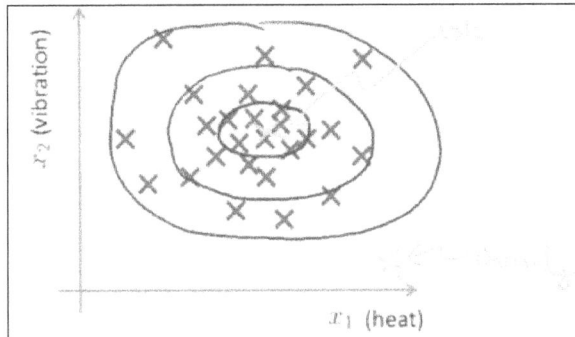

Two-dimensional representation of normal distribution with one single outlier (http://dnene.bitbucket.org/docs/mlclass-notes/lecture16.html)

# Anomaly detection using deep auto-encoders

The proposed approach using deep learning is semi-supervised and it is broadly explained in the following three steps:

1. Identify a set of data that represents the normal distribution. In this context, the word "normal" represents a set of points that we are confident to majorly represent non-anomalous entities and not to be confused with the Gaussian normal distribution.

   The identification is generally historical, where we know that no anomalies were officially recognized. This is why this approach is not purely unsupervised. It relies on the assumption that the majority of observations are anomaly-free. We can use external information (even labels if available) to achieve a higher quality of the selected subset.

2. Learn what "normal" means from this training dataset. The trained model will provide a sort of metric in its mathematical definition; that is, a function mapping every point to a real number representing the distance from another point representing the normal distribution.

Detected based on a threshold, on the anomaly score. By selecting the right threshold we can achieve the desired trade-off between precision (fewer false alarms) and recall (fewer missed detections).

One of the pros of this approach is robustness to noise. We can accept a small portion of outliers in the normal data used for training since that model will try to generalize the main distribution of the population and not the single observations. This property gives us an enormous advantage in terms of generalization with respect to the supervised approach, which is limited to only what can be observed in the past.

Moreover, this approach can be extended to labeled data as well, making it suitable for every class of anomaly detection problems. Since the label information is not taken into account in the modeling, we can discard it from the feature space and consider everything to be under the same label. Labels can still be used as ground truth during the validation phase. We could then treat the anomaly score as a binary classification score and use the ROC curve, and related measures, as benchmarks.

For our use cases, we will make use of auto-encoder architecture to learn the distribution of the training data. As we have seen in *Chapter 4, Unsupervised Feature Learning*, the network is designed to have arbitrary, but symmetric hidden layers with the same number of neurons in both the input layer and output layer. The whole topology has to be symmetric in the sense that the encoding topology on the left side is just mirrored to the decoding part to the right and they both share the same number of hidden units and activation functions:

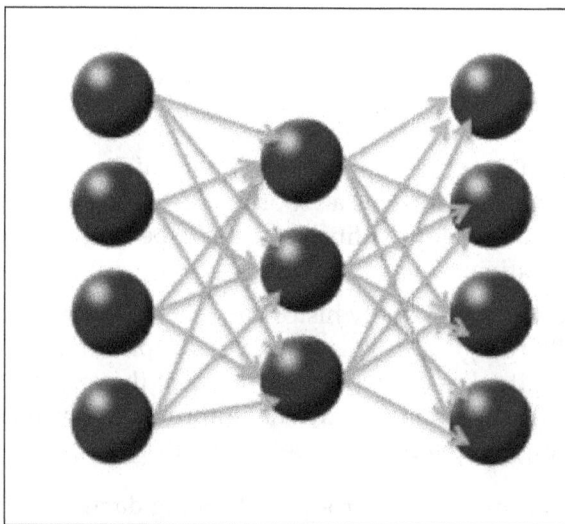

Auto-encoder simple representation from H2O training book (https://github.com/h2oai/h2o-training-book/blob/master/hands-on_training/images/autoencoder.png)

The loss function generally used is the **MSE** (**mean squared error**) between the input and the corresponding neurons in the output layer. This way, the network is forced to approximate an identity function via a non-linear and compressed representation of the original data.

Deep auto-encoders are also frequently used as a pre-training step for supervised learning models and for dimensionality reduction. In fact, the central layer of the auto-encoder could be used to represent the points in a reduced dimensionality, as we will see in the last example.

We can then start making analysis with the fully reconstructed representation that is the result of the encoding and decoding in cascade. An identity auto-encoder would reconstruct exactly the same values of the original point. That would not be very useful. In practice, auto-encoders reconstruct based on intermediate representations that minimize the training error. Thus, we learn those compression functions from the training set so that a normal point is very likely to be reconstructed correctly, but an outlier would have a higher **reconstruction error** (the mean squared error between the original point and the reconstructed one).

We can then use the reconstruction error as an anomaly score.

Alternatively, we can use a trick of setting the middle layer of the network small enough so that we can transform every point into a low-dimensional compressed representation. If we set it equal to two or three, we can even visualize the points. Hence, we can use auto-encoders for reducing the dimensionality followed by standard machine learning techniques for detection.

# H2O

Before we deep dive into the examples, let's spend some time justifying our decision of using H2O as our deep learning framework for anomaly detection.

H2O is not just a library or package to install. It is an open source, rich analytics platform that provides both machine learning algorithms and high-performance parallel computing abstractions.

H2O core technology is built around a Java Virtual Machine optimized for in-memory processing of distributed data collections.

The platform is usable via a web-based UI or programmatically in many languages, such as Python, R, Java, Scala, and JSON in a REST API.

Data can be loaded from many common data sources, such as HDFS, S3, most of the popular RDBMSes, and a few other NoSQL databases.

After loading, data is represented in an `H2OFrame`, making it familiar to people used to working with R, Spark, and Python pandas data frames.

The backend can then be switched among different engines. It can run locally in your machine or it can be deployed in a cluster on top of Spark or Hadoop MapReduce.

H2O will automatically handle the memory occupation and will optimize the execution plan for most of the data operations and model learning.

It provides a very fast scoring of data points against a trained model; it is advertised to run in nanoseconds.

In addition to traditional data analysis and machine learning algorithms, it features a few very robust implementations of deep learning models.

The general API for building models is via the `H2OEstimator`. A dedicated `H2ODeepLearningEstimator` class can be used to build feed-forward multilayer artificial networks.

One of the main reasons why we choose H2O for anomaly detection is that it provides a built-in class very useful for our cause, the `H2OAutoEncoderEstimator`.

As you will see in the following examples, building an auto-encoder network only requires a few parameters to be specified and then it will self-tune the rest.

The output of an estimator is a model, which depending on the problem to be solved, can be a classification model, regression, clustering, or in our case an auto-encoder.

Deep learning with H2O is not exhaustive, but it is quite simple and straightforward. It features automatic adaptive weight initialization, adaptive learning rates, various regularization techniques, performance tuning, grid-search, and cross-fold validation just to name a few. We will explore those advanced features in *Chapter 10, Building a Production-Ready Intrusion Detection System*.

We also hope to see RNNs and more advanced deep learning architecture soon implemented in the framework.

The key points of H2O are scalability, reliability, and ease of use. It is a good fit for enterprise environments that care about production aspects. The simplicity and built-in functionalities make it also well suited for research tasks and curious users who want to learn and experiment with deep learning.

# Getting started with H2O

H2O in local mode can be simply installed as dependency using `pip`. Follow the instructions at `http://www.h2o.ai/download/h2o/python`.

A local instance will be automatically spun at your first initialization.

Open a Jupyter notebook and create an `h2o` instance:

```
import h2o
h2o.init()
```

To check whether the initialization was successful, it should print something like `"Checking whether there is an H2O instance running at http://localhost:54321. connected."`.

You are now ready to import data and start building deep learning networks.

# Examples

The following examples are proof-of-concepts of how to apply auto-encoders to identify anomalies. Specific tuning and advanced design considerations are out of the scope for this chapter. We will take for granted some results from the literature without going into too much theoretical ground, which has already been covered in previous chapters.

We recommend the reader to carefully read *Chapter 4, Unsupervised Feature Learning* and the corresponding sections regarding auto-encoders.

We will use a Jupyter notebook for our examples.

Alternatively, we could have used H2O Flow (`http://www.h2o.ai/product/flow/`), which is a notebook-style UI for H2O pretty much like Jupyter, but we did not want to confuse the reader throughout the book.

We also assume that the reader has a basic idea of how the H2O framework, pandas, and related plotting libraries (`matplotlib` and `seaborn`) work.

In the code, we often convert an `H2OFrame` instance into a `pandas.DataFrame` so that we can use the standard plotting libraries. This is doable because our `H2OFrame` contains small data; it is not recommended when the data is large.

# MNIST digit anomaly recognition

This is a pretty standard example used for benchmarking anomaly detection models.

We have already seen this dataset in *Chapter 3, Deep Learning Fundamentals*. In this case though, we are not predicting which number each image represents, but whether the image represents a clear or an ugly handwritten digit. The goal is identifying badly written digit images.

In fact, in our example, we will discard the response column containing the label (the digit). We are not interested in which number each image represents, but rather how clearly this number is represented.

We are going to follow the same configurations provided in the H2O tutorial at `https://github.com/h2oai/h2o-training-book/blob/master/hands-on_training/anomaly_detection.md`.

We will start with some standard imports of `pandas` and `matplotlib`:

```
%matplotlib inline
import pandas as pd
from matplotlib import cm
import matplotlib.pyplot as plt
import numpy as np
from pylab import rcParams
rcParams['figure.figsize'] = 20, 12
from six.moves import range
```

Next, we are importing the data from the H2O repository (this is a readapted version of the original dataset in order to make it easier to parse and load into H2O):

```
train_with_label = h2o.import_file("http://h2o-public-test-data.
s3.amazonaws.com/bigdata/laptop/mnist/train.csv.gz")
test_with_label = h2o.import_file("http://h2o-public-test-data.
s3.amazonaws.com/bigdata/laptop/mnist/test.csv.gz")
```

The loaded train and test datasets represent one digit image for each row and contain 784 columns representing grayscale values in a scale from 0 to 255 of each pixel of a 28 x 28 image grid plus the last column used as label (the digit number).

We will use only the first 784 as predictors and leave the label only for validation:

```
predictors = list(range(0,784))
train = train_with_label[predictors]
test = test_with_label[predictors]
```

The H2O tutorial suggests a shallow model made of just one hidden layer of 20 neurons using a hyperbolic tangent as an activation function and 100 epochs (100 scans over the data).

The goal is not to learn how to tune the network, but rather understand the intuitions and concepts behind the anomaly detection approach. What we need to understand is that the encoder capacity depends on the number of hidden neurons. A too large capacity would lead to an identity function model, which would not learn any interesting structures. In our case, we are setting a low capacity, from 784 pixels to 20 nodes. This way, we will force the model to learn how to best approximate an identity function by only using a few features representing the relevant structures of the data:

```
from h2o.estimators.deeplearning import H2OAutoEncoderEstimator
model = H2OAutoEncoderEstimator(activation="Tanh", hidden=[20],
ignore_const_cols=False, epochs=1)
model.train(x=predictors,training_frame=train)
```

After we have trained the auto-encoder model, we can predict the digits in the test set, reconstructed using our new reduced dimensionality representation, and rank them according to the reconstruction error:

```
test_rec_error = model.anomaly(test)
```

Let's quickly describe the reconstruction error:

```
test_rec_error.describe()
```

We will see that it ranges between 0.01 and 1.62 with a mean of around 0.02, not a symmetric distribution.

Let's make a scatter plot of the reconstruction error for all of the test points:

```
test_rec_error_df = test_rec_error.as_data_frame()
test_rec_error_df['id'] = test_rec_error_df.index
test_rec_error_df.plot(kind='scatter', x='id', y='Reconstruction.MSE')
```

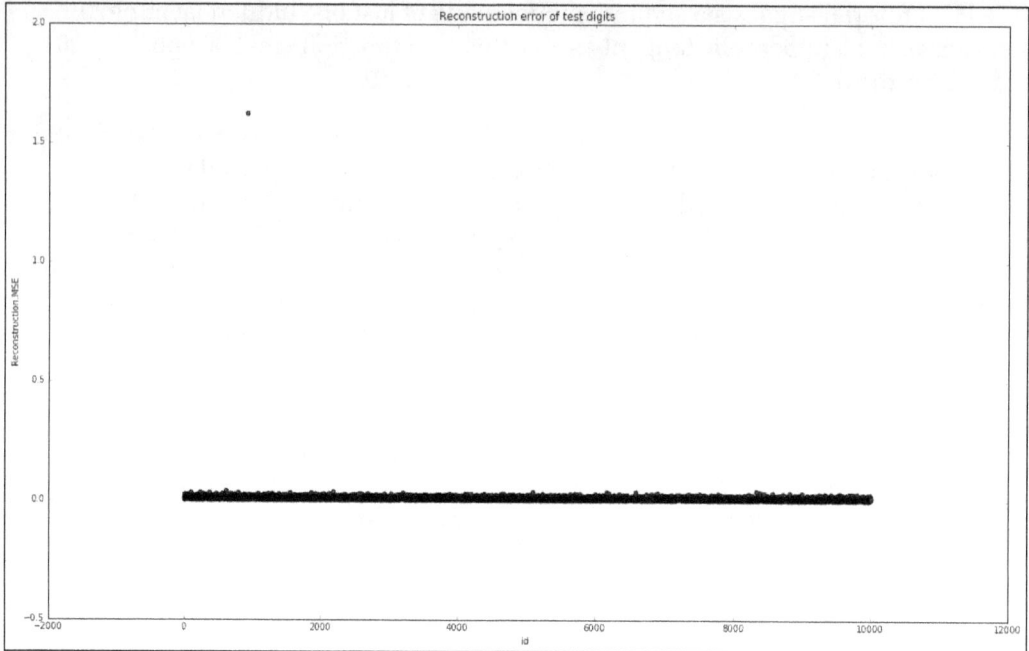

We can see that the test set contains only one obvious outlier, while the rest of the points fall in the range [0.0, 0.07].

Let's join the test feature set, including the label, with the reconstruction error and grab the outlier point and try to reconstruct it using the auto-encoder model:

```
test_with_error = test_with_label.cbind(test_rec_error)
outlier = test_with_error[test_with_error['Reconstruction.MSE'] > 1.0]
[0, :]
outlier_recon = model.predict(outlier[predictors]).
cbind(outlier['Reconstruction.MSE'])
```

We need to define a helper function to plot a single digit image:

```
def plot_digit(digit, title):
    df = digit.as_data_frame()
    pixels = df[predictors].values.reshape((28, 28))
    error = df['Reconstruction.MSE'][0]
    fig = plt.figure()
    plt.title(title)
    plt.imshow(pixels, cmap='gray')
    error_caption = 'MSE: {}'.format(round(error,2))
    fig.text(.1,.1,error_caption)
    plt.show()
```

And plot both the original outlier and its reconstructed version:

```
plot_digit(outlier, 'outlier')
plot_digit(outlier_recon, 'outlier_recon')
```

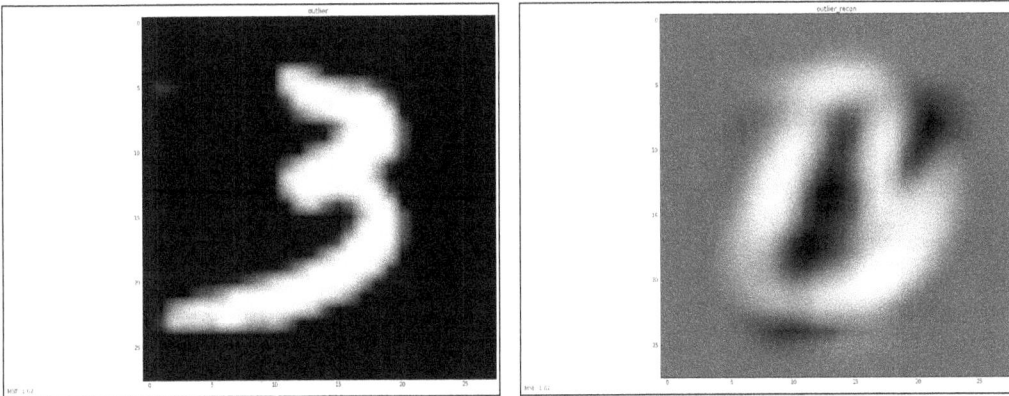

The reconstructed version is very noisy even though the outlier seems to clearly be representing the number three. We will see that it has one particular detail that makes it different from the rest of the other three digits.

Let's zoom into the error distribution of the remaining points:

```
test_rec_error.as_data_frame().hist(bins=1000, range=[0.0, 0.07])
```

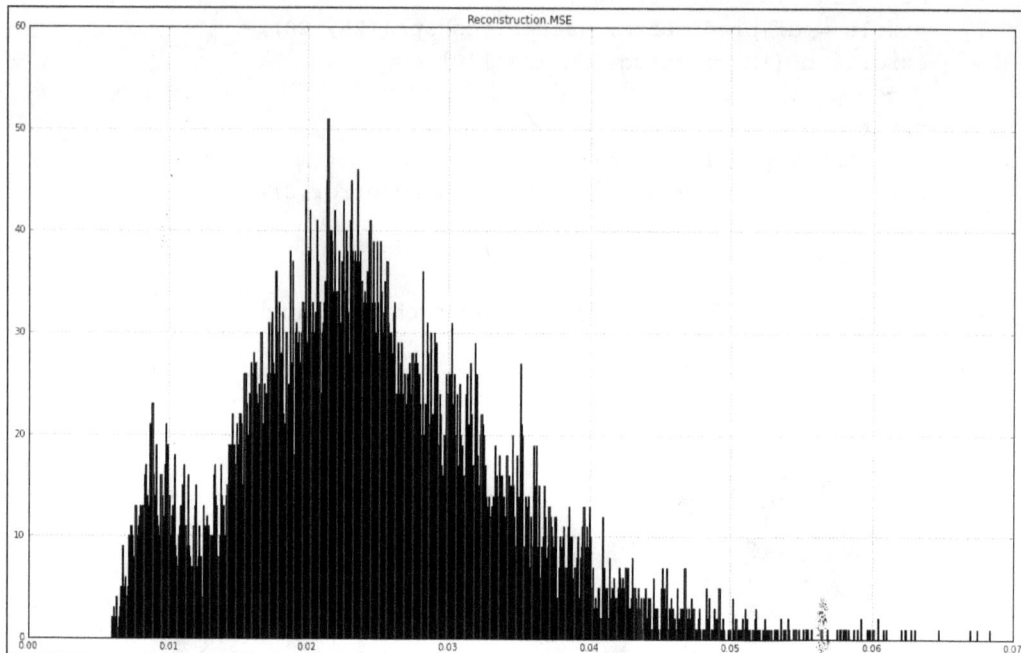

From the distribution, we can split the "central bell" at 0.02 into the "good" digits (on the left) and the "bad" (on the right). The rightmost tail (greater than 0.05) could be considered the "ugly" digits or the most anomalous.

We will now pick some digits of the number three from the "good" subset and compare them with our outlier:

```
digits_of_3 = test_with_error[(test_with_error['C785'] == 3) &
(test_with_error['Reconstruction.MSE'] < 0.02)]
```

In order to visualize multiple digits, we need to extend the plot util into a function that plots a grid of images:

```
def plot_multi_digits(digits, nx, ny, title):
    df = digits[0:(nx * ny),:].as_data_frame()
    images = [digit.reshape((28,28)) for digit in
    df[predictors].values]

    errors = df['Reconstruction.MSE'].values
    fig = plt.figure()
```

```
plt.title(title)
plt.xticks(np.array([]))
plt.yticks(np.array([]))
for x in range(nx):
    for y in range(ny):
        index = nx*y+x
        ax = fig.add_subplot(ny, nx, index + 1)
        ax.imshow(images[index], cmap='gray')
        plt.xticks(np.array([]))
        plt.yticks(np.array([]))
        error_caption = '{} - MSE: {}'.format(index,
        round(errors[index],2))
        ax.text(.1,.1,error_caption)
plt.show()
```

We can now plot both the original and reconstructed values of 36 random digits arranged on a 6 (nx) times 6 (ny) grid:

```
plot_multi_digits(digits_of_3, 6, 6, "good digits of 3")
plot_multi_digits(model.predict(digits_of_3[predictors]).cbind(digits_
of_3['Reconstruction.MSE']), 6, 6, "good reconstructed digits
of 3")
```

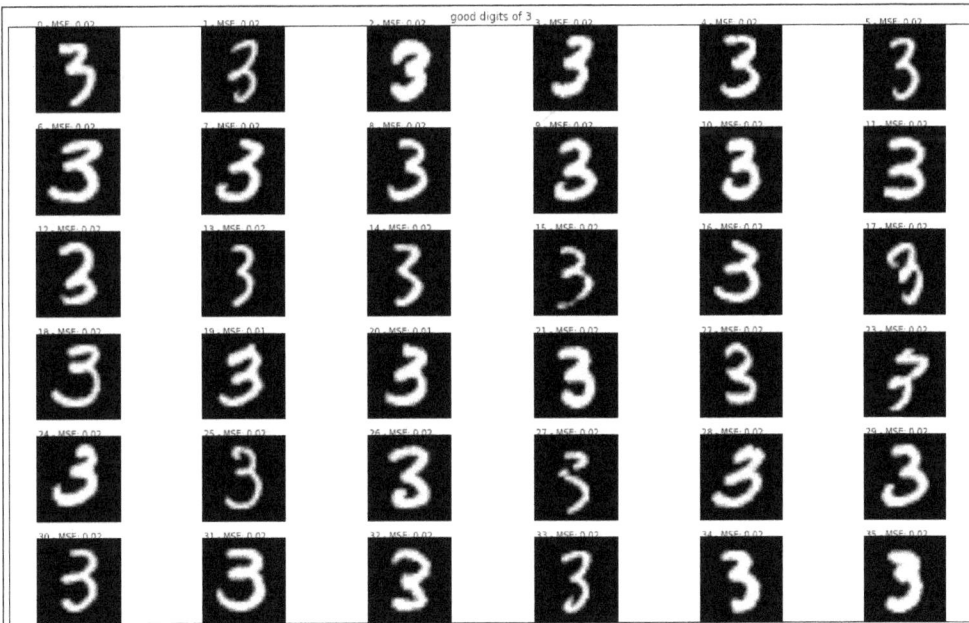

Original good digits of number three

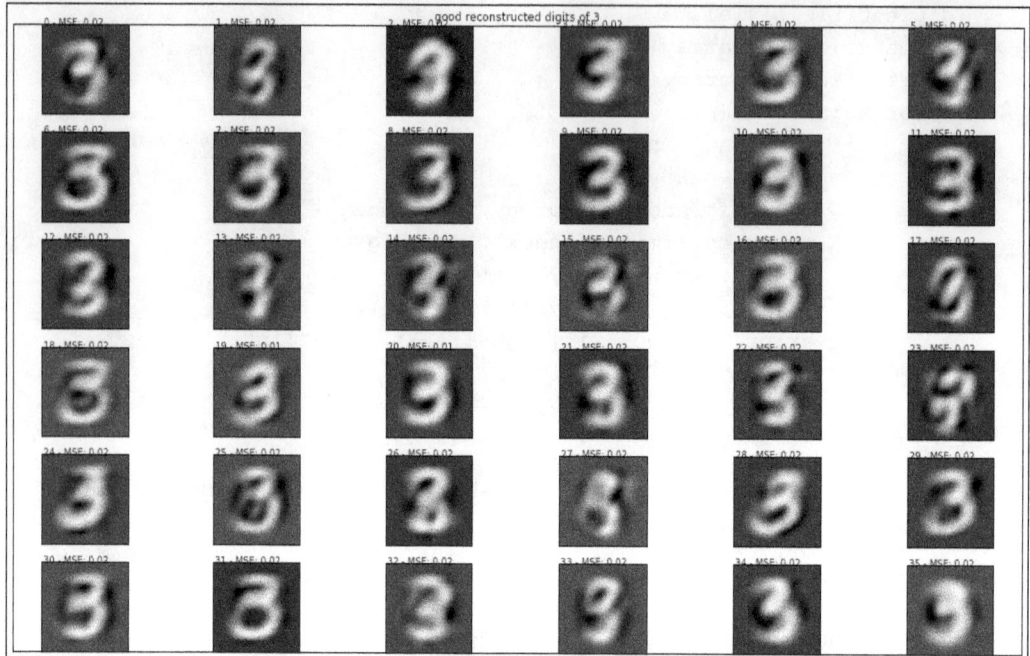

Reconstructed version of the good digits of number three

At first glance, our outlier does not look very different with the good-classified ones. Many of the reconstructed figures look similar to their original representation.

If we look more carefully at the figures, we can observe that none of them have the bottom-left shape of the digit so long to almost touch the corner.

Let's pick the digit with index 1, which scores 0.02, and let's copy the bottom-left part (the last 16 x 10 pixels) from the outlier figure. We will recompute the anomaly score to the modified image:

```
good_digit_of_3 = digits_of_3[1, :]
bottom_left_area = [(y * 28 + x) for y in range(11,28) for x in range
(0, 11)]
good_digit_of_3[bottom_left_area] = outlier[bottom_left_area]
good_digit_of_3['Reconstruction.MSE'] = model.anomaly(good_digit_of_3)
plot_digit(good_digit_of_3, 'good digit of 3 with copied bottom left
from outlier')
```

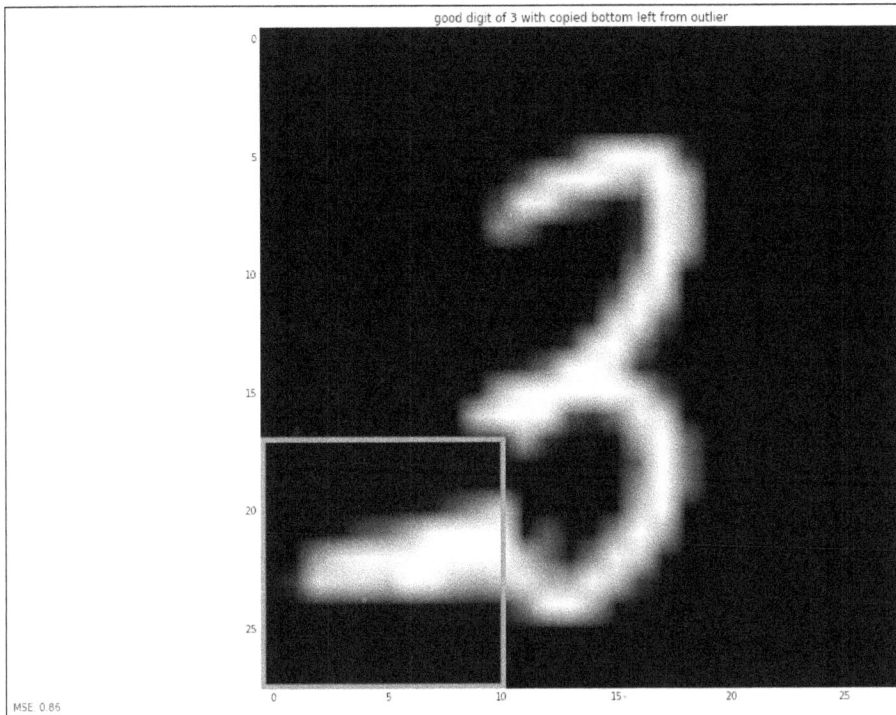

Magically, the MSE went up to 0.86. The remaining contribution to the high anomaly score (~1.62) is probably explained by the abnormal handwriting style.

This explanation means that the model is too sensitive to noise. It marks a digit image as anomalous due to a licit property simply because the training data does not contain enough samples. This is an "outlier" of the outlier detector, an example of a false positive.

This problem can generally be solved using denoising auto-encoders. In order to discover more robust representations, we can train the model to reconstruct the original input from a noisy version of it. We can look at *Chapter 4, Unsupervised Feature Learning*, for more theoretical explanations.

In our use case, we could mask each digit with a binomial sampling where we randomly set pixels to 0 with probability $p$. The loss function will then be the error of the reconstructed image from the noisy version and the original one. At the time of writing, H2O did not offer this feature, nor a customization of the loss function. Hence, implementing it on our own would have been too complicated for this example.

Our dataset contains labels for the digits, but unfortunately it does not have any assessment about the quality of them. We will have to do a manual inspection to gain confidence that our model works fine.

We will grab the bottom 100 (good) and top 100 (ugly) points and visualize them in a 10 x 10 grid:

```
sorted_test_with_error_df = test_with_error.as_data_frame().sort_
values(by='Reconstruction.MSE')
test_good = sorted_test_with_error_df[:100]
plot_multi_digits(test_good, 10, 10, "good digits")
```

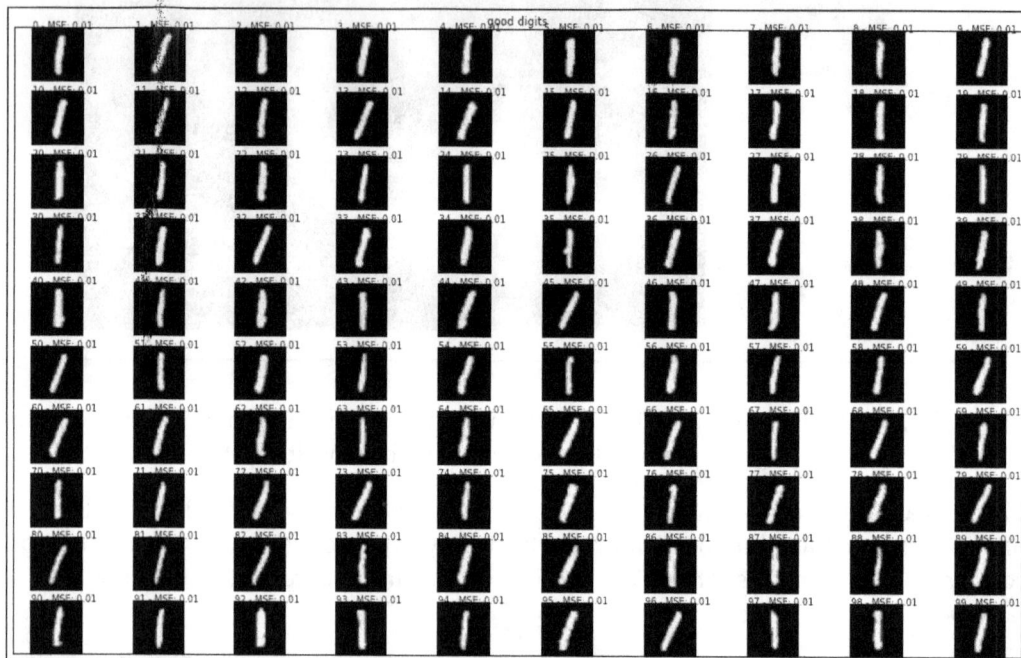

Reconstruction error of the top good digits

```
test_ugly = sorted_test_with_error_df.tail(100)
plot_multi_digits(test_ugly, 10, 10, "ugly digits")
```

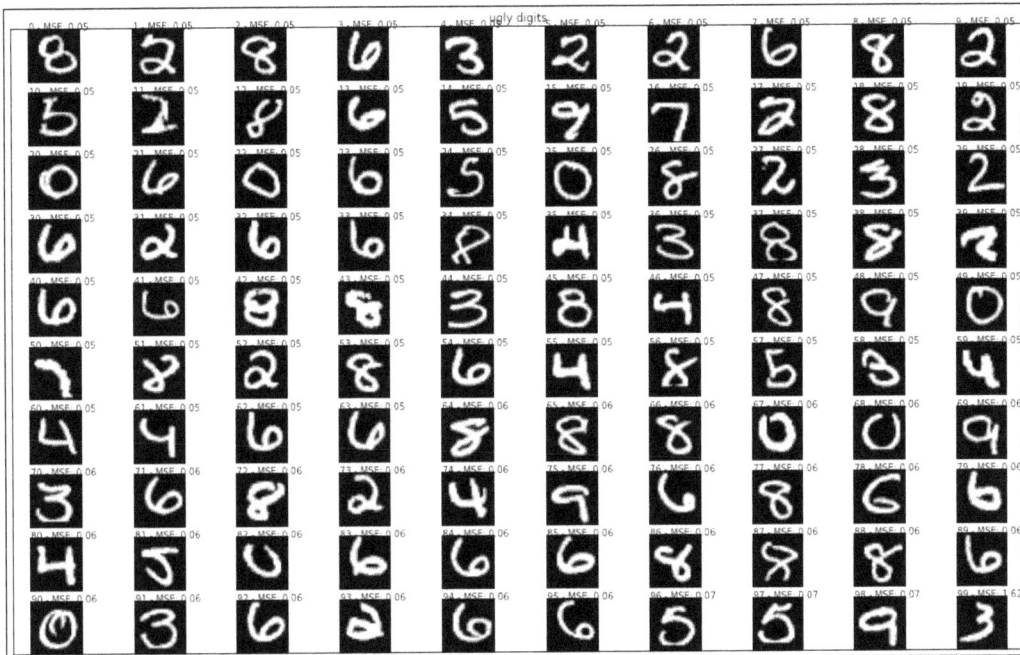

Reconstruction error of the worst ugly digits

From the figures, it is easy to see that "the good" represent number one, which is the easiest digit to write due to its simple structure of a straight line. Thus, digits of number one are less prone to be miswritten.

The bottom group is clearly ugly. The round shapes make it harder to distinguish between similar numbers and it strongly depends on the specific person's handwriting. Thus, those are most likely to represent "anomalies". They are most likely to deviate from the majority of the population's writing style.

Please be careful that different runs may lead to different results due to randomness introduced for scalability reasons due to race conditions generated by the Hogwild! algorithm explained in the following chapter. In order to make results reproducible, you should specify a `seed` and set `reproducibility=True`.

# Electrocardiogram pulse detection

In this second example, we will take a snapshot of data of an electrocardiogram time series specifically prepared from H2O for the anomaly detection use case.

The prepared data is available from the H2O public repository. The original dataset is provided by `http://www.physionet.org/`. Additional references are available at `http://www.cs.ucr.edu/~eamonn/discords/`.

The prepared dataset contains 20 ECG time series of good heartbeats plus three anomalous heartbeats.

Each row has 210 columns representing value samples in an ordered sequence.

Firstly, we load the ECG data and derive the training and test sets:

```
ecg_data = h2o.import_file("http://h2o-public-test-data.s3.amazonaws.
com/smalldata/anomaly/ecg_discord_test.csv")
train_ecg = ecg_data[:20:, :]
test_ecg = ecg_data[:23, :]
```

Let's define a function that stacks and plots the time series:

```
def plot_stacked_time_series(df, title):
    stacked = df.stack()
    stacked = stacked.reset_index()
    total = [data[0].values for name, data in
    stacked.groupby('level_0')]
    pd.DataFrame({idx:pos for idx, pos in enumerate(total)},
    index=data['level_1']).plot(title=title)
    plt.legend(bbox_to_anchor=(1.05, 1))
```

And then plot the dataset:

```
plot_stacked_time_series(ecg_data.as_data_frame(), "ECG data set")
```

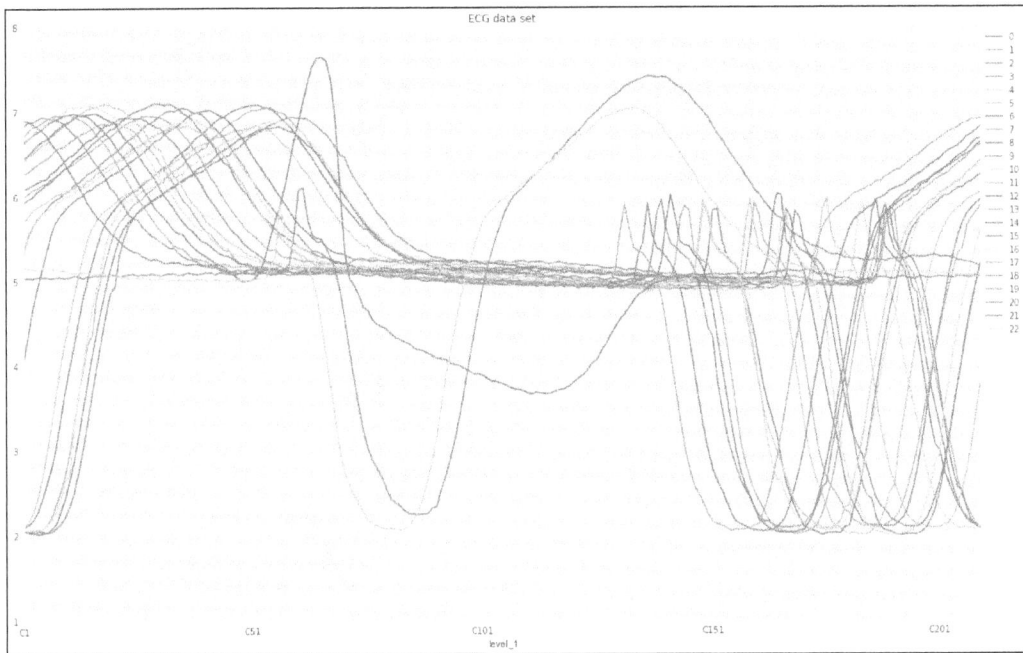

We can clearly see that the first 20 time series are normal while the last three (identified as 21, 22, and 23) are quite different from the others.

Hence, we want to train the model only on the first 20 samples. This time, we will use a deeper architecture made of five hidden layers of respectively 50, 20, and 20, 50 at the edges and two neurons in the middle. Remember that auto-encoders' topology is always symmetric and generally with decreasing layer size. The idea is to learn how to encode original data into a lower-dimensional space with minimum information loss and then be able to reconstruct the original values from this compressed representation.

This time, we will fix the value of the seed for reproducibility:

```
from h2o.estimators.deeplearning import H2OAutoEncoderEstimator
seed = 1
model = H2OAutoEncoderEstimator(
    activation="Tanh",
    hidden=[50,20, 2, 20, 50],
    epochs=100,
    seed=seed,
```

```
        reproducible=True)
model.train(
        x=train_ecg.names,
        training_frame=train_ecg
)
```

We can plot the reconstructed signals as follows:

```
plot_stacked_time_series(model.predict(ecg_data).as_data_frame(),
"Reconstructed test set")
```

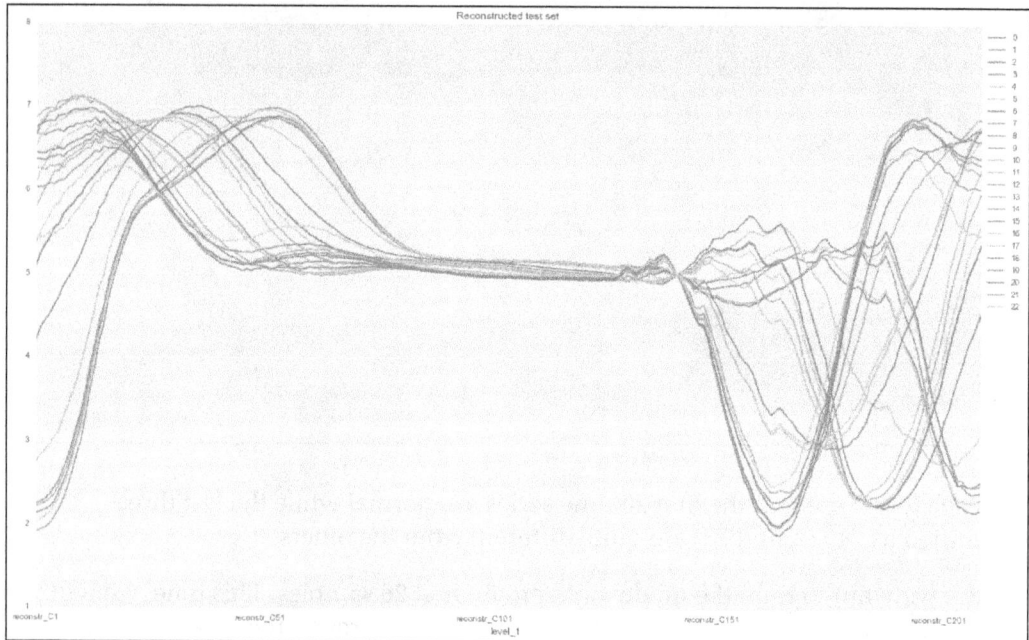

The reconstructed signals all look very similar. The outliers (20, 21, and 23) are now indistinguishable, which means they will have a higher reconstruction error.

Let's compute and plot the reconstruction error:

```
recon_error = model.anomaly(test_ecg)
plt.figure()
df = recon_error.as_data_frame(True)
df["sample_index"] = df.index
df.plot(kind="scatter", x="sample_index", y="Reconstruction.MSE",
title = "reconstruction error")
```

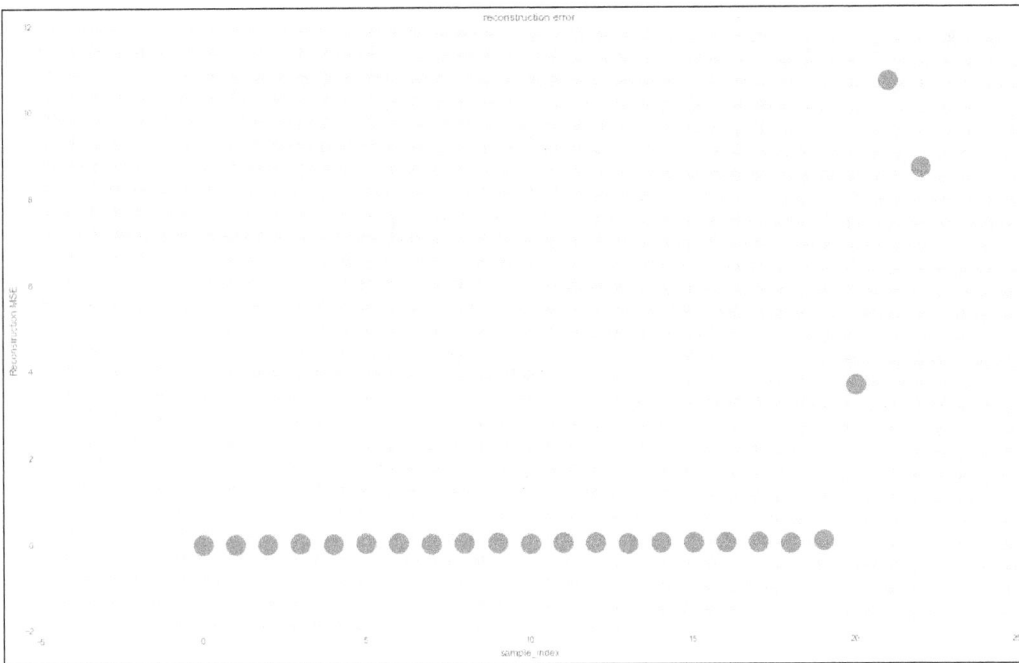

It is very easy to identify the last three points as outliers.

Now let's try to see the problem from a different perspective. By setting the central layer size equal to two, we can then use the encoder output to compress and visualize our points in a two-dimensional plot. We will use the `deepfeatures` API of the trained model to plot a new data frame with the 2D representation specifying the hidden layer index (starting from 0, the middle one is at index 2):

```
from matplotlib import cm
def plot_bidimensional(model, test, recon_error, layer, title):
    bidimensional_data = model.deepfeatures(test,
    layer).cbind(recon_error).as_data_frame()
    cmap = cm.get_cmap('Spectral')
    fig, ax = plt.subplots()
    bidimensional_data.plot(kind='scatter',
                        x= 'DF.L{}.C1'.format(layer+1),
                        y= 'DF.L{}.C2'.format(layer+1),
                        s = 500,
                        c = 'Reconstruction.MSE',
                        title = title,
                        ax = ax,
                        colormap=cmap)
```

```
layer_column = 'DF.L{}.C'.format(layer + 1)
columns = [layer_column + '1', layer_column + '2']
for k, v in bidimensional_data[columns].iterrows():
    ax.annotate(k, v, size=20, verticalalignment='bottom',
    horizontalalignment='left')
fig.canvas.draw()
```

Then we visualize all of the points with the previously trained model with seed 1:

```
plot_bidimensional(model, test_ecg, recon_error, 2, "2D
representation of data points seed {}".format(seed))
```

If we repeat the same procedure by retraining the model with the seed set to 2, 3, 4, 5, and 6, we obtain the following:

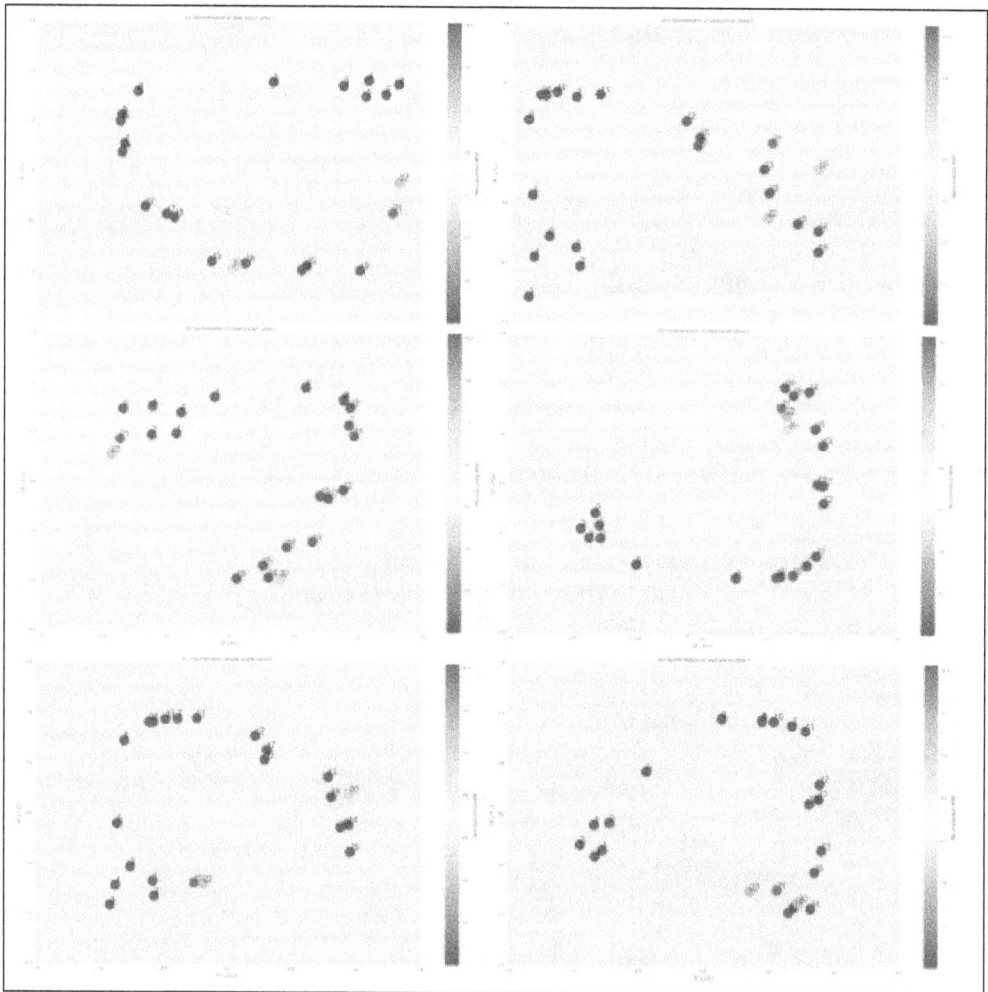

As you can see, each seed gives a totally different two-dimensional representation. What is more interesting is that the outlier points (marked with 20, 21, and 22) always have the same reconstruction error (given by their color). For the model, those are all valid two-dimensional compressed representations that contain the same amount of information and can be decoded into the original time series.

We could then use the auto-encoder for reducing the dimensionality followed by an unsupervised approach (for example, density-based clustering) to group similar points together. By repeating the clustering for each seed, we can then apply a Consensus Clustering to determine which are the points that mostly agree with each other (points that are always clustered together). This approach won't necessary tell you where the anomalies are, but it will help you understand your data and spot clusters of small dimensions that can be further investigated. The smaller and more isolated from the other clusters, the higher the anomaly scores.

# Summary

Anomaly detection is a very common problem that can be found in many applications.

At the start of this chapter, we described a few possible use cases and highlighted the major types and differences according to the context and application requirements.

We briefly covered some of the popular techniques for solving anomaly detection using shallow machine learning algorithms. The major differences can be found in the way features are generated. In shallow machine learning, this is generally a manual task, also called feature engineering. The advantage of using deep learning is that it can automatically learn smart data representations in an unsupervised fashion. Good data representations can substantially help the detection model to spot anomalies.

We have provided an overview of H2O and summarized its functionalities for deep learning, in particular the auto-encoders.

We have implemented a couple of proof-of-concept examples in order to learn how to apply auto-encoders for solving anomaly detection problems.

For the digit recognition, we ranked each image according to an anomaly score given by the model reconstruction error.

A similar approach could also be further extended to applications such as signature verification, author handwriting recognition of manuscripts, or fault detection via image pictures.

The digit recognition example was a type of individual point outlier detection. It used a shallow architecture made of only one single hidden layer.

For the ECG example, we used a deeper architecture and showed an additional detection technique based on the compressed feature representation instead of the fully reconstructed one. We used the encoder part of the network to compress the non-linear relationships of the raw data into a smaller dimensionality space. The newer representation can then be used as a pre-process step in order to apply classic anomaly detection algorithms such as Gaussian Multivariate Distribution. By reducing to a two-dimensional space, we could even visualize the data points and identify anomalies at the frontier of the main elliptical distribution.

Nevertheless, auto-encoders are not the only way of doing anomaly detection using deep learning. You can also follow a supervised approach where you take out part of the information from your data and try to estimate based on the remaining information. The predicted value will represent your normal expected behavior and deviations from this value would represent your anomalies. For example, in case of time series, you could use recurrent neural networks (RNNs), or their evolution in long short-term memory (LSTM), as a regression model to predict what is going to be the next numerical value of a time sequence and then use the error between the predicted and observed value as an anomaly score.

We preferred to focus on this semi-supervised approach because it can be applied to many applications and also because it is nicely implemented in H2O.

Another important detail is that the majority of the code snippets were written for data analysis, manipulation, and visualization. By using H2O, we used the built-in classes to implement deep neural networks in just a couple of lines of code. This is quite impressive compared to the overhead of other frameworks. Moreover, the H2O estimators and models offer a wide range of customizable parameters and different configurations. On the other hand, we found H2O to be quite limited in extending its usage for scopes that are not currently supported. Overall, it is a very promising technology and there is much room for further improvement.

Be aware that the techniques covered in this chapter served only as proof-of-concept for how deep learning could be applied to anomaly detection. There are many gotchas and pitfalls to consider, both technical and practical, when dealing with production data. We will cover a few of them in *Chapter 10, Building a Production-Ready Intrusion Detection System*.

# 10
# Building a Production-Ready Intrusion Detection System

In the previous chapter, we explained in detail what an anomaly detection is and how it can be implemented using auto-encoders. We proposed a semi-supervised approach for novelty detection. We introduced H2O and showed a couple of examples (MNIST digit recognition and ECG pulse signals) implemented on top of the framework and running in local mode. Those examples used a small dataset already cleaned and prepared to be used as proof-of-concept.

Real-world data and enterprise environments work very differently. In this chapter, we will leverage H2O and general common practices to build a scalable distributed system ready for deployment in production.

We will use as an example an intrusion detection system with the goal of detecting intrusions and attacks in a network environment.

We will raise a few practical and technical issues that you would probably face in building a data product for intrusion detection.

In particular, you will learn:

- What a data product is
- How to better initialize the weights of a deep network
- How to parallelize in multi-threading the Stochastic Gradient Descent algorithm with HOGWILD!
- How to distribute computation using Map/Reduce on top of Apache Spark using Sparkling Water
- A few rules of thumb for tweaking scalability and implementation parameters

- A comprehensive list of techniques for adaptive learning
- How to validate both in presence and absence of ground truth
- How to pick the right trade-off between precision and reduced false alarms
- An example of an exhaustive evaluation framework considering both technical and business aspects
- A summary of model hyper parameters and tuning techniques
- How to export your trained model as a POJO and deploy it in an anomaly detection API

# What is a data product?

The final goal in data science is to solve problems by adopting data-intensive solutions. The focus is not only on answering questions but also on satisfying business requirements.

Just building data-driven solutions is not enough. Nowadays, any app or website is powered by data. Building a web platform for listing items on sale does consume data but is not necessarily a data product.

Mike Loukides gives an excellent definition:

> *A data application acquires its value from the data itself, and creates more data as a result; it's not just an application with data; it's a data product. Data science enables the creation of data products.*

> *From "What is Data Science" (https://www.oreilly.com/ideas/what-is-data-science)*

The fundamental requirement is that the system is able to derive value from data—not just consuming it as it is—and generate knowledge (in the form of data or insights) as output. A data product is the automation that let you extract information from raw data, build knowledge, and consume it effectively to solve a specific problem.

The two examples in the anomaly detection chapter are the definition of what a data product is not. We opened a notebook, loaded a snapshot of data, started analyzing and experimenting with deep learning, and ultimately produced some plots that prove we could apply auto-encoders for detecting anomalies. Although the whole analysis is reproducible, in the best case, we could have built a proof-of-concept or a toy model. Will this be suitable for solving a real-world problem? Is this a Minimum Viable Product (MVP) for your business? Probably not.

Machine learning, statistics, and data analysis techniques are not new. The origin of mathematical statistics dates back to the 17th century; Machine Learning is a subset of **Artificial Intelligence (AI)**, which was proven by Alan Turing with his *Turing Test* in 1950. You might argue that the data revolution started with the increase of data collection and advances in technology. I would say this is what enabled the data revolution to happen smoothly. The real shift probably happened when companies started realizing they can create new products, offer better services, and significantly improve their decision-making by trusting their data. Nevertheless, the innovation is not in manually looking for answers in data; it is in integrating streams of information generated from data-driven systems that can extract and provide insights able to drive human actions.

A **data product** is the result of the intersection between science and technology in order to generate artificial intelligence, able to scale and take unbiased decisions on our behalf.

Because a data product grows and get better by consuming more data, and because it generates data itself, the generative effect could theoretically establish an infinite stream of information. For this reason, a data product must also be self-adapting and able to incrementally incorporate new knowledge as new observations are collected. A statistical model is just one component of the final data product. For instance, an intrusion detection system after the anomaly inspection would feed back a bunch of labeled data that can be re-used for training the model in the following generations.

Nevertheless, data analytics is also extremely important in every organization. It is quite common to find hybrid teams of Data Scientists and Analysts within organizations. The manual supervision, inspection, and visualization of intermediate results is a must requirement for building successful solutions. What we aim to remove is the manual intervention in the finite product. In other words, the development stage involves a lot of exploratory analysis and manual checkpoints but the final deliverable is generally an end-to-end pipeline (or a bunch of independent micro-services) that receives data as input and produces data as output. The whole workflow should preferably be automated, tested, and scalable. Ideally we would like to have real-time predictions integrated within the enterprise system that can react upon each detection.

An example could be a large screen in a factory showing a live dashboard with real-time measurements coming from the active machines and firing alerts whenever something goes wrong. This data product would not fix the machine for you but would be a support tool for human intervention.

Human interaction should generally happen as:

- Domain expertise by setting priors coming from their experience
- Developing and testing
- Final consumption of the product

In our intrusion detection system, we will use the data to recommend actions for a team of security analysts so that they can prioritize and take better decisions.

# Training

Training a network means having already designed its topology. For that purpose we recommend the corresponding Auto-Encoder section in *Chapter 4, Unsupervised Feature Learning* for design guidelines according to the type of input data and expected use cases.

Once we have defined the topology of the neural network, we are just at the starting point. The model now needs to be fitted during the training phase. We will see a few techniques for scaling and accelerating the learning of our training algorithm that are very suitable for production environments with large datasets.

# Weights initialization

The final convergence of neural networks can be strongly influenced by the initial weights. Depending on which activation function we have selected, we would like to have a gradient with a steep slope in the first iterations so that the gradient descent algorithm can quickly jump into the optimum area.

For a hidden unit $j$ in the first layer (directly connected to the input layer), the sum of values in the first iteration for the training sample $x$ of dimensionality $d$ would be:

$$h_j = \sum_{i=1}^{d} w_{o,i} x_i$$

Here, $w_{0,i}$ is the initial weight of the $i^{\text{th}}$ dimension.

Since we choose the weights to be independent and identically distributed (*i.i.d.*) and also independent from the inputs, the mean of unit $j$ is:

$$E\left(h_j\right) = \sum_{i=1}^{d} E\left[w_{o,i}\right] E\left[x_i\right] = d\mu_{wo}\mu_x$$

If the input values $x_i$ are normalized to have $\mu_x = 0$ and standard deviation $\sigma_x = 1$, the mean will be $E(h_j)$ and the variance will be:

$$E\left(h_j^{\,2}\right) = \sum_{i=1}^{d} E\left[w_{o,i}^{\,2}\right] E\left[x_i^2\right] = d\sigma_{w_0}^2 \sigma_x^2 = d\sigma_{w_0}^2$$

The output of the hidden unit j will be transformed through its activation function as:

$$y_j = activation\left(h_j + b\right)$$

Here $b$ is the bias term that can be simply initialized to 0 or some value very close to 0, such as 0.01 in the case of ReLU activation functions.

In the case of a sigmoid function, we have very flat curve for large values (both positives and negatives). In order to have a large gradient we would like to be in the range between $[-4, +4]$.

If we draw the initial weights from a uniform distribution $U\left(-\frac{1}{\sqrt{d}}, \frac{1}{\sqrt{d}}\right)$, the variance of unit $j$ becomes:

$$E\left(h_j^2\right) = d\frac{\left(\frac{1}{\sqrt{d}} - \left(-\frac{1}{\sqrt{d}}\right)\right)^2}{12} = d\frac{\left(\frac{2}{\sqrt{d}}\right)^2}{12} = d\frac{\frac{4}{d}}{12} = \frac{1}{3}$$

The probability that $h_j$ will fall outside $[-4, +4]$ is very small. We are effectively reducing the probability of early saturation regardless of the size of $d$

This technique of assigning the initial weights as function of the number of nodes in the input layer $d$ is called uniform adaptive initialization. H2O by default applies the uniform adaptive option which is generally a better choice than a fixed uniform or normal distribution.

If we have only one hidden layer, it is sufficient to just initialize the weights of the first layer. In case of deep auto-encoders we can pre-train a stack of single layer auto-encoders. That is, we create a bunch of shallow auto-encoders where the first one reconstructs the input layer, the second one reconstructs the latent states of the first hidden layer, and so on.

Let's use the label $L_i$ to identify the $i$th layer with $L_0$ to be the input layer, the last one to be the final output, and all the others in the middle to be the hidden layers.

For example, a 5-layer network $L_0 \to L_1 \to L_2 \to L_3 \to L_4$ could be broken down into 2 networks $L_0 \to L_1 \to L_4$ and $L_1 \to L_2 \to L_3$.

The first auto-encoder, after training, will initialize the weights of $L_1$ and will turn the input data into the latent states of $L_1$. These states are used to train the second auto-encoder, which will be used to initialize the weights of $L_2$.

The decoding layers share the same initial weights and bias of the encoding counterpart. Thus, we only need to pre-train the left-half of the network.

Likely, a 7-layer network $L_0 \to L_1 \to L_2 \to L_3 \to L_4 \to L_5 \to L_6$ can be broken down into $L_0 \to L_1 \to L_6$, $L_1 \to L_2 \to L_5$ and $L_2 \to L_3 \to L_4$.

In general, if the deep auto-encoder has N layers we can treat it as a stack of $\frac{(N-1)}{2}$ stacked single-layer auto-encoders:

$$L_{i-1} \to L_i \to L_{N-i} \qquad \forall 1 \leq i \leq \frac{(N-1)}{2}$$

After pre-training, we can train the entire network with the specified weights all together.

# Parallel SGD using HOGWILD!

As we have seen in previous chapters, deep neural networks are trained via backpropagation of a given error generated from a loss function. Backpropagation provides the gradient of the model parameters (weights $W$ and biases $B$ of each layer). Once we have calculated the gradient, we could use it to follow the direction that minimizes the error. One of the most popular technique is **Stochastic Gradient Descent (SGD)**.

SGD can be summarized as following.

1.  Initialize $W, B$.
2.  While convergence is not reached:
    - Get the training example $i$
    - $w_{jk} := w_{jk} - \alpha \dfrac{\partial L(W,B \mid j)}{\partial wjk}$ for any $w_{jk}$ in $W$
    - $b_{jk} := W_{jk} - \alpha \dfrac{\partial L(W,B \mid j)}{\partial w_{jk}}$ for any $b_{jk}$ in $B$

Here $W$ is the weights matrix, $B$ is bias vector, $\nabla L$ the is gradient computed via backpropagation and $\alpha$ is the learning rate.

While SGD is the de-facto most popular training algorithm for many machine learning models, it is not efficiently parallelizable. Many parallelized versions have been proposed in the literature, but most of them are bottlenecked by the synchronization and memory locks amongst processors, without taking advantage of the sparsity of the parameters updates, a common property for neural networks.

In most neural networks problems, the update step is generally sparse. For every training input, only a few weights associated with the neurons that are wrongly reacting are updated. Generally, a neural network is built so that each neuron only activates when a specific characteristic of input is present. As a matter of fact, a neuron that activates for every input would not be very useful.

**HOGWILD!** is an alternative algorithm that allows each thread to overwrite each other's work and provide better performances. Using HOGWILD!, multiple cores can asynchronously handle separate subsets of the training data and make independent contributions to the updates of the gradient $\nabla L$.

If we divide the data dimensionality $d$ into small subsets $E$ of $\{1,...,d\}$ and $x_e$ the portion of the vector $x$ on the coordinates indexed by $e$, we can separate the whole cost function $L$ as:

$$L(x) = \sum_{e \in E} L_e(x_e)$$

The key property that we exploit is that cost functions are sparse in the sense that $|E|$ and $d$ can be large but $L_e$ is calculated only on a much smaller components of the input vector ($x_e$).

If we have $p$ processors, all sharing the same memory and all able to access the vector $x$, the component-wise update would be atomic due to the additive property:

$$x_v \leftarrow x_v + a; v \in \{1,...,d\}$$

That means we can update the state of the single unit without a separate locking structure. A different story is the case of updating multiple components at once where each processor would repeat asynchronously the following loop:

Sample $e$ uniformly at random from $E$.

Read current state $x_e$ and evaluate $G_e(x)$.

For $v \in e$ do $x_v \leftarrow x_v - \gamma b_v^T G_e(x)$.

Here $G_e$ is the gradient $\nabla L$ multiplied by $|e|$. $b_v$ is a bitmask vector where 1 corresponds to a selected index of $e$, and $\gamma$ is the step size, which is diminished by a factor $\beta$ at the end of each epoch.

Because computing the gradient is not instantaneous and any processor may have modified $x$ at any time, we might update $x$ with a gradient computed with an old value read many clock cycles earlier. The novelty of HOGWILD! is in providing conditions under which this asynchronous, incremental gradient algorithm converges.

In particular, it has been proven that the lag between when the gradient is computed and when it is used is always less than or equal to a maximum value, $\tau$. The upper bound value of $\tau$ depends on the number of processors and it converges to 0 as we approach the standard serial version of the algorithm. If the number of processors is less than $d^{1/4}$, then we get nearly the same number of gradient steps of the serial version, which means we get a linear speedup in terms of the number of processors. Moreover, the sparser the input data, the less the probability of memory contention between processors.

In the worst case, the algorithm can always provide some speed improvement even when the gradients are computationally intensive.

You can find more details in the original paper: https://people.eecs.berkeley.edu/~brecht/papers/hogwildTR.pdf.

# Adaptive learning

In the previous paragraphs, we have seen the importance of the weights initialization and an overview of the SGD algorithm, which in its base version uses a fixed value of the learning rate $\alpha$. Both of them are important requirements in order to guarantee a fast and accurate convergence.

A few advanced techniques can be adopted to dynamically optimize the learning algorithm. In particular, we can divide into two types of techniques: the ones that attempt to speed up the learning wherever is convenient and the ones that slows down when near local minima.

If $\theta_t$ represents the quantity we are updating at iteration $t$ (the weights and biases parameters), the general SGD algorithm will update as follows:

$$\theta_t = \theta_{t-1} + \Delta(t)$$

$$SGD : \Delta(t) = -\alpha \nabla L(\theta_{t-1})$$

# Rate annealing

We need to choose $\alpha$. Low values of the learning rate will require a lot of iterations in order to converge with the risk of getting stuck into a local minimum. Having a high learning rate will cause instability. If the algorithm contains too much kinetic energy, the step to minimize $\theta$ would cause it to bounce around chaotically.

Rate Annealing slowly reduces the $\alpha_t$ as we consume data points during training. One technique is to update $\alpha_t = 0.5\,\alpha_{t-1}$ every $k$ samples:

$$Rate\,annealing : \Delta(t) = -\alpha_t \Delta L(\theta_{t-1})$$

Thus, the decay rate would correspond to the inverse of the number of training samples required to divide the learning rate in half.

# Momentum

Momentum takes into account the results of previous iterations to influence the learning of a current iteration. A new velocity vector $v$ is introduced and defined as:

$$Momentum : \Delta(t) = v_t = \mu v_{t-1} - \alpha \nabla L(\theta_{t-1})$$

Here $\mu$ is the momentum decay coefficient. Instead of using the gradient to change position, we use the gradient to change velocity. The momentum term is in charge of speeding up the learning over dimensions where the gradient continues pointing at the same direction and slowing down those dimensions where the sign of the gradient is alternating, that is, those areas corresponding to a region with a local optimum.

This additional momentum term will help reach convergence faster. Too much momentum could lead to divergence though. Suppose we are running SGD with momentum for enough epochs, the final velocity would eventually be:

$$v_\infty = \lim_{t\to\infty} v_t = \lim_{t\to\infty} \mu^t v_0 - \alpha \sum_{k=0}^{t-1} \mu^{t-k-1} \nabla L(\theta_k)$$

It is a geometric series if $\mu$ is less than 1; then the limit will converge to something proportional to:

$$v_\infty \alpha \frac{1}{1-\mu}$$

In this formula, when $\mu$ is close to 1, the system would be moving too fast.

Moreover, at the beginning of the learning, there may already be large gradients (the effect of weights initialization). Thus, we would like to start with a small momentum (for example, 0.5); once the large gradients have disappeared, we can increase the momentum until it reaches a final stable value (for example, 0.9), and keep it constant.

## Nesterov's acceleration

The standard momentum computes the gradient at the current location and amplifies the steps in the direction of the accumulated gradient. It is like pushing a ball down a hill and blindly following the hill slope. Since we can approximate where the ball will land, we would like to take this information into account when computing the gradient.

Let's remember the value of our parameters $\theta$ at time $t$ is given by:

$$\theta_t = \theta_{t-1} + \Delta(t) = \theta_{t-1} + \mu v_{t-1} - \alpha \nabla L(\theta_{t-1})$$

The gradient of $\theta_t$, if we omit the second derivative, can be approximated as:

$$\nabla L(\theta_t) = \nabla L(\theta_{t-1} + \mu v_{t-1} - \alpha \nabla L(\theta_{t-1})) = \nabla L(\theta_{t-1} + \mu v_{t-1}) - \alpha \nabla^2 L(\theta_{t-1})$$
$$\cong \nabla L(\theta_{t-1} + \mu v_{t-1})$$

The update step will be calculated using the gradient at time $t$ instead of $t - 1$:

$$Momentum + Nesterov : \Delta(t) = \mu v_{t-1} - \alpha \nabla L(\theta_t) = \mu v_{t-1} - \alpha \nabla L(\theta_{t-1} + \mu v_{t-1})$$

The Nesterov variation would first make a big step in the direction of the previously accumulated gradient and then correct it with the gradient calculated after the jump. This correction prevents it from going too fast and improves stability.

In the *ball down the hill* analogy, the Nesterov correction adapts the velocity according to the hill slope and speeds up only where possible.

# Newton's method

Whereas single-order methods only use gradient and function evaluations to minimize $L$, second-order methods can use the curvature as well. In Newton's method, we compute the Hessian matrix $HL(\theta)$ which is the square matrix of second-order partial derivatives of the loss function $L(\theta)$ . The inverse Hessian will define the value of $\alpha$ and final step equation is:

$$Newton : \Delta(t) = -H^{-1}L(\theta_{t-1})\nabla L(\theta_{t-1}) = -\frac{\nabla L(\theta_{t-1})}{\left|diag\left(HL(\theta_{t-1})\right)\right| + \in}$$

Here the absolute value of the diagonal is used to ensure the negative gradient direction to minimize $L$. The parameter $\epsilon$ is used for smoothing regions with a small curvature.

By using second-order derivatives, we can perform updates in more efficient directions. In particular, we will have more aggressive updates over shallow (flat) curvatures and smaller steps over steep curvatures.

The best property of this method is that it has no hyper-parameters, except the smoothing parameter which is fixed to a small value; thus it is one dimension less to tune. The major issue is in the computational and memory costs. The size of $H$ is the square of the size of the neural network.

A number of quasi-Newton methods have been developed to approximate the inverse Hessian. For instance, **L-BFGS (Limited Memory Broyden-Fletcher-Goldfarb-Shanno)** stores only a few vectors that implicitly represent the approximation and the history of the last updates of all of the previous vectors. Since the Hessian is constructed approximately from the previous gradient evaluation, it is important that the objective function is not changed during the optimization process. Moreover, the Naïve implementation requires the full dataset to be computed in a single step and is not very suitable for mini-batch training.

## Adagrad

**Adagrad** is another optimization of SGD that adapts the learning rate of each parameter based on the L2 norm of all previous computed gradients on a per-dimension basis.

The value of alpha will depend on the time $t$ and the $i^{th}$ parameter $\theta_{t,i}$:

$$Adagrad : \alpha(t,i) = \frac{\alpha}{\sqrt{G_{t,ii} + \epsilon}}$$

Here $G_t$ is a diagonal matrix of size $d \times d$ and the element $i, i$ is the sum of squares of the gradients of $\theta_{k,i}$ up to the iteration $t - 1$:

$$G_{t,ii} = \left( \sum_{k=1}^{t-1} \nabla L(\theta_{k,i})^2 \right)$$

Each dimension will have a learning rate inversely proportioned to the gradient. That is, larger gradients will have smaller learning rates and vice versa.

The parameter $\epsilon$ is a smoothing term helpful for avoiding divisions by zero. It generally ranges between 1e-4 and 1e-10.

The vectorized update step is given by the element-wise matrix-vector multiplication $\odot$ :

$$Adagrad : \Delta(t) = -\frac{\alpha}{\sqrt{G_t + \epsilon}} \odot \nabla L(\theta_{t-1})$$

The global learning rate $a$ at the nominator can be set to a default value (for example, 0.01) since the algorithm will automatically adapt it after a few iterations.

We have now obtained the same decaying effect of rate annealing but with the nice property that progress along each dimension evens out over time, just like second-order optimization methods.

# Adadelta

One problem with Adagrad is that is very sensitive to the initial state. If the initial gradients are large, and we want them to be large as described in the weights initialization, the corresponding learning rates will be very small from the beginning of the training. Hence, we have to counter-balance this effect by setting high values of α.

Another problem with Adagrad is that the denominator keeps accumulating gradients and growing at each iteration. This makes the learning rate eventually become infinitesimally small such that the algorithm cannot longer learn anything new from the remaining training data.

Adadelta aims to solve the latter problem by fixing the number of accumulated past gradients to some value $w$ instead of $t - 1$. Instead of storing the $w$ previous values, it recursively performs an incremental decaying with the running average at time $t$. We can replace the diagonal matrix $G_t$ with the decaying average of past gradients:

$$E\left[\nabla L(\theta)^2\right]_t = \rho E\left[\nabla L(\theta)^2\right]_{t-1} + (1-\rho)\nabla L(\theta_{t-1})^2$$

Here $\rho$ is the decay constant typically ranging between 0.9 and 0.999.

What we really need is the square root of $E\left[\nabla L(\theta)^2\right]_t + \epsilon$ which approximates the **root mean square** (**RMS**) of $\nabla L(\theta)$ at time $t$:

$$RMS\left[\nabla L(\theta)\right]_t \cong \sqrt{E\left[\nabla L(\theta)^2\right]_t + \epsilon}$$

The update step would be:

$$Adadelta^{(*)} : \Delta(t) = -\frac{\alpha}{RMS\left[\nabla L(\theta)\right]_t}\nabla L(\theta_{t-1})$$

We have defined Δ, the update step, to add to the parameters vector at each iteration. In order to make those equations correct, we shall ensure that the units are matching. If we imagine the parameters to have some hypothetical unit, Δ should be of the same unit. All of the first-order methods considered so far relate the units of Δ to the gradient of the parameters and assume the cost function $L$ to be unitless:

$$units(\Delta) \propto units(\nabla L(\theta)) \propto \frac{1}{units(\theta)}$$

In contrast, second-order methods such as Newton's method use the Hessian information, or an approximation of it, to get the correct units for the update step Δ:

$$units(\Delta) \propto units(H^{-1}L(\theta)\nabla L(\theta)) \propto \frac{\nabla L(\theta)}{\nabla^2 L(\theta)} \propto units(\theta)$$

For the *Adadelta*[*] equation, we need to replace the term $a$ with a quantity proportional to the RMS of Δ(t).

Since we don't know Δ(t) yet, we can only compute the RMS over the same window of size $w$ of Δ(t - 1):

$$RMS[\Delta]_{t-1} = \sqrt{E[\Delta^2]_{t-1} + \epsilon}$$

Where the same constant $\epsilon$ is used and has the purpose of both starting the first iteration when Δ(0) = 0 and ensuring progress even if previous updates are small due to the saturating effect of the accumulating gradients at the denominator.

If the curvature is smooth enough, we can approximate $\Delta(t) \cong \Delta(t-1)$, which changes the equation of Adadelta to:

$$Adadelta: \Delta(t) = -\frac{RMS[\Delta]_{t-1}}{RMS[\nabla L(\theta)]_t} \nabla L(\theta_{t-1})$$

The final Adadelta equation covers many of the properties discussed in previous methods:

- It is an approximation of the diagonal Hessian but uses only the RMS measures of $\nabla L$ and $\Delta$ and only one gradient computation per iteration.

- It always follows the negative gradient as in plain SGD.

- The numerator lags behind by 1 the denominator. This makes the learning more robust for sudden large gradients, which would increase the denominator and reduce the learning rate before the numerator can react.

- The numerator acts as an accelerator term, just like Momentum.

- The denominator acts like the per-dimension decay seen in Adagrad, but the fixed window ensures that progress is always made in every dimension at any step.

In conclusion, there are many techniques for optimizing learning in terms of speed, stability, and the probability of getting stuck into a local optimum. Non-adaptive learning rates associated with Momentum would probably give the best results, but it will require more parameters to be tuned. Adadelta is a trade-off between complexity and performance since it only requires two parameters ($\rho$ and $\epsilon$) and is able to adapt to different scenarios.

# Distributed learning via Map/Reduce

Parallelizing the training in multiple concurrent threads is a great improvement but it is constrained by the quantity of cores and memory available in the single machine. In other words, we can only scale vertically by buying more resourceful and expensive machines.

Combining the parallel and distributed computation enables the desired horizontal scalability, which is theoretically unbounded as long as we have the capability of adding additional nodes.

Two of the reasons why we chose H2O as the framework for anomaly detection are that it provides an easy-to-use built-in implementation of auto-encoders, and it provides an abstraction layer between the functionality (what we want to achieve) and the implementation (how we do it). This abstraction layer provides transparent and scalable implementations that allows to obtain the distribution of computation and data processing in a map/reduce fashion.

If our data is partitioned uniformly in smaller shards in each node, we can describe the high-level distributed algorithm as follows:

1. **Initialize**: An initial model is provided with weights and biases.

2. **Shuffling**: Data can be either entirely available in each node or bootstrapped. We will cover this data replication problem at the end of the paragraph.

3. **Map**: Each node will train a model based on the local data via asynchronous threads using HOGWILD!.

4. **Reduce**: The weights and biases of each trained model are averaged into the final one. This is a monoidal and commutative operation; averaging is associative and commutative.

5. **Validate** (optional): The current averaged model can be scored against a validation set for monitoring, model selection, and/or early stopping criteria.

6. **Iterate**: Repeat the whole workflow several times until a convergence criterion is met.

## H20 Deep Learning Architecture

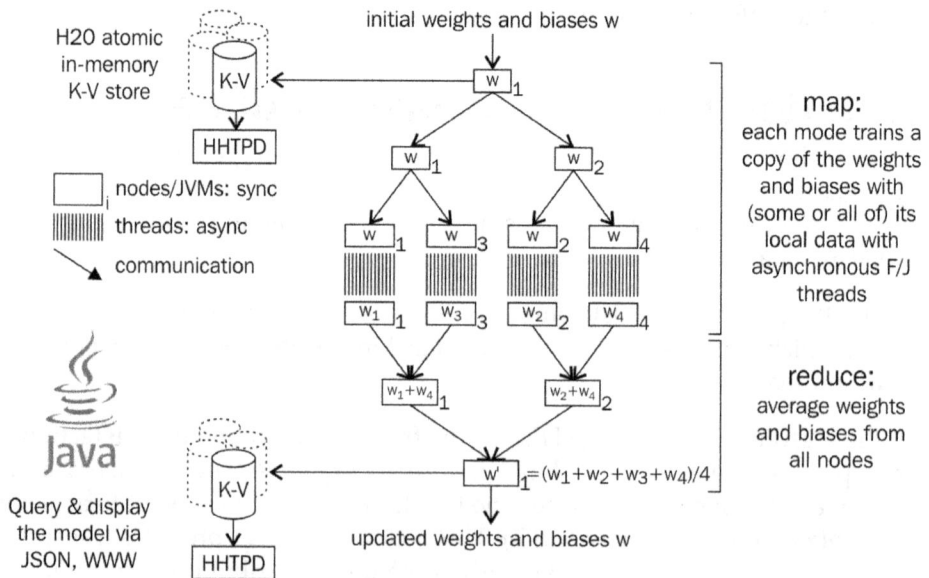

H2O Deep Learning Architecture

The complexity time will be o(n/p + log(p)) per iteration, where n is number of data points in each node and p the number of processors (the nodes). The linear term is the map computation and the logarithmic term the reduce.

In the preceding formula, we are not considering the memory occupation and the expensiveness of the data shuffling. We can ignore the complexity of the model averaging in the reduce step since we assume the model parameters to be small enough compared to the data size. In particular, the size of a model is the number of parameters that corresponds to the number of neurons of the network plus the number of hidden layers (the bias terms). Assuming you have one million neurons, the total size of the model would be less than 8 MB.

The final scalability will depend on:

- Computation parallelism
- Memory buffering
- Network traffic and I/O

Our goal is to find the right trade-off between model accuracy and training speed.

We will use the term iteration to represent the single Map/Reduce step trained only on the specified number of `train_samples_per_iteration`. The parameter `epochs` will define the necessary number of passes over the data to complete the training.

The `train_samples_per_iteration` parameter could correspond to the whole dataset, be smaller (stochastic sampling without replacement), or even be larger (stochastic sampling with replacement).

The value of `train_samples_per_iteration` will affect both the memory occupation and the time between models averaging, that is, the training speed.

Another important parameter is the Boolean flag `replicate_training_data`. If it is enabled, a copy of the whole data will be made available in each node. This option will allow each model to be trained faster.

Another linked parameter is `shuffle_trainingd_data`, which determines whether the data can or cannot be shuffled among nodes.

If N is the number of available nodes and n is the size of the training dataset, we can identify a few operating modes characterized by the special values of `train_samples_per_iteration` and by the activation of `replicate_training_data`:

| train_ samples_per_ iteration | replicate_ training_data | Description |
|---|---|---|
| 0 | False | Only one epoch, averaging over N models built with local data. |
| -1 | True | Each node processes the whole dataset per iteration. This results in training N epochs per iteration in parallel in N nodes. |
| -1 | False | All nodes process only the locally stored data. One epoch corresponds to one iteration. You can have many epochs. |
| -2 | True | Auto-tuning of the number of sample per iteration based on both computation time and network overhead. Full dataset is replicated, with sampling without replacement. |
| -2 | False | Auto-tuning of the number of samples per iteration based on both computation time and network overhead. Only local data is available; it might require sampling with replacement. |
| > 0 | true | Fixed number of samples per iteration sampled from the full dataset. |
| > 0 | false | Fixed number of samples per iteration sampled from only the local available data. |

If $n = 1M$ and $N = 4$, each node on an average will store 25K locally. If we set *samples_per_iteration=200K*, the single Map/Reduce iteration will process 200 K records. That is, each node will process 50K rows. In order to complete one epoch, we will need 5 Map/Reduce iterations corresponding to 20 local training steps.

In the preceding example, each node will have those 50K samples from the local available data with or without sampling depending on whether the local data is greater or smaller than the requested one. Sampling with replacement may negatively affect the accuracy of the model since we would train on a repeated and limited subset of the data. If we enable the replication, we would always have the most data locally in every node, assuming it can fit in memory.

A special case is when we want to process exactly the amount of local data without sampling (*train_samples_per_iteration* = -1). In that case, we would iterate over the same dataset again and again at every iteration, which is redundant for multiple epochs.

Another special case is when `samples_per_iteration` is close to or greater than N * n with replication enabled. In this case, every node would train with almost the whole data or more at each iteration. Similarly, it would re-use almost the same data at every iteration.

For those two special cases, the `shuffle_training_data` is automatically turned on. That is, local data will be randomly shuffled before each training.

To conclude, depending on the size of data we could or could not replicate in every node. H2O offers a smart way to automatically tune and adapt the size of each iteration by balancing the CPU cost and the network overhead. Unless you have some requirement for fine-tuning your system, you probably want to use the self-tuning option.

The distributed algorithm for deep learning will benefit your final model in both accuracy and training speed. Even though you might not have a very large dataset, this distributed approach is something you want to consider for a production system.

# Sparkling Water

Although H2O can run on its own standalone cluster, an enterprise environment would probably already have a distributed data processing cluster. Managing two separate clusters, even if physically on the same machines, can be expensive and conflicting.

**Apache Spark** is nowadays the de-facto computation framework for large datasets and for building scalable data products. H2O includes Sparkling Water, an abstraction layer that lets you model your data and algorithms together with all of the features and functionalities of the native framework but with the capabilities of Spark.

Sparkling Water is an alternative to the ML and MLlib frameworks for doing machine learning and one of the few alternatives for deep learning on top of Spark.

Spark is designed and implemented in Scala. In order to understand the inter-operability of H2O and Spark, we need to refer to the native Scala APIs.

In the Sparkling Water architecture, the H2O context co-exists with the Spark context in the driver node. Also, we now have SparkSession as main entry point in Spark 2. Likely, the H2O and Spark executors co-exist in the worker nodes. As such, they share the same **Java Virtual Machine (JVM)** and memory. The resource allocation and setup could happen via YARN, a Hadoop component used for resource management and job scheduling.

You could build end-to-end pipelines combining both the strengths of Spark and MLlib with the features of H2O.

For example, you might use Spark and H2O together for data munging and alternate different transformation functions. Then do the deep learning modeling in H2O. Ultimately you can return the trained model to be integrated within a greater application.

Spark offers three APIs for storing, modeling, and manipulating data. The typed **RDD (Resilient Distributed Data)**, the DataFrame and the recent unified DataSet API. **DataFrame** is an RDD of objects of type `sql.Row`; thus in this integration, they are considered similarly.

Sparkling Water currently offers the conversion between `H2OFrame` and both RDD and DataFrame, in both directions. When converting an `H2OFrame` to an RDD, a wrapper is created, mapping the column names to the corresponding elements of a specified class type bound in the `Product` trait. That is, you will typically have to declare a Scala case class that acts as container for the data you are converting from the `H2OFrame`. This has the limitation that case classes can only store at most 21 flat fields. For larger tables, you can use nested structures or dictionaries.

Converting an `H2OFrame` into a Spark DataFrame does not require any type of parameter. The schema is dynamically derived from the column names and types of the `H2OFrame`.

Vice versa, the conversion from an existing RDD or DataFrame into an `H2OFrame` requires data to be duplicated and reloaded. Since the `H2OFrame` is registered in a Key/Value store, we can optionally specify the frame name. No explicit type is required to be specified in the case of RDDs since the Scala compiler can infer it.

The column primitive types will have to match according to the following table:

| Scala/Java type | SQL type | H2O type |
|---|---|---|
| NA | BinaryType | Numeric |
| Byte | ByteType | Numeric |
| Short | ShortType | Numeric |
| Integer | IntegerType | Numeric |
| Long | LongType | Numeric |
| Float | FloatType | Numeric |
| Double | DoubleType | Numeric |
| String | StringType | String |
| Boolean | BooleanType | Numeric |
| java.sql.TimeStamp | TimestampType | Time |

Both RDDs and `H2OFrame` share the same memory space in the executor JVMs; it is convenient to un-persist them after the conversion and duplication.

Now that we have understood how the native Scala integration with Spark works, we can consider the Python wrapper.

In the driver program, the Python `SparkContext` will use `Py4J` to start the driver JVM and the Java-corresponding `SparkContext`. The latter will create the `H2OContext` which will then start the H2O cloud in the Spark cluster. After this setup stage, the Python APIs of both H2O and `PySpark` can be used to interact with data and algorithms.

Although `PySpark` and `PySparkling` are good options for developing on top of Spark and H2O in Python, please bear in mind that the Python APIs are wrappers around the JVM executors. Maintaining and debugging complex projects in a distributed environment could be more tedious than sticking with the native APIs could help. Nevertheless, in most cases, the Python API will work just fine and you will not have to switch between Python and the native language.

# Testing

Before we discuss what testing means in data science, let's summarize a few concepts.

Firstly and in general, what is a model in science? We can cite the following definitions:

> *In science, a model is a representation of an idea, an object or even a process or a system that is used to describe and explain phenomena that cannot be experienced directly.*

Scientific Modelling, Science Learning Hub, http://sciencelearn.org.nz/Contexts/The-Noisy-Reef/Science-Ideas-and-Concepts/Scientific-modelling

And this:

> *A scientific model is a conceptual, mathematical or physical representation of a real-world phenomenon. A model is generally constructed for an object or process when it is at least partially understood, but difficult to observe directly. Examples include sticks and balls representing molecules, mathematical models of planetary movements or conceptual principles like the ideal gas law. Because of the infinite variations actually found in nature, all but the simplest and most vague models are imperfect representations of real-world phenomena.*

What is a model in science?, Reference: https://www.reference.com/science/model-science-727cde390380e207

We need a model in order to simplify the complexity of a system in the form of a hypothesis. We proved that deep neural networks can describe complex non-linear relationships. Even though we are just approximating a real system with something more complex than shallow models, in the end this is just another approximation. I doubt any real system actually works as a neural network. Neural networks were inspired by the way our brain processes information, but they are a huge simplification of it.

A model is defined according to some parameters (parametric model). On one hand, we have a definition of a model as function mapping an input space to an output. On the other hand, we have a bunch of parameters that the function needs in order to apply the mapping. For instance, the weights matrix and biases.

Model fitting and training are two terms referring to the process of estimating the parameters of that model so that it best describes the underlying data. Model fitting happens via a learning algorithms that defines a loss function depending on both the model parameters and the data, and it tries to minimize this function by estimating the best set of values for the model parameters. One of the most common algorithm is Gradient Descent, with all its variants. See the previous Training section. For auto-encoder, you would minimize the reconstruction error plus the regularization penalty, if any.

**Validation** is sometimes confused with testing and evaluation. Validation and testing often use the same techniques and/or methodology but they serve two different purposes.

Model validation corresponds to a type of hypothesis validation. We consider our data to be well described by a model. The hypothesis is that, if that model is correct, after having been trained (parameters estimation), it will describe unseen data the same way it describes the training set. We hypothesize that the model generalizes enough given the limits of the scenario in which we will use it. Model validation aims to find a measure (often referred to as a metric) that quantifies how well the model fits the validation data. For labeled data, we might derive a few metrics from either the **Receiver Operating Characteristic** (**ROC**) or Precision-Recall (**PR**) curve computed from the anomaly scores on the validation data. For unlabeled data, you could for instance use the **Excess-Mass** (**EM**) or **Mass-Volume** (**MV**) curve.

Although model validation can be a way to evaluate performances, it is widely used for model selection and tuning.

**Model selection** is the process of selecting among a set of candidates, the model that scores highest in the validation. The set of candidates could be different configurations of the same model, many different models, a selection of different features, different normalization, and/or transformation techniques, and so on.

In deep neural networks, feature selection could be omitted because we delegate to the network itself the role of figuring out and generating relevant features. Moreover, features are also discarded via regularization during learning.

The hypothesis space (the model parameters) depends on the choice of topology, the activation functions, size and depth, pre-processing (for example, whitening of an image or data cleansing), and post-processing (for example, use an auto-encoder to reduce the dimensionality and then run a clustering algorithm). We might see the whole pipeline (the set of components on a given configuration) as the model, even though the fitting could happen independently for each piece.

Analogously, the learning algorithm will introduce a few parameters (for example, learning rate or decay rate). In particular, since we want to maximize the generalization of the model, we generally introduce a regularization technique during the learning function, and that will introduce additional parameters (for example, sparsity coefficient, noise ratio, or regularization weight).

Moreover, the particular implementation of the algorithm also has a few parameters (for example, epochs, number of samples per iteration).

We can use the same validation technique to quantify the performance of the model and learning algorithm together. We can imagine to have a single big vector of parameters that include the model parameters plus the hyper-parameters. We can tune everything in order to minimize the validation metric.

At the end of the model selection and tuning via validation, we have obtained a system that:

- Takes some of the available data
- Divides into training and validation, making sure to not introduce biases or unbalancing
- Creates a search space made up of the set of different models, or different configurations, learning parameters, and implementation parameters
- Fits each model on the training set by using the training data and learning algorithm with a given loss function, including regularization, according to the specified parameters
- Computes the validation metric by applying the fitted model on the validation data
- Selects the one point in the search space that minimizes the validation metric

The selected point will formalize our final theory. The theory says that our observations are generated from a model that is the outcome of the pipeline corresponding to the selected point.

Evaluation is the process of verifying that the final theory is acceptable and quantifying its quality from both technical and business perspectives.

Scientific literature shows how, during the course of history, one theory has succeeded another. Choosing the right theory without introducing a cognitive bias requires rationality, accurate judgment, and logical interpretation.

Confirmation theory, the study that guides scientific reasoning other than reasoning of the deductive kind, can help us defining a few principles.

In our context, we want to quantify the quality of our theory and verify it is good enough and that it an evident advantage with respect to a much simpler theory (the baseline). A baseline could be a Naïve implementation of our system. In the case of an anomaly detector, it could simply be a rule-based threshold model where anomalies are flagged for each observation whose feature values are above a static set of thresholds. Such a baseline is probably the simplest theory we can implement and maintain over time. It will probably not satisfy the full acceptance criteria, but it will help us to justify why we need another theory, that is, a more advanced model.

Colyvan, in his book *The Indispensability of Mathematics*, summarized the criteria for accepting a good theory as a replacement for another based on four major criteria:

1. **Simplicity/Parsimony**: Simple is better than complex if the empirical results are comparable. Complexity is only required when you need to overcome some limitation. Otherwise, simplicity should be preferred in both its mathematical form and its ontological commitments.

2. **Unification/Explanatory Power**: The capacity of consistently explaining both existing and future observations. Moreover, unification means minimizing the number of *theoretical devices* needed for the explanation. A good theory offers an intuitive way of explaining why a given prediction is expected.

3. **Boldness/Fruitfulness**: A bold theory is an idea that, if it was true, would be able to predict and/or explain a lot more about the system we are modeling. Boldness helps us refuse theories that would contribute very little to what we know already. It is allowed to formulate something new and innovative and then try to contradict it with known evidence. If we can't prove a theory is correct we can demonstrate that the evidence does not prove the contrary. Another aspect is heuristic potential. A good theory can enable more theories. Between two theories we want to favor the more fruitful: the one that has more potential for being reused or extended in future.

4. **Formal elegance**: A theory must have an aesthetic appeal and should be robust enough for ad-hoc modifications to a failing theory. Elegance is the quality of explaining something in a clear, economical, and concise way. Elegance also enables better scrutiny and maintainability.

These criteria, in the case of neural networks, are translated into the following:

1.  Shallow models with a few layers and small capacity are preferred. As we discussed in the Network design section, we start with something simpler and incrementally increase complexity if we need so. Eventually the complexity will converge and any further increase will not give any benefit.

2.  We will distinguish between explanatory power and unificatory power:

    ○   **Explanatory power** is evaluated similarly to model validation but with a different dataset. We mentioned earlier that we broke the data into three groups: training, validation, and testing. We will use the training and validation to formulate the theory (the model and hyper-parameters) that the model is retrained on the union of both training and validation set becoming the new training set; and ultimately the final, already validated, model is evaluated against the test set. It is important at this stage to consider the validation metrics on the training set and test set. We would expect the model to perform better on the training set, but having too wide a gap between the two means the model does not explain unseen observations very well.

    ○   **Unificatory power** can be represented by the model sparsity. Explaining means mapping input to output. Unifying means reducing the number of elements required to apply the mapping. By adding a regularization penalty, we make the features sparser, which means we can explain an observation and its prediction using fewer regressors (*theoretical devices*).

3.  Boldness and fruitfulness can also be split into two aspects:

    ○   **Boldness** is represented by our test-driven approach. In addition to point 2, where we try to make clear what a model does and why, in the test-driven approach, we treat the system as a black box and check the responses under different conditions. For an anomaly detection, we can systematically create some failing scenarios with different degrees of anomalousness and measure at which level the system is able to detect and react. Or for time-responsive detectors, we could measure how long it takes to detect a drift in the data. If the tests pass, then we have achieved confidence that it works no matter how. This is probably one of the most common approaches in machine learning. We try everything that we believe can work; we carefully evaluate and tentatively accept when our critical efforts are unsuccessful (that is,. the tests pass).

○ **Fruitfulness** comes from the reusability of a given model and system. Is it too strongly coupled to the specific use case? Auto-encoders work independently of what the underlying data represent, they use very little domain knowledge. Thus, if the theory is that a given auto-encoders can be used for explaining a system in its working conditions, then we could extend it and re-use it for detecting in any kind of system. If we introduce a pre-processing step (such as image whitening), then we are assuming the input data are pixels of an image, thus even if this theory superbly fit our use case it has a smaller contribution to the greater usability. Nevertheless, if the domain-specific pre-processing improves the final result noticeably, then we will consider it as an important part of the theory. But if the contribution is negligible, it is recommended to refuse it in favor of something more reusable.

4. One aspect of elegance in deep neural networks could implicitly be represented as the capacity of learning features from the data rather than hand-crafting them. If that is the case, we can measure how the same model is able to self-adapt to different scenarios by learning relevant features. For example, we could test that given any dataset we consider normal, we can always construct an auto-encoder that learns the normal distribution. We can either add or remove features from the same dataset or partition according to some external criteria generating dataset with different distributions. Then we can inspect the learned representations and measure the reconstruction ability of the model. Instead of describing the model as a function of the specific input features and weights, we describe it in terms of neurons — entities with learning capabilities. Arguably, this is a good example of elegance.

From a business perspective, we really need to think carefully about what the acceptance criteria are.

We would like to answer at least the following questions:

- What problem are we trying to solve?
- How is the business going to benefit from it?
- In which way will the model be integrated within an existing system from a practical and technical point of view?
- What is the final deliverable so that it is consumable and actionable?

We will try to use as example an intrusion detection system and try to respond to these questions.

We would like to monitor a network traffic in real time, taking individual network connections and marking them as normal or suspicious. This will allow the business to have enhanced protection against intruders. The flagged connections will be stopped and will go into a queue for manual inspection. A team of security experts will look into those connections and determine whether it is a false alarm and, in the case of a confirmed attack, will mark the connection under one of the available labels. Thus, the model has to provide a real-time list of connections sorted by their anomaly score. The list cannot contain more elements than the capability of the security team. Moreover, we need to balance the cost of permitting an attack, the cost of damages in the case of an attack, and the cost required for inspection. A minimum requirement consisting of precision and recall is a must in order to probabilistically limit the worst-case scenario.

All of these evaluation strategies have been mainly defined qualitatively rather quantitatively. It would be quite hard to compare and report something that is not numerically measurable.

Bryan Hudson, a Data Science practitioner, said:

> *If you can't define it, you can't measure it. If it can't be measured, it shouldn't be reported. Define, then measure, then report.*

Define, then measure, then report. But be careful. We might think of defining a new evaluation metric that takes into account every possible aspect and scenario discussed so far.

Whilst many data scientists may attempt to quantify the evaluation of a model using a single utility function, as you do during validation, for a real production system, this is not advised. As also expressed in the Professional Data Science Manifesto:

> *A product needs a pool of measures to evaluate its quality. A single number cannot capture the complexity of reality.*

The Professional Data Science Manifesto, www.datasciencemanifesto.org

And even after we have defined our **Key Performance Indicators (KPIs)**, their real meaning is relative when compared to a baseline. We must ponder over why we need this solution with respect to a much simpler or existing one.

The evaluation strategy requires defining test cases and KPIs so that we can cover the most scientific aspects and business needs. Some of them are aggregated numbers, others can be represented in charts. We aim to summarize and efficiently present all of them in a single evaluation dashboard.

In the following sections, we will see a few techniques used for model validation using both labeled and unlabelled data.

Then we will see how to tune the space for parameters using some parallel search space techniques.

Lastly we will give an example of a final evaluation for a network intrusion use case using A/B testing techniques.

# Model validation

The goal of model validation is to evaluate whether the numerical results quantifying the hypothesized estimations/predictions of the trained model are acceptable descriptions of an independent dataset. The main reason is that any measure on the training set would be biased and optimistic since the model has already seen those observations. If we don't have a different dataset for validation, we can hold one fold of the data out from training and use it as benchmark. Another common technique is the cross-fold validation, and its stratified version, where the whole historical dataset is split into multiple folds. For simplicity, we will discuss the hold-one-out method; the same criteria apply also to the cross-fold validation.

The splitting into training and validation set cannot be purely random. The validation set should represent the future hypothetical scenario in which we will use the model for scoring. It is important not to contaminate the validation set with information that is highly correlated with the training set (leakage).

A bunch of criteria can be considered. The easiest is the time. If your data is chronological, then you'll want to select the validation set to always be after the training set.

If your deployment plan is to retrain once a day and score all the observations of the next 24 hours, then your validation set should be exactly 24 hours. All observations after 24 hours would never be scored with the last trained model but with a model trained with the additional past 24 hours' observations.

Of course, only using 24 hours of observations for validation is too restrictive. We will have to perform a few validations, where we select a number of time split points; for each split point, we train the model up to that point and validate on the data in the following validation window.

The choice of number of split points depends on the amount of available resources. Ideally, we would like to map the exact frequency at which the model will be trained, that is, one split point a day for the last year or so.

There are a bunch of operational things to consider when splitting in train and validation set:

- Regardless of whether the data has a timestamp or not, the chronological time should be set by what would have been available at that time. In other words, let's suppose that you have 6 hours of delay between the data generation and the time when it is turned into a feature space for training; you should consider the latter time in order to filter what was before or after the given split point.

- How long does the training procedure take? Suppose our model requires 1 hour to be retrained; we would schedule its training one hour before the expiration of the previous model. The scores during its training interval will be covered by the previous model. That means we cannot predict any observation that happens in the following hour of the last data collected for training. This introduces a gap between the training set and validation set.

- How does the model perform for day-0 malware (the cold start problem)? During validation, we want to project the model in the worst-case scenario instead of being over-optimistic. If we can find a partitioning attribute, such as device ID or network card MAC address, we can then divide users into buckets representing different validation folds and perform a cross-fold validation where iteratively you select one fold of users to validate the model trained with the remaining users folds. By doing so, we always validate predictions for users whose history we have never seen before. That helps with truly measuring the generalization for those cases where the training set already contains a strong signal of anomaly for the same device over past connections. In that case, it would be very easy for the model to spot anomalies but they would not necessary match a real use case.

- The choice of attribute (primary key) on which to apply the partitioning is not simple. We want to reduce the correlation among folds as much as possible. If we ingenuously partition on the device ID, how will we cope with the same user or the same machine with multiple devices, all registered with a different identifier? The choice of partitioning key is an entity resolution problem. The correct way of solving this issue would be to firstly cluster the data belonging to the same entity and then partition such that data of the same entity is never split among different folds. The definition of the entity depends on the particular use case context.

- When performing cross-fold validation, we still need to ensure the time constraint. That is, for each validation fold, we need to find a time split point in the intersection with the other training folds. Filter the training set both on the entity id and timestamp; then filter the data in the validation fold according to the validation window and gap.

- Cross-fold validation introduces a problem with class unbalancing. By definition; anomalies are rare; thus our dataset is highly skewed. If we randomly sample entities, then we would probably end up with a few folds without anomalies and a few with too many. Thus, we need to apply a stratified cross-fold validation where we want to preserve the same distribution of anomalies uniformly in each fold. This is a tricky problem in the case of unlabeled data. But we can still run some statistics on the whole feature space and partition in such a way as to minimize the distribution differences among folds.

We have just listed a few of the common pitfalls to consider when defining the splitting strategy. Now we need to compute some metrics. The choice of the validation metric should be significant with the real operational use case.

We will see in the following sections a few possible metrics defined for both labeled and unlabeled data.

# Labeled Data

Anomaly detection on labeled data can be seen just as a standard binary classifier.

Let $s : R^d \rightarrow R^+$ be our anomaly scoring function where the higher the score, the higher the probability of being an anomaly. For auto-encoders, it could simply be the MSE computed on the reconstruction error and rescaled to be in the range[0,1]. We are mainly interested in relative ordering rather than absolute values.

We can now validate using either the ROC or PR curve.

In order to do so, we need to set a threshold $a$ that corresponds to the scoring function $s$ and consider all of the points $x$ with score $s(x) \geq a$ to be classified as anomalies.

For each value of $a$, we can calculate the confusion matrix as:

| Number of observations n | Predicted anomaly $s(x)$ $\geq a$ | Predicted non-anomaly $(s < a)$ |
|---|---|---|
| True anomaly | True Positive (TP) | False Negative (FN) |
| True non-anomaly | False Positive (FP) | True Negative (TN) |

From each confusion matrix corresponding to a value of $\alpha$, we can derive the measures of **True Positive Rate (TPR)** and **False Positive Rate (FPR)** as:

$$TPR = \text{Recall} = \frac{TP}{TP + FN}$$

$$FPR = \text{False positive ratio} = \frac{FP}{FP + TN}$$

We can draw each value of $a$ in a two-dimensional space that generates the ROC curve consisting of $TPR = f(FPR)$.

The way we interpret the plot is as follows: each cut-off point tells us on the y-axis the fraction of anomalies that we have spotted among the full set of anomalies in the validation data (Recall). The x-axis is the false alarm ratio, the fraction of observations marked as anomalies among the full set of normal observations.

If we set the threshold close to 0, it means we are flagging everything as anomaly but all the normal observations will produce false alarms. If we set it close to 1, we will never fire any anomaly.

Let's suppose for a given value of $\alpha$ the corresponding TPR = 0.9 and FPR = 0.5; this means that we detected 90% of anomalies but the anomaly queue contained half of the normal observations as well.

The best threshold point would be the one located at coordinates (0,1), which corresponds to 0 false positive and 0 false negatives. This never happens, so we need to find a trade-off between the Recall and false alarm ratio.

One of the issues with the ROC curve is that does not show very well what happens for a highly skewed dataset. If anomalies represent only 1% of the data, the $x$ axis is very likely to be small and we might be tempted to relax the threshold in order to increase the Recall without any major effect on the $x$ axis.

The **Precision-Recall (PR)** plot swaps the axis and replaces the FPR with the Precision defined as:

$$Precision = \frac{TP}{TP + FP}$$

Precision is a more meaningful metric and represents the fraction of anomalies among the list of detected ones.

The idea now is to maximize both the axes. On the $y$ axis, we can observe the expected results of the portion that will be inspected, and the $x$ axis tells how many anomalies we will miss, both of them on a scale that depends only on the anomaly probability.

Having a two-dimensional plot can help us understand how the detector would behave in different scenarios, but in order to apply model selection, we need to minimize a single utility function.

A bunch of measures can be used to synthesize this. The most common one is the **area under the curve (AUC)**, which is an indicator of the average performance of the detector under any threshold. For the ROC curve, the AUC can be interpreted as the probability that a uniformly drawn random anomaly observation is ranked higher than a uniformly drawn random normal observation. It is not very useful for anomaly detection.

The absolute values of Precision and Recall being defined on the same scale can be aggregated using the harmonic mean, also known as **F-score**:

$$F_\beta = \left(1+\beta^2\right)\frac{Precision \cdot Recall}{\left(\beta^2 Precision\right)+Recall}$$

Here, $\beta$ is a coefficient that weights to what extent Recall is more important than Precision.

The term $\left(1+\beta^2\right)$ is added in order to scale the score between 0 and 1.

In case of symmetry we obtain the F1-score:

$$F_1 = \frac{2 \cdot Precision \cdot Recall}{Precision + Recall}$$

Security analysts can also set preferences based on minimum requirements for the values of Precision and Recall. In that situation, we can define the Preference-Centric score as:

$$PC\left(r_{min}, p_{min}\right) = \begin{cases} F_1 + 1, r \ge r_{min} \text{ and } p \ge p_{min} \\ F_1, otherwise \end{cases}$$

The PC-score allows us to select a range of acceptable thresholds and optimize the points in the middle based on the F1-score. The unit term in the first case is added so that it will always outperform the second one.

# Unlabeled Data

Unfortunately, most of the times data comes without a label and it would require too much human effort to categorize each observation.

We propose two alternatives to the ROC and PR curves that do not require labels: the **Mass-Volume (MV)** and the **Excess-Mass (EM)** curves.

Let $s : R^d \rightarrow R^+$ be our inverse anomaly scoring function this time, where the smaller the score, the higher the probability of it being an anomaly. In the case of an auto-encoder, we can use the inverse of the reconstruction error:

$$s = \frac{1}{RMSE + \epsilon}$$

Here $\epsilon$ is a small term to stabilize in the case of a near zero reconstruction error.

The scoring function will give an ordering of each observation.

Let $f : R^d \rightarrow [0,1]$ be the probability density function of the normal distribution of a set of i.i.d. observations $X_1,...,X_n$ and $F$ its cumulative density function.

The function $f$ would return a score very close to 0 for any observation that does not belong to the normal distribution. We want to find a measure of how close the scoring function $s$ is to $f$. The ideal scoring function would just coincide with $f$. We will call such a performance criterion $C(s)$.

Given a set $S$ of scoring functions integrable with respect to the Lebesgue measure.

The MV-curve of $s$ is the plot of the mapping:

$$\alpha \in (0,1) \rightarrow MV_s(\alpha) = \inf_{t \geq 0} Leb\left(\left\{x \in X, \mathbb{P}\left(s(x) \geq t\right) \geq \alpha\right\}\right)$$

Here $Leb(s \geq t, \alpha) = Leb\left(\left\{x \in X, \mathbb{P}\left(s(x) \geq t\right) \geq \alpha\right\}\right)$.

The Lebesgue measure of a set $X$ is obtained by dividing the set into buckets (sequence of open intervals) and summing the n-volume of each bucket. The n-volume is the multiplication of the lengths of each dimension defined as the difference between max and min values. If $X_i$ is a subset of a bunch of d-dimensional points, their projection on each axis will give the lengths and the multiplication of the lengths will give the d-dimensional volume.

The MV measure at $\alpha$ corresponds to the n-volume corresponding to the infimum subset of $X$ defined by the threshold $t$ such that the c.d.f. of $s(X)$ at $t$ is higher than or equal to $\alpha$.

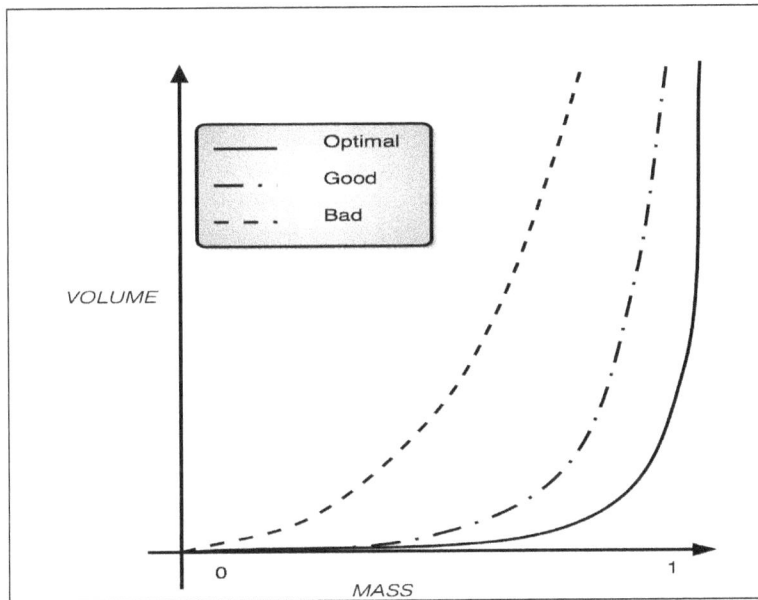

Volume-Mass curve from "Mass Volume Curves and Anomaly Ranking", S. Clemencon, UMR LTCI No. 5141, Telecom ParisTech/CNRS

The optimal MV curve would be the one calculated on $f$. We would like to find the scoring function $s$ which minimizes the L1 norm of the point-wise difference with $MV_f$ on an interested interval $I^{MV}$ representing the large density level-sets (for example, $[0.9, 1]$).

It is proven that $MV_f \leq MV(s) \forall \alpha \in [0,1]$. Since $MV_s$ is always below $MV_f$, the $\arg\min_s \left\| MV_s - MV_t \right\|_{L1(I^{MV})}$ will correspond to the $\arg\min_s \left\| MV_s \right\|_{L1(I^{MV})}$. Our performance criterion for MV is $C^{MV}(s) = \left\| MV_s \right\|_{L1(I^{MV})}$. The smaller the value of $C^{MV}$ the better is the scoring function.

One problem with the MV-curve is that the area under the curve (AUC) diverges for $a = 1$ if the support of the distribution is infinite (the set of possible values is not bounded).

One workaround is to choose the interval $I^{MV} = [0.9, 0.999]$.

A better variant is the Excess-Mass (EM) curve defined as the plot of the mapping:

$$\alpha \in (0,1) \rightarrow EM_s(\alpha) = \sup_{t \geq 0} \mathbb{P}\left(s(x) \geq t\right) - t \, Leb(s \geq t, \alpha)$$

The performance criterion will be $C^{EM}(s) = \|EM_s\|_{L1(I^{EM})}$ and $I^{MV} = \left[0, EM_s^{-1}(0.9)\right]$, where $EM_s^{-1}(\mu) = \inf_{t>0}\left(EM_s(t) \leq \mu\right)$. $EM_s$ is now always finite.

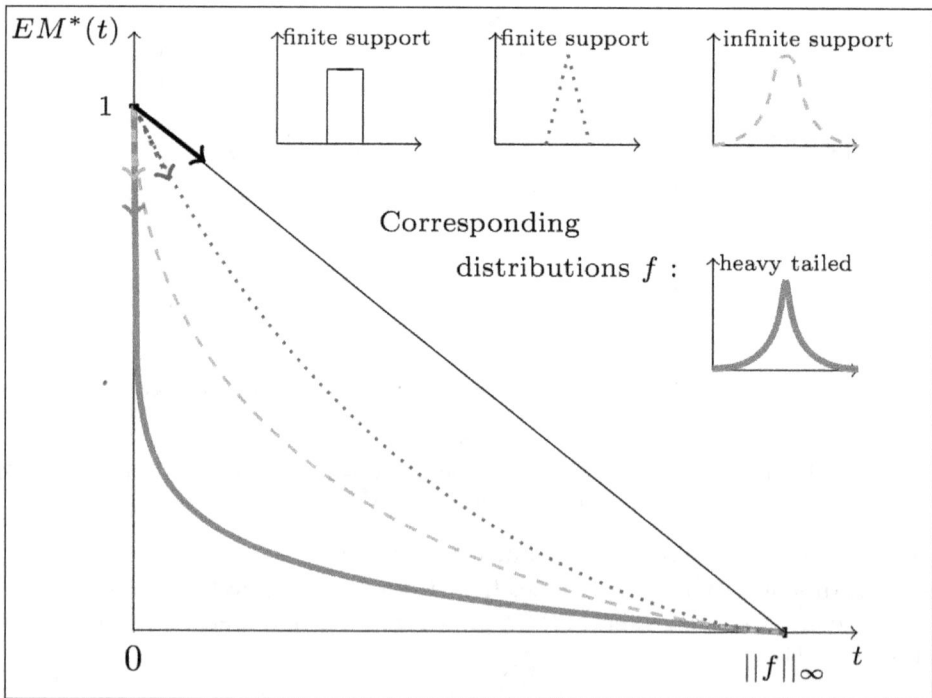

Excess-Mass curve from "On anomaly Ranking and Excess-Mass curves", N. Goix, A. Sabourin, S. Clemencon, UMR LTCI No. 5141, Telecom ParisTech/CNRS

One problem of EM is that the interval of large level sets is of the same order of magnitude as the inverse of the total support volume. This is a problem for datasets with large dimensions. Moreover, for both EM and MV, the distribution $f$ of the normal data is not known and must be estimated. For practicality, the Lebesgue volume can be estimated via the Monte Carlo approximation, which applies only to small dimensions.

In order to scale to large-dimensional data, we can sub-sample training and validation data with replacement iteratively along a randomly fixed number of features $d'$ in order to compute the EM or MV performance criterion score. Replacement is done only after we have drawn the samples for each subset of features.

The final performance criterion is obtained by averaging these partial criteria along the different features draw. The drawback is that we cannot validate combinations of more than $d'$ features. On the other hand, this feature sampling allows us to estimate EM or MV for large dimensions and allows us to compare models produced from space of different dimensions, supposing we want to select over models that consume different views of the input data.

# Summary of validation

We have seen how we can plot curve diagrams and compute aggregated measures in the case of both labeled and unlabeled data.

We have shown how to select sub ranges of the threshold value of the scoring function in order to make the aggregated metric more significant for anomaly detections. For the PR-curve, we can set the minimum requirements of Precision and Recall; for EM or MV we arbitrarily select the interval corresponding to large level-sets even if they don't have a directly corresponding meaning.

In our example of network intrusion, we score anomalous points and store them into a queue for further human inspection. In that scenario, we need to consider also the throughput of the security team. Let's suppose they can inspect only 50 connections per day; our performance metrics should be computed only on the top 50 elements of the queue. Even if the model is able to reach a recall of 100% on the first 1,000 elements, those 1,000 elements are not feasible to inspect in a real scenario.

This situation kind of simplifies the problem because we will automatically select the threshold that gives us the expected number of predicted anomalies independently of true positive or false positives. This is the best the model can do given the top N observations most likely to be anomalies.

There is also another issue in this kind of threshold-based validation metrics in the case of cross-fold validation, that is, the aggregation technique. There are two major ways of aggregating: micro and macro.

Macro aggregation is the most common one; we compute thresholds and metrics in each validation fold and then we average them. Micro aggregation consists of storing the results of each validation fold, concatenating them together and computing one single threshold and metric at the end.

The macro aggregation technique also gives a measure of stability, and of how much the performance of our system changes if we perturb by using different samples. On the other hand, macro aggregation introduces more bias into the model estimates, especially in rare classes like anomaly detection. Thus, micro aggregation is generally preferred.

# Hyper-parameters tuning

Following the design of our deep neural network according to the previous sections, we would end up with a bunch of parameters to tune. Some of them have default or recommended values and do not require expensive fine-tuning. Others strongly depends on the underlying data, specific application domain, and a set of other components. Thus, the only way to find best values is to perform a model selection by validating based on the desired metric computed on the validation data fold.

Now we will list a table of parameters that we might want to consider tuning. Please consider that each library or framework may have additional parameters and a custom way of setting them. This table is derived from the available tuning options in H2O. It summarizes the common parameters, but not all of them, when building a deep auto-encoder network in production:

| Parameter | Description | Recommended value(s) |
| --- | --- | --- |
| activation | The differentiable activation function. | Depends on the data nature. Popular functions are: Sigmoid, Tanh, Rectifier and Maxout.<br><br>Each function can then be mapped into the corresponding drop-out version. Refer to the network design section. |

| Parameter | Description | Recommended value(s) |
|---|---|---|
| hidden | Size and number of layers. | Number of layers is always odd and symmetric between encoding and decoding when the network is an autoencoder.<br><br>The size depends on both the network design and the regularization technique.<br><br>Without regularization the encoding layers should be consecutively smaller than the previous layer.<br><br>With regularization we can have higher capacity than the input size. |
| epochs | Number of iterations over the training set. | Generally, between 10 and a few hundreds. Depending on the algorithm, it may require extra epochs to converge.<br><br>If using early stopping we don't need to worry about having too many epochs.<br><br>For model selection using grid search, it is better to keep it small enough (less than 100). |
| train_samples_per_iteration | Number of training examples for Map/Reduce iteration. | This parameter applies only in the case of distributed learning.<br><br>This strongly depends on the implementation.<br><br>H2O offers an auto-tuning option.<br><br>Please refer to the *Distributed learning via Map/Reduce* section. |
| adaptive_rate | Enable the adaptive learning rate. | Each library may have different strategies. H2O implements as default ADADELTA.<br><br>In case of ADADELTA, additional parameters rho (between 0.9 and 0.999) and epsilon (between 1e-10 and 1e-4) must be specified.<br><br>Please refer to the Adaptive Learning section. |
| rate, rate_decay | Learning rate values and decay factor (if not adaptive learning). | High values of the rate may lead to unstable models, lower values will slow down the convergence. A reasonable value is 0.005.<br><br>The decay factory represents the Rate at which the learning rate decays across layers. |

| Parameter | Description | Recommended value(s) |
|---|---|---|
| `momentum_start`, `momentum_ramp`, `momentum_stable` | Parameters of the momentum technique (if not adaptive learning). | When exists a gap between the momentum start and the stable value, the momentum ramp is measured in number of training samples. The default is typically a large value, for example, 1e6. |
| `Input_dropout_ratio`, `hidden_dropout_ratio` | Fraction of input nodes for each layer to omit during training. | Default values are 0 for input (all features) and a value around 0.5 for hidden layers. |
| `l1, l2` | L1 and L2 regularization parameters. | High values of L1 will cause many weights to go to 0 while high values of L2 will reduce but keep most of the weights. |
| `max_w2` | Maximum value of sum of squared weights incoming for a node. | A useful parameter for unbounded activation functions such as ReLU or Maxout. |
| `initial_weight_distribution` | The distribution of initial weights. | Typical values are Uniform, Normal, or UniformAdaptive. The latter is generally preferred. |
| `loss` | The loss function to use during back-propagation. | It depends on the problem and nature of data.<br><br>Typical functions are CrossEntropy, Quadratic, Absolute, Huber. Please refer to the Network design section. |
| `rho_sparsity`, `beta_sparsity` | Parameters of the sparse auto-encoders. | Rho is the average activation frequency and beta is the weight associated to the sparsity penalty. |

These parameters can be tuned using search space optimization techniques. Two of the most basic, popular and supported by H2O techniques, are grid search and random search.

Grid search is an exhaustive approach. Each dimension specifies a limited number of possible values and the Cartesian product generates the search space. Each point will be evaluated in a parallel fashion and the point that scores the lowest will be selected. The scoring function is defined by the validation metric.

On the one hand, we have a computational cost equals to the power of the dimensionality (the curse of dimensionality). On the other hand, it is embarrassingly parallel. That is, each point is perfectly parallelizable and its run is independent from the others.

Alternatively, randomly choosing points in a dense search space could be more efficient and can lead to similar results with much less computation. The number of wasted grid search trials is exponential in the number of search dimensions that turned out to be irrelevant for a particular dataset. Not every parameter has the same importance during tuning. Random search is not affected by those low-importance dimensions.

In random search, each parameter must provide a distribution, continuous or discrete depending on the values of the parameter. The trials are points sampled independently from those distributions.

The main advantages of random search are:

- You can fix the budget (maximum number of points to explore or maximum allowed time)
- You can set a convergence criterion
- Adding parameters that do not influence the validation performance does not affect the efficiency
- During tuning, you could add extra parameters dynamically without have to adjust the grid and increase the number of trials
- If one trial run fails for any reason, it could either be abandoned or restarted without jeopardizing the entire tuning algorithm

Common applications of random search are associated with early stopping. Especially in high-dimensional spaces with many different models, the number of trials before to converge to a global optimum can be a lot. Early stopping will stop the search when the learning curve (training) or the validation curve (tuning) flattens out.

Because we can also constrain the computation budget we could set criteria like: *stop when RMSE has improved over the moving average of the best 5 models by less than 0.0001, but take no more than 1 hours.*

Metric-based early stopping combined with max runtime generally gives the best tradeoff.

It also common to have multi-stage tuning where, for example, you run a random search to identify the sub-space where the best configuration might exist and then have further tuning stages only in the selected subspace.

More advanced techniques also exploit sequential, adaptive search/optimization algorithms, where the result of one trial affects the choice of next trials and/or the hyper-parameters are optimized jointly. There is ongoing research trying to predetermine the *variable importance* of hyper-parameters. Also, domain knowledge and manual fine-tuning can be valuable for those systems where automated techniques struggle to converge.

# End-to-end evaluation

From a business point of view what really matters is the final end-to-end performance. None of your stakeholders will be interested in your training error, parameters tuning, model selection, and so on. What matters is the KPIs to compute on top of the final model. Evaluation can be seen as the ultimate verdict.

Also, as we anticipated, evaluating a product cannot be done with a single metric. Generally, it is a good and effective practice to build an internal dashboard that can report, or measure in real-time, a bunch of performance indicators of our product in the form of aggregated numbers or easy-to-interpret visualization charts. Within a single glance, we would like to understand the whole picture and translate it in the value we are generating within the business.

The evaluation phase can, and generally does, include the same methodology as the model validation. We have seen in previous sections a few techniques for validating in case of labeled and unlabeled data. Those can be the starting points.

In addition to those, we ought to include a few specific test scenarios. For instance:

- **Known versus unknown detection performance**: This means measuring the performance of the detector for both known and unknown attacks. We can use the labels to create different training sets, some of them with no attacks at all and some of them with a small percentage; remember that having too many anomalies in the training set would be against the definition of anomalies. We could measure the precision on the top N elements in the function of the percentage of anomalies in the training set. This will give us an indicator of how general the detector is with respect to past anomalies and hypothetical novel ones. Depending on what we are trying to build, we might be interested more on novel anomalies or more on known ones.

- **Relevance performance**: Just scoring enough to hit the threshold or being select in the top priority queue is important but the ranking also matters. We would like the most relevant anomalies to always score at the top of the queue. Here we could either define the priorities of the different labels and compute a ranking coefficient (for example, Spearman) or use some evaluation technique used for Recommender Systems. One example of the latter is mean average precision at k (MAP@k) used in Information Retrieval to score a query engine with regards to the relevance of the returned documents.

- **Model stability**: We select the best model during validation. If we sample the training data differently or use slightly different validation dataset (containing different types of anomalies) we would like the best model to always be the same or at least among the top selected models. We can create histogram charts showing the frequency of a given model of being selected. If there is no obvious winner or a subset of frequent candidates, then the model selection is a bit unstable. Every day, we might select a different model that is good for reacting to new attacks but at the price of instability.

- **Attack outcome**: If the model detects an attack with a very high score and this attack is confirmed by the analysts, is the model also able to detect whether the system has been compromised or returned to normalcy? One way of testing this is to measure the distribution of the anomaly score right after an alert is raised. Comparing the new distribution with the older one and measuring any gap. A good anomaly detector should be able to tell you about the state of the system. The evaluation dashboard could have this information visualized for the last or recently detected anomalies.

- **Failure case simulations**: Security analysts can define some scenarios and generate some synthetic data. One business target could be "being able to protect from those future types of attacks". Dedicated performance indicators can be derived from this artificial dataset. For example, an increasing ramp of network connections to the same host and port could be a sign of **Denial of Service (DOS)** attack.

- **Time to detect**: The detector generally scores each point independently. For contextual and time-based anomalies, the same entities might generate many points. For example, if we open a new network connection, we can start scoring it against the detector while it is still open and every few seconds generate a new point with the features collected over a different time interval. Likely, you will collect multiple sequential connections together into a single point to score. We would like to measure how long it takes to react. If the first connection is not considered anomalous, maybe after 10 consecutive attempts, the detector will react. We can pick a known anomaly, break it down into sequentially growing data points, and then report after how many of those the contextual anomaly is raised.

- **Damage cost**: If somehow we are able to quantify the impact of attack damages or savings due to the detection, we should incorporate this in the final evaluation. We could use as benchmark the last past month or year and estimate the savings; hopefully this balance will be positive, in case we have deployed the current solution since then or the real savings if the current solution was deployed in this last period.

We would like to summarize all of this information within a single dashboard from where we can make statements such as: *Our anomaly detector is able to detect previously seen anomalies with a precision of 76% (+- 5%) and average reacting time of 10 seconds and novel anomalies with precision of 68% (+- 15%) and reaction time of 14 seconds. We observed an average of 10 anomalies per day. Considering the capability of 1,000 inspections per day, we can fill the 80% of the most relevant detections corresponding to 6 anomalies within just 120 top elements of the queue. Of these, only the 2 out of 10 that compromise the system are included in this list. We can then divide the inspections in 2 tiers; the first tier will respond immediately of the top 120 elements and the second tier will take care of the tail. Standing to the current simulated failing scenarios, we are protected in 90% of them. Total saving since last year corresponds to 1.2 million dollars.*

# A/B Testing

So far, we have only considered evaluation based on past historical data (retrospective analysis) and/or based on simulations with synthetic dataset. The second one is based on the assumption of a particular failure scenario to happen in the future. Evaluating only based on historical data assumes that the system will always behave under those conditions and that the current data distribution also describes the stream of future data. Moreover, any KPI or performance metric should be evaluated relative to a baseline. The product owner wants to justify the investment for that project. What if the same problem could have been solved in a much cheaper way?

For this reason, the only truth for evaluating any machine learning system is A/B testing. A/B testing is a statistical hypothesis testing with two variants (the control and variation) in a controlled experiment. The goal of A/B testing is to identify performance differences between the two groups. It is a technique widely used in user experience design for websites or for advertising and/or marketing campaigns. In the case of anomaly detection, we can use a baseline (the simplest rule-based detector) as the control version and the currently selected model as variation candidate.

The next step is to find a meaningful evaluation that quantifies the return of investment.

> *"We have to find a way of making the important measurable, instead of making the measurable important."*
>
> Robert McNamara, former US Secretary of Defense

The return of investment will be represented by the uplift defined as:

$$uplift = KPI\left(variation\right) - KPI\left(control\right)$$

It is the difference between the two KPIs that quantifies the effectiveness of the treatment.

In order to make the comparison fair we must ensure that the two groups share the same distribution of the population. We want to remove any bias given by the choice of individuals (data samples). In the case of the anomaly detector, we could, in principle, apply the same stream of data to both the two models. This is not recommended though. By applying one model you can influence the behavior of a given process. A typical example is an intruder who is first detected by a model, and as such, the system would react by dropping his open connections. A smart intruder would realize that he has been discovered and would not attempt to connect again. In that case, the second model may never observe a given expected pattern because of the influence of the first model.

By separating the two models over two disjoint subsets of data, we make sure the two models cannot influence each other. Moreover, if our use case requires the anomalies to be further investigated by our analysts, then they cannot be duplicated.

Here, we must split according to the same criteria as we have seen in the data validation: no data leakage and entity sub-sampling. The final test that can confirm whether the two groups are actually identically distributed is A/A testing.

As the name suggests, A/A testing consists on re-using the control version on both the two groups. We expect that the performance should be very similar equivalent to an uplift close to 0. It is also an indicator of the performance variance. If the A/A uplift is non-zero, then we have to redesign the controlled experiment to be more stable.

A/B testing is great for measuring the difference in performance between the two models but just the model is not the only factor that influence the final performance. If we take into account the damage cost model, which is the business core, the model must be accurate on generating a prioritized list of anomalies to investigate but also the analysts must be good on identifying, confirming and reacting upon.

Hence, we have two factors: the model accuracy and the security team effectiveness.

We can divide the controlled experiment into an A/B/C/D test where four independent groups are created, as follows:

|  | Base model | Advanced model |
| --- | --- | --- |
| **No action from security team** | Group A | Group B |
| **Intervention from security team** | Group C | Group D |

We can compute a bunch of uplift measures that quantify both the model accuracy and security team effectiveness. In particular:

- `uplift(A,B)`: The effectiveness of the advanced model alone
- `uplift(D,C)`: The effectiveness of the advanced model in case of security intervention
- `uplift(D,A)`: The effectiveness of both advanced model and security intervention joint together
- `uplift(C,A)`: The effectiveness of the security intervention on the low-accuracy queue
- `uplift(D,B)`: The effectiveness of the security intervention on the high-accuracy queue

This is just an example of meaningful experiment and evaluations you want to carry out in order to quantify in numbers what the business really cares about.

Furthermore, there are a bunch of advanced techniques for A/B testing. Just to name a popular one, the multi-armed bandit algorithm allows you to dynamically adjust the size of the different testing groups in order to adapt to the performance of those and minimize the loss due to low performing groups.

# A summary of testing

To summarize, for an anomaly detection system using neural networks and labeled data, we can define the following:

- Model as the definition of the network topology (number and size of hidden layers), activation functions, pre-processing and post-processing transformations.

- Model parameters as the weights of hidden units and biases of hidden layers.

- Fitted model as the model with an estimated value of parameters and able to map samples from the input layer to the output.

- Learning algorithm (also training algorithm) as SGD or its variants (HOGWILD!, adaptive learning) + the loss function + regularization.

- Training set, validation set and test set are three disjoint and possibly independent subsets of the available data where we preserve the same distribution.

- Model validation as the maximum F-measure score from the ROC curve computed on the validation set using model fitted on the training set.

- Model selection as the best validated model among a set of possible configurations (1 hidden layer Vs. 3 hidden layers, 50 neurons Vs. 1000 neurons, Tanh Vs. Sigmoid, Z-scaling Vs. Min/Max normalization and so on...).

- Hyper-parameters tuning as the extension of model selection with algorithm and implementation parameters such as learning parameters (epochs, batch size, learning rate, decay factor, momentum...), distributed implementation parameters (samples per iteration), regularization parameters (lambda in L1 and L2, noise factor, sparsity constraint...), initialization parameters (weights distribution) and so on.

- Model evaluation, or testing, as the final business metrics and acceptance criteria computed on the test set using model fitted on both training and validation set merged together. Some examples are the precision and recall for just top N test samples, time to detection, and so on.

- A/B testing as the uplift of evaluation performances of a model with respect to a baseline computed on two different, but homogeneous, subsets of the live data population (the control and variation groups).

We hope that we've clarified the essential and most important steps to consider when testing a production-ready deep learning intrusion detection system. These techniques, metrics, or tuning parameters may not be the same for your use case, but we hope that the thoughtful methodology can serve as a guideline for any data product.

A great resource of guidelines and best practices for building Data Science systems that are both scientifically correct and valuable for the business is the Professional Data Science Manifesto: www.datasciencemanifesto.org. It is recommended the reading and reasoning around the listed principles.

# Deployment

At this stage, we should have done almost all of the analysis and development needed for building an anomaly detector, or in general a data product using deep learning.

We are only left with final, but not less important, step: the deployment.

Deployment is generally very specific of the use case and enterprise infrastructure. In this section, we will cover some common approaches used in general data science production systems.

# POJO model export

In the Testing section, we summarized all the different entities in a machine learning pipeline. In particular, we have seen the definition and differences of a model, a fitted model and the learning algorithm. After we have trained, validated, and selected the final model, we have a final fitted version of it ready to be used. During the testing phase (except in A/B testing), we have scored only historical data that was generally already available in the machines where we trained the model.

In enterprise architectures, it is common to have a Data Science cluster wherein you build a model and the production environment where you deploy and use the fitted model.

One common way is to export a fitted model is **Plain Old Java Object (POJO)**. The main advantage of POJO is that it can be easily integrated within a Java app and scheduled to run on a specific dataset or deployed to score in real-time.

H2O allows you to extract a fitted model programmatically or from the Flow Web UI, which we have not covered in this book.

If model is your fitted model, you can save it as POJO jar in the specified path by running:

```
model.download_pojo(path)
```

The POJO jar contains a standalone Java class of the base class `hex.genmodel.` `easy.EasyPredictModelWrapper`, with no dependencies on the training data or the entire H2O framework but only the `h2o-genmodel.jar` file, which defines the POJO interfaces. It can be read and used from anything that runs in a JVM.

The POJO object will contain the model class name corresponding to the model id used in H2O (`model.id`) and the model category for anomaly detection will be `hex.` `ModelCategory.AutoEncoder`.

Unfortunately, at the time of writing this chapter, there is still an open issue over implementing the Easy API for AutoEncoder: `https://0xdata.atlassian.net/` `browse/PUBDEV-2232`.

Roberto Rösler, from the h2ostream mailing list, solved this problem by implementing its own version of the `AutoEncoderModelPrediction` class as:

```
public class AutoEncoderModelPrediction extends AbstractPrediction {
    public double[] predictions;
    public double[] feature;
    public double[] reconstrunctionError;
    public double averageReconstructionError;
}
```

And modified the method `predictAutoEncoder` in the `EasyPredictModelWrapper` as:

```
public AutoEncoderModelPrediction predictAutoEncoder(RowData data)
throws PredictException { double[] preds =
preamble(ModelCategory.AutoEncoder, data);
    // save predictions
    AutoEncoderModelPrediction p = new AutoEncoderModelPrediction();
    p.predictions = preds;
    // save raw data
    double[] rawData = new double[m.nfeatures()];
    setToNaN(rawData);
    fillRawData(data, rawData);
    p.feature = rawData;
    //calculate and reconstruction error
    double[] reconstrunctionError = new double [rawData.length];
    for (int i = 0; i < reconstrunctionError.length; i++) {
    reconstrunctionError[i] = Math.pow(rawData[i] - preds[i],2); }
    p.reconstrunctionError = reconstrunctionError;
    //calculate mean squared error
    double sum = 0; for (int i = 0; i < reconstrunctionError.length;
    i++) {
```

```
        sum = sum + reconstrunctionError[i];
    } p.averageReconstructionError =
      sum/reconstrunctionError.length;
    return p;
}
```

The custom modified API will expose a method for retrieving the reconstruction error on each predicted row.

In order to make the POJO model to work, we must specify the same data format used during training. The data should be loaded into `hex.genmodel.easy.RowData` objects that are simply instances of `java.util.Hashmap<String, Object>`.

When you create a `RowData` object you must ensure these things:

- The same column names and types of the `H2OFrame` are used. For categorical columns, you must use String. For numerical columns, you can either use Double or String. Different column types are not supported.

- In case of categorical features, the values must belong to the same set used for training unless you explicitly set `convertUnknownCategoricalLevelsToNa` to true in the model wrapper.

- Additional columns can be specified but will be ignored.

- Any missing column will be treated as NA.

- The same pre-processing transformation should be applied to the data as well.

This last requirement is probably the trickiest one. If our machine learning pipeline is made of a bunch of transformers, those must be exactly replicated in the deployment. Thus, the POJO class is not enough and should also be accompanied by all of the remaining steps in the pipeline in addition to the H2O neural network.

Here is an example of a Java main method that reads some data and scores it against an exported POJO class:

```java
import java.io.*;
import hex.genmodel.easy.RowData;
import hex.genmodel.easy.EasyPredictModelWrapper;
import hex.genmodel.easy.prediction.*;

public class main {
  public static String modelClassName = "autoencoder_pojo_test";

  public static void main(String[] args) throws Exception {
    hex.genmodel.GenModel rawModel;
```

```
    rawModel = (hex.genmodel.GenModel)
    Class.forName(modelClassName).newInstance();
    EasyPredictModelWrapper model = new
    EasyPredictModelWrapper(rawModel);

    RowData row = new RowData();
    row.put("Feature1", "value1");
    row.put("Feature2", "value2");
    row.put("Feature3", "value3");

    AutoEncoderModelPrediction p = model.predictAutoEncoder(row);
    System.out.println("Reconstruction error is: " +
    p.averageReconstructionError);
    }
}
```

We have seen an example of how to instantiate the POJO model as a Java class and use it for scoring a mock data point. We can re-adapt this code to be integrated within an existing enterprise JVM-based system. If you are integrating it in Spark, you can simply wrap the logic we have implemented in the example main class within a function and call it from a map method on a Spark data collection. All you need is the model POJO jar to be loaded into the JVM where you want to make the predictions. Alternatively, if your enterprise stack is JVM-based, there are a few util entry points, such as `hex.genmodel.PredictCsv`. It allows you to specify a csv input file and a path where the output will be stored. Since `AutoEncoder` is not yet supported in the Easy API, you will have to modify the `PredictCsv` main class according to the custom patch we have seen before. Another architecture could be like this: you use Python to build the model and a JVM-based application for the production deployment.

# Anomaly score APIs

Exporting the model as a POJO class is one way to programmatically include it in an existing JVM system, pretty much like the way you import an external library.

There are a bunch of other situations where the integration works better using a self-containing API, such as in a micro-services architecture or non-JVM-based systems.

H2O offers the capability of wrapping the trained model in a REST API to call specifying the row data to score via a JSON object attached to an HTTP request. The backend implementation behind the REST API is capable of performing everything you would do with the Python H2O API, included the pre and post-processing steps.

The REST API is accessible from:

- Any browser using simple add-ons, such as Postman in Chrome
- curl, one of the most popular tools for client-side URL transfers
- Any language of your choice; REST APIs are completely language agnostic

In spite of the POJO class, the REST API offered by H2O depends on a running instance of the H2O cluster. You can access the REST API at `http://hostname:54321` followed by the API version (latest is 3); and the resource path, for example, `http://hostname:54321/3/Frames` will return the list of all Frames.

REST APIs supports five verbs or methods: `GET`, `POST`, `PUT`, `PATCH`, and `DELETE`.

`GET` is used to read a resource with no side-effects, `POST` to create a new resource, `PUT` to update and replace entirely an existing resource, `PATCH` to modify a part of an existing resource, and `DELETE` to delete a resource. The H2O REST API does not support the `PATCH` method and adds a new method called `HEAD`. It is like a `GET` request but returns only the `HTTP` status, useful to check whether a resource exists or not without loading it.

Endpoints in H2O could be Frames, Models, or Clouds, which are pieces of information related to the status of nodes in the H2O cluster.

Each endpoint will specify its own payload and schema, and the documentation can be found on `http://docs.h2o.ai/h2o/latest-stable/h2o-docs/rest-api-reference.html`.

H2O provides in the Python module a connection handler for all the REST requests:

```
with H2OConnection.open(url='http://hostname:54321') as hc:
  hc.info().pprint()
```

The hc object has a method called `request` that can be used to send `REST` requests:

```
hc.request(endpoint='GET /3/Frames')
```

Data payloads for `POST` requests can be added using either the argument `data` (x-www format) or `json` (json format) and specifying a dictionary of key-value pairs. Uploading a file happens by specifying the `filename` argument mapping to a local file path.

At this stage, whether we use the Python module or any REST client, we must do the following steps in order to upload some data and get the model scores back:

1. Import the data you want to score using the POST /3/ImportFiles by using an ImporFilesV3 schema, including a remote path from where to load data (via http, s3, or other protocols). The corresponding destination frame name will be the file path:

```
POST /3/ImportFiles HTTP/1.1
Content-Type: application/json
{ "path" : "http://s3.amazonaws.com/my-data.csv" }
```

2. Guess the parameters for parsing; it will return a bunch of parameters inferred from the data for the final parsing (you can skip and manually specify those):

```
POST /3/ParseSetup HTTP/1.1
Content-Type: application/json
{ "source_frames" : "http://s3.amazonaws.com/my-data.csv" }
```

3. Parse according to the parsing parameters:

```
POST /3/Parse HTTP/1.1
Content-Type: application/json
{ "destination_frame" : "my-data.hex" , source_frames : [ "http://
s3.amazonaws.com/my-data.csv" ] , parse_type : "CSV" , "number_
of_columns" : "3" , "columns_types" : [ "Numeric", "Numeric",
"Numeric" ] , "delete_on_done" : "true" }
```

4. Get the job name from the response and poll for import completion:

```
GET /3/Jobs/$job_name HTTP/1.1
```

5. When the returned status is DONE, you can run the model scoring as:

```
POST /3/Predictions/models/$model_name/frames/$frame_name HTTP/1.1
Content-Type: application/json
{ "predictions_frame" : "$prediction_name" , "reconstruction_
error" : "true" , "reconstruction_error_per_feature" : "false" ,
"deep_features_hidden_layer" : 2 }
```

6. After parsing the results, you can delete both the input and prediction frames:

```
DELETE /3/Frames/$frame_name

DELETE /3/Frames/$prediction_name
```

Let's analyze the input and output of the Predictions API. `reconstruction_error`, `reconstruction_error_per_feature`, and `deep_features_hidden_layer` are specific parameters for AutoEncoder models and determine what will be included in the output. The output is an array of `model_metrics` where for AutoEncoder will contain:

- **MSE**: Mean Squared Error of the predictions
- **RMSE**: Root Mean Squared Error of the predictions
- **scoring_time**: Time in mS since the epoch for the start of this scoring run
- **predictions**: The frame with the all the prediction rows

# A summary of deployment

We have seen two options for exporting and deploying a trained model: exporting it as a `POJO` and incorporating it into a JVM-based application or using the REST API to call a model which is already loaded into a running H2O instance.

Generally, using `POJO` is a better choice because it does not depend on a running H2O cluster. Thus, you can use H2O for building the model and then deploy it on any other system.

The REST API will be useful if you want to achieve more flexibility and being able to generate predictions from any client at any time as long as the H2O cluster is running. The procedure, though, requires multiple steps compared to the `POJO` deployment.

Another recommended architecture is to use the exported `POJO` and wrap it within a JVM REST API using frameworks such as Jersey for Java and Play or `akka-http` if you prefer Scala. Building your own API means you can define programmatically the way you want to accept input data and what you want to return as output in a single request, as opposed to the multiple steps in H2O. Moreover, your REST API could be stateless. That is, you don't need to import data into frames and delete them afterwards.

Ultimately, if you want your POJO-based REST API to be easily ported and deployed everywhere, it is recommended to wrap it in a virtual container using Docker. Docker is an open source framework that allows you to wrap a piece of software in a complete filesystem that contains everything you need to run: code, runtime, system tools, libraries and everything you need to have installed. In such a way, you have a single lightweight container that can always run the same service in every environment.

A Dockerized API can easily be shipped and deployed to any of your production servers.

# Summary

In this chapter, we went through a long journey of optimizations, tweaks, testing strategies, and engineering practices to turn our neural network into an intrusion detection data product.

In particular, we defined a data product as a system that extracts value from raw data and returns actionable knowledge as output.

We saw a few optimizations for training a deep neural network to be faster, scalable, and more robust. We addressed the problem of early saturation via weights initialization. Scalability using both a parallel multi-threading version of SGD and a distributed implementation in Map/Reduce. We saw how the H2O framework can leverage Apache Spark as the backend for computation via Sparkling Water.

We remarked the importance of testing and the difference between model validation and full end-to-end evaluation. Model validation is used to reject or accept a given model, or to select the best performing one. Likely, model validation metrics can be used for hyper-parameter tuning. On the other hand, end-to-end evaluation is what quantifies more comprehensibly how the full solution is solving real business problems.

Ultimately, we did the last step—to deploy the tested model straight into production, by either exporting it as a POJO object or turning it into a service via a REST API.

We summarized a few lessons learnt in the experience of building robust machine learning systems and deeper architectures. We expect the reader to use those as a basis for further development and customized solutions according to each use case.

# Index

Boltzmann machine (BM) 120-125, 83

# C

character-based models, language modeling
  about 185
  data, preprocessing 186
  data, reading 186
  example training 192
  LSTM network 187, 188
  sampling 191
  training 189, 190
collective anomaly 299
Connectionist Temporal
      Classification (CTC) 198
contextual anomaly 299
contractive autoencoders
  about 112, 113
  reference link 114
convolutional layers
  about 139-148
  pre-training 163
  stride and padding 148, 149
Convolutional Neural Networks (CNN) 84
Computing Processing Units (CPUs) 1
cross-entropy method 22

# D

data collection 10
DataFrame 342
data modeling
  collective anomaly 299
  contextual anomaly 299
  point anomaly 299
  techniques 299
data processing 10
data product 324-326
Data Science systems
  reference link 370
decision trees 16, 17
deep auto-encoders
  used, for anomaly detection 301-303
deep belief networks
      (DBN) 83, 133, 134, 197
deep learning 25
  about 70, 71
  algorithms 83, 84

feature learning 73-82
fundamental concepts 72
deep learning, applications
  about 84
  object recognition and classification 86-89
  speech recognition 84-86
deep neural networks (DNN) 197
denoising autoencoders 111, 112
deployment
  about 370
  conclusion 376
  POJO model export 370-373
  REST API 373-375
detection modeling
  about 299
  semi-supervised 300
  supervised 300
  unsupervised 300
discrete cosine transform (DCT) 196
distributed learning
  via Map/Reduce 337-341
dynamic games
  about 263-268
  Epsilon greedy 271, 272
  experience replay 268-270

# E

early game playing AI 209, 210
Efficient BackProp
  reference link 110
end-to-end evaluation
  about 364, 366
  A/B testing 366, 368
energy based model (EBM) 119
examples, anomaly detection
  about 305
  Electrocardiogram pulse detection 316-321
  MNIST digit anomaly recognition 306-315
Excess-Mass (EM) 356
explanatory Power 347, 348

# F

False Positive Rate (FPR) 354
feature engineering 101
formal elegance 347
fruitfulness 347, 349